WEAVERS OF REVOLUTION

WEAVERS OF REVOLUTION

The Yarur Workers and Chile's Road to Socialism

PETER WINN

New York   Oxford
OXFORD UNIVERSITY PRESS
1986

Oxford University Press

Oxford   New York   Toronto
Delhi   Bombay   Calcutta   Madras   Karachi
Petaling Jaya   Singapore   Hong Kong   Tokyo
Nairobi   Dar es Salaam   Cape Town
Melbourne   Auckland

and associated companies in
Beirut   Berlin   Ibadan   Nicosia

Library of Congress Cataloging-in-Publication Data
Winn, Peter.
Weavers of revolution.
Bibliography: p.   Includes index.
1. Textile workers—Chile.   2. Yarur Manufacturas Chilenas de Algodón.
3. Employee ownership—Chile—Santiago.   4. Socialism—Chile.
5. Chile—History—1920– .   I. Title.
HD8039.T42C478   1986   338.7'67721'098331   85–18832
ISBN 0-19-503960-2

Printing (last digit): 9 8 7 6 5 4 3 2 1

Printed in the United States of America

The consciousness of a worker is not a curve that
rises and falls with wages and prices; it is the accumulation of a lifetime of experience and socialization, inherited traditions, struggles successful and
defeated. . . . It is this weighty baggage that goes
into the making of a worker's consciousness and provides the basis for his behavior when conditions ripen
. . . and the moment comes.

—E. P. Thompson

PREFACE

Like many projects, this one began by accident. In February 1972 I was on my way to Uruguay with the intention of completing research on the nineteenth century that would turn a doctoral dissertation on British influence into a book. During the flight between Lima, Peru, and Santiago, Chile, I was engaged in conversation by a group of Americans who were going to Chile for a political tour of Salvador Allende's democratic revolution. They were to visit the first factory seized by its workers after Allende was elected, and they invited me to join them. This book is the result of that unexpected visit to the Yarur cotton mill.

I spent most of that day at the Yarur factory talking with the workers and their leaders about their experience. As I listened to the workers tell their story, I was struck both by their eloquence and its significance. They would never write their memoirs, but they were as articulate as any politician and more likely to tell the truth—if one took the time to listen. Recording the history of the inarticulate had become fashionable among historians of earlier eras, who often drew upon fragmentary records and ingenious interpolations of data, yet no one was seizing the opportunity to record the history that these workers were making. I remember thinking to myself, "This is the kind of history one should be doing of the revolutionary process, not the view from the presidential palace, but history from the bottom up. After all, if this is a 'proletarian revolution,' as Chilean leftists claim, then these workers are its central protagonists." I resolved that if I ever returned to Chile for research, this was the project I would undertake.

During the weeks that followed, the explosion of the Tupamaro civil war in Uruguay made it impossible for me to proceed with my original plans, so I decided to stay in Chile and do a historical study of the Yarur mill. As I explored that history, its scope and significance grew. I found that Yarur was the first modern cotton textile mill in Chile and the base of one of the most powerful economic empires in that country. I discovered that Yarur had long been a symbol of social struggle, an arena where contrasting visions of production and labor relations clashed. I learned that the Yarur workers were not only the first workers to seize their factory after Allende's election but also the first to force the socialization of their enterprise, despite presidential opposition, and the first to inaugurate worker participation in the management of their enterprise. I met weavers who had imposed their vision of revolution on politicians, and spinners who had been born peasants and in their lifetimes had experienced both an industrial revolution and a transition toward socialism. Through the local history of the Yarur mill, I realized, much of the modern history of Chile could be illuminated.

Teaching responsibilities interrupted my research, but I returned to Chile in mid-1973 and resumed my study—although in the very different and more difficult context of the death throes of the revolutionary process. My research was first altered and then ended by the military coup of September 11, 1973, and its repressive aftermath. I persisted in my efforts for several months, but it was not possible to do an oral history of workers in General Pinochet's Chile. When I tried to return to the Yarur mill for further research, I was denounced anonymously, detained by the army, and taken at bayonet-point to a regimental barracks, where I was interrogated at midnight by its commander. After three days of interrogation and investigation, he informed me, "We have no proof that you have committed a crime, exactly speaking, Professor Winn, but talking with workers, interviewing union leaders, all this is very suspicious. We do not want *anyone* talking to our workers," he stressed, bringing my research to an abrupt end. "For that reason, the government has decided that it is best that you leave the country within twenty-four hours." As a result, I was unable to obtain many interviews I had planned. The record of others vanished during their difficult exit from Pinochet's police state. Nor have I been able to return to Chile for additional research.

Still, the interviews and notes collected during those months of research were voluminous and rich. The transcription and translation of many hours of interviews proved a lengthy process, and the integration of this rich record of workers' experiences with a more general interpretation of Chilean history was an absorbing but time-consuming task. As a consequence, it is only now that I am able to present my research—and the Yarur workers' story—to the public at large.

Any project conceived under such circumstances and executed over so long a period of time inevitably accumulates many debts, and this one is no exception. Many individuals and institutions in Chile contributed to this book, and I wish that I could acknowledge them all. Space poses one constraint, politics another. Given the state of Chilean affairs, it might be a disservice to acknowledge their aid and advice in these pages. They know who they are and I know how invaluable their assistance was. I hope that the contents of this book will be recompense enough for their help.

It is much easier to thank the institutions and individuals in the United States who contributed to this book. Princeton University's generous leave policy for junior faculty made the initial research possible, while the Tinker Foundation's Postdoctoral Fellowship Program enabled me to begin distilling my research in the hospitable context of Columbia University's Institute of Latin American Studies. I owe special thanks and a debt of gratitude to Columbia University's Research Institute on International Change, which supported the writing of this book for four years and offered both constructive criticism and continuing faith—in addition to providing a scholarly community conducive to creative work. Frank and Nita Manitzas, Barbara Stallings, and Carol Smith contributed in different ways to the success of my research efforts.

Many of my colleagues at Tufts, Yale, and Columbia Universities read all or portions of the manuscript, as did many colleagues in the field. I am indebted to them all, but it is beyond the scope of this preface to acknowledge them all individually, although the detailed commentaries of Shane Hunt, Edward Malefakis, Kenneth Maxwell, Daniel Mulholland, and Howard Solomon deserve special mention. I do want to underscore, however, the multiple contributions of three special friends—Richard Locke, Martin Sherwin, and Isser Woloch—without whose encouragement, support, and advice this book might never have reached fruition. And in particular, I want to thank Sue Gronewold—my "in-house" editor, toughest critic, and closest companion—whose many-faceted contributions to this book are woven into its words and into the fabric of our life together.

Lastly, I would like to thank Nancy Lane and Susan Gyarmati for editorial advice that made this a far better book, my protests notwithstanding. I am also grateful to Henry Krawitz and Cecil P. Golann for their precise and sensitive copy editing. The photographs are all my own, but I am indebted to Jerry Berndt for his enhanced reproductions.

But, most of all, I would like to thank the workers of Ex-Yarur, who trusted me to tell their story. When they are able to read it, I hope they will feel that their trust was not in vain.

Cambridge, Massachusetts　　　　　　　　　　　　　　　　　　　　P.W.
December 1985

CONTENTS

ABBREVIATIONS

AIFLD	American Institute for Free Labor Development
ALALC	Latin American Free Trade Association
ANEF	National Association of State Employees
A.P.I.	Popular Independent Action party
CEREN	*Cuadernos de la Realidad Nacional*
CIA	(U.S.) Central Intelligence Agency
C.I.E.	Special Investigations Commission, Ministry of Economy
CORA	Agrarian Reform Corporation
CORFO	State Development Corporation
CTCh	Chilean Workers Confederation
CUP	Popular Unity Committee
CUT	National Labor Confederation
DGT/DOS	Department of Social Organizations, General Labor Secretariat, Ministry of Labor
DINA	National Intelligence Directorate
DIRINCO	National Directorate of Industry and Commerce
EURE	*Estudios Urbanos y Regionales*
FENATEX	National Textile Workers Federation
FOCh	Chilean Workers Federation
FRAP	Popular Action Front
FRENAP	Private Enterprise Front
FTR	Revolutionary Workers Front
GAP	President Allende's personal guard
INCHITEX	Textile Institute of Chile
ITT	International Telephone and Telegraph Corporation
JAP	Price and Supply Committees
JJCC/Jota	Communist Youth organization
MAPU	Movement for Popular United Action
MIR	Revolutionary Left Movement
ODEPLAN	National Planning Ministry
PADENA	National Democratic party
PIR	Party of the Left Radicals
RCA	Radio Corporation of America

SAYMCHA	S.A. Yarur, Chilean Cotton Manufacturers
SCSSSABC/DSA	Superintendency of Insurance Companies, Limited Corporations and Chambers of Commerce, Department of Limited Corporations
Ses. Extra.	Special Session of Congress
Ses. Ords.	Ordinary Session of Congress
SOFOFA	National Manufacturers' Association
U.T.E.	State Technical University

WEAVERS OF REVOLUTION

INTRODUCTION:
A FACTORY SEIZED,
A REVOLUTION
TRANSFORMED

On Monday, the twenty-sixth of April 1971, Chileans awoke to surprising headlines: The workers of the Yarur cotton mill, the country's largest, had seized their factory and were demanding its immediate socialization by the Allende government. A cause of alarm to some and celebration to others, the seizure (*toma*) of Yarur was viewed by all as a turning point on the "Chilean road to socialism." Since Allende's election as Chile's president some eight months before, there had been seizures of farms by peasants anticipating land reform and *tomas* of vacant suburban lots by squatters seeking homes. There had even been a few takeovers of factories that had been abandoned or closed by their owners.

Yarur was different. Its owners had neither fled the country nor ceased production; they had neither stopped paying wages nor gone bankrupt. Nor was Yarur an unimportant industry or a special case, an exception to that revolution by democratic rules that Salvador Allende had promised Chile's economic elite. On the contrary, the Yarur mill was the nation's largest cotton textile plant, a strategic industry that supplied the armed forces and hospitals with uniforms and bedding, the flour mills with sacks and knitting mills with yarn, and the populace with inexpensive cotton cloth.

Not only was Yarur an important industry; it was also a symbolic one. To some, it symbolized the creativity and contribution of Chile's entrepreneurs. Juan Yarur was a Chilean Horatio Alger. Founder of the first modern cotton mill in Chile, he turned it into the base of one of the country's greatest fortunes. In the process, a Palestinian peddler became a captain of Chilean

3

industry, a rags-to-riches story that accompanied and symbolized the nation's industrial development. So fabled was the family's wealth by 1971 that "tan rico como Yarur" ("as rich as Yarur") had become a Chilean saying. By then the Yarur mill had become the base of a family economic empire, which included Chile's second largest bank, insurance companies, radio stations, and real estate, in addition to an array of textile factories and distributors. To many Chileans, the Yarurs symbolized both the success of the nation's entrepreneurs and their contribution to its development.

Other Chileans agreed that the Yarur story was emblematic of the evolution of their country's private sector, but they viewed it less as a cause for celebration than as a cautionary tale. To them, Yarur symbolized the "monopoly" and "dependent" character of Chilean capitalism and its sweetheart relationship with the Chilean state at the expense of its competitors, consumers, and workers. Although they acknowledged the entrepreneurial genius of the firm's founder, they stressed that state assistance was the real secret of his success. Yarur's political influence had secured his business protective tariffs, cheap foreign exchange, and favorable regulation. The result was a protected "national" industry that could not compete with cheaper foreign goods, but was tied to foreign capital and dependent on the importation of machinery, spare parts, and raw materials.

Although technically a public company, Yarur was run as a family firm in patrimonial style, a central enterprise in an economic empire notorious for its shrewd but shady management. By 1971, this Yarur economic empire was one of the largest and most powerful in Chile, and the Yarurs were counted among the dozen financial "clans" that dominated the Chilean economy. To Allende's economic advisers, this history and position marked the Yarur mill as a prime target for nationalization by a government committed to gaining control of the "commanding heights" of the Chilean economy, "declaring war on monopolies," and placing the nation's industries "at the service of the people."

To the mill's workers, Yarur's significance was less abstract but equally salient. It was their world, one ruled with an iron hand by omnipotent and capricious owners who demanded deference in addition to discipline and loyalty in addition to production. To them, the mill represented a steady job in a country plagued by unemployment, but it was a job that exacted its pound of flesh in return for low wages and limited benefits. On the factory floor, the workers were controlled by the Taylor System, in which every movement was regulated and each moment monitored, converting them into optimally efficient extensions of the machines they tended. The introduction of *taylorismo* a decade before had produced the biggest and bitterest strike in the factory's history, with more than a thousand workers fired and blacklisted in its wake.

But strikes were few and far between at the Yarur mill. Social control of the workers was ensured by a combination of paternalism and repression. Loyalty to the *patrón* was rewarded, but it was demonstrated by informing on fellow workers. Only a company union was tolerated, and discussion of an independent union or national politics was prohibited, along with criticism of the Yarurs or of working conditions in the factory. "Deviance" from this norm of unquestioning loyalty was reported by informers and punished by harassment, transfer to undesirable sections, suspension, and dismissal. As a result, Yarur was notorious for its repressive politics, rigid social control, and exploitative working conditions.

Although the social politics of the Yarur mill reflected the paternalistic vision of its owners, it also relied on the complicity of the Chilean state. The Labor Code of 1931 gave the state broad authority to regulate labor relations and to ensure union democracy, projecting the state as the neutral arbiter of the conflict between labor and capital. Yet, with rare exception, these powers had been invoked by venal officials, beholden politicians, or conservative governments to confirm the absolute authority of the Yarurs over their workers. On three occasions, the election of presidents heading coalition governments with leftist participation triggered workers' movements that counted on state support to redress the power imbalance between labor and capital at Yarur, only to be disappointed—and defeated.

These intertwined histories of the Yarurs, their workers, and the Chilean state—recounted in the background chapters—were part of the mind-set of the actors in the 1970–71 drama and helped shape their expectations and behavior. Amador Yarur, anxious "to be what his father had been," was determined that history should repeat itself. His veteran workers feared this would be the case and were reluctant to risk themselves in yet another losing cause. Leftist leaders, locally and nationally, were determined to break with this past and to fulfill their pledge to construct a New Chile—even at the Yarur mill.

In 1970, the election of Salvador Allende—itself a reflection of the rise of the Left and the leftward shift of the Center nationally—detonated a new and more powerful workers movement at the Yarur mill. It was led by a new generation of younger workers, more urban and better educated than the old, more typical of the new working class that had emerged in Chile during the preceding years. It was these "Youngsters" (*jóvenes*) who persuaded the "Old-timers" (*viejos*) that with a *compañero presidente* they could defeat the Yarurs and win an independent union. In the wake of Allende's election, the blue-collar workers regained control of what had been a company union and forced the Yarurs to accept the first authentic collective bargaining in a decade, negotiations that resulted in major gains in wages and working conditions. During these same months, S.A. Yarur's five hundred employees organized the first white-collar union in the firm's history. By the end of 1970, a repressed group of textile workers had cast aside their apparent passivity and crowned a year of struggle with success—a local social triumph made possible by the national political victory of the Chilean Left.

Within months of those achievements, moreover, the workers' movement at Yarur had moved beyond these historic aspirations to new and more revolutionary goals, translating the abstract planks of the Popular Unity program into their own concrete reality. By April 1971, the Yarur workers were ready for the structural transformation that Allende had promised them during his campaign—the socialization of their mill—a step that embodied their understanding of the meaning of the Chilean revolution. To the workers of Yarur, the seizure and socialization of their mill were like the fall of the Bastille—a dreamed-of but scarcely imaginable event that freed them from the shackles of their past and dissolved the very contours of their world into pure possibility. Ex-Yarur, their socialized factory, where they created their own vision of "democratic socialism," was a dream of workers who had never before dared to dream. This book is the story of the birth—and death—of their dream.

It is also a case study in revolution from below. Following the election of Salvador Allende on a platform promising a democratic road to socialism, the Yarur mill was the first factory to be seized by its workers as a way of securing its socialization and the first to experiment with worker co-management. It was an industry in the vanguard of a revolution from below that powerfully influenced the pace, direction and outcome of the Chilean revolutionary process.

Most students of the Chilean revolution have viewed it in partisan political terms, blaming Communists or Christian Democrats, Socialists or Nationalists, the extreme Left or the far Right, for its changing course and tragic conclusion.[1] What these divergent interpretations have in common is their perspective: They are essentially views from above, which assume that national political actors were the important players in the revolutionary drama, and ignore the relative autonomy of local actors and movements.

Yet the history of the Yarur mill during the months that followed Allende's election and inauguration suggests a more complex interpretation, one in which the workers' revolution from below, with its own internal dynamic, played a major role. The Chilean revolution reached a turning point in April 1971, with the seizure of the Yarur mill by its workers and its socialization by the Allende government, using executive decree powers to circumvent an opposition-controlled Congress. A wave of factory seizures followed, all demanding immediate socialization and forcing Allende to choose between his carefully controlled and phased strategy for socialism and a confrontation with his central mass base. As a consequence, the timetable for structural transformation was accelerated, and the revolutionary process was radicalized; in response, the Center moved right and the middle classes embraced counterrevolution.

National political actors, from President Allende and his ministers to party and labor leaders, played major roles in this turning point, but so did the workers of the Yarur mill. As Allende was acutely aware, the Yarur drama revealed as unresolved the crucial questions of revolutionary leadership and strategy. In its wake, it was unclear who was determining the pace and direction of the revolutionary process and who was deciding its strategy and tactics. Within the Popular Unity coalition and government, autonomous yet overlapping centers of authority appeared to coexist uneasily and compete for ascendancy. Within the revolutionary camp as a whole, the Yarur *toma* and its aftermath underscored the tension between revolution from below and revolution from above, the contest between workers and politicians, the clash between leaders and masses and their differing visions of the revolutionary process. It was a tension that was never resolved, and in the end it proved fatal to the Chilean revolution. For all these reasons, the Yarur *toma* marked a turning point in the Chilean revolution, and its workers were central protagonists of this drama.

This book is *their* story, which I have tried to tell as much as possible through their eyes and in their words, in an effort to preserve the authenticity of their reality and to convey the reality of their experience. Although some labor historians of Latin America have pursued similar goals, none have utilized the same methods—combining oral history with the factory study. Most research in Latin American labor history to date has involved institutional, statistical, or ideological approaches to workers' lives. These studies have added to our knowledge and laid the foundations of the field, but they are largely views from above or analyses from outside, too general or too abstract to capture the concrete historical experiences of workers, both in themselves and in relation to more global historical events and processes.

The history of labor in Chile is a good example of both the accomplishments and limitations of existing scholarship.[2] Some studies have sketched the outlines of the origins and development of labor organizations and militancy in Chile, but have based frequently tendentious interpretations on a slender body of evidence.[3] Others have demarcated the pattern of wages and prices, strikes, and voting behavior[4] or analyzed labor relations or the ties between labor and political parties.[5] There have also been a few useful biographies of national union leaders[6] and some suggestive writings based on survey data.[7]

These studies constitute contributions to scholarship, but almost all are descriptions of a labor iceberg from the tip that appears above the national waterline. Leaders, institutions, ideologies, statistical averages, and structures are discussed. With rare exception, the workers themselves—the presumed protagonists of labor history—appear in these studies only as institutional, theoretical, or statistical abstractions; the concrete and complex realities of their experience are conspicuous by their absence. Where oral history interviews have been used, their purpose has generally been to add color to otherwise traditional studies or to bear political witness to traumatic national events.

The alternative is to fuse history from above with history from below. In this book I have combined the microhistory of the factory study with the insights of oral history, integrating them with national perspectives and written sources. Within this context, I have tried to reconstruct the experience of the workers of the Yarur mill during a particularly salient period of their history—and Chile's. Along the way, I have sought to illuminate such neglected areas of Latin American labor history as the history of work, the formation of consciousness, and divisions within the working class reflecting differences in character, worldview, and politics.

Within the arena of the Yarur mill, I have explored as well the relationship between classes and assessed the role of the state in the contest between labor and capital. The struggles of workers do not take place in a vacuum, nor can their experience be understood in isolation from the history of capital and the contest between labor and capital for control of the state. In Chile, labor, capital and the state formed an eternal triangle, within which the destiny of the Yarur workers was decided. I have also examined the relationship between changes within the industry and changes in the economy, polity, and society outside its walls, including the relationship between workers' movements from below and national labor organizations and political parties.

A well-chosen case study can also illuminate more global historical events and processes—national and international, economic or political. The Yarur mill was a classic example of the import substitution industrialization and paternalistic labor organization that characterized the Popular Front and postwar eras. The impact of foreign technologies and managerial models, international conflicts and multinational corporations on developing economies is revealed in the factory's history. Four of Yarur's five workers' movements followed national elections perceived by the workers as leftist victories, and they cast light from below on Chile's political course.

In order to illuminate this complex history and capture the workers' experience, I have made use of a variety of sources, written as well as oral. I have drawn on available statistical materials, including published and unpublished S.A. Yarur statistics and data culled from the company archives. Government statistics were another source, particularly data from the Min-

istries of Economy and Labor, from the Superintendency of Public Corporations and the Textile Committee of the State Development Corporation
(CORFO). Census and election returns were also used, as were the data
compiled by the Textile Institute of Chile (INCHITEX), the private-sector
business association, and W. R. Grace's Chilean textile subsidiary. I have
made use of correspondence found in the company archives and in the Ministry of Labor archives; and I have utilized as well the minutes of union
meetings, of the S.A. Yarur Board of Directors and of the state mediation
board, along with the minutes of Ex-Yarur's Administrative Council and
Coordinating Committee.

The annual reports of S.A. Yarur and other public companies were
researched, as were the annual reports of the Society for the Promotion of
Manufacturing (SOFOFA) and the Textile Institute of Chile. The reports of
government investigators and state labor inspectors were also consulted.
Although the police archives were not open to me, police reports occasionally
appeared or were quoted in Labor Ministry files, congressional documents,
or court records; and a few reports of the company police were turned up.
The reports and notes of journalists and scholars who visited the Yarur mill
were often of interest. Notarial and judicial archives were utilized, as were
the texts of congressional debates and presidential speeches. Chilean, Peruvian, Bolivian, and American periodicals—ranging from daily newspapers
and weekly magazines to specialized trade publications and the Arab community press—proved important repositories of fact and opinion. Worker
flyers, pamphlets, and newspapers were valuable sources for the history of
Yarur workers' movements.

But first and foremost, I have relied on oral history, conceived of neither
as folklore nor as sacred text, but as a historical source like any other, whose
information and arguments have to be evaluated in the same way as a historian
would evaluate a written text.[8] My study is based largely on oral history
interviews, some of which were recorded on tape and others noted down by
hand. During the course of my research, I conducted more than two hundred
interviews, including multiple interviews with many individuals. There were
interviews with political and labor leaders at the national and local levels,
with state labor inspectors and ministry officials, with mill owners and
managers, with people who knew the Yarurs in Peru and Bolivia, and with
those who did business with them in Chile. There were interviews, too,
with local storekeepers and residents of the neighborhoods surrounding the
Yarur mill and housing developments and also interviews with the families'
of Yarur employees.

Most of all, I interviewed workers—blue-collar and white-collar, male
and female, Old-timers and Youngsters, leftists and rightists, skilled and

unskilled, weavers and spinners, leaders and rank and file. It was their words that largely shaped my understanding of the Chilean experience. It is their experience that shapes this book: the story of the creation of "Ex-Yarur: Territory Free of Exploitation"—a turning point in the Chilean revolution.

I

ORIGINS: CAPITAL, LABOR, AND THE STATE

1

PALESTINIANS IN
THE PROMISED LAND

When the workers toppled Juan Yarur's larger-than-life statue from its pedestal in the Plaza Yarur and took over the factory that bore his name, they not only inaugurated a new epoch in their own lives. They also brought to a close an era that had begun in 1937, when Juan Yarur opened Chile's first modern cotton mill. Yarur had come to Chile from neighboring Bolivia three years before at the invitation of the government of President Arturo Alessandri, which was interested in promoting domestic industries as a solution to the intense economic problems generated by the Great Depression. The trip from the barren highlands of Bolivia to the fertile valleys of Chile was brief, but for Juan Yarur it marked the end of a far longer journey that had taken him halfway across the globe.

Juan Yarur Lolas was born in 1896 in the holy town of Bethlehem, then part of Ottoman Palestine. He was the oldest of three sons born to Carlos Yarur and Emilia Lolas, and although he was not born in a manger, neither was he from a wealthy family. The Yarurs were Christian Arabs and, like many of their community, lived off the religious tourist trade. Carlos Yarur was a maker and seller of pearl-shell trinkets whose prosperous business employed twenty artisans; his wife came from a less wealthy family of farmers and fishermen. The Yarurs were comfortable enough to send Juan and his brother Nicolás to the Kaiser Wilhelm School that German missionaries had founded near Bethlehem and that Juan Yarur attended through secondary school.[1]

As a teenager, he helped out in the family business; and when his father died, he set up on his own, selling religious souvenirs to the pilgrims who came to Bethlehem. It was a business that offered little scope for Juan Yarur's budding entrepreneurial talents. By 1912, moreover, the Ottoman Empire was at war in the Balkans and was torn by ethnic tensions. The sixteen-year-old Juan Yarur, with his younger brother, Nicolás, left Palestine to escape both the imperial draft and Turkish intolerance of the empire's Christian Arab minority.[2]

The young Yarur brothers wandered through Europe peddling religious trinkets and then took ship for America to escape the gathering war clouds on the Continent. Like most Arab immigrants of this era, they knew little of the lands to which they were headed and based their choice of destination on the presence of relatives who could help them get a start in the New World. Juan and Nicolás Yarur had a married older sister in Chile and a cousin in Bolivia. With no other star to guide their journey from Bethlehem, they set sail for Chile and by 1914 had settled in Bolivia. There, with the money they had brought with them, the Yarur brothers opened a small store in the highland tin mining center of Oruro.[3]

Juan Yarur spent two long decades in the Andean highlands of Bolivia and southern Peru, transforming himself from a Palestinian peddler into a Latin American industrialist along the way. In booming Oruro, during World War I, he became a wholesaler, supplying imported textiles to the shopkeepers and peddlers who sold cheap goods to Bolivia's miners and peasants. When the war ended, Juan Yarur took his pregnant wife to the more clement clime of Arequipa, the commercial capital of southern Peru, a better place to raise a family.[4] In Arequipa, Juan Yarur began to work with the Saids, who had emigrated there from Bethlehem three decades before, and by 1918 had become one of the major importers of southern Peru, specializing in textiles for the Indian peasantry of the densely populated highlands.[5] From the Saids, he learned the import trade, along with the use of recent Arab immigrants as a loyal, low-cost distribution network. From them he also learned that a public position as Arab community leader could further private economic ends.[6] The Saids were impressed by Juan Yarur's entrepreneurial talents, and when the Yarur brothers returned to Oruro in 1920, it was as junior partners in the prestigious import house of Said & Sons, with responsibility for the Bolivian market.[7]

In Bolivia in 1929, the importers became industrialists. As distributors of imported textiles, the Saids and Yarurs were aware of the large market for heavy flannels and other rough cotton goods among the poor peasants of the Andean highlands, which was being satisfied by imports from overseas. When the opposition of foreign-owned textile factories and domestic political enemies blocked the Said request for a Peruvian concession, the Yarurs used the contacts that they had developed with influential Bolivians to secure an exclusive concession in La Paz, where there was no existing cotton mill to oppose them and where a nationalist government favored industrial development.[8]

In 1929, Said & Yarur's La Paz cotton mill opened with the aid of an exclusive Bolivian concession, American machinery and technicians, and local loans. For two years, the Yarurs, who managed the mill, struggled to overcome unsuitable workers, resistant consumers, financial difficulties, and their own inexperience. They were helped by the Great Depression, which left a bankrupt Bolivia without the foreign exchange to import textiles, but it was the Chaco War (1932–35) that made their fortune. This conflict between Bolivia and Paraguay over the oil-rich Chaco Desert put their idle looms and spindles to work making uniforms and blankets for the Bolivian army. It also converted their cotton mill into a strategic war industry, which the government subsidized by giving them scarce dollars at an artificially low rate of exchange—dollars that were supposed to be used to import raw materials and spare parts, but could also be sold on the black market for windfall profits.[9] "The Chaco War was a bonanza for Said & Yarur," a former employee recalled.[10] By its close, Juan Yarur had become economically powerful, politically influential, and socially acceptable. He had also established connections with American bankers, manufacturers and exporters that would make his next industrial venture far easier than his first.[11]

Equally important were the experience gained and the lessons learned. At bottom, the Yarurs' Bolivian mill was a school for industrialists, a classroom in which they learned how to found and manage an industry—how to secure a concession, select machinery, shape a labor force, master modern technology, run a mill, and distribute its production. "For us the La Paz factory was a big leap," affirmed Nicolás Yarur, "because we never had a factory before."[12]

Although some of these lessons were the common stock of industrial entrepreneurs everywhere, others were specific to Latin America. In La Paz the Yarurs learned that in order to secure a concession one had to offer something to everyone—a cotton market to farmers, jobs to labor, foreign exchange savings to governments, and development to nationalists. They also learned to found an industry with government subsidies, foreign credits, and local loans without putting up capital of their own. They learned how to shape a docile and disciplined work force out of ill-educated rural migrants and how to cast labor relations in a paternalistic mold. They learned, too, that women workers were less expensive, more malleable, and equally skilled mill hands. They learned, moreover, to place their trust in American technology and technicians.

Bolivia also taught the Yarurs that there were more ways to profit from a Latin American industry than by selling its products—particularly where foreign exchange was scarce and could be secured from a friendly government at a subsidized rate of exchange. Most of all, La Paz taught them the importance of the Latin American state to the fortunes of private entrepreneurs—and thus the importance of securing political influence. The Yarurs' Bolivian mill was not just a school for industrialists; it was a school for *Latin American* industrialists.

It was also where Juan Yarur established himself as an entrepreneur who could successfully mount a modern textile industry where none existed, amid the constraints of Andean instability and underdevelopment. In 1933, when the Alessandri government wanted capitalists who could create a modern cotton industry in Chile, it sought out the Palestinian entrepreneur and invited his firm to establish a similar industry in the territory of Bolivia's wealthier neighbor. Juan Yarur's pilgrimage from Bethlehem to Bolivia may have been long and arduous, with many years spent wandering in the Andean wilderness, but his entry into the city of St. James was triumphal.

A PALESTINIAN'S PROGRESS

It was in April 1933 that Juan Yarur set out from La Paz for Santiago, Chile. Although the two countries were neighbors, the journey between their capitals was difficult, and the contrast in landscapes striking. To descend from the stark and barren Bolivian plateau, some 14,000 feet above the sea, to the fertile Pacific valleys of central Chile, reminiscent of his native Mediterranean, was to enter a different world. For an Arab emigrant who had wandered so long in the frozen deserts of Bolivia, Chile's verdant valleys must have seemed the promised land.

Although the differences in landscape and climate might have been reason enough for the trip, "the purpose behind this journey to Chile," Juan Yarur confided to a Santiago journalist, "refers to the possible installation of a cotton spinning factory, along the lines of our La Paz factory," a project that would represent an investment of twenty million Chilean pesos ($800,000). The installation of such a mill, Yarur affirmed, would promote "the cultivation of cotton, solve part of the unemployment problem and produce a good savings for the country, which was now forced to purchase for itself in foreign markets what could be produced right here." In this way, his industry would contribute "a modest grain of sand to the industrial progress of the country."[13] It was an argument that Juan Yarur had perfected in Bolivia and would repeat many times in Chile—to bankers and journalists, mayors and ministers, congressmen and presidents.

In talking to Alessandri's finance minister, Gustavo Ross, however, Juan Yarur was preaching to the converted. Ross was well aware that Chile was the most depressed nation in a depressed world, a country whose extreme dependence on mining exports (principally copper and nitrates, which together accounted for almost 90 percent of export earnings) had made it particularly vulnerable to the collapse of international trade during the preceding years. Between 1929 and 1932, the value of Chile's exports had fallen by 88 percent, mining output by three-quarters, and domestic production as a whole by almost half. During this same period, the price of staples doubled, real wages fell by some 40 percent, and unemployment soared, with three-quarters of Chile's miners out of work. The Great Depression struck hardest at those Chileans least able to bear the burden, but few escaped its ravages unscathed, and faith in the economic system itself was shaken.[14]

The Alessandri government was also aware that such a profound economic trauma could cause dangerous social tremors in Chile because the political earthquake detonated by the Great Depression was responsible for its own existence. In 1931 such unrest had toppled the seemingly impregnable rule of the Chilean strongman, General Carlos Ibáñez del Campo. One year later, the continuing economic crisis had provoked a revolution, led by a charismatic army colonel with the unlikely name of Marmaduke Grove, who had proclaimed Chile the hemisphere's first socialist state. Although Grove's "Socialist Republic" only lasted twelve days before it was overthrown by a more conservative coup, the sudden fashionableness of "socialism" among the middle class and the strong response that Grove's revolutionary populism had evoked in the urban masses threw a scare into Chile's traditional elites. One result was the election of Arturo Alessandri, the upper-class industrialist and reformer who had been ousted as too radical a decade earlier, as the last hope of the status quo. Another consequence was the conversion of even the *laissez-faire* commercial elite to the gospel of domestic industry and the catechism of state economic intervention.[15]

That was why Gustavo Ross, Alessandri's finance minister and strongman, who spoke for those commercial elites, had invited Juan Yarur to Chile and was prepared to promote a Yarur effort to establish Chile's first modern cotton textile industry as part of the Alessandri government's strategy of substituting domestic manufactures for foreign imports.[16] With his help, Juan Yarur secured the duty-free importation of spinning machinery and a low tariff on imported looms, plus a million-dollar loan from the Banco de Chile, the nation's leading private bank, with which to finance the construction of his Santiago factory.[17] With this local support in hand, Juan Yarur was able to obtain his machinery on long-term credit—and at a depression discount—from the same American manufacturers who had supplied his Bolivian mill. In the end, his Chilean factory was financed almost entirely by local bankers and foreign manufacturers, so that the Arab entrepreneurs only had to put up "a few thousand dollars of [their] own."[18] Banco de Chile advances also enabled the Yarurs to buy out the Saids. As a result, when the first yard of cloth rolled off the production lines on January 7, 1937— Juan Yarur's saint's day—it bore the stamp of "Yarur Brothers," a family firm in which Juan Yarur was the largest shareholder, served as president, and acted as general manager.[19]

Santiago, a city of half a million with a perfect climate and a stunning natural setting, was where Juan Yarur decided to build his cotton mill. It was a shrewd choice, at once Chile's political capital, financial center, railway hub, and largest market. The site that Juan Yarur chose for his factory was on the southern edge of the city, then an area of open fields—*puro pasto*[20]— west of the Carmine industrial zone, close to the Central Railway Station, and bordering on the Zanjón de la Aguada canal and Circumnavigation Railway. It was an ideal location, which assured him of water for the mill's cooling system, accessible railway transportation to its suppliers and markets, and nearby working-class communities from which to recruit an initial labor force.[21]

During those first years of establishing his infant industry, Juan Yarur consolidated a set of business relationships that would outlast his lifetime. Internationally, he maintained the links with the Morgan Guaranty Trust and American cotton dealers and machine manufacturers that had served him well in Bolivia.[22] The Banco de Chile became his local banker, and through it the Yarurs were able to forge a close relationship with Saavedra Benard, an established distributing firm, which had recently come within the bank's orbit.[23] With the transformation of the Yarur Brothers partnership into a public corporation in 1941, Juan Yarur created further links between his Arab enterprise and prominent Chileans that would stand his family business in good stead. Its board of directors included Arturo Phillips, general manager of the Banco de Chile, as vice president, as well as other influentials from the interlocking worlds of business and politics.[24] Going public, however, neither altered the family character of the business nor lessened Juan Yarur's control. At bottom, this legal transformation concentrated the power of decision in the hands of Juan Yarur while protecting the interests of his two brothers, who gradually sold off their shares and used the proceeds to buy textile mills of their own.[25]

During those early years, Juan Yarur's principal problem was selling his mill's expanding production of cotton textiles and yarn. As in Bolivia, consumer resistance to wearing apparel cut from domestic cloth was part of the problem, but the low price of Japanese textiles, which sold in Chile for the price Yarur paid for his raw cotton, was the central dilemma. As in La Paz, Juan Yarur overcame these obstacles with the aid of the state and a timely war. Tariff protection enabled the Yarur mill to meet the Japanese competition after 1939, but it was World War II that made his fortune.

For Chile, global conflict might mean scarce foreign exchange, consumer shortages, and rapid inflation; but for Yarur, the benefits of World War II far outweighed its costs. Pearl Harbor banished his Japanese rivals from the

Chilean market more decisively than any tariff, effectively restricting the market to a small number of domestic producers whose installed capacity was insufficient to keep pace with consumer demand. Conceived in the Great Depression and born under the sign of the Popular Front, the Yarur mill came of age under the aegis of global conflict.[26]

World War II completed what the Great Depression had begun: the transformation of Chile's industries into the leading sector of its economy. Shortages of imported consumer goods and wartime demand for Chilean copper impelled this industrial surge, but state promotion and protection also played a major role.[27] During the war years, the state emerged as the principal source of investment credit and as the chief risk taker in projects of uncertain profitability, long gestation, or large initial investment. In addition, policymakers recognized the new centrality—and continued un-competitiveness—of Chile's industries in a complex network of governmental protection and state subsidies, ranging from tariffs and import quotas to multiple exchange rates and cheap dollars for machinery, spare parts, and raw materials. By the war's close, a Chilean road to industrialization had been constructed, paved by the state and paid for by the consumer in the form of higher prices.[28]

Among Chile's cotton mills, Juan Yarur's was particularly well placed to take advantage of wartime opportunities and governmental policies. The combination of protected markets and limited domestic competition with its excess capacity, enterprising management, and financial solidity spelled greatly increased production, sales, and earnings for Yarur, Inc. Between 1941 and 1944, receipts almost tripled while costs only doubled, yielding reported annual net profits that averaged 42 percent despite Yarur's stock-piling of spare parts and building of a sizable reserve fund.[29]

By 1945, the Yarur mill was producing at the limits of its installed capacity in three round-the-clock shifts and still not meeting consumer demand for its products. During the war, the machinery that could enable Yarur to satisfy this increased demand was simply not available as American manufacturers retooled for the war effort. In 1944, however, the end of the conflict was in sight, and the Yarur directors signed contracts for the new machinery that would enable Yarur, Inc., to claim an even larger share of the growing Chilean market despite the expansion of competitors and emerg-ence of new rivals.[30]

In the postwar struggle for preeminence, moreover, Yarur, Inc., had one asset that none of its competitors could match—Juan Yarur, a master businessman at the height of his powers. Even his rivals recognized him as "a born entrepreneur,"[31] and a Communist labor leader, one of his bitterest antagonists, affirmed: "He was the best business strategist I have ever seen, a true business genius."[32]

Juan Yarur was not just a "business genius." He was also a shrewd political operator. He had taken pains to build bridges to the dominant political figures of the Right and Center, giving generously to political campaigns in return for congressional allies and governmental access. He had maintained good relations with successive governments of varying political persuasions and had ensured the protection of his firm's interests. With the election of the aging caudillo, Carlos Ibáñez del Campo, to his second presidency in 1952, the political influence of Juan Yarur and the Arab-Chilean community reached its zenith. Yarur was an intimate of the new chief executive, for whom the door to the presidential palace was always open.[33]

Juan Yarur did not hesitate to use his political influence to advance his business interests. When Ibáñez's minister of labor tried to enforce the president's own labor code at the Yarur mill, he was forced to resign.[34] When Chile's foreign exchange difficulties led the Ibáñez government to barter Chilean nitrates for Egyptian cotton and centralize its allocation in a government agency, it made the state the arbiter of textile fortune and the Yarur mill the chief beneficiary of a system that placed a premium on political pull.[35] Although not enough raw cotton was imported to meet the requirements of Chile's textile industries, the Yarur mill often received more than it needed. As a result, Juan Yarur was in a position to sell surplus cotton on the black market and to dictate terms to the smaller mills, which became totally dependent on Yarur for their own inputs of cotton and yarn. His stranglehold on Chile's cotton imports was the source of both windfall profits and a dominant market position. "Ruthlessness" was the word that one competitor used to describe Yarur's business style.[36]

Although other textile magnates had more capital and more modern mills, the decade following World War II belonged to Juan Yarur. During these years, he not only emerged as a captain of industry, but as a banker as well. In 1946, Juan Yarur took over the Banco de Crédito e Inversiones, a failing commercial bank founded in 1937 by a group of Italian immigrants to provide credit for small businesses; and, with the help of the Arab community, he transformed it into a highly profitable, but very personal, financial instrument. By 1954, Juan Yarur had erected the twin pillars—the textile mill and bank—on which his family's economic empire would rest.[37]

On August 21, 1954, while driving along fashionable Providencia Avenue, Juan Yarur was stricken by a heart attack. His American sedan spun out of control and crashed into the curb, where the Arab magnate died unexpectedly at the age of fifty-eight. He left behind a growing economic empire with a solid industrial and financial base.

In the end, however, Juan Yarur's chief legacy may have been his entrepreneurial model. He demonstrated that in an economy that combined industrialization and inflation with tariff protection, import quotas, and price controls, windfall profits could be earned by the shrewd accumulation and sale of raw materials and product inventories. He also showed that the pairing of an industrial monopoly with a closely controlled bank was the key to economic power in postwar Chile—in combination with the political influence that he cultivated assiduously and wielded shrewdly.

Juan Yarur was a master of all these techniques and strategies. By the time he died, his wealth, genius, and power were proverbial; and Juan Yarur had become a Chilean legend, a Palestinian Horatio Alger who had "made his America" in Santiago.

FATHER AND SONS

Juan Yarur died before he could complete the creation of the economic empire that he had founded. He left behind three adult sons, all of whom had some business experience, but none of whom inherited their father's combination of entrepreneurial genius and personal charm. In other ways, Juan Yarur's entrepreneurial legacy was hard for his sons to imitate, yet impossible to ignore. He had branded his business style indelibly on his cotton mill. Juan Yarur held the accounts in his head and his clients in the palm of his hand. He knew every detail of the business and made his deals out of his pocket—the one with the wallet that contained the little pieces of paper with the business data that only he knew. Within the factory, although "he seemed like just another worker," his word was law, and his subordinates were totally dependent on his will and favor, without autonomous authority or power of decision. As an expression of Juan Yarur's personality and a reflection of his talents, this personalistic way of running the factory was fine. As a system of business management, however, "it was organized disorganization," one of his top aides recalled.[38]

Moreover, times had changed. Juan Yarur's untimely death coincided with the passing of an era in Chile's economic history. The import substitution boom came to an end with the Korean peace; and the years that followed were shaped by falling copper exports, galloping inflation, and industrial stagnation, the latter a reflection of declining real incomes and eroded consumer purchasing power.[39] By 1954, consumer demand no longer exceeded the factory's output, and the competition for this limited market was far greater than before. Yarur's sons inherited a cotton mill of declining profitability that could no longer afford the managerial inefficiencies and low labor productivity of the past.[40] This was the view of Jorge Yarur Banna, the most talented of Juan Yarur's sons, who took over the family business after his father's death. It reflected not only the changed economic realities of the Chilean textile industry but also Jorge Yarur's personality, training, and experience.[41]

"Don Jorge" was the best businessman of Juan Yarur's sons and his father's equal in financial matters, but there the resemblance ended.[42] Where his father was a self-made entrepreneur and personalistic manager, Jorge Yarur was a university-educated lawyer and corporate executive. Don Juan's death gave Jorge Yarur the opportunity to modernize his father's cotton mill. He was comfortable with professional expertise, aware of the importance of a quality staff and prepared to delegate authority to skilled subordinates. He was an experienced banker, who had taken courses in business administration introduced recently in Chile from the United States. Jorge Yarur's model was the modern American corporation that he had studied, and he set out to reshape S.A. Yarur in its image.[43]

Juan Yarur's death coincided as well with the dawning of the age of the transnational corporation, an expansion epitomized not only by the multiplication of foreign subsidiaries but also by the export of its example and the merchandising of its methods. Juan Yarur had always looked to the United States for his technical models and depended heavily on American expertise. In 1956, Jorge Yarur followed his father's precedent but for radically different purposes. He hired American experts to advise him on the modernization of the family cotton mill, with Price, Waterhouse, the prestigious international accounting firm, acting as management consultants.[44]

At S.A. Yarur, an old-fashioned family firm and factory, their recommendations included the reorganization of both administration and production to improve the efficiency of the former and the productivity of the latter. The methods of the modern American corporation—cost accounting, operations research, computer processing—were introduced for the first time, and the administration of the industry was reorganized. New departments—production planning, industrial engineering, data processing—were created; and Chilean professionals hired and trained to staff them. The structure of decision making was rationalized to improve the flow of information, the delegation of responsibility, and the resolution of problems.[45]

Jorge Yarur's American consultants identified the low productivity of labor at the mill as the biggest threat to the profitability of Yarur, Inc., and recommended the Taylor System, with its work norms and time-motion controls, as a remedy for this problem, one that would allow the Yarurs to produce the same amount of cloth and yarn with half the work force—and half the labor costs. Consultants from another American transnational, Burlington Mills, supervised installation of the new system of work beginning in 1962.[46] It took three years, $300,000 in consulting fees, and the biggest strike in Yarur's history; but by 1965 the labor force had been halved and its productivity more than doubled. With minimal new capital investment, the Yarurs had greatly reduced their unit costs while improving the utilization of the firm's past investment in imported machinery. In the process, a talented group of Chilean technicians had been trained, and the quality of the work force was upgraded. From a management viewpoint, the Taylor System was a brilliant success.[47]

On the surface, it appeared as if Juan Yarur's mill were being transformed utterly, turning its back on his personalistic and paternalistic business style and embracing instead the American model known in Chile as "rational business administration," which "was very fashionable at that time."[48] Appearances were deceiving. It was one thing to replicate on paper the structure of an impersonal American corporation, but something else to implement it in a family firm run by brothers with disparate talents, differing personalities, divergent business visions—and the same ambition: "to be what their father had been."[49]

The clash between Jorge and Amador Yarur was not just sibling rivalry, nor merely a personality conflict or power struggle. At bottom, it was a contest between two entrepreneurial visions and business styles: the personalism of Juan Yarur versus the impersonal corporate model of his middle son. To Jorge Yarur, his father's business style was both outmoded and uncongenial, and his own desire for a modernization of management was a business necessity as well as a personal preference; to Amador, his brother's importation of foreign models seemed out of tune with the Chilean character and a betrayal of his father's legacy, as well as alien to his own personality and incompatible with his talents. Underconfident and ill-educated, Amador Yarur was unprepared to compete with his better-qualified older brother for ascendancy within a modern managerial structure. If S.A. Yarur went the way of the American corporation, there was little doubt who would dominate it. If it remained the personalistic business that Amador had learned at his father's side, the outcome might be different.[50]

Whether their struggle was over power or management philosophy, the results were the same—a competition for ascendancy and a conflict of authority that made a mockery of the clear lines of command on the organizational charts. Jorge Yarur was president of the firm; Amador, manager of the mill. "Here in the factory they did not speak to each other," one senior employee recalled, "and many times one gave an order, and the other gave an opposite order. There was no unity of command."[51] Instead, there was a running battle between the two Yarur brothers and their adherents among the employees. Jorge Yarur placed his trust in "the students," the score of university graduates who had entered the company recently. They were given special training and responsible positions. Amador Yarur emerged as the champion of his father's veteran employees, who owed their positions more to loyalty than to ability and felt as threatened as Amador himself by the new style of management that Jorge Yarur was trying to impose on Don Juan's mill.[52]

Amador Yarur might not be able to oppose his brother's modernizing mission openly, but as manager of the mill he was able to undermine it—and Jorge Yarur's authority in the process. Although the contest for control of the family textile industry continued for several years, Amador Yarur gradually won the day. Jorge Yarur might be the better businessman and more powerful personality, but he was too fully engaged at the family bank to best his brother at daily palace intrigues.[53] He remained president of Yarur, Inc., but "at bottom, it was Amador who ruled here," one of Jorge's partisans lamented.[54]

Amador Yarur had no objections to the final stage of his brother's planned transformation of their father's mill—an expansion and modernization program that would increase the mill's productive capacity by 70 percent and replace its antiquated machinery with modern equipment capable of manufacturing the synthetic blends that were increasingly in demand throughout Latin America. The Taylor System's improvement of productivity made Yarur the most efficient cotton mill in Chile, ready and able to dominate the domestic market. At the same time, the prospective formation of a Latin American common market—which filled most Chilean textile manufacturers with a dread of Colombian competition—encouraged the Yarurs to pursue their expansion plans with vigor.[55] With their labor costs halved and operations modernized, the Yarurs were optimistic about their competitive position and future prospects.

Then, in June 1963, the Yarurs bought W. R. Grace's Caupolican Textiles, their traditional rival—largely with Yarur, Inc., capital—and these ambitious plans for the transformation of their father's mill were postponed.[56] Jorge Yarur withdrew from the contest for control of the Yarur mill and focused his attentions instead on the Caupolican mills, where he could realize his vision of a modern textile industry without having to overcome his brother's resistance. By the end of 1963, each of the Yarur Banna brothers had his own textile mill.[57]

AMADOR'S MILL

As a consequence, the factory that the workers seized in April 1971 was neither Juan's nor Jorge Yarur's—it was Amador's mill. Juan Yarur may have founded it, and Jorge Yarur may have modernized it, but it was Amador who ruled it, and he stamped it with his own likeness. On the surface, he combined his father's legacy with his brother's changes, but Amador Yarur colored this complex inheritance with his own personality and concerns.

In 1971 most of Amador's mill seemed similar to the factory that his father had built in 1936 and expanded a decade later. The imposing two-story administration building, with its neoclassic facade, marbled hallways, and monogrammed glass still displayed its now dated elegance, with only the presence of a computer and a few air conditioners to mar its period-piece air. It overlooked and contrasted with the nondescript factory buildings, with their functional grays and greens. The sprawling production plant still looked the same, its lack of air-conditioning betrayed by the noise, humid heat, and cotton dust that filled the enormous weaving and spinning rooms. Much of the machinery was also the same, antiquated equipment whose life had been extended by periodic overhauls. But even the names on the new machines revealed that the Yarur mill still depended on foreign technology, as well as on imported raw materials.

There were some changes of significance. In a closed room off the spinning section was a laboratory that exercised a quality control absent in Juan Yarur's day, part of the changes made by the American efficiency experts who had overseen the rationalization of production methods during the preceding decade. The most visible physical change, however, lay across Avenida Club Hípico from the administration building. Where Juan Yarur's old sports stadium had once been, a new finishing plant now stood. Completed in 1969, it was an impressively modern building with air-conditioning and the latest American equipment. Equally evident, but less impressive, was its idle and underutilized machinery, a reflection of the new plant's capacity to finish 13 million meters (27 percent) more cloth than the Yarur mill could weave. Also questionable was the purchase of expensive new equipment designed to process the polyester weaves that the rest of the mill could not produce.

The explanation for this seeming irrationality lay in the Yarur drive for control of the cotton industry, which had led them to take over W. R. Grace's Caupolican mills in 1963. During the years that followed, the money that should have been invested in the expansion and modernization of Amador's Santiago mill flowed south instead in a misguided effort to transform Jorge's Caupolican Chiguayante factory. As a consequence, the planned expansion and modernization of the Yarur mill remained impressive on paper, but delayed in practice and incoherent in execution. Amador Yarur talked of buying modern shuttleless looms, but with consumer demand stagnant, inflation accelerating, and profits falling, the imbalance between weaving and finishing sections seemed likely to continue for the foreseeable future. As a result, in 1971, Amador's mill spun and wove the same pure cotton yarn and cloth that his father had produced in 1937 and with technologies as outdated as the machinery.[58]

The financial position of the enterprise that the workers wanted socialized in 1971 seemed equally problematic. The ability of the Yarur mill to sell its products in an era of slackening demand and tight credit remained striking. As the annual reports stressed, Yarur retained the loyalty of its clientele, in part because it enjoyed a virtual monopoly of the cheaper cotton goods with assured markets—overalls for workers, sacks for flour mills, sheets for hospitals, denims for jeans, and flannels for the armed forces—in part because of its known quality and shrewd advertising. In real terms, however, the reported value of Yarur sales decreased by one-quarter between 1964 and 1970, a drop that was reflected in a declining profit rate that fell below 3 percent in 1970.[59] As a consequence, Yarur, Inc., was forced to borrow increasingly after 1966, and, by 1970, it owed sums equal to 60 percent of its capital plus reserves. By 1971, the Yarur mill was reporting only enough earnings to cover current expenses and seemed incapable of meeting its rising debt payments without additional loans from the family's Banco de Crédito, which already held more than three-quarters of the textile firm's domestic debt.[60]

Amador Yarur blamed his enterprise's financial difficulties on government price controls in an era of escalating costs, a complaint echoed by other textile entrepreneurs.[61] But government experts suggested that these calculations were more self-interested than accurate, and political leaders suspected "the textile monopoly" of fixing prices and speculating on the black market.[62] Although government investigators early in 1971 concurred with Amador Yarur's conclusion that a hefty price rise—or new loan—was needed to keep S.A. Yarur solvent, they blamed its declining profitability on inflated operating costs and onerous sales commissions. Subsequent investigations revealed alleged overinvoicing of imports, use of fictitious suppliers, tax evasion through the transfer of shares to dummy foreign corporations, the abuse of preferential foreign exchange rates, and illegal foreign loans. The payment of "excessive commissions" to distributors linked to the Yarurs was yet another practice alleged by government investigators to typify the milking of the public corporation for private purposes.[63] Suspicions that all was not what it seemed at Yarur, Inc., were heightened by the refusal of Amador Yarur to permit an outside audit or to comply with generally accepted rules of accounting.[64] The real "profits of this industry," the head of the Data Processing Department concluded from his own calculations, "were different from the annual reports."[65] S.A. Yarur might be a public corporation with thousands of shareholders, but in 1971 it seemed to be run in the private interests of the Yarur family.

Although efforts to cover questionable financial practices may have played a major role in the peculiar way S.A. Yarur was managed, so did Amador Yarur's character. Insecure and suspicious, Amador distrusted the technically skilled, better-educated employees and valued loyalty above competence in his subordinates. The result was a personalistic management that concentrated power and decision making in the hands of Amador Yarur, whose rulings often seemed arbitrary and capricious. It was a style that demoralized the industry's best employees while turning the rest into servile instruments of Don Amador's will, sycophants who held their positions more through favoritism than competence and responded with unquestioning obedience—and indecisive administration. Amador Yarur may have accepted the existence of the new professional departments mandated by the Burlington and Price, Waterhouse modernization plans, but he tried to control their activities and limit their purview.[66]

In 1970, therefore, the Yarur mill presented a paradoxical picture, one in which the anachronistic and the contemporary, efficiency and irrationality, coexisted uneasily side by side.[67] Yet, despite these paradoxes and problems, Amador's mill remained Chile's principal cotton textile industry, producing as much as one-third of the nation's cotton yarn and cloth. By 1971, it had consolidated a virtual monopoly over the less expensive lines of pure cotton goods while maintaining its strong position as a supplier of cotton yarn to the country's many knitting mills. The factory that the workers seized on April 25, 1971, was both a strategic industry and an economic force to be reckoned with.

AN EMPIRE OF PAPER AND CLOTH

By 1971, moreover, the Yarur factory was not just an isolated cotton mill. It was also a vital part of one of Chile's largest and most powerful economic empires—an empire built on paper money and woven of cotton cloth. Juan Yarur had begun its creation in 1946, when he used his textile mill's wartime profits to acquire the Banco de Crédito e Inversiones, but he died before he could complete the task.

As a result, it was Jorge Yarur who built this empire, constructing it around the textile mill his father had founded, the bank that he had acquired, and the family holding company that the Yarur Banna brothers had created to administer their joint inheritance. By 1954, the Yarur mill was already "the principal textile industry in the country."[68] During the next decade its resources were used to acquire three other textile plants, including those of its chief competitor.[69] During this same decade, Empresas Juan Yarur (Juan Yarur Enterprises) was transformed from a passive family trust into an aggressive investment company, whose growing portfolio reflected the expansion of Yarur holdings.[70]

The Banco de Crédito e Inversiones became the motor and balance wheel of this enlarged family economic empire, and it was there that Jorge Yarur concentrated his talents and time. A banker by temperament, Jorge Yarur proved the perfect person to construct and consolidate a Yarur economic empire during an era in which Chile's industries were stagnating and its economy was being divided among powerful "clans," each with its own bank.[71] In his capable, if ruthless hands, the Banco de Crédito was transformed from a modest commercial bank catering to the needs of small business into a powerful financial instrument of family economic empire. "We made the bank," he boasted later.[72] Don Jorge also converted it into a Yarur milch cow, a source of personal profits, venture capital, and loans for the Yarur family and its proliferating enterprises. The Banco de Crédito not only advanced the Yarurs and their companies large sums but also invested its funds directly in these ventures, purchasing large blocs of shares, which the depositors and shareholders of the bank financed but the Yarurs controlled.

Jorge Yarur used every legal means—and some that were dubious—to maximize the bank's assets and channel them into the coffers of the Yarur textile enterprises, several of which were in need of continual capital infusions during the 1960s. In some years, more than three-quarters of the Banco de Crédito's loans went to family members and enterprises, often at less than the normal bank rate and with no pressure for repayment.[73] It was this ability to mobilize other people's savings for Yarur purposes on a vast scale that made the Banco de Crédito so valuable an instrument of economic empire. "It was sure financing," one former bank inspector explained wryly.[74]

By 1960, the Yarurs were already ranked among the eleven financial "clans" that dominated the Chilean economy. A decade later, they had moved up on that very short list although they were still a rung below the top three. Unlike most of Chile's leading economic groups, whose diversification of investments was striking, the Yarur holdings were concentrated in two sectors—finance and textiles.[75]

In the financial sector, the Yarur Banna brothers controlled the Banco de Crédito e Inversiones and the Banco Llanquihue de Puerto Montt, which together formed the second largest private bank in Chile in assets, deposits, and investments. They also controlled an auxiliary financial group that included a major savings and loan association, two large investment companies, and four insurance companies.[76]

The Yarur economic empire had been founded on textiles, and the textile sector remained its greatest strength. By 1970, the Yarurs had secured the ascendancy over the cotton textile industry that they had sought since the founding of the Yarur mill in 1937. Between the Yarur and the Caupolican

Chiguayante mills, they virtually monopolized the production of cheaper cotton goods while carving out a significant share of the more expensive lines as well. With the Caupolican Renca plant, the Yarurs claimed a sizable share of the growing market in cotton-synthetic weaves, and the acquisition of Química Industrial gave them their own source of polyester fibers. Their links with Saavedra Benard, Distribuidora Talca, and Luis Portaluz—Jorge Yarur was vice president of the first, the second was controlled by Arab entrepreneurs who were close to the Yarurs, and the third was a totally dependent subcontractor of Juan Yarur Enterprises—brought their leading distributors within their orbit. The chain of Yarur retail outlets completed the picture of vertical integration—from the fiber to the consumer.[77]

The cotton textile enterprises of the Yarur Banna brothers, moreover, were complemented by the woolen mills controlled by the junior branches of the family—the Yarur Kazakias and Yarur Asfuras, the children of Juan Yarur's younger brothers. Through Textil Progreso, Fabrilana, Bellavista Tomé and FIAP-Tomé, the Yarurs claimed a major share of Chile's woolens industry, including the popular synthetic blends.[78] In addition, through interlocking directorates and bank loans, the Yarurs had acquired influence in Textil Viña, an old rival noted for high-quality cotton goods; in Sedamar, the manufacturer of the best-quality artificial silk in Chile; and in Chiteco's knit goods business.

Through ownership or influence, the Yarurs sat on the boards of directors of five of Chile's fifteen largest textile enterprises and were linked by inter-locking directorates with eight others.[79] They had also consolidated a dom-inant role in the Instituto Textil de Chile (INCHITEX), the industry's business association, which Jorge Yarur had founded in 1963 and then presided over.[80] By 1970, the Yarurs were the ascendant economic group within an industry that was so highly oligopolistic that it was the example chosen by economists to illustrate the increasing concentration of ownership in Chile.[81]

The Chilean textile industry was not only concentrated in a few hands; it was heavily concentrated in *Arab* hands. About 80 percent of cotton textile production, for example, was controlled by three families who traced their origins to the Bethlehem region of Palestine. In 1970 they divided the Chilean market and cooperated more than they competed with each other. As one Christian Democratic deputy affirmed, during a 1966 congressional debate on textile price-fixing: "It might not be a formal monopoly that they have organized, but it is a monopoly in fact."[82]

This informal monopoly was facilitated by ethnic ties and social links. The Yarur ascendancy within the Chilean textile industry was paralleled by their community leadership. "The Yarur group is the most important group of the Arab community," concluded a knowledgeable study of the Arab economic role in Chile, "both for its economic power and for serving as the 'guide' for the activities of the other entrepreneurs."[83] The Yarurs were the first to found a modern textile industry, the first to use that industry as the base for acquiring a bank, the first to use their bank as an agency of capital formation for takeovers of other textile industries, the first to extend that control to their distributors, and the first to introduce the Taylor System into their mills. The other major Arab entrepreneurs—Hirmas, Sumar, and Said—followed the Yarur lead although none were able to attain the latter's level of wealth and power. Imitation was the sincerest form of flattery.

The Yarurs had come a long way from their trinket shop in the little town of Bethlehem. They had found their promised land some 9000 miles from their native Palestine. By 1971, their wealth had become so proverbial that "rich as Yarur" had become a common Chilean saying. Although the true extent of their personal fortunes was unknown, it was generally assumed that they were among the largest in Chile.

The Yarurs' wealth had also become more visible. Juan Yarur preferred to live simply, residing in an unpretentious house and driving his own Chevrolet. The contrast with his sons was striking. The Yarur Bannas lived in a manner that advertised their wealth and asserted their status, a style that became synonymous with ostentation and luxury—although to many among the Chilean elite it merely confirmed their distaste for these *turco* parvenus. The popular press celebrated the life-style that expressed this wealth, but also hinted at its immorality and "Oriental" decadence. In the end, their wealth created more envy than admiration, but it did purchase the Yarur Bannas access to the corridors of power.

Juan Yarur had learned early in his Latin American career that political influence was the key to economic success. His sons continued his policy of contributing generously to the major parties and politicians of the Right and the Center and of cultivating close relations with political leaders and state bureaucrats. Influential Chileans enjoyed their table and sat on their boards of directors. The Yarur radio station, Radio Balmaceda, boosted political careers with its endorsements. The sizable advertising budgets of the Yarur enterprises enabled their owners to influence the editorial policies of major newspapers and magazines.[84]

The Yarur goal was to ensure privileged access to policymakers and implementers no matter which president ruled or which party governed. Politicians and civil servants who enjoyed Yarur largesse rewarded their generosity by looking after their interests. Jorge and Amador Yarur may have lacked their father's charisma, but they possessed resources and connections that made them powerful players in Chile's political game, and they were usually able to get their way. The Yarurs were powerful because they were rich, and they were feared because everyone knew that they were willing to use both wealth and power ruthlessly to advance their interests.

When the workers seized the Yarur mill in April 1971, they were confronting not just the diminutive boss of an aging cotton mill, but one of Chile's wealthiest and most powerful families as well. The temerity of their challenge did not escape them. Since the factory was founded in 1937, the Yarurs had crushed all efforts to organize an independent union. It was a history that formed part of the collective memory of the Yarur workers who seized their factory on that April Sunday, as well as one that many of those who stood guard around the Yarur mill that night had "lived in the flesh."[85]

2

THE MAKING
OF THE OLD-TIMERS

On the morning of April 25, 1971, the Yarur workers held an unprecedented union assembly. Unanimous in its conclusions, this meeting soon led to the seizure and socialization of the Yarur mill. Yet this apparent unanimity was deceptive. Among the 1500 Yarur blue-collar workers who packed the nearby C.I.C. union hall on that fateful Sunday were many who did not favor taking over the mill and still others who understood the actions they had voted for differently from the young union leaders. These divergent positions and perceptions expressed differences in consciousness, which, in turn, reflected differences in origin, age, upbringing, and experience. The Yarur workers might seem to speak with one voice, but the reality was more complex.

In 1971 there were two groups of workers at the Yarur mill—the Old-timers (*viejos*) and the Youngsters (*jóvenes*)—labels that reflected different generations of experience. The Youngsters knew only Amador's mill and the Taylor System, whereas most Old-timers remembered Juan Yarur and a less demanding system of work. All the Old-timers were survivors of the 1962 strike, and many of them had lived through one or more of the earlier worker movements at the mill; the Youngsters had never experienced a labor conflict with the Yarurs.

Even a category such as "Old-timer" obscured important differences. Some of the Old-timers had been at the factory since it first opened in 1937; others had entered it during the postwar expansion or the last years of Juan Yarur's life. Even where they had experienced the same labor struggles, they had often been on opposite sides of the conflict and drawn different lessons from it. Yet, despite these differences and the unique individuals they produced, most of the Old-timers had shared and been shaped by salient common experiences.

32

DON JUAN'S PEOPLE

The Old-timers of 1971 were all survivors—of the Yarurs' repressive paternalism, of the Taylor System, and of the successive defeats suffered by worker movements at the Yarur mill. For the most part, the Old-timers were Juan Yarur's "people." Many of them had been recruited by him personally, an experience they still remembered.[1]

Although youth and height, "a more or less good appearance," and parental permission were requisites for a job at his mill, that was not all Juan Yarur "was looking for."[2] He wanted a malleable and loyal labor force that could be shaped into a disciplined and obedient instrument of production and would be receptive to the paternalistic style of labor relations he had perfected in Bolivia. In La Paz, the solution had been to recruit illiterate Indian women fresh from the countryside. In Santiago, Juan Yarur sought their functional Chilean equivalent in teenage girls from the families of recent rural migrants, who were expected to embrace a model of labor relations similar to that of landlord and peasant, in which the omnipotent but benevolent *patrón* conferred a special relationship on his dependent work force in return for their unquestioned loyalty and hard work for long hours at low pay.[3] As María López, who entered the factory as a teenager from the rural south a few years after it opened, recalled: "If you were young and passed your health exams and if you seemed like a good sort of person they took you immediately, but especially if you were from the south of Chile, because they said that people from the south were hard workers, very honest, and loyal to their *patrón*."[4]

Although most of the mill's initial work force of one thousand was recruited among the teenage girls of the surrounding neighborhoods, increasingly the children of southern peasants and Mapuche indians joined their ranks. In a country with accelerating rural migration and chronic high unemployment, there were always applicants for a steady factory job.[5] Generally, preference was given to relatives or friends of Yarur workers, which reinforced the image of the industry as an extended family linked by reciprocal bonds of favor and obligation, or else to rural migrants who arrived at the factory gates with a scrawled reference from some local notable, who vouched for their good character and conduct. In both cases, the new workers would be bound to good behavior by a sense of personal obligation to the person who had recommended them, as well as by their new loyalty to the *patrón* who had given them a job.[6]

The new workers were introduced to the unfamiliar rhythms and routines of factory work by experienced machine operators or by one of the foreign technicians whom Juan Yarur favored, whose main task was finding the right

job for new workers and winnowing out unsuitable ones. Those who remained
had to adjust to long hours of monotonous work—twelve hours a day at
first, eight hours a day after 1941—in the hot and humid mill, with the
noise of the machines deafening their eardrums and the cotton dust filling
their lungs.[7]

Still, years later Old-timers recalled their work at Juan Yarur's factory
with a fondness absent from their feelings about their labors at Amador's
mill. Although nostalgia for their youth probably played a part, there were
also more solid reasons for these positive memories. By the standards of the
day, the Yarur mill was modern, yet there was little pressure to produce,
as neither foremen nor machine operators received incentive pay, and costs
could be passed on to the consumer.[8] Most of the labor force were teenagers
who worked to help support their frequently large families and who were
grateful for the opportunity to earn a regular wage. Yarur workers also valued
their posts because they had "a steady job" that paid them "all year round;
the factory never closed."[9] Moreover, although the wages were low and there
were few fringe benefits, the pay at the Yarur mill was better than domestic
service, the only other job available to the uneducated lower-class women
who comprised the majority of the labor force. Besides, stressed Blanca
Bascuñan, "You had much more liberty here than as a domestic servant . . .
who is often little more than a slave."[10]

For most of them, teenagers who lived at home, it was also a liberation
from the supervision and isolation of their families. "We were all young
girls," recalled Rosa Ramos, "and there was so much *compañerismo* in those
days."[11] Juan Yarur's mill was a social center as well as a workplace. Young
men worked alongside them, and many workers found their mates as well
as their friends at the mill.

There were workers for whom their "plain wage" with "no fringe benefits,
not even overalls," did not suffice and who remembered their work in Juan
Yarur's mill as "very hard."[12] Yet even a worker such as Alicia Navarrete,
the sole support of seven younger siblings, who maintained that the wages
he paid her were "a misery" and that she was "exploited," remembered Juan
Yarur fondly.[13] "In reality, he was a good man, Don Juan," her friend Blanca
Bascuñan recalled with a smile. "I am not going to deny his merits. He was
very fond of the Old-timers, very fond."[14]

To the Old-timers, Juan Yarur was every inch the paternalistic *patrón*,
an omnipotent but benevolent boss with whom each had a special personal
relationship. It was an image that Don Juan cultivated with care. Each day
he toured the factory, stopping to talk with one worker, to pat another on
the back, to enquire about the family of a third. As he passed, workers
could approach their *patrón* with special requests—for time off, for a loan,
for a change of work section. Juan Yarur never refused these requests, always

turning to the supervisor or personnel chief and audibly telling him to grant it, although he might later countermand that order. Nor did he ever punish or fire a worker himself, leaving such tasks to his subordinates and seeming sympathetic if the worker appealed to him to reverse the decision.[15] As a result, workers saw him as the "good *patrón*" whereas the supervisor or personnel manager who executed Yarur's orders was viewed as the "the bad guy of the picture."[16]

This sense of a special relationship was reinforced by special treatment. Don Juan would leave a "client or friend . . . to attend to a worker," one of his closest collaborators recalled. "Direct treatment was his style."[17] So was apparent generosity in a worker's time of need, ranging from advances against their wages to time off without pay. At Christmas, he gave the workers presents of shoes for their children.[18] After World War II, he also "gave" them company housing, in the Población Juan Yarur, although in reality he was merely fulfilling a law requiring every industry to invest a certain percentage of their profits in housing for their workers.[19] For those blue-collar workers (*obreros*) who were in his favor, there was also the plum of getting friends and relatives jobs at the mill and the dream that their loyalty would one day be rewarded by promotion to employee (*empleado*) status, with its additional material benefits and social prestige.[20]

In addition, pretty women workers could aspire to a very special relationship with Don Juan, who "was very Arab in his ways" and "had his harem here in the factory," whose members were rewarded with presents and the best work assignments, as well as the prestige of being "Don Juan's *querida*," or mistress.[21] Generally, the women who graced this harem had been chosen as factory "Spring Queens" at one of the two annual festivals that Juan Yarur celebrated with his workers—the other being his saint's day. These ritual acts of shared celebration both symbolized and reinforced his paternalistic image in the eyes of the workers, as well as their sense that they enjoyed a special relationship with him. Juan Yarur not only gave them a party, but "came and danced and drank, just like us."[22] As one worker put it: "Together with him we were content."[23] It was no accident that many Old-timers identified with their *querido patroncito*—("dear little boss")—rather than with their co-workers.

"For me Juan Yarur was the prototype of paternalism. He had a paternalistic system that was very well worked out, and he knew how to carry himself with the personnel," one of his close collaborators in that system concluded. "As a result, he always could solve the labor conflicts on his terms because he always had the support of certain sectors of workers in the industry."[24] A strategy of divide and conquer was the underside of paternalism's organic unity of *patrón* and worker. At bottom, the purpose behind Juan Yarur's system of recruitment, socialization, and social control was to create a labor force composed of *apatronados*—"the boss's people"—who chose loyalty to their *patrón* over solidarity with their *compañeros* and believed that "good understanding ought to reign between Capital and Labor," whose natural harmony of interests reflected their complementary economic roles.[25]

Typical of these *apatronados* was José Lagos, who as a teenager was hired personally by Juan Yarur in 1937. "When my father left me at the factory gate that first day," Lagos recalled, "he turned to me and said: 'Son, Juan Yarur is a clever man and a good *patrón*. Always be loyal to him and you will never go wrong.' I never forgot his words."[26]

When Yarur's "paternalistic system" proved insufficient to prevent a majority of his workers from wanting an independent union, as in 1939, Don Juan showed the repressive side of his paternalism. During 1939 and 1940, one-fifth of the blue-collar workers were fired on one pretext or another although those who went to him repentant were later hired back on condition that they "behaved and not get involved ever again in these things."[27] As a way of combatting the union, Juan Yarur formed the "Mutual Juan Yarur," an ostensibly autonomous mutual aid association run by company employees, which workers were pressed to join or risk losing their jobs. Once his loyalists controlled the union, he allowed the mutual to fade away and embraced the union whose formation he had opposed so fiercely, transforming it into a "yellow" (company) union, which occupied the legal space of the independent blue-collar union but served an opposite function—social control instead of class representation.

When the emergence of a new and more powerful workers' movement in 1946 and 1947 demonstrated that neither the attractions of paternalism nor the moribund company union were enough to keep an independent union from his factory's gate, Juan Yarur responded with even more drastic measures. Once again, suspect workers were purged—and this time they were not taken back. In choosing their replacements—and the new workers recruited as part of the postwar doubling of the expanded factory's labor force—Juan Yarur put a heavier stress on screening for the characteristics that he thought made for loyal workers.

This time, moreover, the system of social control was made more comprehensive and more repressive. A network of informers composed of Yarur loyalists was established in both the work sections and the new company housing to spy on their co-workers so that "disloyalty" could be detected and dealt with before a new workers' movement could be formed. The *serenos* (watchmen) were transformed into a company political police who spied on "suspicious gatherings" and filed reports on suspect workers. The mutual was revived and made a test of worker loyalty and the agency for the allocation of welfare benefits. These were measures that largely transformed the atmosphere at the Yarur mill. The relaxed days of optimistic paternalism were gone forever, replaced by a system of social control that Juan Yarur hoped would be proof to the growing class consciousness and radical politics of Chile's workers. "It was then that fear entered the factory," one Old-timer recalled.[28]

Juan Yarur's more pervasive system of social control made its mark, but what the Old-timers remembered most was the initiation ceremony required for joining the mutual, a precondition for getting and keeping a job at the Yarur mill. About a month after Luz Castro entered the Yarur mill in 1948, she and ten of her co-workers were called out of the spinning section and told that "we had to go and swear." A Yarur employee then led them down to a darkened room in the basement of the administration building, where they found "Padre" Concha, a Yarur employee dressed as a priest, and parallel lines of male and female workers waiting to take their oath. "On a table they had put a black cloth and on top of the black cloth was Our Lord crucified on a cross and below the Christ was a skull," she recalled. "So we had to sit down or stop in front of the table and put our hands on the table and the little Padre Concha made us swear." If the setting was an odd one for initiation into a mutual aid association, the oath that the pseudopriest administered was stranger still: "In the first place they made me swear that I would be faithful to the bosses, not to participate in anything against the boss, neither politics, nor unions . . . and we all had to say: 'I swear by God and by this banner!' "[29]

Although the more sophisticated workers did not take seriously what they considered a bizarre "Oriental rite," even they affirmed that among the ill-educated rural migrants who entered the factory in large numbers at this time, there were "many people who because of it preferred to leave the mill rather than betray Don Juan."[30] Bogus or real, effective or not, "the *calavera*" (crucifixion) as it was known among the workers, came to symbolize Juan Yarur's increasingly repressive paternalism and underscored the lengths to which he was prepared to go to prevent "his" workers from organizing the independent union that might challenge his social hegemony.[31]

WORKER MOVEMENTS, YARUR MEASURES

Yet, despite the attractions and punishments of Don Juan's paternalistic system, again and again a majority of "his" workers tried to organize a union independent of company control. There were several reasons why Juan Yarur's "well worked out . . . paternalistic system"[32] didn't always work well, and at the Yarur mill they were mutually reinforcing. Chile was a country where the law of the land legitimated union organization, and workers were heirs to a long tradition of class struggle and labor organization linked to political

parties of the Left. The workers who formed the first Yarur union back in
1939 were political innocents, but they took for granted that it was "our
right to have a union to defend us."[33] Even a seeming *apatronada*, such as
Isabél Torres, who never took part in the worker movements at the mill,
was embarrassed "that here the union was run by the bosses."[34]

Within this context, the only way for Juan Yarur to sustain a rigidly
anti-union posture was to keep his workers isolated from the class culture
and politics swirling around them. That was the intent of Juan Yarur's
policies of selective recruitment and social control, but it proved impossible
to enforce. In part, this was because his recruiting principles and screening
procedures were not foolproof. Reinaldo Jara might have been "a cowboy
from Angol," a backward rural southern province, and thus a perfect candidate for the Yarur mill; but the future leader of the 1947 Yarur workers'
movement had been converted to communism during the Great Depression
by some unemployed miners whom he met in the mountains before migrating
to Santiago.[35] Juan Yarur understood that the tide of rural migration that
was engorging Chile's cities was also a migration of consciousness, but this
migration was more complex than his recruiting strategy allowed. Many of
the sons and daughters of peasants who arrived at the Yarur gates in search
of work were not what they seemed, even where, like Laura Coruña, a Yarur
"favorite" who "betrayed him" in joining a workers' movement, they came
from families with a history of conservative politics. "What good did it do
my father to be loyal to the *patrón*?" she had concluded from her family's
poverty. "One must be loyal to one's own class."[36]

But even many of the peasant children who arrived in Santiago with
little working-class consciousness and less political awareness soon lost their
innocence. Although few were educated, most were literate enough to read
the leftist and labor press. Even more influential in reshaping their attitudes
and assumptions was the rich oral tradition around them. Juan Yarur might
limit what co-workers would dare say to new recruits, but from their friends
and neighbors they learned about the new world they had entered and were
initiated into the culture of the class that they aspired to join.

Juan Yarur might place his company housing under surveillance, but
the Población Yarur housed less than 10 percent of the factory's *obreros*. The
rest lived in working-class communities beyond Juan Yarur's control—in
the inner city's decaying one-room *conventillos* or cell-like *cités*, or else in the
new suburban squatter settlements, the rent-free *callampas* (wild mushrooms),
which sprang up overnight on vacant lots, such as "La Victoria" in nearby
San Miguel. The experience of living in such a community, with its class
culture and populist politics—as well as its continuing struggle for electricity, running water, and other public services—produced a different mind-
set from that which Juan Yarur wanted his workers to have.[37]

Although the working class world in which they lived encouraged many of his workers to favor a union of their own, their experience within the factory where they spent their days often reinforced that predisposition. Juan Yarur might seem a benevolent *patrón* who never punished "his people," but that was because he delegated the enforcement of discipline and social control to his subordinates, who often "were very tyrannical."[38] In Juan Yarur's system, the *Jefe* became a petty despot whose arbitrary power to punish workers by abusing them, transferring them to a less desirable job, or getting them suspended or fired for real or imagined failings left the workers feeling vulnerable and powerless.

The worst threat of all was "to be sent to Welfare" to see Daniel Fuenzalida, the martinet personnel and welfare chief, who was widely regarded as "the worst man that ever was in the industry." To the vulnerable workers, Fuenzalida "was the king of the factory . . . and all the people trembled before him." As a result, "when they saw that another *compañera* had a problem, they didn't try to defend her."[39] In reality, Fuenzalida was Juan Yarur's hatchet man, who fired workers and denied the requests that Yarur had ostensibly approved, "because a *patrón* never wants to appear bad in front of his people," an *apatronado* leader explained.[40] Most workers did not realize that Yarur and Fuenzalida were "a combination," allowing Don Juan to have his benevolent image and yet keep his strict social control too.[41] But the workers were fully aware of feeling anxious, angry, and impotent in the face of the arbitrary abuses of his subordinates. The response of many workers to the repressive side of Juan Yarur's paternalistic system of social control was to believe that "we needed a union to protect us."[42]

"But the most important problem was the economic problem," stressed Reinaldo Jara, who in 1947 organized the most powerful challenge to Juan Yarur's system of social control that the mill owner ever confronted. "Yarur wages were very low—not by comparison with other textile industries, they were all badly paid—but by comparison with the cost of living."[43] During the decade of the 1940s, Chile experienced an inflation of more than 400 percent whereas the price of necessities rose even more sharply. Blue-collar wages did not keep pace, and many Yarur workers found it increasingly hard to make ends meet, particularly if they had families to support. The inadequate wages of Yarur workers were reflected in impoverished living conditions, which were typical of the Chilean working class during this era.[44] The Yarur workers whom Reinaldo Jara knew lived in partitioned one-room shacks and survived on a diet of bread, beans, pasta, and *cazuela*, a soupy stew with a potato and onions. They could not afford to pay a doctor, dress their children decently, or educate them well.[45] Nor did they have confidence that the future would be any better. On the contrary, their real wages seemed to drop with each year's raise.[46]

In view of such working and living conditions, worldview, and expectations, it was not surprising that, despite Juan Yarur's best efforts, most of his workers wanted to have an independent union to represent them and were prepared to support a "free union" movement if they thought that it could succeed. But given their belief in the omnipotence of their boss, they had to be persuaded that they would enjoy the outside help that would redress the imbalance of power between Juan Yarur and themselves. Although the support of other labor organizations, particularly the national textile workers federation (FENATEX) and the Confederation of Chilean Workers (CTCh) or Central Unica de Trabajadores (CUT), was essential, it was insufficient in itself to allay worker fears. The central role in labor relations that Chilean labor legislation gave to the state meant that workers had to believe that their efforts would also enjoy state support.[47]

Significantly, the three workers' movements that confronted Juan Yarur with demands for an independent union and authentic collective bargaining followed national elections of presidents—Pedro Aguirre Cerda in 1938, Gabriel González Videla in 1946, and Carlos Ibañez del Campo in 1952—who were supported by coalitions that included leftist parties and whose governments were expected to be prolabor and sympathetic to popular movements. Whenever the Yarur workers perceived an opening to the Left nationally, they tried to take advantage of the political moment to challenge the social politics of the Yarur mill. The result was a series of intense social struggles that indelibly marked the Old-timers of 1971—and shaped Amador Yarur's attitudes on how to handle worker challenges as well.

The three workers' movements that broke the paternalist peace of Juan Yarur's mill had different origins, politics, and characters, as well as differing dynamics, plots, and dramatics. Yet, despite these differences of detail, they followed the same course. It was a pattern that was set in the very first conflict between Juan Yarur and his workers—the workers' attempt to organize a union during 1939 and 1940—and it was repeated with variations in the years 1946–47 and 1952–53.

All three movements were organized from below by Yarur workers, but with the advice and assistance of national labor unions. Although the movements themselves were nonpartisan, their leaders were more political—ranging from "some kind of socialists"[48] in 1939 and 1940 to Communist in the years 1946–47 and Popular Socialist in the 1952–53 period. Each had unique demands, such as the elimination of the night shift for women workers in 1939 and the firing of the company police chief in 1953,[49] but they all shared a common goal: to secure the authentic union representation and collective bargaining that were their legal rights under the Chilean Labor Code, which the first Yarur union president called "one of the social conquests won by the working class through bloody combats."[50]

Initially, these movements received the state support that they expected and "with the aid of the Labor authorities"[51] were able to secure the union balloting that they sought. In the years 1939–40 and 1946–47, they were even able to elect insurgent slates to union office. They then pressed for the collective bargaining that would constitute company recognition and the fruits of their victory. But Juan Yarur would not accept defeat or allow "anyone to tell him how to run his industry."[52] Faced with an independent union leadership, he responded by denying their legitimacy, intimidating their supporters with firings and strong-arm squads, and stonewalling their efforts to win a contract with the increases in wages and benefits that would consolidate their position and demonstrate the value of an independent union to their rank and file. At the same time, Don Juan created a parallel organization, the infamous Mutual Juan Yarur, to divide the workers and undermine the union, offering increases in wages and benefits to workers who joined his mutual aid association and threatening to dismiss those who refused.[53]

Confronted with this Yarur intransigence and counterattack, the union leaders invoked state mediation on the advice of their mentors in the national labor movement. When the state Conciliation Board failed to break the deadlock, the workers took the steps allowed them under the Labor Code. In 1939 they went on strike for a fortnight and then accepted binding governmental arbitration. In 1947 a formal flaw in their procedures prevented the union leaders from securing the "legal strike" they sought and persuaded them to accept state arbitration instead. It made little difference to the outcome, which was the same in both cases: an arbitration award that granted the workers a part of their wage demands but denied them the job security and independent union leadership they sought.[54]

While the workers' movement was preoccupied with the complex legal formalities of the Labor Code, Juan Yarur was using his wealth to secure "the collaboration" of venal state labor inspectors and his political influence to block governmental enforcement of the workers' rights under Chile's labor laws.[55] After the "resolution" of these conflicts, governments that were moving to the Right nationally failed to protect union activists from dismissal or to prevent the bribing of some worker leaders and the ouster of the remaining insurgent officers in elections that made a mockery of the labor laws. Within twelve to sixteen months of their initial "victories," both insurgent movements had gone down to defeat, and the paternalistic peace of unquestioned company control was restored to the Yarur mill.

The 1952–53 movement did not even get that far. When Clodomiro Almeyda, the Socialist labor minister, refused to accede to Juan Yarur's demands that the union balloting be held within the factory and be supervised by state labor inspectors that he would name, Yarur used his political pull with his intimate friend President Carlos Ibáñez to oust Almeyda and his top aides.[56] Under Almeyda's successor, the promised elections were never held, and the firing and intimidation of dissident workers were ignored. Beyond the differences between the three movements was their common fate: All three failed to survive Juan Yarur's attacks in large part because the state support that they had counted on to enforce the Yarur workers' rights under the Labor Code deserted them in response to Juan Yarur's wealth and power and the shifting sands of national politics.

This was a lesson that the Old-timers who survived these defeats learned through bitter experience. For those like José Lagos, who had not joined these movements, their defeat confirmed the wisdom of placing "loyalty to the *patrón*" over solidarity with one's *compañeros*.[57] But even workers who had participated in the movements came to similar conclusions. For some, it was a conversion experience that reflected their gratitude to "Don Juan" for "taking [them] back."[58] For others, this change of heart reflected a disillusionment with the independent union's lack of support or prospects for success. To Alicia Navarrete, the central reason for their defeat was that "we didn't have anyone to help us."[59] The leftist parties and unions were too weak and often too divided as well, and despite initial promises of state assistance, Juan Yarur "had the support of the government and as a consequence nothing came of it."[60]

Although their interpretations of the experience varied, Juan Yarur's basic message had gotten through to all: He would brook no disloyalty, accept no independent union, and defeat any insurgent movement, no matter how sizeable its support, euphoric its initial victory, or promising its early prospects. After these defeats, "people were so demoralized that they didn't want to get involved in anything," recalled Alicia Navarrete, "because we were always going to lose."[61] In their wake, even workers such as Juana Garrido, who still believed in "our cause," had learned to feign loyalty and "to keep my thoughts to myself."[62] By 1954, those who had failed to learn this lesson were gone from the Yarur mill, along with the insurgent movements they had championed. The Old-timers who remained were all *apatronados*—out of conviction or calculation. When Juan Yarur died, in August 1954, "his" union and "his" workers were securely under his paternalistic control.

DON JORGE AND MR. TAYLOR

Juan Yarur's sons didn't just inherit a factory. They also inherited some thirty-five hundred workers, a system of social control, and a style of production. As the new head of the family mill, Jorge Yarur set out to change all three.

A large majority of the blue-collar workers were women, whom Juan

Yarur had preferred as machine operators because they earned 30 percent less than men for the same work, were more reliable, and were more receptive to Don Juan's paternalistic charms. Although many of the workers of 1954 were relative newcomers to the mill, Old-timers predominated, and the average age of the work force was over thirty-five.[63] Many of these Old-timers were ill-educated or even illiterate, and most were *apatronado* in their mentality, the product of selective recruiting and careful socialization.[64]

Juan Yarur had turned these loyalists into guardians of his paternalistic social order by encouraging them to inform on their co-workers.[65] Many loyalists, however, were not very productive as workers, and most of them lacked the education to handle the more modern technologies and work methods that Jorge Yarur envisioned for the mill's future.

During Juan Yarur's last years, Jorge Yarur had urged his father to update his labor force and modernize his methods of managing it.[66] Don Juan was aware of the need to keep up with changing times.[67] Under his son's prodding, he began to require literacy in new *obreros* and to recruit better-educated technicians. But, for the most part, Juan Yarur had resisted his son's suggestions, believing that the old ways were best—and more in keeping with his own personality and inclinations.[68]

His father's sudden death in 1954 gave Jorge Yarur the opportunity to put his industrial vision into practice. First, he formed his own group of aides, most of whom had better training and more modern ideas than his father's cronies. Then he began to modify the most eccentric and anachronistic aspects of Don Juan's paternalism. The pseudorcligious oath of loyalty before a skull and crucifix died with its creator, whose special claim on his workers was commemorated instead by a larger-than-life statue financed by their "voluntary" contributions. The mutual itself remained, but it was de-emphasized as an instrument of social control and relegated to a subsidiary position as an agency of social welfare.[69]

In its place, Jorge Yarur relied increasingly on a refurbished company union to distribute benefits and control the work force, a shift that brought Yarur into line with current Chilean business practice. This was combined with an effort to lend the company union leadership greater legitimacy in the eyes of the workers. Benefits that Juan Yarur might have channeled through the mutual as gifts of the *patrón* were now presented to the workers as "conquests won" by these "Yellow" union leaders in collective bargaining. The new company union leaders were allowed to compete with each other for votes and vied with each other in securing favors for their followers. By and large, they were a younger and more popular lot, typified by Mario Leníz, an affable mustachioed fat man, whose political style resembled that of a ward boss.[70]

These changes reflected not only the differences between Jorge Yarur's ideas and his father's but the evident difference in their personalities as well. Where Don Juan was a charismatic figure with an easy way with his workers, his most talented son was aloof and cold.[71] He was not the man to carry on Juan Yarur's backslapping paternalism with its illusion of intimacy between the workers and their *patrón*.

Jorge Yarur was also not a sentimentalist where costs, competence, and productivity were concerned. He was notorious for firing new workers just before they had completed a year at the mill so as not to have to pay them vacation benefits.[72] Under Juan Yarur, about 60 percent of the blue-collar work force were women, many with long years of service, who were paid 30 percent less than men. But when the Ibañez government, in the mid–1950s, passed legislation granting women workers equal pay for equal work and six month maternity leaves, Jorge Yarur began to phase them out because "they were becoming too protected."[73] Nor was he indulgent of longtime Yarur loyalists of questionable competence. Under Jorge Yarur, performance became the criterion for promotion, and a growing number of graduates from the State Technical University (U.T.E.) were hired for supervisory and technical posts, threatening the careers of his father's underqualified employees and foreclosing the *empleado* dreams of blue-collar *apatronados*.[74]

These personnel changes were preludes to Jorge Yarur's most decisive break with his father's mill: the transformation of its system of work. At bottom, Jorge Yarur's principal concern was reducing costs so as to restore his textile mill's profitability in an era of stagnant consumer demand, increasing raw material prices, and growing domestic competition. Price, Waterhouse, the American management consultants whom Jorge Yarur had hired to advise him on the modernization of the industry, estimated that there were twice as many *obreros* in the mill as necessary and concluded that their wages and benefits were depressing company profits.[75] The solution they counseled was to introduce the system of standardized work norms pioneered in the United States by Frederick Taylor and implemented with great success in Colombia, whose textile industry was both more productive and more profitable than Chile's. For the job, they recommended Burlington Mills, which had played a seminal role in the modernization of the Colombian industry.[76]

In January 1962, Burlington's Technical Advisory Service began to install a modified version of the Taylor System in the Yarur mill, starting in the spinning section, where the production process began. First, "time and motion" studies were carried out to determine the optimal work method and production standard for each task. Then the workers were taught how to do their jobs without wasting a moment or a movement. Workers were given points for each production task and paid a small bonus for each day they earned enough points. Those who could not meet the norms were weeded

The Taylor System halved the blue-collar labor force, isolating the workers from each other and converting them into extensions of the multiplied number of machines they now tended.

out, their places taken not by new machine operators, but by the increased output of the *obreros* who remained. Many Yarur workers found themselves tending three or four times as many machines as before, and in the factory as a whole the company's expectation was that the new system of work would double productivity and halve labor costs.[77]

The Taylor System might be a capitalist's dream, but it was a worker's nightmare. Machine operators experienced this increase in industrial efficiency as an infernal speedup that exhausted their energies and exceeded their capacities. This speedup was hardest on the older workers, who no longer had the strength and stamina to sustain such an intensified work load.[78] Worker distress at the speedup was compounded by the accompanying changes in environmental conditions and social relations. Windows were closed to create a controlled environment "because some Yankee technicians arrived and said that a lot of air was entering, which cut the thread and all those things."[79] The Burlington experts were technically correct, but as the Yarurs refused to spend money on air-conditioning the plant, a big increase in heat, noise, and cotton dust resulted, which increased fainting, deafness, and brown lung disease.

Compañerismo was another casualty of the Taylor System—and paternalism perished with it as well. There was no longer time to talk with other workers, and the foremen were now paid bonuses based on the productivity of their workers. With their own incomes—and futures—dependent on their ability to get their workers to double or triple their productivity, the Yarur *Jefes* became intolerant of those who could not meet the new norms even if faulty machinery or inferior raw materials were to blame. "They treated us like animals," was the way one ten-year veteran put it. "The foreman walked behind you, watching you, shouting at you, hurrying you, even hitting one young woman . . . We were really tormented."[80]

The worst torment of all was losing one's job. "Being called to the office" was what even veteran workers who had long taken their job security for granted now began to fear. "We knew what this meant: suspended or fired," explained one Old-timer.[81] During the preceding two years, the Yarurs had cut back on new hiring in preparation for the installation of the Taylor System, but that reduction in the work force had been by attrition.[82] This was different. "First they began to dismiss two or three a week, then four and then ten a week."[83] For the Old-timers, the handwriting on the mill wall seemed clear: Those who could not double or triple the number of machines they tended would lose their jobs notwithstanding their past service and loyalty to the Yarurs. "They were going to fire people and you didn't know if it would be you," one veteran weaver explained. "But you knew that they had to cut one or two thousand machine operators."[84]

For the Old-timers, being fired at an age when they could not count on finding another job was the ultimate nightmare. It was compounded at Yarur by awareness of their double vulnerability. Many lived in subsidized company housing and believed that they would lose it if they lost their jobs. "I was afraid that I would have to live in a shantytown," recalled one old *apatronada*, who had always remained loyal to the Yarurs.[85] Suddenly, the annuity for years of service, which the insurgent movements had demanded in vain and the company union leaders failed to press on a resistant boss, loomed large— as did the need for an independent union. "We needed a free union because we no longer had Don Juan to protect us," explained José Lagos, a Yarur loyalist who had entered the factory with its founding.[86]

It was a revealing comment, which many Old-timers echoed. They had been loyal to Juan Yarur because he had been loyal to them. This loyalty had been based upon an implicit social contract: loyalty for job security. Now his sons had broken that pledge and dissolved that compact—and with it the paternalistic cement that held the factory's social system together. Even Amador Yarur, who "talked, laughed and made jokes" with the workers and in general tried to imitate his father, was now seen as a "hypocrite who shook hands with you but nothing more."[87] To these Old-timers, Juan Yarur was "a more open type, more understanding, more humane"; his "sons were different. They only looked out for money, that is what interested them."[88] It was for that reason, a former Yarur loyalist with twenty years in the storeroom concluded, that "people began to change and to look for other perspectives."[89] Suddenly, even old *apatronados* began to see the importance of an independent union and to feel that the time had come to fight for it.

The introduction of the Taylor System and the changes that it wrought in the work experience, perceptions, and expectations of the Old-timers explained the emergence of a powerful new workers' movement in 1962— the only insurgent movement at the Yarur mill that did not follow a leftist national political victory, but on the contrary took place under the presidency of Jorge Alessandri, the most conservative government to rule Chile since the factory's founding. The profound ramifications of the Taylor System also explained the intensity of the 1962 movement and its culmination in the longest and most bitter strike in Yarur history. It was the new system of work that explained, too, the presence of so many Old-timers on the picket lines during the wintry July of 1962, including many who had never before questioned their loyalty to the Yarurs and many others who had sworn after earlier defeats "never to get involved again."[90]

THE STRIKE OF '62

The Old-timers were joined on the picket lines by newer workers, many of whom had entered the mill after the death of Juan Yarur. Even Mario Leníz, the company union president, recognized that this "generation of 1962" was significantly more radical than his own. "There was a political awakening all over Chile at that time. People became enthusiastic about new ideas . . . and you know that youth is socialist by nature, that it is always making demands on behalf of the poor." He was also convinced that "it was precisely because we had so many young people in the industry that the strike of '62 erupted here."[91]

There were other reasons, too, but some of them came too close to Lemus's company union for him to accept. Wages so low that "some of the *compañeros* couldn't afford to eat lunch"[92] galvanized some of these newer workers into activity. The "ambience of fear"[93] and humiliation at "the way we were treated" mobilized many more.[94] Their discontent found a target in the company union, whose *apatronado* officers had "sold themselves to the boss instead of defending the interests of the workers."[95] The Taylor System may have led many Old-timers to adhere to the 1962 movement, but it was "because of the union question once again"[96] that the Yarur mill was shut down on July 8, 1962.

The "union question" had lain dormant for a decade despite the emergence during that period of a new national labor confederation, the Central Unica de Trabajadores (CUT), whose leaders discouraged a renewed social struggle at the Yarur mill as "premature."[97] But, by 1962, all agreed that the situation inside the factory had ripened—"Yarur was like a kettle that had been boiling for some time"[98]—and a group of Communist activists, who had remained in contact with provincial labor leaders, began to prepare for a showdown. Significantly, the "struggle platform" adopted by the national CUT conference held in January 1962 stressed three demands of particular relevance to Yarur workers: job security, free unions and the elimination of work norming (the Taylor System).[99] It was a program around which all Yarur workers—young and old—could rally.

During the first months of 1962, the movement leaders organized underground, spreading a structure of cells throughout the mill, utilizing women's aprons to transmit messages and the factory's sports league to communicate between work sections. The leftist press began a propaganda campaign against Yarur labor practices, and the CUT publicly pledged its support and privately gave freely of its advice and resources.[100] All this was a prelude to the unprecedented act of running an insurgent slate in the July union elections. National attention was focused on them by congressional charges that state labor officials were complicit in rigging the Yarur union balloting.[101]

The election, held as usual in the industry gym with the same labor inspectors, was a textbook of intimidation. Yet insurgent support was so widespread that they were confident they had won. When it became clear that the results had once again been rigged, the response of the expectant workers was immediate. With a spontaneity and resolve that surprised even their mentors from the CUT and the Communist party, they stopped their machines, cast off years of passivity, and walked off their jobs into the torrential rain of a winter's night.[102] For the first time in more than two decades, the Yarur mill was on strike.

In many ways, the "strike of '62" was similar to the first Yarur strike in 1939. Management efforts to use strikebreakers led to physical confrontations. The local labor conflict became a national cause célèbre, discussed in newspapers and debated in Congress, a political litmus test that each party tried to exploit for its own advantage. The 1962 walkout also ended in a stalemate, which was resolved by a state intervention that the strikers initially viewed as a victory. Common to both conflicts was the Yarurs' ability to restore their social control with governmental assistance, buying the loyalty of some insurgent leaders and firing others, purging the factory of activists and intimidating a demoralized rank and file into passivity.

But there were also significant differences between the two strikes. The 1962 strike lasted longer—nine weeks instead of two—which placed a premium on the social solidarity and political support that the strikers received from other workers and allies. The conflict was also more intense in its passions and bitter in its emotions. As a consequence, the physical confrontations were more violent and vengeful. Company employees ran down pickets and shot several of them. Vigilante squads beat up workers on the other side, attacked their houses, threw bags of excrement through their windows, and threatened their families. The result was a social struggle in which neutrality was impossible, and the polarization between "Reds" (Insurgents) and "Yellows" (Loyalists) penetrated the minds and psyches of the Yarur workers.

Other differences reflected the divergent political and legal contexts of the two strikes. In 1962 a conservative government was in power, and its probusiness sympathies were clear from the start. Unlike the 1939 strike, moreover, the 1962 work stoppage was illegal, a "wildcat" strike undertaken without the state approval specified in the Labor Code and led by union officers whose election was not recognized by the relevant state agencies. This meant that the strikers enjoyed no legal protection and could be fired for being absent from work.

On September 11, 1962, Colonel Armando Baeza, the military interventor appointed by the Alessandri government to oversee resumption of production at the Yarur mill, ordered the industry's *obreros* to report for work. But when the returning strikers arrived at the factory, "the Interventor had people line up there at the factory gate" where "there was a man with a book who looked up our names and said: 'You enter, you no.' "[103] That day, some two hundred activists, including two of the insurgent candidates for union office, were barred from the mill for alleged "crimes" committed during the strike. Other activists were required to sign new contracts as if they were new workers, costing them their seniority and leaving them vulnerable to being fired without cause for six months.

During the months that followed, more than one thousand workers were fired from the Yarur mill on one pretext or another. These dismissals paralleled the advance of the Taylor System through the factory, which the new personnel chief later admitted was no mere coincidence: "According to our calculations we were working with 1200 machine operators too many, which represented an extra cost for the industry. If there had not been a way to fire them, we would have had to eliminate them little by little over time."[104] With one stroke, the Yarurs both eliminated the most militant workers and reduced their labor force to the optimal number needed under the Taylor System. "In the end," Jorge Yarur conceded, "the strike helped us."[105]

The Alessandri government did keep its promise to hold new union elections, which the insurgents won handily despite Yarur threats and blandishments. But a misguided sense of union democracy led the insurgents to divide their votes among ten candidates whereas the *apatronados* intelligently concentrated their far smaller number of votes among a slate of three. As a result, although the insurgents elected three directors, the Yarur loyalists elected two. It was to prove a "fatal error."[106]

Amador Yarur, like his father before him, refused to accept the adverse electoral verdict, and now it was he—not his brother Jorge—who was setting labor policy at the family mill. When Jorge Yarur was unable to break the strike, his younger brother took over the task. Jorge Yarur was willing to give modern labor relations a chance, but Amador wouldn't hear of it.[107] "He said that the people weren't ready for a free union, that you had to guide them" and warned that "if you didn't, you would not have social peace in the factory," one top aide recalled.[108] It was the voice of Juan Yarur speaking through his youngest son, and, with the support of the senior supervisors—"who were afraid of the union delegates in each section, afraid that there wouldn't be any authority anymore"—he carried the day.[109]

Don Amador's methods also echoed his father's. First, he denied the insurgents the fruits of their victory, stonewalling the first real collective bargaining in fifteen years. Then he paralyzed the union by ordering his loyalists to stay away from its meetings, thus denying the insurgents the legal quorum needed for passing budgets, revising bylaws, or calling strikes. Taking another leaf from his father's book, Amador Yarur now formed a parallel organization, the misnamed "United Independent Committee," and warned all workers who wished to keep their jobs to stay away from the union meetings and attend those of "his Committee" instead. At the same time, the physical intimidation of union supporters increased, and those workers who refused to be pressured into passivity were fired one by one.

When even these steps failed to produce the censure of the leftist union officers that he sought, Amador Yarur reached still deeper into his father's bag of tricks and persuaded the original insurgent leader, Horacio Zuñiga, "a talented but vain man," who resented being displaced by the younger Pepe Muñoz as head of the movement, to "sell out."[110] Zuñiga's switch of sides not only demoralized his former followers but also gave the Yarur loyalists a majority on the union board of directors. A few months later, this Yellow victory was consolidated by an electoral triumph that was preceded by the firing of scores of insurgent sympathizers, accompanied by gross intimidation, and followed by another wave of dismissals, which included Pepe Muñoz and his remaining followers.

The 1962 workers' movement was over, but its lessons lingered on. For almost all involved, it was a traumatic experience, as well as the event that consolidated the Taylor System and confirmed Amador Yarur's increasingly repressive system of social control. Moreover, it was the experience that shaped Amador Yarur's labor policies during the years that followed.

The conclusions that the Old-timers drew from 1962, however, varied with their worldview and experience. For most of those who had remained loyal to the Yarurs, the 1962 strike and its aftermath confirmed the wisdom of their choice and consolidated still further their *apatronado* mind-set. It also deepened their anti-Communist politics, reflecting the polarization between "Reds" and "Yellows" that the 1962 strike had so accentuated. Yarur loyalists such as Daniel Gómez congratulated themselves on their choice of sides, took pleasure in lording it over the remaining Reds in their work section, and basked in the reflected power and prestige of the Yarurs.[111]

Yet there were others who had taken the boss's side in 1962 who were appalled by Amador Yarur's vengeance and disillusioned by his deviousness, "so different from Don Juan."[112] Amador Yarur's ruthlessness and his lieutenants' brutality had stripped his benevolent mask and destroyed the organic ties of mutual loyalty that had bound many Old-timers to his father. "Never again were the people totally convinced, as they had been before by all that coaxing" of the Yarurs, Yolanda Gajardo stressed.[113] Some former *apatronados* were even radicalized by the experience. Iris Valenzuela "began to rebel in [her] heart . . . to see such wickedness on the part of the *jefes* and the bosses."[114]

For the workers who went down to defeat with Pepe Muñoz, the 1962 movement had been a heroic, but devastating experience. Even for those movement supporters who survived the Yarur purge—by luck, favor, or a strategic switch of sides—the experience was traumatic. Many knew that they were there on sufferance, that "in the moment that we least expected it, we could be thrown out."[115] Others, including old Yarur loyalists, were transferred to inconvenient shifts, undesirable work sections, and uncongenial foremen. Even former favorites complained that "they no longer had goodwill toward me; rather they hated me. They gave me the hardest jobs and tried to crush my spirit."[116] These workers retained their jobs, but they paid a heavy price for their disloyalty.

There were others who had gone out on strike who had been disillusioned by the experience. Some learned never to trust leftist leaders who might later sell out; others grew to mistrust Communists who might manipulate a spontaneous workers' movement for their own political ends. Many Old-timers were once again convinced that their *patrón* was omnipotent and that mere workers were too weak to challenge him, confirming their resolve never again to get involved in so hopeless a task as an insurgent movement at the Yarur mill.

Many of them, however, harbored deep resentments under an *apatronado* exterior, and their growing sense that the inequality of wealth and power between rich and poor was unjust drew them to a populist worldview, which looked for a benevolent elite leader to redress this imbalance, whether that leader was a Christian Democrat such as Eduardo Frei or a Socialist such as Salvador Allende. There were many now at Yarur who agreed with Iris Valenzuela when she said: "I had to listen to them because I had to work . . . but the only thing that I thought was that some day I would be able to demonstrate my ideas."[117]

The political ideas and identifications of many Yarur workers were also shaped by their growing awareness during the strike of whom their political allies and enemies were. They had sat in the spectator benches in Congress when a Communist deputy had stressed that "the way in which different deputies vote . . . will be sufficient to define them. Thus all of Chile will know where every party, politician, and candidate stands: if they are with the rich or with the poor, if they are with the empire of the Yarurs or with the free union that the majority of their workers have elected democratically."[118] The complicity of the Alessandri government in the strikebreaking and purge that followed underscored this local lesson in national politics.

The strike of '62 and its traumatic aftermath taught the Yarur workers once again that the Chilean state played a decisive role in the struggle between labor and capital. For some, this was a radicalizing experience that pushed them into political activity; but for most of the Old-timers, the lesson had the opposite effect. In the future they would not hazard their jobs, homes, and dreams unless they were convinced that the government would protect them. Some of the Old-timers of 1970 were *apatronados* out of conviction, and others out of calculation, but all would remain loyal to Amador Yarur until that time came.

3

THE CHILEAN ROAD
TO SOCIALISM[1]

When the Yarur workers seized their mill in April 1971, they did so with the expectation that the Chilean government, under President Salvador Allende, would support their bold act. They had anticipated state support in the past, when all they were demanding was their legal rights under Chile's Labor Code, but they had been sorely disappointed.

During the decades since the factory's founding, ill-paid and venal state labor inspectors had turned a blind eye to Yarur violations of the labor laws and repression of union democracy while a permeable state that had been colonized by special interests and governments responsive to Yarur wealth and power had promoted and protected Yarur interests. In the process, the state's authority as the arbiter of labor relations under the Chilean Labor Code was used to reinforce the hegemony of capital instead of to redress the imbalance of power between the Yarurs and their workers.

Yet when the workers decided to challenge Amador Yarur's control of his cotton mill in 1971, they were convinced that this time would be different. For the first time, a self-proclaimed "workers' government" ruled Chile, dominated by the Left and pledged to socialist revolution. For once, they could count on a *"compañero presidente"* in La Moneda.

The election of Salvador Allende Gossens as president of Chile in September 1970 took most Americans by surprise. Allende was an avowed Marxist, the candidate of a coalition dominated by the Communist and Socialist parties, and had campaigned on a platform of peaceful revolution. Nothing like it had ever happened in the Western Hemisphere, and Washington's alarm reverberated throughout the continent. Yet although many Chileans were worried at the prospect of a Marxist president, to them it did not come as a total surprise. Allende's triumph represented the culmination

of decades of Socialist and Communist participation in Chile's pluralistic
political system. It was a victory made possible by the evolution of mass
politics, economic structures, and social expectations. At bottom, Allende
was elected on a platform of democratic socialism because of the failure of
less radical alternatives to solve the chronic problems of postwar Chile:
dependency and stagflation, economic inequality and social inequity, the
concentration of wealth and the persistence of poverty, the hegemony of the
rich and the powerlessness of the poor.

THE LONG MARCH OF THE CHILEAN LEFT

By 1970, the Chilean Left had completed a long march through the political
wilderness. The isolated movement of northern nitrate miners at the turn
of the century had become a national political force. The essentially urban
organization of the 1930s now reached into rural estates and Indian villages.
From the political expression of the organized working class, the Chilean
Left had been transformed into a political movement that included significant
sectors of the middle class and the intelligentsia, the peasantry and the urban
lower class. Ideologically, the Chilean Left had completed a sinuous journey
from the revolutionary anarchism of the turn of the century "resistance
societies" through the mild reformism of the Popular Front (1938–41) and
creole populism of Carlos Ibáñez (1952–58) to a socialism that combined a
commitment to Marxism-Leninism with a Western European parliamentary
road and the anti-imperialism and nationalism of a Third World revolution.

   Along the way, the Left had tried a variety of political strategies, with
varying results. It had sponsored general strikes and a military coup, endorsed
class coalitions and proletarian unity, formed national labor confederations
and local community organizations, relied on elitist vanguards and mass
parties, engaged in guerrilla warfare and parliamentary politics, embraced
ideological purity and programatic compromise, proffered revolutionary zeal
and populist promises. Some of these strategies had brought the Left tran-
sitory gains and even governmental participation, but none had won them
power. Some of them had secured their working-class supporters modest
increases in living standards and life chances, but none had brought them
socialism. Still others had failed utterly and on several occasions had provoked
a ruthless repression of leftist movements and their mostly working-class
supporters.

   The path the Left had taken had not been straight and narrow. Rather,
it had experienced a cyclic pattern of victories and defeats, advances and
retreats. By 1970, the Chilean Left had survived three cycles of success and
failure, acceptance and repression, which had molded its traditions and

leaders, ideology and organization. One cycle had taken the Left from the rebellion and repression of the northern miners at the turn of the century through the militant organization of workers and class politics that culminated in the radicalization of the Chilean Workers Federation (FOCh) and the founding of the Communist party during the decade that followed World War I. A second cycle of repression and revolution began with the crushing of these leftist movements by Ibáñez after 1927 and ran through the twelve-day Socialist Republic of 1932 and the founding of the Socialist party in the wake of its defeat. A third cycle, of coalition governments and political isolation, reform and repression, spanned the three decades from the Popular Front of 1938 to the Popular Unity of 1970.

It was this last cycle that had formed the leftist leaders of 1970 and still shaped their politics and perspectives. For many of them, it was their "long march," during which they had been forced to confront both success and failure and to modify their theories and alter their practice. In many respects, the trajectory of the Left during these decades was reflected in the career of Salvador Allende, its standard-bearer for much of this period. "Salvador is a man formed in this long struggle," one old Socialist comrade underscored.[2]

Allende was born in 1908 in Valparaíso, Chile's leading port and second largest city, into an established, but not wealthy, family, which counted several leaders of the Masons and the Radical party among its members. It was from his father, a lawyer and public defender, that he acquired his political vocation and commitment to social reform. "It was at my father's funeral, when I was twenty-four," Allende recalled, "that I vowed to dedicate my life to the social struggle."[3] At that age, he was already a socialist activist, released from jail to attend his father's burial.

Allende's political radicalization had begun at age fifteen through a friendship with an aging anarchist shoemaker. But it was as a medical student in Santiago that he was introduced to Marxism and became a confirmed socialist. "The medical students, with their awareness of malnutrition and disease, were the most advanced politically," he explained.[4] "We read Marx and talked politics and anatomy." Equally important was his exposure to "the tragedy of poverty." "As a student," Allende recalled, "I lived in poor neighborhoods as a boarder and came to know at close quarters the misery, lack of housing, lack of medical care, and lack of education of the Chilean people. My studies taught me that socialism was the only solution to these problems and that Chile had to find its own road." By the time Allende graduated from medical school in 1932, with a thesis on the social causes of ill health, he had acquired a political faith and a reputation as a leftist leader.

In 1932, Allende was expelled from the university for political activities, fought for his cousin Marmaduke Grove's brief "Socialist Republic," and was jailed in the struggles that followed. A year later, he became one of the founders of the Socialist party and its organizer in his hometown of Valparaíso, from where he was elected to Congress in 1937, at the age of twenty-nine. The following year, Allende became minister of health in Pedro Aguirre Cerda's Popular Front government, an experience that was seminal for his politics and career.

The Chilean Popular Front was a Center-Left coalition that included both the Socialist and Communist parties, but was dominated by the centrist Radicals, who, once in power, lost their zeal for reform. The Popular Front failed to satisfy the expectations of social change and economic betterment that it had raised among Chile's workers and peasants. Its contradictory coalition soon broke into its component parts as the Radicals moved to the Right and the Left divided into feuding factions. The Popular Front ended with Pearl Harbor, leaving as its political legacy a Socialist-Communist rivalry that exploded into open hostilities once the cold war began.

During this long decade of fratricidal warfare within the left and factional feuding within the Socialist party, Allende became Socialist party chief (in 1942) and a senator (in 1945), the leader of those Socialists who opposed the anti-communist line of the majority, arguing that "a divided Left could not win power."[5] He remained loyal to this political vision during the cold war years of Communist persecution by Radical President Gabriel González Videla, earning the trust of Chile's Communists in return. In 1952, when most Socialists backed Carlos Ibáñez, Allende ran for president with Communist support but received only 6 percent of the vote. During the years that followed, Allende became the apostle of leftist unity, blessing the reunification of the labor movement in the Central Unica de Trabajadores (CUT), reuniting the factious fragments of his Socialist party and leading them into the Popular Action Front (FRAP), a new leftist coalition. By 1970, he had run for president twice more as the candidate of this Socialist-Communist alliance, increasing his vote totals and improving his showing with each campaign. In 1958 he polled first among male voters and might have been elected had it not been for the candidacy of a defrocked radical priest. In 1964, he won 39 percent of the vote, attracting the support of more than half a million Chileans, but lost to Christian Democrat Eduardo Frei. In the political maneuvers that followed, Allende was elected President of the Senate, the highest position to which a leftist had ever been voted in Chile, a success that symbolized the long journey of the Left to legitimacy, respectability, and influence.

From each of these experiences, Allende and the other leftist leaders extracted important lessons. Although Grove's Socialist Republic had been a brief episode with few concrete achievements to its credit, even the Communists (who opposed it) later admitted that "it was an important political event that announced a new set of possibilities."[6] To Allende, who won his political spurs fighting for it, the Socialist Republic was also a personal experience of revolutionary practice that would sustain his faith through four decades of parliamentary politics.[7]

The Popular Front, the Left's first experience of government, was a formative one for Allende and the "generation of '38." For Salvador Allende, the Popular Front, despite its limitations, was decisive, teaching him "the importance of an alliance between the workers and the middle class" and convincing him that "in Chile it was possible to construct socialism within the existing political institutions." Unlike some of his Socialist comrades, Allende considered the Chilean Popular Front "a relative success," whose chief defect was that it "was dominated by the bourgeois Radical party" instead of by "the proletarian [Socialist and Communist] parties." He decided to devote the rest of his political career to reconstructing that class coalition and Center-Left alliance on firmer social and political foundations.[8]

The postwar decade of leftist feuding, political repression, and populist disappointment taught different lessons. The decline of leftist strength persuaded Allende that "the success of the popular movement in Chile depended on the unity of the parties of the working class, despite the differences and rivalries among them."[9] The unity of the Left became the guiding principle of Salvador Allende, the only major Western Socialist leader willing to ally himself with the Communists during the cold war. Meanwhile, the Communists learned from González Videla's betrayal not to place their trust in centrist parties and opportunistic leaders.[10] At the same time, the anti-Communist Socialist majority found out that Ibáñez's populists were no more trustworthy as allies than Radical politicians.[11] By the 1958 elections, the various factions of the Left had learned from bitter experience that only by uniting their forces under a leader from their own ranks could they hope to win power and change Chile.

By then, Allende had also learned another important lesson: that if he hoped to construct socialism and do it democratically, he would have to persuade the Chilean people of its necessity and superiority. The Left might still press for ameliorating reforms and make bread-and-butter demands on behalf of their working class followers, but they had to begin to prepare the way for a democratic socialism.[12] In 1952, Salvador Allende proposed the expropriation of Chile's American-owned copper mines on the floor of the Senate, fusing socialism with nationalism and seizing on an issue that dramatized the need for structural change in Chile. He continued to make the same points year after year as the support for socialism grew and the political spectrum shifted increasingly to the Left.

Although its course had not been steady or its road easy, over this long period the electoral strength of the Left had grown until it was superior to the Right and almost the equal of the Center, accounting for almost two-fifths of the electorate in 1964's presidential balloting.[13] The distance traveled by the Left was equally apparent in organizational terms. Between its founding in 1922 and 1970, the Moscow-line Communist party had transformed itself from a small proletarian vanguard party with a narrow social and geographical base among the miners of the far north into a national mass party of workers, peasants, and professionals that commanded almost 400,000 votes (16 percent of the 1969 congressional balloting) and claimed about 100,000 members and almost an equal number in its active youth wing.[14] The less disciplined and more diverse Socialists had reconciled their internal differences sufficiently to unite their warring factions into the Left's second largest party, one that received almost 300,000 votes (12 percent) in the 1969 parliamentary elections. They remained a heterogeneous party with largely middle-class leaders and mostly skilled working-class and lower-middle-class followers, but with growing support among peasants and *pobladores* (urban poor) and increasing strength in the outlying provinces. Ideologically, the Socialist party now defined itself as "Marxist-Leninist" although it still contained sizable populist and social democratic elements.[15] Both Marxist parties had participated in governmental coalitions and parliamentary blocs along the way, gaining legitimacy and experience in the process.

The Chilean Left was the beneficiary as well of profound structural changes. Between 1920 and 1970, both the size and composition of the Chilean electorate were transformed. During these five decades, the number of registered voters expanded from 10 percent to 36 percent of a population that grew from 3.7 million to 9.7 million. Women were granted the franchise in 1949, and the electorate jumped by more than half, but female voters were less supportive of leftist candidates than their male counterparts. More positive for the Left were the reforms of 1958, which established a single official secret ballot, and 1962, which made voter registration obligatory, simplified, and permanent. These reforms discouraged electoral fraud and encouraged an effective working-class, peasant, and lower-class suffrage that had often been more formal than real.[16] Together, these reforms created the context for a doubling of the electorate between 1952 and 1970, the vast majority of whom came from the lower social strata. The political implications of these reforms were seen in the decline of the Right's rural vote and in increased peasant support for the Center and the Left, a shift that reflected as well the social costs of the postwar modernization of Chilean agriculture.

Other historical processes also encouraged this political revolution. During these decades, Chile became progressively more urban, with 70 percent of its population living in cities by 1970, one-third in Santiago alone. The urban lower class was easier for the Left to reach and more likely to respond to its appeals than their rural counterparts. These same years saw the formation and growth of an industrial working class, which became the central social base for the Marxist Left. They also witnessed the parallel rise of a labor movement closely linked to the Communist and Socialist parties. Although estimates varied,[17] 500,000–700,000 workers, some 20 to 30 percent of the labor force, were unionized, the overwhelming majority united in the 4200 local unions affiliated with the Central Unica de Trabajadores (CUT), the Marxist-led national labor confederation founded in 1953.

These statistics, though impressive, obscured the relative weakness of the national labor movement within the complex system of state-regulated labor relations established by the Chilean Labor Code of 1931. Prohibited by law from organizing plants with fewer than twenty-five workers, engaging in industry-wide collective bargaining, or calling solidarity strikes, the CUT and its constituent federations focused much of their resources, time, and energies on national issues and politics. It was a system that placed a premium on political influence and a weakness that tied the labor movement to the leftist parties that claimed to speak for the working class. If one of the CUT's functions was to win the support of the parties of the Left for worker demands, another was to mobilize the support of their members for the Left's policies and candidates. Significantly, the Left's rise in electoral strength paralleled the growth of the CUT. In the 1969 congressional balloting, leftist parties received almost one-third of the vote, more than double their 1953 showing.[18] Clearly, a leftward shift of the electorate had taken place in the interim.

THE FAILURE OF REFORM

Equally important by then was the radicalization of the Center, the balance wheel of Chilean politics. Like the rise of the Left that it paralleled, this shift reflected both changes in Chilean society and the failure of more moderate measures to solve contemporary Chile's enduring economic and social problems. During the postwar years, populism and Christian Democracy, modernized capitalism and bureaucratic clientelism, foreign corporations and Chilean technocrats all tried—and failed—to provide adequate answers.

From 1938 to 1952, the centrist Radical party dominated Chilean politics, placing three successive presidents in La Moneda, but failed to solve these difficult dilemmas.[19] By 1952, the Radicals' economic strategy of deficit spending, expanded public employment, and protected import substitution was exhausted; and their political practice of opportunistic alliances, governmental corruption, and a bloated bureaucracy was discredited. Economically and politically bankrupt, the Radicals watched their electoral strength ebb as a disillusioned middle class turned to the antipolitics of the aging strongman, Carlos Ibáñez del Campo.

From 1927 to 1947, Ibáñez had been an authoritarian rightist, but he was returned to power in 1952 as an antiparty populist with the support of the most radical faction of the divided Socialists and the votes of substantial sectors of the working class. The election of a "popular" president raised worker expectations, but a year later the aging *caudillo* jettisoned his Socialist advisers, reversed their economic policies, and, amid runaway inflation, moved toward the conservative fiscal measures and American advisers that he had favored during his first presidency (1927–31).

The result was a classic austerity program, whose burdens were borne primarily by those Chileans who could least afford the sacrifice—wage workers and salaried employees. Their declining living standards, in combination with the opposition of urban entrepreneurs and rural landowners to the restriction of credit and state subsidies, doomed Ibáñez and his stabilization plan to political defeat.

The failure of personalistic populism to solve Chile's chronic economic problems gave the Right one final chance to demonstrate that a modernized capitalism with minimal governmental regulation and extensive foreign investment was the answer. In the 1958 elections, the conservative entrepreneur Jorge Alessandri defeated Allende by a thin margin in a four-way race. But even a capitalist president, pursuing probusiness policies, could not induce Chilean—or foreign—investors to risk their capital in modernizing Chile's inefficient industries. As a consequence, Alessandri soon ran aground on the familiar reef of stagflation. At the same time, the conservative social policies of "Don Jorge" failed to come to grips with the flood of rural migrants or the decline in mass living standards. When the anticipated surge in prosperity failed to materialize, popular discontent grew, along with strikes, demonstrations, and land seizures—to which Alessandri's response was repression, as the Yarur workers could attest.

The capitalist's candidate and paternalist president, Alessandri, had failed to restore dynamism to the economy, stability to prices, or cohesion to society. As a consequence, from 1962 on, the political tide ran to the Left as Chileans turned to more radical solutions to their country's chronic problems. As the 1964 presidential election approached, the only question was whether they would choose Christian Democratic reform—or socialist revolution.

The prospect of a Marxist victory led a worried Chilean elite to back the presidential bid of Eduardo Frei, a centrist Christian Democrat running on a platform of Alliance for Progress social and economic reforms, which promised Chileans a "revolution in liberty" that would solve the nation's problems without running the risk of a "Marxist dictatorship." Washington and Rome also backed Frei as "the last best hope" to save Chile from communism. Eduardo Frei's statesmanlike manner and "American" media campaign, along with the attraction of his party's reform program and uncorrupted image, won him a majority of the vote—with the support of the Right and the assistance of an anti-Communist scare campaign aided and advised by the CIA.[20] A few months later, congressional elections gave the new president a majority in the Chamber of Deputies and a clear mandate for his "revolution in liberty."

Although his party's left wing viewed Christian Democracy as a "third way" between an avaricious capitalism and a totalitarian communism, in which technocratic direction and a mixed economy would avoid the evils of both the uncontrolled market and state socialism, Eduardo Frei himself remained a man of the center, linked to the modernizing sector of Chile's business elite, ambivalent about the reforming thrust of his party's program, and hostile to its more radical definitions. He retained the rhetoric of "peaceful revolution," but the reforms that his government initiated were intended to rescue Chile's dependent capitalism, not to replace it. "Development" was the watchword of this program, and a key Frei goal was the modernization and expansion of Chile's inefficient and stagnant industries and agriculture through state planning and regulation, promotion of foreign investment, and provision of liberal credits and technical assistance.[21]

Central to this economic strategy was increased social spending on housing construction and an agrarian reform intended to expropriate inefficient large estates. The Frei land reform was designed to create a rural middle class of peasant producers who would serve as a market for domestic manufactures.[22] Equally important was the projected "Chileanization of copper," on the surface a nationalistic purchase of a majority share in the country's giant copper mines, but at bottom a strategy to induce the American copper corporations to produce the increased mineral exports that would fund the Christian Democrats' victimless strategy of economic modernization and social reform.[23]

If this strategy were to succeed, not only would Chile reap economic gains without social conflict, but the Christian Democrats would also benefit politically. Their political strategy aimed at nothing less than the transformation of Christian Democracy into the hegemonic political force that would bar both Left and Right from power. Above all, this strategy relied on an unprecedented campaign of mass mobilization calculated to incorporate the unorganized rural peasants and urban slum dwellers into the political system under Christian Democratic colors.

To succeed, the Frei strategy required the cooperation of both capital and labor, whose shared sacrifices—through controls on wages and prices — would contain inflation and finance the program. Not surprisingly, both capital and labor responded to the Frei government's strategy ambivalently, taking advantage of the opportunities it offered to advance their interests while avoiding the sacrifices it demanded for the Christian Democratic vision of the public good. Moreover, active state promotion proved insufficient to infuse entrepreneurial dynamism into a dependent Chilean capitalism accustomed to government credits at negative interest rates, oligopolistic control of protected markets, and windfall profits from monetary manipulations and financial speculations. The Yarurs were a good case in point.[24]

As a result, by 1970 the Christian Democratic strategy lay in ruins. Between 1966 and 1970 economic growth declined by half, while inflation soared to over 30 percent and unemployment rose to 8 percent. Despite record copper earnings, budget deficits expanded, leading the Frei government to contract spending on public works and social services. Housing construction, a dire Chilean need and initial Frei success story, was cut back after 1967. A slow and limited land reform disappointed more peasants than it satisfied, and recrudescent inflation generated the heightened social conflict that the Christian Democrats had hoped to avert.[25]

Under these circumstances, the political mobilization of previously unorganized peasants and *pobladores* (urban poor) did not always redound to the benefit of the Christian Democrats. By 1970, one-third of the organized peasants were members of Marxist unions, and leftist banners flew from suburban shantytowns. Far from achieving the definitive political breakthrough they had planned, the Christian Democrats saw their share of the vote fall from 43 percent in 1965 to less than 30 percent in 1969.[26]

Equally important was the growing alienation of Christian Democratic leaders and activists. For many idealistic Christian Democrats, their first taste of power had proved a frustrating and disillusioning experience, as elite opposition, bureaucratic inertia, and partisan politics combined to slow the pace of change and restrict the scope of reform. The party's left-wing *rebelde* and *tercerista* factions were convinced by this experience that a more radical assault on the status quo was needed. When their proposals for a "noncapitalist road of development" and a "People's Alliance of all the Lefts"— Christian and Marxist—were rejected, the *rebelde* faction bolted the Christian Democrats and in 1969 formed the United Popular Action Movement (MAPU)—with the intention of negotiating an electoral alliance with the Marxist Left.[27]

The secession of the *rebeldes*, many of whom had long histories and important positions in the party, was a big shock to the Christian Democrats. In order to mollify the *terceristas*, their leader, Radomiro Tomic, was nominated as the party's presidential candidate for 1970. Tomic then endorsed an electoral program closer to Allende's in 1970 than to Frei's in 1964.

The Christian Democrats were not the only center party to move Left after 1964. After losing badly with a right wing candidate in 1964, the Radicals found themselves in grave danger of ceding their role as the representative of the middle class center to the Christian Democrats. Gradually, the Radical party began to move to the Left in search of a political raison d'être, out of fear of political extinction and under pressure from its own "revolutionary" youth wing, which was influenced by the revolutionary currents swirling around Latin America in the decade of Che Guevara and the Cuban Revolution. In 1965 the Radicals agreed to back Allende's candidacy for president of the Senate in return for leftist support of their candidate in the Chamber of Deputies. To the old Radical *políticos*, the success of this deal demonstrated the advantages of a new alliance with the Marxist Left.

The stage was set for the formation of the Popular Unity—a heterogeneous Center-Left coalition built around the Socialists, Communists, and Radicals, but including the MAPU and several small social democratic and populist groupings as well. The creation of the Popular Unity signified the end of the Chilean Left's long march through the political wilderness following the disintegration of the Popular Front in 1941. During the preceding two decades, the Left had rebuilt its labor and political organizations, overcoming internal differences and rivalries, constructed new social alliances, and designed a more coherent and independent program. Capitalizing on the popularity of Salvador Allende and the policy failures of governments of the Right and Center, the Left had honed its political appeals and increased its electoral strength. In 1969, with the formation of the Popular Unity, it became a credible contender for power.

¡"UNIDAD POPULAR! VENCEREMOS!"

At bottom, the Popular Unity represented a modified 1930's Popular Front strategy, given another chance in the very different conditions of 1970. The failure of Chile's dependent capitalism to resolve the country's basic problems during the intervening decades had brought Chilean politics full circle, but this time with a more radical cast and more revolutionary goals.

Where the Popular Unity differed dramatically from the Popular Front was in its diagnosis of, and cures for, these chronic ills. The failures of Ibáñez's populism, Alessandri's "free enterprise," and Frei's reformed neocapitalism to solve Chile's problems gave the Popular Unity license to conclude that they were systemic, to blame them on Chile's dependent capitalism, and to maintain that democratic socialism was the only solution.

The Popular Unity program embodied this socialist solution in concrete proposals. Economic dependence would be combatted by an aggressive extension of state control. The "recuperation of the nation's basic riches" from foreign control would be accomplished by nationalization. The acquisition of Chile's giant American-owned copper mines, begun by the Frei government, would be completed and extended to the country's iron, nitrate, and coal mines. Foreign trade would also come under government control, as would the large enterprises that dominated domestic distribution of imported goods.

Public ownership was also the Popular Unity's solution to the domestic concentration of wealth and power. Chile's private banks and insurance companies, which had monopolized credit in the interest of the reduced number of financial "clans"— such as the Yarurs—that controlled them, would also be nationalized. A "social property area" would be created through the acquisition of the "strategic industrial monopolies," along with the service sector enterprises that "have a strong influence on the nation's social and economic development." This creation of "a dominant public sector" would ensure state control of "the commanding heights of the economy."[28]

It would also enable a Popular Unity government to implement policies calculated to end Chile's economic stagflation and to give national economic development priority over private pecuniary gain. Within the social property area, state planning would replace "the irrationality of the market" as a regulating mechanism, and the power of governmental policies would influence as well the far larger number of enterprises that would remain in the private sector or be incorporated into a new mixed sector of joint public-private ownership. In agriculture, the Christian Democratic land reform would be accelerated, intensified, and extended to the poorest rural groups, with a preference given to cooperative ownership. Together, these measures would accomplish "the central objective of . . . the Popular Unity," which "is to replace the present economic structure and to end the power of monopoly capitalism together with that of the landowner, in order to begin the construction of socialism."[29]

If socialism was one watchword of the Popular Unity program, democracy was the other. Chile's centralized and bureaucratized state was to be transformed by institutional changes calculated to increase popular participation and power. At the national level, the bicameral congress would be replaced by a single chamber "People's Assembly," whose representatives would be subject to recall. Similar assemblies would be established at the regional and local levels, their authority enhanced by a decentralization of power. "The new power structure will be built up from the grassroots by extending democracy at all levels," the program stressed.[30] The creation of organizations in workplaces and residential neighborhoods would ensure that this new power would be exercised directly by the people themselves. Economic democracy would be guaranteed by worker participation in the administration of the public sector enterprises and in the planning process. Less precise and more visionary than the economic program, the Popular Unity's political plank reflected the belief of many leftists that "the revolutionary changes required by Chile can only be carried out if the people of Chile take power into their own hands and exercise it in a true and effective manner."[31] Together they constituted a blueprint for a transformation of old structures that would culminate in a new "Chilean Road" to a socialism compatible with the nation's pluralistic traditions.

Socialism might be the Popular Unity's ultimate solution to Chile's problems, but along *la via chilena* its program promised a variety of populist palliatives. The duality of the Popular Unity—at once socialist and populist—was evident in the rhetoric of its program and clear in the first "Forty Measures" that it promised to take on becoming the "Popular Government." Ten of these measures pledged nothing more radical than good government— an end to corruption and the abuse of power. Another group promised more extensive and less expensive social benefits—vacations and retirement pay, housing and medical care. The egalitarian thrust of the Popular Unity was revealed in pledges to guarantee free milk, medical care, and basic education to all Chilean children and in its boast that "in the New Chile, only children will be privileged." The program's stress on the redistribution of wealth and power was also apparent in promises to abolish regressive taxes, use price controls—not wage freezes—to contain inflation, and implement policies that would eliminate unemployment and increase real incomes. Although the Popular Unity program was often vague on the means, its message was that the transformation of economic and political structures would enable the Popular Government "to resolve the immediate problems of the great majority."[32]

Populism, socialism, and nationalism: a patchwork platform for a heterogeneous political coalition calculated to appeal to an equally varied electorate. The Popular Unity's program reflected its political strategy: an alliance of the middle and lower classes, blue- and white-collar workers, intellectuals and peasants. It contained something for almost everybody and particular assurances to the non-Marxist middle class that a Popular Unity victory would benefit them and hurt only "monopolists" and "imperialists." The ritualistic formula of *el pueblo* ("the people") papered over the underlying contradiction between a long-term goal of worker-peasant hegemony and the short-term need for an alliance with the middle sectors. It was a platform made for Salvador Allende—by leaders who did not want him to run.

By 1970, Allende had run for president unsuccessfully three times. During those two decades in the political limelight, opinions about him had hardened. One 1970 survey indicated that two-thirds of the middle class would not vote for Allende under any circumstances,[33] but many workers viewed him as their symbolic standard-bearer and took his candidacy for granted. Leftist independents like Inés Castro, a middle-aged weaver at the Yarur mill, defined themselves not as Socialists or Communists, but as *allendistas*. "He is the only politician I ever trusted and the only one that I have ever voted for—or would vote for," she affirmed.[34]

Most Popular Unity leaders, on the other hand, were not so enthralled at the prospect of a fourth Allende candidacy.[35] To the dominant left wing of his own Socialist party, Allende was "too bourgeois" and "insufficiently revolutionary," while the social democratic right wing distrusted his Communist ties.[36] The Radical party and the MAPU expected their candidates to get the nomination as a reward for joining a largely Marxist coalition.[37] Even the Communists, who had sustained Allende's candidacy for two decades, expressed the general view: ¿*"Hasta cuando Allende?"* ("How long do we have to go on losing with Allende?") and favored a reassuring Radical or a fresh ex-Christian Democratic face in 1970.[38]

It was with justice that Allende later boasted: "It was the people who chose me. My own party was against me. The leaders of the Popular Unity were against me. But the people made me their candidate."[39] As Senator Volodia Teitelboim, a leading Communist, admitted: "Allende was chosen . . . because he was the voice of the people. Because if you talked with a peasant or a worker, in Valdívia or in Bellavista or in Magallanes, they said: "Well, yes of course the candidate has to be Salvador Allende." Allende's candidacy wasn't the product of "back room politics," Teitelboim stressed. "He is a man who won himself a name among the people."[40]

Allende already knew his opponents. Radomiro Tomic, Frei's more radical rival, was the Christian Democratic candidate, running on a platform that included the nationalization of the copper mines, the deepening of the agrarian reform, and the creation of a mixed economy with worker participation. The Right had toyed with the idea of supporting a right wing Christian Democrat, as in 1964, but Tomic's nomination and program put an end to such thoughts. Instead, the National party chose former president Jorge Alessandri as the standard-bearer of the conservative cause. "¡Alessandri Volvera!" ("Alessandri Will Return!") soon began to appear on the walls of Chile's better neighborhoods. The presidential campaign had begun.[41]

Allende's political advisers were convinced that there were two conditions essential to his victory in 1970: the formation of a Center-Left class coalition that would enable him to transcend the limits of his leftist constituency and mostly working-class base plus a three-way race with the Right and the Christian Democrats each running separate candidates. The creation of the Popular Unity satisfied the first of these conditions; the nomination of Tomic and Alessandri, the second. It remained to be seen, however, whether Allende could win.[42]

The pattern of the campaign was soon clear. Alessandri had most of the press, all the elite, and the United States Embassy; Tomic had the government apparatus, the Church, and the party faithful; but Allende had the walls, streets, and slums of Chile. Both Allende and Tomic focused their attacks on Alessandri; both Allende and Alessandri ignored Tomic, convinced that the election was between the two of them.

From the outset, Alessandri was the strong favorite. The United States Embassy even spoke of an absolute majority for Don Jorge.[43] Alessandri seemed the perfect candidate. The son of the most popular Chilean politician of the century, a successful businessman, and a former president, he was the embodiment of Chile's patrician past. Alessandri's image called up an era of tranquillity and tradition and promised a future that resembled the secure past and not the uncertain present. This impression was reinforced by his campaign platform, which denounced "political demagogues" as responsible for Chile's problems, exuded confidence that the return of an austere authority figure would solve them, and proposed a moratorium on change and a return to conservative economics. At the same time, it was expected that his slick, heavily financed media campaign would "sell" Alessandri to a substantial number of lower-class and peasant voters—especially the women—projecting a strong but grandfatherly image of the enlightened aristocrat and paternalistic *patrón*, whose wisdom, experience, and firmness would guarantee their welfare. It was an image conveyed in posters of Alessandri in judicial robes, hands extended to the adoring masses, assuring them: "I am with you."

The seventy-three-year-old Alessandri, however, proved to be "the perfect candidate" only until he began his campaign. Increasingly, the aging Alessandri seemed less the measured modernizer than the anachronistic conservative, less the grandfatherly *patrón* than the doddering aristocrat. The Left dubbed him *el momio* ("the mummy"), and the name stuck. As the campaign wore on, Alessandri's support eroded although his advisers remained confident of victory up to election day.

At first glance, it appeared as if any deterioration in Alessandri's support would benefit Radomiro Tomic, who could seize the center ground between an aging conservative and a Marxist revolutionary, projecting a "modern" image of responsible and responsive reform. A founder of his party and leader of its left wing, a university professor and ambassador in Washington, a good Catholic and family man, Tomic could project an image that was as respected as Alessandri's aristocratic executive or Allende's concerned physician. Tomic also expected to pick up leftist support as the campaign progressed, and he emerged as the only real alternative to Alessandri.

Once again, appearances were deceiving. Tomic's program and political stance were too far to the Left to win the allegiance of the Right, and his pompous style and United States ties were an anathema to the Left. At the same time, Tomic's Catholicism—pushed in posters in which Tomic resembled a priest granting benediction to the worker and peasant flock gathered below—made him unacceptable to many middle-class Radicals, with their anticlerical tradition. At bottom, however, Tomic's problem was that the middle ground that he sought to occupy was disappearing as a consequence of the very political polarization that his candidacy had accelerated.

Moreover, Allende refused to fade. His campaign had begun badly. The wounds of the Popular Unity's nomination struggle did not heal rapidly, and it appeared as if the support that he would receive from some of its parties would be halfhearted and inefficacious at the polls. Worse still was the defeatism among the Popular Unity leadership. Allende's candidacy had been pressed on them from below over their objections and against their instincts. If the "people's choice" were to emerge victorious, "the people" would have to win it for him.

To the surprise of the pundits, that was precisely what began to happen. Despite an antiquated public relations approach, little media time, and less favorable press coverage, Allende's campaign began to gather momentum—just when the slicker, more heavily financed efforts of his opponents began to run out of steam. In part, this was due to Allende himself, who never wavered in his belief that he would win. Campaigning tirelessly, he took his message of populism and socialism, of a peaceful revolution with *empanadas y vino tinto* ("red wine and meat pies") to the far corners of Chile, varying his approach with his audience, but always with wit and humor. Short and bespectacled, a notorious womanizer and a mediocre public speaker, Allende was neither charismatic nor eloquent. But he *was* a charming and experienced campaigner, projecting an image of dignity and concern. After more than three decades of public life, moreover, Salvador Allende knew the Chilean people, and they knew him.

Allende's campaign was powerfully assisted by the Communist party, which assured him of a disciplined and dedicated group of political workers. But mostly it was "the people" themselves who took over his campaign and made it—and Allende—their own.[44] Throughout the country, they formed thousands of local Popular Unity Committees (CUPs), which made up in grass-roots strength what the Allende campaign lacked in funds, sophistication, and dynamism at the top. Incorporating party members and independents, *allendistas* and the politically uncommitted who favored *los cambios*—"the changes" proposed in the Popular Unity program—the CUPs saturated the working-class and lower-class neighborhoods with their posters and propaganda, campaign speeches and cultural events. Gradually, their chants of "*¡Unidad Popular! Venceremos!*" ("Popular Unity! We Will Win!") became more powerful and more confident. It was the new politics in the service of an old politician, but all for a New Chile.

Pasted on crumbling walls and plastered over public buildings in work-ing-class districts, painted on construction sites and along the river walls and park walks, the messages of the Allende campaign seemed to be every-where that a worker turned, with their promises of populist benefits and visions of socialist transformations. By September, it was clear that Allende had won the battle of the poster and the paintbrush, while the election had become too close to call.

4

EL COMPAÑERO
PRESIDENTE

The elections took place in an atmosphere of heightened expectation. As returns began to come in from the capital's poorer districts and the country's outlying provinces, Allende moved into a narrow lead that he never lost— capturing 36.3 percent of the vote to Alessandri's 34.9 percent and Tomic's 27.8 percent. By midnight, Allende supporters were flooding into the streets to celebrate their long-awaited victory—the "popular triumph" that many of them thought they would never live to see.

"I was still celebrating . . . the following morning," recalled Alma Gallegos, a Communist and former Yarur worker:[1] "When Compañero Allende was elected, my husband came looking for me . . . and we went out together to turn things upside down." As they soon discovered, they were not alone: "It was like a carnival. It was something we had never expected. It was something that those of us who lived that moment will remember all our lives. It was a joy that couldn't fit inside one, to see all the *compañeros* embracing each other—whether they were poor or hungry or well dressed . . . And we shouted out right there in the street: "Long live the Popular Unity! Long live Compañero Allende!" The message of the triumphant workers and slum dwellers who took over the streets of Santiago that night was clear: The politics of deference was past, and a revolution had begun. Chile would never again be the same.

Not all Chileans shared their euphoria. A stunned elite reacted to Allende's election with disbelief, dismay, and alarm. Investment ceased, the stock market fell precipitously, and consumer sales plummeted, with the exception of airline tickets for foreign destinations. Most of the middle class shared the elite's anxieties although many were ambivalent about the electoral outcome and uncertain of its implications.

The reaction of Chile's workers, peasants, and *pobladores* was less equivocal, but equally complex. Although thousands shared Alma Gallegos's euphoria, for many their jubilation was mixed with caution, even apprehension. One leathery-faced peasant confided that when the news of Allende's election reached the Central Valley estate on which he worked, he "celebrated the good news by *"tomando una copa"* [drinking a glass] to the new president-elect, but *"calladito"* [very quietly] so that the *patrón* would not know."[2] A revolution might be about to begin, but the old power structure still ruled most of the land, and the poor and powerless who had voted for "Chicho" Allende still had to hide their loyalties. Even among the urban working class there were many who continued to practice discretion. "The rich have so much power," thought Jaime Riscal, a Yarur weaver who had kept his job by maintaining an *apatronado* facade. "Better to wait and see what happens."[3]

For much of Chile, the two months that separated Allende's election from his inauguration were a time of watchful waiting. Although Tomic immediately recognized Allende's victory, Alessandri maintained an ominous silence, and his campaign manager declared that "the electoral process is not finished."[4] Allende had won a plurality, but not a majority of the votes. This meant that his election had to be confirmed by the Chilean Congress, which had the power to choose between the two leading candidates. In the past, it had always ratified the electoral results, but in the wake of Allende's "popular triumph," rumors of congressional deals and military coups abounded.

They were lent credence by reports that the United States was behind the efforts of the Chilean elite to nullify the electoral verdict. Although the State Department denied such American involvement, the rumors were true. With a mandate from President Nixon, who told CIA Director Richard Helms that "he wanted something done and he didn't much care how,"[5] the CIA set in motion a "two-track" policy designed to prevent Salvador Allende from becoming president of Chile. Track I was a "constitutional coup," persuading the Christian Democrats to break with tradition and vote in the Congress for the runner-up, Jorge Alessandri, as president.[6] Track II was a military coup and "between October 5 and October 20, 1970, the CIA made 21 contacts with key military and Carabinero [police] officials in Chile" in a concentrated effort to promote it.[7] Lastly, in order to justify either a congressional or a military coup, efforts were made to "create a coup climate by propaganda, disinformation, and terrorist activities intended to provoke the left" and by promoting the economic crisis that would execute Nixon's instructions to "make the economy scream."[8]

A major financial panic was set off, with the aid of an irresponsible speech by Frei's finance minister, but from that point on the CIA plots went awry.

Track I began to unravel when key Chilean actors failed to play their assigned roles. Tomic remained steadfast in his recognition of Allende's victory, and Frei proved indecisive and vacillating, despite the urgings of the United States ambassador.[9] Moreover, Allende refused to be provoked and made his supporters follow suit. Instead, he played his cards brilliantly, warning darkly of civil war if his victory at the polls were overturned in the back rooms or barracks while giving in to Christian Democratic demands for a "statute of guarantees" that included both political freedoms and job security for Christian Democratic civil servants. When Frei was unable to persuade his party to reject this compromise of Christian Democratic votes for Popular Unity assurances, it was clear that Track I was unlikely to succeed.

This left only the possibility of a military coup, which even the CIA's own operatives considered remote, given the constitutionalist views of Commander in Chief René Schneider and his deputy, General Carlos Prats. The CIA supported plots headed by General Camilo Valenzuela, commander of the Santiago garrison, and by General Roberto Viaux, a neo-Fascist leader retired for leading a rebellion against President Frei, both of which revolved around attacks on General Schneider.[10] Valenzuela failed in two attempts to kidnap Schneider, and when Viaux's gunmen killed the army commander two days before the Congress was to elect Chile's next president, his assassination rallied "the Army firmly behind the flag of constitutionalism."[11]

The murder of Chile's army commander also guaranteed Allende's election in the Congress on 26 October 1970, with Christian Democratic support, as a shaken country tried to reaffirm the democracy that it had taken for granted. Even the ruthless, if covert, exercise of power by the United States, in alliance with the Chilean Right, had failed to prevent Salvador Allende from becoming the first democratically elected, Marxist chief executive in the history of the hemisphere.

Inauguration Day was a study in contrasts, as well as a foretaste of things to come. Inside the ornate Senate chamber, a funereal Eduardo Frei, impeccably dressed in morning coat, placed the red, white, and blue presidential sash on his successor, whose election he had opposed. Allende, defying tradition in a business suit, was sober and dignified as he accepted the badge of office before the assembled members of the Congress and representatives of the Chilean armed forces and some sixty foreign governments, including the United States. Then Chile's first Marxist president, a Grand Master of the anticlerical Masons and a founder of the Socialist party, sat in a seat of honor in the musty eighteenth-century cathedral while Cardinal Raúl Silva Henriquez led a special ecumenical service that called for "justice for all brothers." From the cathedral, Allende made his way to the presidential palace through cheering crowds, many of whom had been waiting since dawn to get a glimpse of their new president. Then, from the balcony of La

Moneda, Allende declared: "The people have arrived with me to the presidential palace," and he proclaimed himself a *"Compañero Presidente."*[12]

The Chilean masses might rejoice that they had a *compañero"* for president, and socialists might celebrate a Marxist in La Moneda, but Allende's abilities as a traditional politician were likely to be equally important on the "long march through bourgeois institutions." Fortunately for the Left, such old-fashioned politicking was Allende's strength. Although the foreign press pictured Salvador Allende as a socialist revolutionary in a business suit, in many ways he was the Lyndon Johnson of Chilean politics. By the time he became president, Allende had done everything else in Chilean politics. He had been a deputy and senator, cabinet minister and party head, and had served as president of the Senate before becoming chief executive. After a political career that spanned five decades, he knew all the important political actors—their strengths, weaknesses, and peculiarities—and understood, too, how his country's social and political institutions operated. Like LBJ, Allende enjoyed a well-deserved reputation as a master political manipulator; even his opponents proclaimed him *"la mejor muñeca que hay"* ("the best wheeler-dealer there is").[13]

Salvador Allende would need all these old-fashioned political skills to lead his people to the New Chile. Although he inherited an executive office so powerful that it was referred to as "a six-year elective monarchy," as head of a heterogeneous multiparty coalition he was as weak as any Italian premier. The Popular Unity, moreover, lacked the congressional majority needed to legislate its program, and both the courts and the bureaucracy, drawn from the social elite and political opposition, could block governmental decrees and undermine policy initiatives. The press and mass media were mostly under the control of his opponents, and the loyalty of the armed forces was uncertain although the existence of conspirators was sure. From such a weak political position, it would be difficult to navigate a democratic road to socialism through "bourgeois institutions" designed to protect the existing system.

Allende's task was made more difficult by the economic constraints he had inherited. Chile's economy was dependent on exports, imports, and capital flows that were largely controlled by a hostile United States. Foreign corporations and Chile's own economic elite retained the capacity to sabotage the government's economic strategy, which envisioned a mixed economy and counted on the cooperation of Chile's capitalists to get a stagnant economy moving again.

Given a Popular Unity political strategy that counted heavily on economic success to build an electoral majority for socialism, these economic constraints were of central political importance. Moreover, Allende's economic team of inexperienced socialist theoreticians had little time to learn their new jobs and no room for failure. The nationwide municipal elections in April 1971, only five months after the inauguration, were seen by all concerned as a key test of the government's popularity and mandate for change.

As a consequence, although the Allende government's long-term goal might be to prepare the way for the democratic construction of socialism, its initial aims were both more modest and more urgent: economic revival, political consolidation, and social conciliation. Pedro Vuskovic, an independent socialist and United Nations economist, was named minister of economy and charged with the design of a strategy compatible with these political priorities and economic constraints. His initial task was clear: overcome the financial crisis and economic recession that the Allende government had inherited.

Salvador Allende understood the importance of a revived economy, but his initial preoccupation was to restore political stability to a nation shaken by the events that preceded his inauguration and to consolidate a government whose legitimacy had been challenged by opponents at home and abroad. During his first weeks in office, Allende crafted his conduct to reassure the uneasy and restore political normalcy. He played down socialism, projecting an image of moderation and stressing the need to proceed slowly and with restraint. During this initial period, his revolutionary acts were more symbolic than substantive, and his policies more populist than socialist. By Christmas, the specter of political instability had been banished.

It was not until the final days of 1970 that Allende turned to his agenda of structural change, moving with a swiftness and execution that took his opponents by surprise. On December 21, Allende proposed a constitutional amendment expropriating the multimillion dollar American investment in Chile's large copper mines. Then, on New Year's Eve, *el compañero presidente* promised the Chilean people a special year-end "bonus": the nationalization of the country's private banks, using the mechanism of the stock market to acquire their shares, as in any capitalist takeover. The next day, he flew to the southern coal mines of Lota-Coronel to announce to cheering miners that the government had just purchased a controlling share of their mines from their Chilean owners. Within a fortnight, the Allende government had bought out the private shareholders of Chile's only steel mill and made public plans to purchase the nation's second largest iron mine from Bethlehem Steel. In February, Allende had Agriculture Minister Jacques Chonchol move his headquarters to southern Cautín, the epicenter of spreading rural land seizures. There Chonchol told impatient peasants and Mapuche Indians that the government would speed up the expropriation of land but remain within the letter of the Frei agrarian reform law. By the end of March, Allende's commitment to carry out the Popular Unity's program of structural change was clear, as was his intention to do it legally.

By then, the Allende government had begun its promised "recuperation of Chile's basic riches" from mostly American hands, started to acquire private banks and foreign-owned industries, and accelerated the agrarian reform. Allende had selected for early action only those measures and targets most likely to attract the broadest popular support while provoking the least entrepreneurial resistance. It was a strategy calculated to project an image of a revolution without sacrifice, whose only victims would be the old oligarchs, the new monopolists, and the Yankee imperialists. On the eve of the April 4 elections it was clear that Allende had initiated a profound revolution from above, but it was equally evident that he was committed to a carefully controlled, phased, and legal process of structural change.

By April, Pedro Vuskovic's short-term economic policies also looked like a success. The economy was showing signs of revival, with production increasing and unemployment declining. Together with the Allende government's strict price controls on essential consumer goods, real wage and salary raises generated an increase in consumer purchasing power that fueled the economic upturn, dispelling the air of crisis and replacing it with a cautious optimism.

Allende's first five months as president seemed a signal success. His moderation, strict adherence to legality, and efforts to restrain his more militant followers had reassured and won approval among the middle classes. At the same time, his populist policies and style brought him increased support among workers, peasants, and *pobladores*, and his symbolic forays into outlying provinces scored points with the citizens of these previously neglected areas. Even his enemies gave him reluctant praise, and one old Communist called Allende's first five months in office "the most brilliantly played in Chilean history."[14]

With economic prosperity reviving, political stability restored, income redistribution underway, and structural changes begun, the Popular Unity was ready to face the electorate and seek a mandate for *la via chilena*. By then, even the Yarur mill seemed ready for the democratic road to socialism.

II

THE WORKERS
ORGANIZE

5

DON AMADOR AND
THE YOUNGSTERS

Amador Yarur was short and squat. To his face, the workers all addressed him deferentially as "Don Amador," but behind his back they called him *"el chico de plomo"* ("the little lead midget") "because he was little, wore lead blue suits, and was *so heavy*," one dyer explained.[1] Amador had learned the business at his father's side and tried to imitate Don Juan's style of labor relations but lacked his way with people. He was not unintelligent, but he had neither the vision nor the self-confidence to blaze a new trail. Considered a "weak and insecure person" by his top aides, he was "very impressionable" and "more influenced by Juan Yarur's ideas" than was his older brother, Jorge.[2]

Yet even Juan Yarur might have been hard put to make his paternalistic system work in the new era of the sixties, with its raised expectations and political effervescence, and Amador was merely a parody of his father. As his own personnel chief admitted: "He wanted to continue with the same system and to continue controlling the union with a vision of labor relations that was already anachronistic."[3] The 1962 strike had been a traumatic experience for Amador Yarur, shaking his self-image as the beloved *patrón*. His experience had taught Amador Yarur that although the old ways were best, a heightened vigilance and constant repression were required to maintain a paternalistic vision of social peace in a changing Chile. It might not be possible to seal the factory off from the leftist currents swirling around its walls, but systematic surveillance, exemplary punishments, and periodic purges might keep them under control.

Both *empleados* and *obreros* were well aware of what one top aide called Amador's "psychosis" of anticommunism.[4] Amador Yarur's obsession with worker disloyalty and Communist conspiracies was cultivated by "his cabal," which advised Amador Yarur to combine a highly repressive paternalism with a modern system of work.[5] For almost a decade this apparently contradictory combination seemed highly successful.

At the point of production, control of the blue-collar workers was ensured by the Taylor System, which not only regulated every motion they made, but also monitored every moment they spent on their shift. Extensions of the perpetual motion machines they tended, the workers had no time to talk on the job and no lunch break in which to socialize: "We had to go running to the aisle to get our little pitcher of tea when the cart passed by—a sandwich and a pitcher of tea—that was lunch," a veteran weaver recalled. "At each turn you took a little bite and a little gulp of tea, and so it went for eight hours without stopping . . . That was the System!"[6] As Yarur foremen now earned bonuses of their own if their section met its quota, they rode herd over their workers with what one finishing section worker called "a slave-driver" mentality. "If one lost time or went to the bathroom and were there three minutes, they called you out and warned you."[7] Between the demands of the Taylor System and the surveillance of their foremen, Yarur workers had no opportunity even to talk with each other during working hours, let alone conspire against their boss or organize a new insurgent movement.

The counterpoint to the rigors of the Taylor System was Amador Yarur's show of paternalism. In a frank imitation of his father, Amador Yarur made twice daily tours of the factory, distributed gifts on holidays, and granted the annual raise on Juan Yarur's saint's day.[8] He also built a new sports stadium and a modern company housing development. Social activities were sponsored for workers and their families, and both educational allowances and university scholarships were awarded by the company, which also opened a "satellite school," which trained children of Yarur workers for jobs at the mill. Many of these expenditures were required by law after 1964, but all were presented to the workers as "gifts of the *patrón*" and thus proofs of his benevolence, as were the advances against future wages and the ultimate favor at the Yarur mill—promotion to *empleado* status.[9]

Even in their own terms, these "gifts" were double-edged, instruments of social control as well as expressions of benevolence. Their intent was to bind workers to their boss by ties of gratitude, hopes of obtaining benefits, and fears of losing those already granted. More generally, they can be understood as part of Amador Yarur's effort to seal his workers off from the mainstream of working class culture, with its labor militancy and leftist politics. Workers who lived in company housing and played in the Juan Yarur Stadium were less likely to fraternize with workers from other enterprises. The apprentice school not only guaranteed jobs to workers' children, but also gave the Yarurs an opportunity to screen and socialize them before they entered the factory. These benefits, moreover, were granted in exchange for loyalty, as the workers themselves were well aware.

What made Amador Yarur's paternalism a particularly insidious system of social control was his definition of "loyalty": Loyal workers were those who were willing to inform on their co-workers. Amador Yarur's "addicts" competed for his favor by bringing him these tales: "There was always a long line of people outside his door waiting to pour poison into his ear," Julio Solar recalled, "telling him that this one is a Red, that this other is a Communist, things he liked to hear."[10]

The web of *soplones* (informers) began on the factory floor as one new recruit discovered when the machine operator to whom he was apprenticed told him in secretive tones: "Whatever little thing you hear—about political parties, about plots, about unions, about anything—tell me." What impressed Guillermo Jordan about this encounter was that "he wasn't my foreman, or my department head, or boss, or anything special, but just a simple person the same as me, who dedicated himself to take down all this type of information and bring it to 'El Hombre.' "[11] "The Man" was Amador Yarur, and it was on a base of such "simple workers" that his network of informers was constructed, supplemented by the reports of foremen and guards, supervisors and social workers. It was a network that penetrated every work section and reached beyond the factory gates into the company housing projects, athletic facilities, and social clubs, making workers afraid to talk to each other and distrustful even of seemingly close *compañeros*—and that was the most effective means of social control of all.

Amador Yarur had "an elephant's memory" and "he who fell into disgrace with him was finished," a former loyalist explained.[12] Workers suspected of "disloyalty"—a sin that encompassed everything from vague expressions of discontent to discussions of leftist politics or union organization—might be suspended without warning, docked a day's pay, or summarily dismissed; or else they might find themselves transferred to an inconvenient shift or to a less desirable work section. They might also be sent to a punishment section, such as "Siberia," an unheated and damp underground storeroom where they toted heavy cotton bales or salt sacks all day, or "the Pool," a utility section of reserve labor for miscellaneous tasks, which Amador Yarur transformed into a place where suspect workers cleaned latrines until they tired of the humiliation and quit. At bottom, these were exemplary punishments, warnings to other workers that this is where disloyalty led, with dismissal the direst threat of all. Although firing a worker was a last resort, made more difficult after 1964 by Christian Democratic labor legislation, a pretext could always be found—or invented—and a stream of workers exited from the Yarur mill during the years that followed.[13] Worker passivity was the goal, and it was ensured by demonstrating the costs of any other course.

Equally important was the careful recruitment and initiation of new workers. By 1968, Yarur was only hiring males under twenty-five years of age, who had at least six years of schooling and had never worked in a textile mill before. These criteria not only secured the mill educable young men with the physical strength and learning skills to meet the demands of the Taylor System, but it also made sure that Yarur was "the only source of their professional education."[14] As before, wherever possible, preference was given to relatives of Yarur workers or to rural migrants from the conservative south, both of whom were deemed likely to embrace Amador Yarur's paternalistic system.

Nothing, however, was left to chance. All new workers, irrespective of their manner of recruitment, underwent a three-month apprenticeship, which was part vocational training, part initiation, and part socialization. It was an experience that tested their politics as well as their vocational aptitude. Héctor Mora's initiation into the social politics of the Yarur mill in 1964 was typical. A few days after he entered the factory he was taken with one hundred other new recruits to a room in the administration building where Lucia Cabello, an old Yarur loyalist, told them "it was necessary that we understood some things about Yarur." Their orientation consisted in an explanation of "who were the Yellows and who were the Reds." "The Yellow," they were told, "was the responsible person, who worked hard and took care of the enterprise's property, a person who recognized that the *patrón* was giving them everything that they deserved. The Reds," on the other hand, were "the Communists. They were the guys who operate on the sly, even prepared to knife their boss in the back if necessary." The conclusion to be drawn was underscored: "The obligation of all of you is that if at any time you discover a Communist, you must denounce him immediately."[15] Armando Carrera was taken aside by his foreman; Jorge Lorca was taken to a dinner party where Amador Yarur himself spoke. The settings and words differed, but the message remained the same: "One had the obligation to inform on one's co-workers."[16]

It was an obligation that was tested during a new worker's trial period in the mill, as Heraldo Romo found out. "They sent people to make friends with you, who then began to talk about the boss to see if you would voice your opinions and reveal who you were," he recounted.[17] "So one day this guy comes up to me and begins to speak about the boss. He said: 'The bosses are exploiters, what they pay us is a disgrace, but here one has to suffer in silence. I disagree with that. How can they pay us such crap with all the work they give us? What do you think?' " Romo had been warned this might happen and so pleaded ignorance and refused to be provoked. But as he walked away, he thought to himself: "So one had to keep one's doubts to oneself here. That's all." It was a conclusion that led to passivity, the underlying aim of Amador Yarur's selective recruitment and *apatronado* initiation. Romo might walk away from the encounter proud of having "escaped the trap," but it had served Amador Yarur's purposes all the same.

A passive and isolated work force, carefully selected and socialized, purged of suspect elements, disciplined by the Taylor System, and represented by a moribund company union; a paternalistic *patrón* who dispensed favors and largesse at his pleasure in return for unconditional loyalty, but who punished disloyalty with righteous anger; a network of informers that covered both the work sections and the company housing; and a structure of scaled punishments for transgressions against the *patron* or his social politics that ranged from a verbal warning to summary dismissal and blacklisting— these were the central elements in Amador Yarur's system of social control.

To all appearances, "Don Amador's system" worked well, yielding a dividend that combined passivity with productivity. Other textile entrepreneurs imitated it, labor leaders feared it, and his workers obeyed it. In 1968, an American researcher cited it as "a fine example of how paternalistic social relations can be integrated with modern technology."[18] Three years later it was all in ruins. No one had reckoned on the Youngsters.

THE YOUNGSTERS

In 1960, some four thousand *obreros*, with an average age of forty, worked at the Yarur mill. By 1970, the number of blue-collar workers had dropped below two thousand; and their average age, below thirty.[19] Clearly, a dramatic demographic change had taken place during the intervening decade. Although there was still a substantial number of Old-timers at Yarur, Youngsters now comprised the majority of the labor force. The installation of the Taylor System, which required physically strong and self-directed workers, had compelled Amador Yarur to hire a new generation of *obreros*.

The new workers were not only younger than the Old-timers; they were also different. Few of them were women, a reflection of the Yarur response to the equalizing of pay rates between the sexes and the establishment of six-month maternity leaves. None of them was illiterate, and almost all had completed primary school; moreover many of them had some secondary education, and some were even taking courses at the State Technical University. Nor were these merely statistical differences. "The new people, which included the army of unemployed that came straight from high school, came to the factory with a different mentality from the Old-timers," explained Raúl Guerra, himself a perfect example of the new working class that he described.[20] It was not just that they were better educated and thus more self-confident, but also that their childhood and adolescence, upbringing and experience had been different, and as a consequence so were their world-view and politics.

Although Amador Yarur preferred to recruit the children of peasants who had recently migrated to Santiago from the paternalistic rural south, they were less likely to have the educational qualifications that the new system of work required. As a consequence, he had to hire workers who might be the children of migrants, but who had been brought up in cities or were themselves second-generation urban working class. They had grown to maturity in working-class communities, where the nature of neighboring and social interactions transmitted, reinforced and consolidated a strong sense of working-class identity and social solidarity. Socialized within a distinct subculture, they formed part of a new working class, which stood on the shoulders of the old and represented the culmination of its dreams, traditions, and life experience, but which took them for granted and wished to transcend them. Unlike their parents, they had grown up working class.

Some of them were from provincial cities and brought with them to Santiago the distinctive worldviews of the northern mining center of An-tofagasta, the southern industrial city of Concepción, or the central Chilean ports of Valparaiso or San Antonio, which had their own class cultures and "traditions of struggle."[21]

Many more had grown to maturity in Santiago's suburban "Red Belt," itself the product of rural migration and industrial growth. The overcrowding and high rents of the inner-city slums forced postwar migrants and impoverished workers to seek living space as squatters on vacant lots on the outskirts of the capital. By 1970, Santiago was ringed by such squatter settlements, many of which had evolved into permanent *poblaciones*, transforming areas such as San Miguel into vast working-class bedroom suburbs. [22]

Growing up in a working class *población* in San Miguel, the "Red County" close to the Yarur mill, as many of the Youngsters had, was a powerful formative experience. The language and politics of class were all around, as were the habit of solidarity and tradition of struggle. The influences of school and church were typically less important than those of family and friends, and even these experiences sometimes reinforced the prevailing sense of class community. Adult expectations and peer group interactions both encouraged a strong sense of class identity, and the child's experience of the world outside often corroborated the lesson that Chile was a class society.

For most, working-class consciousness began at home. It was relatives, friends, and neighbors who formed their initial images of Chilean society and their place within it. Froilán Garrido's father was a Socialist, and "at home there were conversations between father and child," he recalled. "We were always surrounded by these ideas."[23] Héctor Mora's mother was a Communist sympathizer who "made me see many things" and had two

Communist friends—a miner and a factory union leader—who "talked a lot to me" and "lent me books," he remembered.[24] Antonio Soto's family lived down the street from the Palestros, the Socialist leaders of San Miguel, and he was influenced by their words and example. Relatively few of the Yarur "Youngsters" were brought up in families of party activists, but most could at least look back to an important figure in their past who, like Jacobo Valenzuela's father, "never belonged to a political party," but whose "ideas were those of a man of the Left."[25] But even those who grew up in families without political loyalties often had relatives who taught them that Chile was divided into "the rich and the poor" and that they, as "poor people," should "side with the poor."[26] "One must be loyal to one's *compañeros*," was the way that Ricardo Berro's brother put it.[27] The words might differ, but the informing idea was the same. The jokes cracked, the curses uttered, the songs sung—all used the language of class and embodied a vision of a class society that shaped one's worldview.

By comparison, school and church were weak influences, whose conservative messages were often undermined by their bearers. In most working-class districts, schools were overcrowded, understaffed, and lacking in resources. Teaching techniques were antiquated, with rote learning the norm and patriotism the goal. Many school teachers, moreover, were leftists who tried to infuse an elitist and irrelevant curriculum with their own concerns and perspectives. The Catholic church, to which most Chileans nominally belonged, was particularly weak among working-class males, whose religious experience was often limited to the major rites of passage and annual holidays. Although many priests in working-class districts were staunch anti-Communists who preached the Christian Democratic gospel of social harmony and peaceful reform, others were leftists who shared with the Marxists their critical view of capitalist society, if not their "statist" prescription for the New Chile.[28]

Parents might be the shaping force of childhood, but for most of the urban Yarur Youngsters peers were the dominant influence of adolescence. Many spoke of the influence of friends with more developed ideas than their own, but it was the age group associations of adolescence that seemed the most powerful shaper of attitudes and opinions of all. The most widespread of these teenage institutions was the neighborhood sports club, where male working-class adolescents spent much of their leisure time. At once an athletic association and a social center, the club was an organization that could be mobilized for political purposes as well. The first political demonstration in which Juan Lazo marched was with his neighborhood athletics club.[29]

The sports club might be more common, but (after 1958) the Communist Youth was more strategic.[30] Combining teenage social life with cultural and political education, the *Jota* (after its abbreviation J.J.C.C.) was the Boy Scouts, church group and finishing school for many working-class children. A multifaceted answer to the needs of adolescence, it fused class consciousness and Marxist politics with generational solidarity and personal development to form a committed political cadre for the future. Few Yarur workers had been members of the Communist Youth, but several of those who had subsequently became leaders at the mill. Although he eventually quit its ranks, it was in the Communist Youth that Raúl Oliva developed the skills as an ideologue and organizer that he later employed with such success at Yarur.[31]

With its ideology of class struggle and theology of collective salvation, the Jota offered answers to the questions of adolescence that reinforced the messages of childhood and linked them to an adult world of political practice. Although the combined memberships of the Communist and Socialist Youth never exceeded 150,000,[32] they were seminal institutions whose impact extended well beyond their membership, coloring red the ground on which other adolescents worked, studied, and played. Every member had the obligation "to orient" a "mass front"—a student organization or sports club—making the Jota at once a training ground and a proving ground. It was a Communist Youth member who persuaded Juan Lazo's sports club to join "the march against inflation" in 1963, and it was an encounter with a Jota leader at a national student government meeting that introduced Jorge Lorca to the political cause that he would later espouse.[33]

Not all working-class children grew up to become Communists or Socialists, but most males who were raised in such class communities emerged into adulthood with a consciousness of class and a leftist politics. Their adult experiences as young workers and residents of a class community reinforced this consciousness. Working-class residential patterns, social institutions, and living patterns enclosed a worker's leisure hours within a context and language of class. The common problems of the Chilean working class household—inadequate nutrition, housing, transportation, and medical care—made concrete their shared sense of social solidarity and struggle. This pattern of daily life, moreover, was punctuated by periodic class rituals that ranged from solidarity campaigns that raised funds for striking workers to marches and demonstrations that linked their own struggles to those of other workers and other generations, underscoring as well the bond between their class and leftist politics.

During the decade of the sixties, Chile's urban culture became less insular and more cosmopolitan. On the one hand, this reflected a growing participation in the consumer culture promoted by foreign corporations and local elites. Their better education and greater exposure to international youth culture left this new working class with higher material aspirations than their parents although they often blamed their failure to possess the objects they coveted on the inequities of the capitalist system and the inequalities of Chilean society. Their materialism, however, was balanced by a romantic political idealism inspired by the Cuban Revolution and the heroic model of Che Guevara. More self-consciously ideological than their fathers and less patient with the slow gains of decades of struggle, this new working class was at once more revolutionary, yet closer to *embourgeoisement*.

Always a powerful influence on young workers, the communities in which they lived were particularly important as sources of class values and models when these were repressed at their workplace. Growing up working class and living in class communities would make all the difference to many Youngsters at the Yarur mill. This was even true for the children of Yarur workers, who were assumed to have absorbed an *apatronado* worldview at home. By 1970, however, this younger Yarur generation was more like their peers than their parents. In part, this was due to their own exposure to the class culture all around them, which even cloistered company housing could not prevent. But, in many cases, it was also because of their own experience of growing up in a Yarur household.

"The truth is I grew up with ill will toward the enterprise," Manuel Fernández, the son of a seeming Yarur loyalist, confessed. "From the time I was a child I listened to my father commenting on how things were here [at Yarur]." It was not a happy memory. "He was in a rage all the time because the supervisors treated him so badly and he couldn't defend himself because if he did he would be fired and a man of my father's age couldn't find another job . . . and so he arrived home each day telling us all this and that fed my feelings against the factory, against the boss."[34] The son became a weaver at the Yarur mill anyway because he married early and "needed a job," but he was not about to be taken in by Amador Yarur's show of paternalism. Other second-generation Yarur workers despised their parents for submitting to such humiliations or were embarrassed by a father's loyalty to his boss at the expense of his *compañeros*.

Still others were influenced by the strike of 1962, which they had witnessed as children, although the lessons they drew were often not those Amador Yarur intended. One young weaver viewed that bitter struggle as a heroic example to be emulated; another saw it as a noble failure to be transcended by his generation. Many Yarur workers' children had been traumatized by what they had observed, and Julio Menéndez refused to accept subsidized company housing "because in that time there were *compañeros* who had been fired and together with the job they took away their house, so that they were left in the street."[35] Although their memories and the lessons they drew from them differed, what these second generation Yarur workers had in common was an alienation from their work and a resentment of their boss. By 1970, coming from a Yarur family was no longer a guarantee of *apatronado* consciousness or worker loyalty.

Amador Yarur was equally mistaken about the mind-set of many of the young rural migrants who entered the mill after 1964. Like his father, Amador Yarur recruited recent migrants from the farms and towns of the south of Chile because he assumed that they would embrace at his mill the paternalism for which that region was known. But the rural south of 1968 was not the same as that of 1948, and neither were many of the young migrants that it sent to the Yarur mill.

The postwar decades had witnessed a far-reaching transformation of Chilean agriculture, with mechanization increasing the productivity and decreasing the size of the rural labor force, whose real wages declined by almost half between 1940 and 1960, deepening rural poverty. As at the Yarur mill, this rural modernization meant the expulsion of redundant laborers, the straining of patron-client ties, and the erosion of the paternalistic system of social relations that had dominated rural Chile for centuries. It also meant rural "overpopulation" and the mass migration of the landless and jobless to the cities of central Chile. These new rural migrants often carried with them a worldview that was different from the deferential mind-set of their predecessors, a consciousness shaped not only by the paternalistic assumptions of their childhood, but also by the new rural realities that had cost their parents jobs and homes.[36]

Jorge Lorca had been a rural schoolboy from a conservative home who "maintained an image of the worker and his *patrón*, in which the *patrón* was a humane person who looked at his workers as human beings like him, and there was such harmony between them that the burdens were light and there was nothing abnormal to complain about." But once he went to work as a rural laborer to support his widowed mother, Lorca's worldview changed. "I worked in vineyards, I worked in grain harvests," he recounted, "and it was there that I began to know real peasants, peasants who didn't know how to read or write . . . And it was there that I began to realize the social problems that we have, seeing this land of misery in which the rural worker was immersed and the land of abundance in which the capitalist or *patrón* lived and the differences between them." Lorca also became aware "with what disdain the [rural] capitalist treated his workers, as if they were merely things that were serving his interests, which had nothing of the human being in them, because they were totally dehumanized. They treated the rural worker like a beast; the more they could extract from them, the better."[37]

In the end, it was this critical vision of Chile's rural realities that Jorge Lorca would take with him when he moved to Santiago in search of educational opportunities, not the idealized image of the paternalistic *patrón* that he had been brought up with, and that Amador Yarur probably read in the broad face and placid eyes of the young farm boy from the south. To all appearances, Lorca seemed a perfect Yarur recruit: the educated son of a conservative father and apolitical mother, who had been a student government president and star soccer player in rural Curicó. But his mind-set was different from his father's, and a chance meeting with a young Communist at a national conference of vocational school student leaders had given new form to this divergent worldview, one at odds with the social system at the Yarur mill.[38]

Jorge Lorca may have been particularly articulate about his evolution, but he was not alone in bringing to the Yarur mill from his rural community ideas that differed from the deferential peasant ideal of Amador Yarur. In some cases, it was a leftist schoolteacher who was the source of these "new ideas," but more often it was a returning relative or friend who had gone to work in the city or the mines. By the mid-1960's, moreover, transistor radios, political parties, and peasant unions were penetrating the Chilean countryside, linking previously isolated rural communities to the radical currents sweeping the nation. Ibáñez's and Alessandri's electoral reforms transformed a captive peasant electorate into a constituency to be captured. Together with Frei's promise of agrarian reform and legalization of peasant organization, they set off a competition between Left and Center for the political allegiance of the rural laborer that was instrumental in the transformation of peasant mentalities.

Peasant unions multiplied, along with rural strikes and land seizures. The migrants who arrived in Santiago from this changing countryside were bearers not only of the old paternalistic values, but of a new rural populism as well, with its rough sense of social justice, its stress on the inequalities between rich and poor, and its nonideological focus on the concrete problems of daily life.

If the worldview that this new generation of rural migrants took with them from their country homes no longer fit the paternalistic mold, the ideas with which they arrived in Santiago often differed even more from Amador Yarur's ideal. Leaving a peasant community for the big city was an adventure most often taken by the young and impressionable, who frequently learned much from the people and experiences encountered along the way. For many, it was a two-stage journey whose first stop was the nearby provincial town. When Jorge Lorca left the fields of Curicó, he "began to work on a railway gang repairing the sleepers on the line." It was not just the work that was different from his past experience as a harvester, but his co-workers as well. "There I also encountered Communist *compañeros*. We used to talk after working hours, discussing and arguing, and they confronted me with the fact that I had been following the wrong road." As a consequence, he decided to go to Santiago, get a job, and finish his schooling, but now as a budding leftist, who no longer shared the paternalistic views of his father.[39]

Nor did this learning experience stop at the city limits. The search for housing, the first step for all new arrivals, was often a traumatic and radicalizing process, which involved banding together with other recent rural migrants and homeless urban poor to seize vacant suburban lands; erecting shacks in the face of police repression; and then pressing the government for sewers and schools, paved roads and public transportation, medical clinics and permanent dwellings. During the 1960s, a growing number of these *tomas* were organized by political movements, as were the *campamentos* that they produced. In the shantytowns of Santiago, moreover, the recent rural migrants mixed with earlier arrivals and second-generation urban workers, and they gradually absorbed the distinctive culture and politics of the Chilean working class.[40] By the time the job-seeking rural migrants arrived at the gates of the Yarur mill, their worldview was often very different from the paternalistic mind-set that Amador Yarur prized.

It was on this complex ground of raised expectations, implicit class consciousness, and explicitly radical politics that the Youngsters' lessons of working at the Yarur mill was inscribed. This was an experience of exhausting labor and iron discipline on the factory floor and rigid social control elsewhere, one that confirmed the messages of their upbringing about exploitation and class without offering them legitimate channels to express their discontent and defend their interests.

Unlike the Old-timers, the Youngsters were sufficiently strong and well educated to handle the rigors and self-direction of the Taylor System. Those who survived the initial shaking-out process soon adjusted to its harsh self-discipline, internalized its work norms, and grew accustomed to earning the 20 percent bonuses paid for meeting their work quotas. Yet the very intensity of the Taylor System and the exhaustion that it produced were sources of alienation. The Youngsters might be better able than the Old-timers to bear the physical and psychic burdens of the Taylor System, but they still regarded it as exploitative—"too much work for too little pay."[41] They were also less accepting than the Old-timers of the great gap between their bosses' wealth and their own poverty and were less inclined to regard this unequal division of the fruits of their labor as either just or immutable. On the contrary, because their material aspirations were greater than those of the Old-timers, they were less satisfied with the "few pesos of the incentive [bonus],"[42] and because they were more Marxist in their worldview, they were more likely to see the Yarurs' luxurious life-style as the cause of their own modest living standards.

The alienation that many Youngsters felt at having to "work like slaves"[43] so that Amador Yarur could become "even more a millionaire" and "live like a king,"[44] was compounded by the rigid social control on the factory floor. If the inhuman regulation of the Taylor System was hard to bear, the inhumane enforcement of it was intolerable. "What bothered us most were the foremen," Raúl Guerra affirmed.[45] The better-educated Youngsters looked down on many of them as unqualified Yarur "addicts" who "rose to their posts by informing on other *compañeros*."[46] They bristled at being ordered around, resented being monitored every minute, and were infuriated at being forced to submit to the often arbitrary will of the foreman, their immediate "exploiter," who drove the workers harder so that he could earn a larger bonus.[47] Even Jorge Lorca, who maintained that "physically the work wasn't hard," was humiliated and enraged by Amador Yarur's system of social control.[48] "The problem was moral, mental . . . the problem lay in what they did to denigrate you"—techniques that ranged from harassment to punishment. To many Youngsters, "the whole factory was like a prison," with the foremen as the guards and the informers the trustees of the warden, Amador Yarur.[49]

But where the Old-timers had learned to suffer these humiliations in silence, there came a moment when many of the Youngsters refused to put up with it. In part, it was because they were younger and thus more willing to take risks than the Old-timers, who were serving time until their retirement; in part, it was because they were more confident of finding another job. But it was also because they had never experienced a traumatic defeat at the hands of the Yarurs. "When I entered the factory, it was at the time that everyone was scared because of the strike of '62," and no one had the will to say anything, let alone organize anything," one young mechanic recalled. Initially he, too, had accepted this state of affairs. "But with time . . . more Youngsters began to arrive at the mill, new people with another mentality, without that fear that the Old-timers had already made part of themselves."[50]

It was from this new generation of workers—more educated and confident, class-conscious and politically aware—that an insurgent movement would emerge to challenge Amador Yarur and his repressive paternalism. Significantly, like the earlier workers' movements at the mill, the new one, too, would focus on "rescuing the union."[51] As one young activist put it: "If the union is a company union, who will defend the worker? *No* one!" was his rhetorical reply.[52] In 1969, the Youngsters set out to change that once and for all.

6

THE YOUNGSTERS
START A MOVEMENT

In the wake of the 1962 strike, Amador Yarur had tried to restore the company union as a major pillar of his system of social control. The mutual was abolished, and its welfare functions were transferred to the union, which also became a channel for a widening range of fringe benefits and a vehicle for a growing number of social activities. There was even a show of collective bargaining, with all the legal formalities observed, as they were in the annual elections. But the occasional airing of grievances and promotion of a seemingly populist leader such as Hector Duarte—a 1962 strike activist who had switched sides and been trained by the "American Institute"[1]—could not obscure the fact that the contract "negotiations" were managed, the elections manipulated, and the gripe sessions choreographed. Worker interest in the union declined, and as Amador Yarur's sense of vulnerability diminished, so did the company's. By 1968 the company union was so unimportant that Personnel Chief Eugenio Stark did not even mention it to a foreign researcher, and by 1970 it was virtually moribund, with less than 10 percent of the members attending its meetings.[2]

There had been few challenges to Amador Yarur's control of "his" union since the defeat of the 1962 movement. The Communist organization at the mill was virtually wiped out by the repression that followed. Still, shortly thereafter a small group of Socialists entered the Conos section and "ran candidates for union office almost every year because we knew the workers wanted to change this situation," recalled Emilio Hernández, who had become a Socialist in 1962 in his hometown in northern Chile, "where the entire workers' movement is unionized."[3] Some of these insurgent candidates had even been elected, with the aid of anonymous leaflet campaigns, "but then Yarur went and bought them afterward."[4] "To one he gave an auto,

92

to another a house . . . valuable things to a blue-collar worker," another Socialist activist explained.[5]

The most recent—and, for Hernández, the most painful—of those experiences had taken place in 1967, when "we nominated a *compadre* of mine, Juan Quilodrán." With the help of an informal network of "honest *compañeros*" in other sections, Quilodrán was elected union director, but, to Hernandez's dismay, "he sold out . . . and very cheaply . . . after two months without being received by Amador Yarur and . . . because he saw that all the other directors were already bought by the boss." It was an experience that persuaded Hernández and his friends that sporadic campaigns for isolated "independent" candidates were both futile and demoralizing. Only a new workers' movement with the strength and will "to recover the blue-collar union" and confront Amador Yarur could make a difference.[6]

It was Raúl Oliva "who began the battle here," affirmed Héctor Mora, one of his first recruits. Only when Oliva took charge in 1969 did the Youngsters begin to organize a movement with the explicit aim of regaining control of the company union. Raúl Oliva was the perfect person for the job. Raised in the southern city of Concepción, a leftist stronghold that boasted the most radical student movement in Chile, Oliva had joined the Communist Youth as a teenager, but left it in angry disillusionment over the Moscow-line Chilean party's denunciation of Che Guevara as a "CIA agent." In 1968 he transferred his loyalties to the Socialist party, where the "revolutionary" left wing had gained control, and "they gave young people a chance."[7] Oliva soon emerged as one of their most promising worker cadres, with party connections and access to student circles that were unusual for a blue-collar worker.[8]

Oliva had known the Yarur workers and their struggles even before he moved to Santiago to study electrical engineering at the State Technical University and took a job at the mill. In 1962 he had been part of a committee that brought food and other solidarity donations from Concepción to the Yarur strikers. In the wake of the strike, he had been hired at Yarur as an assistant supervisor, but he was demoted to electrician for protesting his *Jefe*'s abuse of workers "because I always had this rebel streak."[9] Such unheard of acts quickly won Oliva a reputation as a "gutsy guy" with his co-workers and as "a troublemaker" with his bosses.[10] Only the new Christian Democratic job security legislation and a Socialist labor inspector kept him from being fired on one occasion, and Oliva's whispered threat to his *Jefe* that he would "get him outside" and "put him away" protected Oliva from further persecution.[11]

Tall and powerfully built, articulate and forceful, Oliva was a natural leader, with the political sophistication and organizational experience to lead an insurgent movement at the Yarur mill. He was also well educated, ideologically aware, and highly intelligent, a "worker intellectual."[12] A risk taker by temperament, Oliva was further emboldened by his upwardly mobile self-image, the result of an education and marriage that strengthened his conviction that he "was not going to spend the rest of his life in this factory."[13] His outspoken courage within his section had won him the respect of his co-workers, and his job as an electrician specializing in the factory's ventilating system gave him the opportunity to range through the mill—and make contact with workers in all sections—denied the machine operators. By 1969, when the Popular Unity was deciding on its program and presidential candidate, Raúl Oliva was ready to begin organizing a clandestine movement at the Yarur mill, proceeding with an uncharacteristic caution that bore witness to a system of social control so effective that "no one dared say anything at all to anybody."[14]

This was even true of close friends. But gradually Oliva began to transform friends into comrades. One was Héctor Mora, who both worked with Oliva on the night shift and studied in the same program at the State Technical University (U.T.E.). He had been raised in a town near Santiago by a widowed mother with leftist sympathies and Communist friends, but had learned "to keep [his] ideas to [him]self' at the Yarur mill. "Raúl and I used to go out together, and we were very friendly, but we never touched political themes . . . what with the fear and distrust here," Mora recalled. "But once, when I went to his house to study, I saw some things that struck me . . . for example, many political books, and at times he played music, but purely revolutionary music. So from then on I began to scrutinize him, but without saying anything to him." At times Mora was tempted to risk it, but then he thought: "It could be a trap. Who can assure me that the *compañero* isn't one of those many informers who is getting me to reveal myself so that he can denounce me and cost me my job." It took Oliva a long time to overcome this Yarur paranoia, "but in the end he convinced me that he had ideas that were at bottom the same as mine," Mora recounted. "But neither he nor I talked about them except for those very important details of books and records," silent symbols of political beliefs. "I even became very nosy and looked through some of his notebooks—he draws well—and there were some drawings of Che Guevara . . . until one day he confronted me and there it was."[15]

Oliva and Mora began to build their movement slowly, taking advantage of chance encounters. "Once on a bus far from the factory, I overheard a *compañero* raving against the system here inside the mill . . . ranting against Yarur and all that," Oliva recounted. "Well, he sees me and the guy just falls apart completely. He turns to his buddy and says: 'I just lost my job.' " Oliva acted instinctively. "When he got off the bus, I got down too . . . and although he denied knowing me, I said to him: '*Compañero*, I see from your face that you fear that I may . . . inform on you. I tell you *compañero* . . . we should extract some useful advantage from your imprudence. I am also in the same spot—both here and there [in the mill]—why don't we get together tomorrow where we can talk?' 'O.K.,' he said. 'In the house of my sister in the Población San Joaquín at such a time.' We got together there, we conversed, and it was done." Raúl Oliva had another recruit for his fledgling movement.[16]

"In this way we were able to detect some *compañeros* in whom we felt confidence, with whom we joined forces," Oliva explained. Some of these workers were from other sections "and in that way we continued to organize." Once a worker was recruited into the clandestine movement, his task was to identify and recruit others in his work section. "In which *compañero* in your section do you have confidence?" Oliva would ask. "Well, I trust this one and this one." "Good. Then observe them, *compañero*. See if they are trustworthy and in the bathroom or someplace like that throw them some things and then speak to them," he would instruct his new recruits. "You must push forward. You don't gain anything letting off steam in a bus."[17]

By the end of 1969, "we were some ten people—that's all," Oliva recalled. "We had people in Conos, in Dyeing, in the Maintenance Shop, and in the Electric Shop, and that was it." Although they had diverse personalities and politics, they all came from working-class homes and leftist backgrounds. All of them were younger and better educated than the average Yarur *obrero*, and several of them were students at the State Technical University (U.T.E.). "We only had a small group of people here, but they were all young people, all fighters," Oliva stressed.[18] It was ten against Yarur.

As Allende was beginning his underdog national campaign, Raúl Oliva was starting his own at the Yarur mill. Its goal was "to liberate the union here. We didn't look beyond that—'Liberación Sindical' [Union Liberation]—that's what we called our group." He pointed it toward the union elections to be held in December 1970, developing a strategy based on the presence of the Youngsters at the Yarur mill. His reasoning was clear. "The Old-timer, who had lived through '62, was a frightened man." For that reason, Oliva's movement would be composed entirely of "young people, all people new to the mill, who had not suffered themselves the repression of 1962, which had inflicted such deep wounds."[19] "*Compañeros*, they have already thrown out or retired most of the *compañeros* of '62," Oliva remembered telling a meeting of his group, but "there are many young people, new people, people just like us, who will struggle. So now we are going to go once more into the breach, *compañeros* . . . and the next union election we will . . . do it." "In other words, we risked ourselves," Oliva explained.[20]

The risk was all too clear to the members of his small band. "Our task was to identify gradually all the *compañeros* who had similar ideas and to speak to them and convince them to join our struggle. That is to risk all for all," Mora stressed, "to risk your job because if you made a mistake with even one person, you would be cut the next day." Within their own sections, they had a good sense of which workers were likely recruits. "We all spoke with some others, and we made no mistakes," Mora recalled.[21]

The difficulty was far greater in so controlled a factory as Yarur when they tried to identify likely workers in other sections. "We had to be extra careful here" because "we were on unknown ground." Oliva's solution was to become an amateur detective. "We used to hold brief meetings among ourselves and when we had someone in mind . . . Raúl secured their address and went to Barrio X, where the guy lived, and talked with his neighbors and got precise information about him." Some of these investigations convinced them not to approach the worker in question, but "many times we found to our surprise that the guys were old members of leftist parties," Mora recounted. In that case, there was no longer any doubt, and we confronted the *compañero* at once and told him about us, and of course he joined us at once. In this way, our little group grew over time."[22]

By the final weeks of the presidential campaign, more than 120 workers had joined the "Union Liberation" movement, which had extended its activities from organization to disseminating information, electoral campaigning and raising rank-and-file consciousness.[23] Although they tried to reach out to other shifts, the base of the movement remained the night shift, "which has always been at the top of the barricades here."[24] As in previous clandestine worker movements at the mill, the 1970 movement used the anonymous pamphlet to reach their co-workers without revealing their own identities. "We worked together, writing it in our meetings," Oliva recalled. "Then we sent the leaflets to be printed at the municipal offices of San Miguel," whose Socialist mayor, Tito Palestro, had long backed the Yarur workers' struggles against their boss.[25]

But the hardest part was not writing and printing *La Firme*, as their broadsheet was called, but getting it to the workers. They "divided the papers" among themselves "so many for this one, so many for that one," smuggled them into the factory, and left them in the bathrooms and other places where they would reach a wide audience—although "many *compañeros* didn't even dare to throw them into the bathrooms because when they left, the next person in might inform on them."[26] This led Raúl Oliva to invent an ingenious solution to the problem of distributing "the papers." "As I worked here in things to do with ventilators, and it was common practice to cut the electricity for an entire section turning off the ventilators, I used to cut the electricity and put the leaflets inside those giant ventilators and then turn the current back on." A rain of papers followed, with *La Firme* leaflets showering down on the production floor as far as half a block away.[27]

This eruption of clandestine leftist activity in a factory where such politics were banned and from which they had long been banished worried Amador Yarur. Every time *La Firme* appeared, a group of workers was fired, but it was always people who were innocent of involvement in the movement, victims of their curiosity in reading the pamphlet or of the vindictiveness of some informer. When it became too dangerous to distribute *La Firme* within the factory, Oliva arranged for it to be handed out in the surrounding streets by San Miguel Socialists. The factory's security apparatus was mobilized to identify the culprits, the Yarur strong-arm squad of boxers and other athletic loyalists was revived to combat it, but without visible success in stemming the spread of the "red virus" or in discovering its bearers. "We kept on and little by little got our message across," Mora recounted.[28]

It was a message that increasingly joined their campaign for an independent union to Allende's campaign for the presidency. Issues of *La Firme* linked the onerous working conditions and repressive atmosphere in the factory to Alessandri, "the bosses' candidate," who had broken the 1962 strike during his first presidency, while identifying Tomic with the failed economic policies and unfulfilled reform promises of Eduardo Frei. Allende, *La Firme* insisted, was "the workers' candidate," reminding them that he had supported their strike in 1962 and spoken out against the repression in the plant that followed. Other leaflets talked about the Popular Unity program—inexpensive housing and free medical care, increased wages and controlled prices, free milk and educational opportunities for their children, and for themselves the paid vacations and retirement annuity that the Yarurs had long refused to grant. Still other issues spoke of socialism as a solution to the problems of both the Yarur workers and their country and promised a "people's government" that would bring an independent union to the factory and the Yarurs' reign of terror and exploitation to an end.[29]

It was within this atmosphere of heightened expectation that Salvador Allende paid an unprecedented campaign visit to the Yarur mill in August 1970. Traditionally, the Yarur ban on political activity within the factory was broken only by the ritual campaign speech of the rightist and centrist candidates favored by the Yarurs, whose presence and introduction of the candidate amounted to a tacit endorsement in the eyes of the workers. It was one of the few times that the production lines were shut down at the mill. Alessandri and Frei had both been welcomed by the Yarurs in this way, as had a host of lesser figures of the Right and Center, all of whom had also benefited from generous Yarur campaign contributions calculated to ensure Yarur access to power. Leftist candidates did not receive such Yarur support and usually had to make do with a speech in the public square beyond the factory gate under the watchful eye of the enterprise's security guards. But 1970 was different. Worried about the possibility of an Allende victory, Amador Yarur decided to hedge his bets and make a small contribution to the latter's campaign in the belief that this would protect his factory from socialization if the Left won. For the same reason, he allowed Allende to speak at the mill.[30]

The visits of Alessandri and Tomic were decorous rituals, which persuaded the workers that the aging ex-president was Don Amador's favorite. Allende's appearance was different in form and more dramatic in content. "When Alessandri came, they stopped the factory and brought all of us to listen to him. When Tomic came, they did the same," recounted Armando Carrera. But when Allende came, of course not: All of the factory remained working. Only those who were not working that shift could attend"—if they dared. "The people were afraid to go there" because "in order to enter [the hall] you had to pass through a little corridor" where the members of the strong-arm squad were lined up. "They just stood there, without saying anything, but they inhibited the people." These silent sentinels, moreover, were not posted there purely for effect. "In the end, on whatever excuse, they approached people and asked for their identification. Many people left. Who is going to go in there when those guys are noting down the names of those who do?"[31] They might want to hear "Chicho" Allende, but with "Chico" Yarur, discretion was the better part of valor.

If one of Amador Yarur's purposes was making sure that "Allende didn't get so large a number of people,"[32] another was identifying the leaders of the clandestine movement. For them, Allende's visit posed a difficult dilemma. If they did not attend his speech and did not urge others to do so, the small turnout might demoralize the committed and discourage the undecided. But if they revealed their identities, they risked losing their jobs and decapitating their movement prematurely. Some of the movement leaders favored discretion, arguing that "we are not here so that Allende will win, but rather we are here because there has to be a new internal movement at Yarur." "Whether or not Allende was elected, we were going to go on strike here," Raúl Oliva insisted.[33] But most of them "were convinced that if Allende didn't win, there was no possibility of a strike and that a large number of us were going to get booted out of here. It was all or nothing," Mora argued. They decided to attend and urged the others to do likewise. After passing through the gauntlet of Yarur loyalists outside the hall, "all of us very nervous," they found to their surprise that "the Training Hall was filled, and it must hold about five hundred people."[34] More than one-quarter of the Yarur *obreros* was willing to risk their jobs in order to hear Salvador Allende. They would remember his words.

Amador Yarur was surprisingly gracious to Allende in his introduction, telling the workers that he had known "Salvador" since his youth and addressing the Socialist standard-bearer in the intimate *tu* form reserved only for family and close friends. But Allende was too shrewd and experienced a politician to be trapped by this show of intimacy. He began by returning the pleasantries, bantering with Amador Yarur in a friendly and familiar fashion. "But if I am elected, Amador," he said, darkening his tone, "although we may be very good friends, I will take this industry away from you. It will belong to the workers and to the people of Chile."[35] There was more—about the increase in social security benefits, the nationalization of banks and mines, about medical care and housing—but what the workers remembered was "that if he won the government, he was going to take the factory away from them, that he was going to pay them a good price, but he was going to requisition the industry. So the *patrón* knew it and we knew it," one Old-timer recalled.[36] Stunned silence had greeted his announcement. "We felt joy, but Don Amador was there, so we couldn't applaud," she explained.

Only four workers out of five hundred dared to applaud Allende's speech. but it was clear to all that it had been "a great triumph, both for Allende and for the movement." Right in front of his workers, right there in his own factory, "Allende had told 'El Chico' that he was going to take the industry away from him."[37] The word soon spread through the mill to workers who had been afraid or unable to attend, shattering Amador Yarur's image of omnipotence and triggering worker dreams.

Allende's visit was the turning point for the Union Liberation movement. "After that our work was easier, even though we were marked by the boss," Héctor Mora recalled.[38] "We campaigned more openly and with increasing success." In its aftermath, moreover, *La Firme* was joined by a partner in clandestine labor journalism, *El Despertar Obrero* (The Workers Awakening), put out by a group of independent leftists whose politics were close to that of the Guevarist MIR (Movement of the Revolutionary Left).[39] Its sudden appearance took the *La Firme* group by surprise. "From one day to the next a pamphlet appeared here called *El Despertar Obrero*," Mora recalled. "It shared the same political orientation as we were giving and was a more or less similar piece of work . . . All of which made us think that there must be another group of workers working underground just like us." They located them in the weaving and spinning sections, "and we all got together and held meetings together and our numbers grew."[40] Moreover, as the *Despertar Obrero* group was strongest in the work sections where the *La Firme* group was weakest—weaving and spinning—the two movements were complementary and greatly strengthened by their merger.

It was a union that not only swelled their ranks, but also buoyed their spirits and emboldened their actions. "It was then that we said: 'OK, let us lift up our heads. If they cut us they will have to fire 120 workers' . . . and so we declared war."[41] The Allende campaign had brought the Yarur workers' movement up from underground, but the benefits were mutual, and the relationship was symbiotic. Chile's workers might have been responsible for Allende's nomination and surging campaign, but he could claim credit, in turn, for enlarging and accelerating the workers' movement at the Yarur mill. The workers were convinced that their chances of "liberating the union" were bound up with Allende's electoral fortunes, but the Popular Unity's last-minute surge was dependent upon worker support.[42]

As September drew near, even the optimists in the movement, such as Héctor Mora, began to worry. "I personally was losing my sense of certainty that he was going to win," Mora confessed.[43] "Because as the election approached, the campaign of terror against him—based more than anything on anticommunism—grew, and it was so well orchestrated . . . and seeing that the great majority of workers had so little political clarity . . . and I said to myself: 'We had always let ourselves be fooled, and most likely one more time the bourgeoisie was going to fool the working class.'" But, instead of being paralyzed or demoralized by these fears, Mora and his *compañeros* redoubled their efforts. "I said: 'Bueno, if Allende loses, we are all going to lose,' because we had already revealed ourselves . . . and as they had fired more than a thousand [after the 1962 strike], why wouldn't they cut 150 or 200 now?" There was no turning back. Instead, "as it was already approaching the presidential election, we pulled out all the stops and risked everything."[44] It was the kind of intense, grass-roots campaigning that was responsible for Allende's narrow election victory on September 4, 1970.

The liberating effect of Allende's "Popular Triumph" was clear even in so tightly controlled a factory as Yarur. As soon as "Compañero Allende was elected, everything changed all at once," Oliva admitted. "The guys now came out in the open . . . they identified with *allendismo* at once."[45] This shift to the Left found its local expression in a broadened support for the insurgent movement at the Yarur mill. "Immediately, there was a flood here in the factory," Oliva recalled. "We discovered those who had supported Allende at once, and on finding us these people switched to our side." Armando Carrera agreed: "The impact of Allende's victory was to open up the possibilities of a struggle, to persuade people to support us openly," he explained.[46]

Allende's election freed many Yarur workers from the fears that a lifetime at the Yarur mill had inscribed on their consciousness. Even Old-timers now came out of their populist political closets, "because we saw that Compañero Allende was going to help us."[47] Alicia Navarrete had hidden her leftist sympathies for decades, but now she believed a Communist friend who told her: "Now you have to have confidence because a *compañero* has won election who is going to be with us." "So then and there I lost my fear. We all did," she affirmed.[48] Like the past insurgent movements at the Yarur mill, the

1970 movement took off with the election of a Chilean president perceived by the workers as "someone who would protect us," balancing the power of the Yarurs with the strength of the state.

The prospect of an Allende presidency had an equally profound, but opposite, effect on Yarur loyalists, especially on the Yellow leaders of the company union. "As our spirits rose, the morale of these guys fell," Oliva recalled. "They got scared when Allende won and the situation changed radically; the balance began to tilt the other way."[49] This double shift in the factory's political balance impelled the leaders of the insurgent movement into a more open opposition and accelerated their organization of a campaign directed at attaining within the Yarur union what had been won in the nation—the election of a leftist leadership.

Although the underground "Union Liberation" movement led the way, for many it was a spontaneous process that generated new activists who felt that it was up to the workers themselves to seize the time. One of those was Emilio Hernández, who had become a Socialist in his northern adolescence and led a small group in Conos, but who was not a member of the broader movement before Allende's election and had hidden his politics until then. "Right after Comrade Allende won, we began with the union question," Hernández recounted. "At the next union meeting four people attacked the company union officers, without having had any contact between them—Jorge Lorca of Weaving, Enrique Granados of Maestranza (Maintenance Shop), Armando Carrera, and I (from Conos). We were the ones who spoke out . . . just because we felt deeply about it and at that moment of Popular Triumph had more guts to throw it up to them."[50] When a veteran Yellow leader, María Noriega, accused Hernández, a personal favorite, of ingratitude, he retorted angrily that "this thing had to come to an end." Carrera backed him up, and Lorca and Granados joined in. Carrera, like Hernández, a wiry young Socialist from the mining zone, and Granados, another urban-born leftist, were part of the *Firme* group whereas Lorca, a popular, stockily built soccer star from rural Curicó, was one of the *Despertar Obrero* leaders. But none of them had ever made their views public, and all realized that after speaking out at the union meeting there was no turning back. They had to recapture the union, or else they would lose their jobs.[51]

After the meeting, Hernández analyzed the situation over beers with three friends, all of them Socialist sympathizers from Conos. They agreed that it was time to unite all the activists in one big movement, but that they were too inexperienced to know how. "Why don't we go to the [working-]class institutions that might be able to help us, like the CUT or the party?" Hernández had suggested. They decided to go to the CUT, but they were aware that the CUT leadership included Christian Democrats and "in order not to fall into their hands we spoke with Manuel Dinamarca of the

Socialist Party." To their surprise, the Socialist labor leader told them that he was already in contact with two Socialist militants from Yarur with a similar mission. Dinamarca agreed with their decision "to get organized" and asked them to bring "a group of eight *compañeros* whom we trusted" to a meeting that he would arrange with the other activists. The social control at Yarur was so great that Hernández and his friends could not come up with four more names "in whom they had confidence," so they decided "to bring in the people who had spoken up in the meeting."[52]

Lorca didn't tell Hernández of his *El Despertar Obrero* ties, nor did Carrera and Granados explain their *La Firme* links, but that was not the only surprise in store for Hernández and his friends. "When we arrived at the meeting, there was Raúl Oliva," with whom the Socialist party was already working through Victor Zerega, its labor committee head, and Marisol Bravo, Socialist Youth leader from the Economics Institute of the University of Chile. After this meeting, the various Yarur groups decided to merge their efforts. Their expanded and consolidated movement became bolder in its actions and more deliberate in its organization.[53]

Gradually, they extended their network, incorporating workers who expressed themselves in support of Allende or in opposition to the Yarurs. "Each time we had a meeting, we each brought one more person," Hernández recounted.[54] Meeting in safe places, such as the Socialist Party headquarters or borrowed union halls, the group of activists gradually grew in size and scope. During the two months between Allende's election and inauguration, the clandestine movement at Yarur spread to every section of the factory, binding them to the movement with personal ties.

This expanding web of personal relationships was the way the movement's underground organization was enlarged, but it was not the chief means by which its ideas were spread. This honor was reserved for the new enlarged *La Firme*, rebaptised *La Firme de Yarur*. No longer a simple flyer, but now a folded, four-page underground newspaper, *La Firme* began to appear more regularly and to assume a more constant format. It was polemical investigative journalism at its most basic, featuring exposés of the Yellow union leaders, overbearing supervisors, strong-arm squad members, and the company police.[55] "We distributed about fifteen issues, where we ran down half the world," Hernández recalled.[56] "*La Firme* was good because it was entertaining"—and it was effective because it eroded respect for the agents of the Old Regime while puncturing their image of omnipotence and offering an example of rebellion.[57]

As the movement spread, so did *La Firme's* coverage, with the workers themselves playing the role of investigative journalists. Reading and reporting for *La Firme* came to be a sign of support for Allende nationally and for the movement in the factory, as well as a concrete way of contributing to both causes. The fulcrum of this "new politics" at Yarur was the young leaders who had emerged from the rank and file, like Emilio Hernández, whom one *apatronada* leader likened to "a hen with its chicks," because he was always surrounded by "kids coming up to me to pass me scraps of paper with information." Hernández and his *compañeros* also "took up collections inside [the mill] in order to finance *La Firme* because it cost us a lot to send it to be done up outside."[58] The days of running it off on a mimeograph machine were over as the movement itself entered a new phase.

This open collection of funds and information inside the hitherto sacrosanct Yarur mill was a sign of the emergence of the Union Liberation movement from underground in the wake of Allende's victory. Initially, *La Firme* was distributed outside the factory by Socialist students. Now Yarur workers replaced them, and as the movement grew in size and scope, its members began to distribute the newspaper inside the mill as well. It was not just "the guys" who "came out in the open . . . when Allende was elected." "In the end, we did too," Oliva explained.[59] "We went public because we were distributing *La Firme* . . . and after they knew who the people were who were distributing it, why should we hide?" Before Allende's election, their fear of being fired had led the movement activists to maintain a low profile, but afterward they grew in boldness as they became confident that "now the Turk won't fire us just like that."[60]

Their intuitions were correct, but in many ways that was the most remarkable change of all at the Yarur mill. In the past, Amador Yarur would have immediately fired any worker even suspected of taking part in an insurgent movement, let alone an *obrero* with the temerity to challenge his system of social control openly within the factory walls. But now, uncertain of the future, Yarur hesitated to take reprisals against the known leaders of the movement although he continued to try and intimidate the rank and file into passivity.[61]

Amador Yarur's unaccustomed restraint confirmed the daring of the workers' movement, giving its leaders the confidence to orient their struggle toward their ultimate objective: recapturing the blue-collar union from company control. As befitted a movement conceived within Allende's *via chilena*, they planned to accomplish this transfer of power legally and democratically, using existing institutions. The annual union elections were scheduled for mid-December, a few weeks after Allende's inauguration. They began to plan their election campaign.

But Amador Yarur was biding his time, waiting to see what would happen. In the interim, he was marshaling his forces, intimidating rank-and-file workers and trying to isolate the movement leaders. The message behind his method was clear to the movement activists: "If Chicho [Allende] didn't become president, we were all dead ducks."[62]

For the Yarur workers' movement, therefore, the weeks between September 3 and November 4 were filled with mixed emotions—euphoria with tension, optimism with fear. Acutely aware of the links between national politics and their own local prospects, they sought guidance ɑnd help from political parties and the national trade union leadership. For the same reason, they embarked on a campaign to raise the political consciousness of the Yarur workers, getting them to see their own situation as part of a broader national picture. In October, *La Firme* began to expand its coverage: "One page was dedicated to the internal situation [in the factory]; the other, to support of the [Allende] government and the Popular Unity program, to explaining the benefits that it would bring us," Armando Carrera explained. "We had to combine the two and not just look at the internal situation, but rather to view it together with national realities. If, at that moment, the Left was playing that card, we had to play it too—every way we could."[63]

In response to a CUT appeal and under the guidance of their Socialist advisers, the movement also began to transform its organizations in each work section into informal "Watchdog Committees," whose task was to guard against industrial sabotage and to gather information about production irregularities that might be contributing to the growing economic crisis, which the Left saw as politically motivated and calculated to create conditions for a coup. During these weeks of plots and rumors, the leaders of the Yarur workers' movement waited and watched, ready to respond to the call for action, yet aware that the fate of their movement might well be decided outside the factory gates. When Allende's election was confirmed by the Chilean Congress, they celebrated his triumph as their own.

7

"*¡GANAMOS!*"— "WE WON!"

On November 4, the leaders of the Yarur movement who worked the night shift joined the joyous crowds that lined the streets of downtown Santiago for a glimpse of their *compañero presidente*. The assassination of General Schneider only a few days before made them realize that it had been a close call, so mixed in with their celebration was a collective sigh of relief.

They had come a long way in less than a year. During that time, the handful of clandestine conspirators had become a strong and growing movement that spanned the industry's three shifts and many work sections. In the process, a group of dedicated activists had been organized, leaders had emerged, and the rank and file had begun to be educated for the new era. They had founded an underground newspaper, linked up with national labor and political organizations, and survived the efforts of Amador Yarur to repress their movement and suppress its message. By Allende's inauguration, moreover, the blue-collar workers' movement had emerged from underground to challenge openly Amador Yarur's system of social control and to prepare for their next objective—"to rescue the union, which was still *apatronado.*"[1]

Allende might be president of Chile, but inside the Yarur mill the old regime still ruled. Raúl Guerra spoke for most of the Yarur activists when he affirmed: "The only thing that we wanted was to liberate ourselves somehow."[2] A few of the most radical leaders talked of "seizing the factory," but most agreed with Héctor Mora that "the most important task was to win back the union because what do we gain by seizing the industry when the immense majority of workers and the union itself were controlled by the boss? So it was better to begin from above, through the union," he reasoned.[3] It was a task that they began as soon as a *compañero presidente* was installed in La Moneda. "For us, the inauguration of Allende was a signal to push ahead with our plans to reclaim the company union," explained Emilio Hernández. "If 'Chicho' could win the presidency, I said to myself, then we could win the union—above all now that we had a *compañero presidente* to help us."[4]

What made Allende's inauguration and the impetus it imparted to the Yarur workers' movement particularly timely was that it coincided with both the union election and the negotiation of a new contract. The insurgents decided to take advantage of the latter to increase the visibility, credibility, and popularity of their candidates for union office while testing their strength among the rank and file. The negotiation of the new contract would keep the committee members in the public eye and give them both campaign issues and platforms, making them logical choices as candidates for union office. At the same time, the movement could take advantage of Chilean labor law to protect its candidates, for no workers could be fired after the formal presentation of contract demands.[5]

Although it was usually the union officers who negotiated the annual contract, a little-used clause in the labor code allowed the union assembly "to elect other members to the negotiating committee."[6] The five insurgent candidates took the lead in denouncing the existing contract and proposing a set of bolder demands calculated "to offer something for everyone," completely upstaging the Yellow union officers. When it came time to choose the negotiating committee, the "Popular Unity Five" were elected by acclamation.[7]

Although the overwhelming victory of their candidates "was very auspicious" and convinced several movement leaders that their rank-and-file support was far greater than expected, they still feared that "the political maturity of the *compañeros* was insufficient to elect five Popular Unity candidates."[8] They decided to be cautious. "Clearly, Amador Yarur had already chosen his coterie to be elected," they reasoned. "So we decided that we should run only three candidates to be sure of winning control of the union."[9] It was a shrewd strategy, which the Yarurs themselves had used in the past. Choosing the three candidates, however, proved a more difficult task. Initially a balanced slate representing the three main production divisions — Lorca (Weaving), Peña (Spinning) and Mora (Finishing)—all three leftist independents—was selected. But "on the eve of the nominations the Communist party, which played no part before . . . suddenly insisted on presenting a candidate," Emilio Hernández recounted. "The sectarian criterion prevailed," he lamented, "so we had to remove Peña and put in Lorenzo Calderón who had done very little until then and besides was from the same work section as Mora."[10]

Surprisingly, the *apatronados*, who were divided by personal rivalries, nominated six candidates, a tactical error, as the 1962 workers' movement had learned to its cost. "If they really had been well organized," explained one movement leader, "the Yarur loyalists would have run no more than five or even only three to win a majority, but they left six names in and that diminished greatly the votes for each of them."[11] In the end, however, the electoral outcome hung on organization, not tactics, and revolved around issues as well as personalities.

Only a month separated the nominating assembly from the union elections, little enough time for the insurgents to transform a clandestine movement of uneven strength into a public campaign organization that could match the scope and penetration of Amador Yarur's experienced network of loyalists and supervisors. The only way for the insurgents to do it was from below, hazarding their jobs on a victory at the polls. As election day neared, the web of underground activists surfaced in a "section-by-section campaign," which spanned the factory.[12]

By then they had transcended sectarian politics, personal rivalries, and sectional provinciality to perfect an organization whose efficiency and solidarity they were justifiably proud of. Nobody missed meetings; nobody "went around boasting or telling what they were doing."[13] "In the end, we were about eighty, all committed activists," Emilio Hernández recalled. "But most of us were Youngsters. So we had a problem: how to reach the Old-timers."[14]

There might be more Youngsters than Old-timers at the Yarur mill, but the Old-timer had more votes. A clause inserted into the company union statutes to guard against such an insurgent movement gave workers with more than five years at the mill ten votes to allocate among the candidates for the five positions on the union board of directors—twice as many as each Youngster had. "It was for that reason that all of us Youngsters fought to win over the Old-timers . . . that was our great struggle . . . and as all the Old-timers were terrified, we were afraid that we would lose." The Youngsters' fears were intensified by their awareness that "we were all on the list of eighty to be thrown out of the factory" and that those fired in 1962 had been blacklisted and "were still without a job" in 1970, forced "to earn a living going around selling fruit or vegetables," Armando Carrera underscored. "To lose the election was to lose everything—and it all depended on the votes of the Old-timers."[15]

The Old-timers of 1970 were all survivors—of the Taylor System, of Yarur's repressive paternalism, of the purges that had followed the failure of previous workers' movements. The election of Salvador Allende had led some Old-timers to think that this time it would be different, but most had learned from bitter experience not to challenge the Yarurs, and many had convinced themselves over the years that loyalty, not militancy, was the best way to advance their own individual interests. It would be hard to persuade them differently, but that was what the Youngsters had to do if their campaign were to succeed. The atmosphere of mistrust and repression made it difficult for the Youngsters to talk with the Old-timers directly. They had to rely on *La Firme*.

"The role of *La Firme*," explained Jorge Lorca, "was to clarify the picture for the *compañeros*, to demonstrate that they were exploited, to demonstrate to them how the company union officers took advantage of them and of their posts in order to play Amador Yarur's game, to demonstrate to them how important it would be to have someone who would really represent them, to demonstrate to them also the importance of reclaiming the union from the Yellows."[16] The Youngsters proceeded on the assumption that "the Compañero Old-timer was only terrorized on the surface . . . So we were really frank in the pamphlets . . . we tried to interpret the class interests, and we put it in the simplest way possible . . . by means of this consciousness-raising, we gradually convinced people."[17]

To be sure that *La Firme* reached all of the workers in the factory, the Youngsters devised a more elaborate distribution system, in which some activists were in charge of bringing the leaflet into the mill, and others were responsible for distributing it from there.[18] Still, recalled Emilio Hernández, "one thing was missing: that the *compañeros* pick up the flyers and take them home to read." The problem was to get the Old-timers to overcome their ingrained fear of the Yarur system of social control. "So . . . we decided that we had to read it publicly, right here in the factory, so as to demonstrate that we had lost all fear of the boss." The Bienestar [Welfare] office outside the work sections was traditionally the headquarters for the Yarur chief of social control and thus the most risky place to attempt such a show. "So one day we all sat down in Bienestar and began to read *La Firme* . . . and sat there laughing at all the digs and everything." This show of Youngster macho had the desired effect: "After that everyone read it, even the supervisors read it," Hernández recalled with a laugh.[19]

As the election date approached, *La Firme* moved from a general attack on the Yarur system to the specifics of the campaign. "Every day pamphlets appeared telling the story of our candidates and debunking the others. We put the names of the management's candidates with lines through them crossing them out and said: 'For These No!' And we put the names of our candidates in large letters: 'For These Yes!' And by means of a war of pamphlets we convinced many [Old-timers]."[20] Convincing the Old-timers of the justice of their cause was one thing, persuading them to vote for the insurgent slate was something else again, as the Youngsters became aware. "The *compañeros* who were Old-timers had experienced in the flesh all the exploitation and repression that was Yarur, so we didn't have any problem to convince them that things *ought* to change." The problem was to convince them that things *could* change—and without risk for them," explained Emilio Hernández.[21]

The Youngsters' problems were exacerbated by Amador Yarur's counteroffensive, a propaganda campaign calculated to play on the very fears that years at the Yarur mill had ingrained into the consciousness of the Old-timers. "They began to circulate rumors that Don Amador was waiting for our election because he was going to fire a mob of people and that he had already bought us and that all this was just an act that we were doing as opposition candidates . . . and many believed these rumors."[22] It was Jorge Lorca, in many ways the most attractive of the insurgent candidates—young, handsome, educated, and athletic—who aroused the most suspicions in Old-timer eyes, suspicions that were the mirror image of his qualities. "There were rumors that Lorca had completed secondary school and that therefore he was going to come to an arrangement with the bosses, sell out to the *patron*, and leave the factory. Because, with a high school education, why would he remain here?" reasoned the Old-timers.[23]

Nor were these just rumors. Amador Yarur was doing everything possible to transform his propaganda into prophecy. It was Jorge Lorca whom he approached first. "Some days before the elections, a messenger from Yarur, someone I knew, arrived at my room in the Población Yarur. But I was out at a meeting with the *compañeros*, and when I returned, he had gone, promising to return in about an hour and asking me to be sure to be there." Lorca suspected "that Yarur has sent him to do something," so he hopped in a taxi to borrow a friend's tape recorder, which he "hid and left running, so when this messenger came back I recorded the entire conversation." It "was very clear and not at all subtle," Lorca recalled. "He said to me: 'El Chico sends me to tell you that he is ready to pay you fifty million pesos [$5000 U.S.] in cash, plus a house, but only if you will switch sides. And that is only the beginning. Later, there will be other things coming.'" Lorca tried to keep him talking, to get both more information and more incriminating evidence. "So I told him that it was very little, that I needed a bit more," and the messenger promised to "transmit to El Chico what I had said." It was the last that Jorge Lorca ever heard about his pieces of silver. Amador Yarur "was no fool, so he must have realized what was going on," the insurgent candidate concluded.[24]

For those who remembered how Amador Yarur broke the 1962 workers' movement, his strategy was clear. Running only three candidates for five positions might win the insurgents a majority on the union board of directors, but it would be a bare majority, vulnerable to any one of the movement candidates selling out. Having failed to achieve his objective with Lorca, Yarur turned his attentions to Héctor Mora, this time utilizing a more subtle approach and prominent messenger. "Mario Leníz, the Welfare head [and former company union president], came to the laboratory where I worked and told me: 'Look, Don Amador wants to talk with you . . . At such and such an hour he will wait for you at Las Vertinientes,' a restaurant outside Santiago, with a pool and a casino, a nice place in the hills," Mora recounted. A car would call for him at his house and take him back, all paid for by Amador Yarur "so there would be no problem." After talking with Raúl Oliva, Mora told Leníz that he "couldn't go that day, but that maybe it could be another day. 'Of course,' Leníz replied. 'No problem.'"[25]

All the problems were in Mora's head—and in the social history of the Yarur mill. It might have been pure paranoia, but despite the restaurant's fine reputation, Mora's fantasies of his trip were all nightmares—of thugs or photographers: "What if he takes out a roll of bills, and even though I don't accept them, he has a photographer there who takes a picture of him and me with the money," Mora worried. So he kept putting Leníz off "until finally they realized that I was only talking, that I didn't have the slightest desire to go."[26] Amador Yarur had finally met a group of worker leaders whom he could not buy. El Chico would have to try another tack.

Amador Yarur knew that if he could not buy Lorca or Mora, a longtime Communist like Lorenzo Calderón was unlikely to succumb to his blandishments. But the insurgents had only nominated three candidates, and if he could not bribe one of them, he could accomplish his objective equally well by frightening one of them out of the race. His target was the small, thin Calderón. It was all done "Chicago style, like a gangster movie," was the way Lorca put it.[27] "A few days before the election, four men got out of a car where Calderón's wife was shopping and seized her right there and told her that if her husband didn't retire from the thing, it was going to cost her dear."[28]

"So the woman arrives at our meeting in a state," Mora recalled, but the Communist candidate was determined "not to give in to the boss." So "we went with Calderón's wife to the newspapers and the radio to denounce the deed," making political capital out of this capitalist crime. Unfortunately for Mora: "Just at that moment my wife turned on the radio . . . so when I returned home, I had a drama on my hands! Afterward she didn't want to go out, not even to go shopping. And I began to worry, too, that what had happened to Calderón's wife might happen to my wife. It began to be a psychosis, and unfortunately my wife has a nervous ailment, including a weak heart, so I began to be worried, even worried that something might happen in my house . . . I have three little girls, you see. So I had a double problem: in the factory and in my house." Yarur's gangland tactics might have failed with Calderón, but they came close to driving Mora out of his mind—and the race. "Every day she told me to withdraw," he recalled. But with "the support of the *compañeros*," he persevered, and his fears never materialized.[29]

A more visible threat was "the strong-arm squad," composed of specially recruited boxers and other brawny Yarur loyalists, which Amador Yarur had revived during the presidential campaign "to calm the spirits of the guys," as one Yarur loyalist put it.[30] When the union election campaign began, the strong-arm squad increased in numbers, weapons, and visibility. It had been revived, the insurgents believed, "with the intention of entering into action as in the strike of 1962," when pitched battles were fought between partisans on either side of the picket lines.[31] Certainly, the Yarur strong-arm squad seemed menacing to the insurgent leaders. "They threatened us and thought to liquidate us just like that," Lorca recalled. "They got together and waited for us at the corners . . . in each corner four or five of them, but they never dared to do anything. They showed us that they were going around with revolvers in their belts, but they didn't go any further than that . . . we never let them provoke us into a confrontation—as happened in 1962. Things just remained tense."[32]

The Yarurs had rarely been reticent in the past about using the stick when the carrot failed them, which made their comparative restraint in 1970 all the more striking. The explanation for the lack of violence, Lorca insisted, lay in the changed political context: "Because of the change of government . . . the police didn't give any great help to Amador Yarur. It wasn't like '62, when the whole police force was in the palm of his hand . . . Owing to this, the strong-arm squad didn't act, because if they had acted, they were going to go straight to jail because conditions were very different from '62."[33] The inauguration of a Popular Government placed the power of the state for once squarely on the side of the workers, altering the balance of power between capital and labor at the Yarur mill.

As a consequence, neither Yarur's bribes nor his threats deterred the workers' movement. On the contrary, the Left was able to turn these Yarur tactics to its own advantage, both in the factory election campaign and in the nation at large. The threat to Calderón's wife by Yarur thugs may have frightened Mora's spouse, but their denunciation on national radio was powerful proof of the Popular Unity's charge that Chilean capitalists were criminals who should be expropriated. The same was true of Amador Yarur's tape-recorded attempts to bribe Jorge Lorca, who "took the tape recording to the CUT," which broadcast it on the radio and "squeezed it for all it was worth at the national level—how the capitalist works, how he bribes."[34] Within the mill, moreover, the fact that Amador Yarur had tried to buy Jorge Lorca and failed went a long way to reassuring Old-timers who had resisted voting for him; moreover, the resolution of both attempts punctured Amador Yarur's image of omnipotence and strengthened worker convictions that under *el compañero presidente* the power of the state was on their side.

But there were several strings still remaining to Don Amador's bow. The rumors of mass firings reminded the Old-timers that what had happened in 1962 could happen again. The revival of the strong-arm squad might not frighten the insurgents, but it might well intimidate the Old-timers. In combination with Don Amador's system of surveillance and informing, these tactics could limit Old-timer interactions with the insurgent candidates and activists.   The candidates themselves, moreover, were to be isolated, as Jorge Lorca found out. "In my section the foremen prohibited the rest of the *compañeros* from conversing with me. No one could talk with me during the eight hours of work, and the one *compañero* who did was sent to the office . . . and told that if he did it again, he would be removed from the section." Then, "two days later," Lorca recounted, "they sent me to the Pool . . . there they tried to undermine me morally. They sent me to clean different work sections, to wash windows outside with the rain and the frost. They sent me to clean lavatories, things like that. The idea was to denigrate me, to demoralize me."[35]

If the idea behind sending Lorca to the Pool was to isolate him politically, it backfired. Sent out to clean different work sections, he used it as an opportunity to campaign. "I talked with the *compañeros*. At times I didn't even do the job; the *compañeros* did it for me," he related. Making a virtue of necessity, Lorca transformed his punishment into a living lesson of why the Yarur workers needed an independent union to defend them. "In the end," he laughed, "it seems the bosses realized that it was better if I were in my own section because . . . in the Pool I could move through the other sections . . . and talk with the other *compañeros* . . . a possibility that I did not have in my own section . . . So they had me there [in the Pool] for a week, and then they returned me to Weaving until the election."[36]

As election day approached, despite the atmosphere of fear and mistrust that enveloped the factory, the movement leaders were confident that they were making progress. Increasingly they found Old-timers saying: "If in the end we lose, we aren't going to lose anything and if the Youngsters sell out, well, things will continue the same as before, that's all."[37] This was even true of "the women, who appeared to be Yellows, but only out of fear," Carrera stressed. "Many times we found that the *compañeras* would say to us: 'We will give you our vote, but don't tell anyone.' 'Agreed, that's the way it will be,'" the Youngsters replied.[38] But would it? The Yarur loyalists were predicting a landslide victory, and it was impossible for the insurgents to know how many of those promised votes would actually be cast for their candidates—and whether they had persuaded enough of the Old-timers to win the election.

December 17 was election day, and the presence of the national press underscored that its significance transcended the factory walls. The balloting was held at the Pizarreño Union Hall, a shift of locale away from the traditional factory site which was itself a sign that the times had changed —and a harbinger of an honest vote. "The place was completely filled, and with twelve Labor Inspectors inside and the place loaded with Carabineros outside . . . it seemed like a national election . . . something really important," Héctor Mora recalled.[39]

It was clearly important enough for both sides to pull out all the stops, rules or no rules. The labor inspectors attested that there was no undue pressure to vote, but there was certainly a lot of electioneering going on around the voting booths. "We were making propaganda everywhere," Emilio Hernández recalled. "We were distributing *La Firme* in the polling place itself."[40] But then that was where "the Yellows went around buying votes, saying to people that they shouldn't vote for the Communists—and Allende was already president!" recalled Carrera indignantly.[41] Meanwhile, within the factory itself "that day . . . the Yellows took people out of work to make propaganda for them during working hours, and, besides, they brought sick people on stretchers to the polling place to vote; they carried them there! Luckily they didn't bring the dead!"[42]

The tabulating of the ballots was more orderly, but had a drama all its own. It "was really something," remembered Carrera, "what with the tension here when the count began and when we saw that they began to count pure Yellow votes—a thousand Yellow votes, five hundred Yellow votes and nothing of ours appeared."[43] It was nine o'clock at night, and it had been a long day. The tension told on the candidates, and "Lorca had an attack of nerves and began to cry . . . and with the place packed. I have never seen anything like it," Hernández affirmed.[44] "But at last, when it was ten o'clock at night already, all of our votes began to appear." First "pure bullet votes for Calderón,"* which made the other activists think "the worst of the Communist Party . . . but finally the votes for Lorca and Mora began to appear—a pile of our votes!"[45]

In the end, it was the electoral landslide that the Yarur loyalists had predicted, but they were the ones buried by it. "We captured more than 80 percent of the people," Hernández recounted. "Our three candidates each got more than three thousand votes and the two Yellow candidates who

---

*Workers could either "bullet" all their five or ten votes for one candidate or divide them among several candidates.

headed their list didn't even get three thousand votes between them. So it was really a beating," a victory that not only exceeded leftist expectations, but even outdistanced their wildest dreams.[46] After all his fears, Lorca received the most votes and was elected president of the newly "liberated" union, with Mora as secretary and Calderón as treasurer. The insurgent movement had reclaimed the Yarur blue-collar union from company control.

As the dimensions of their triumph became clear, the tensions that had dominated the day gave way to euphoria. "Afterwards . . . we left the polling place marching," Hernández remembered. "We marched from there to the factory and then marched around the factory shouting slogans against the exploiters and against the Yellows."[47] It was these sounds of defiant celebration that brought the night shift their first news of the electoral outcome. "The night shift was working, but they hadn't been able to work tranquilly, all of them awaiting the election results . . . and here the night shift . . . has been the stronghold of the honest *compañeros* . . . so all of them worried."[48] Amador Yarur had "reinforced the guards at the gates . . . and some *compañeros* in the heat of victory came by with the desire to break in with the news," Mora recalled.[49] It was a scenario for confrontation that was averted by the new union officers in their first act as elected leaders. "'No,' we told them. 'Let us talk with the porters and supervisors.' So we said to them: 'Look, we have just been elected officers, and we want to enter to put up notices on the bulletin board, just the official results, nothing more. Not to commit any act. No reason for you to worry.' So they gave in and we entered." It was a scene that they long remembered. "We all sang the national anthem, and I put on the bulletin board: ¡*Ganamos*! [We Won!]," Hernández recounted.[50] For those who had lived the labor history of the Yarur mill, it was a historic occasion.

It was only the beginning of their celebration. "The whole night shift stopped work and filled Bienestar, and then they all went outside" into the balmy summer night. "Some of them cried. It was very moving . . . and there we greeted the dawn celebrating the victory."[51] For Mora, who had nearly dropped out of the race because of his wife's anxiety, the triumph was particularly satisfying: "I arrived home at about six in the morning, and my wife hadn't slept at all. The first thing she asked me was how it had turned out. So I said to her: 'We won going away, and now you have to believe me!' She jumped for joy—even more than I."[52]

If the running of only three candidates had been a test of worker consciousness, "to see how we did,"[53] the insurgents' landslide victory was a clear reply. "Evidently, we committed the error of not having enough confidence in the *compañeros*," Mora later confessed. "But now it was only a problem of the two . . . of those whom Yarur had put in before, only Osvaldo Troncoso and José Muñoz were reelected as directors."[54] After so decisive a

show of popular support, the new leftist leadership of the union was unwilling
to tolerate "even one Yellow as [union] director."[55] At first, it seemed as if
the two might resign in the face of popular pressure, but Amador Yarur
would not hear of it. Rather than accept the electoral verdict and come to
terms with the new leadership, he ordered Troncoso and Muñoz to fight a
rearguard action. "Even if only one of my leaders is left, he has to remain
in my union," Yarur reportedly instructed his supporters.[56] They were to
remain on the union board at all costs and by whatever means. It was an
invitation for further confrontation—one that the newly confident leftist
leadership was only too willing to accept. No sooner had they assumed their
new posts than they began to look for issues on which the two remaining
Yellow leaders could be censured, the only way that they could be removed
from office.

Ovaldo Troncoso, the former company union president, immediately
provided the Left with the pretext it was looking for. Two days after the
election, recounted the union minutes,[57] "as a result of rumors that a group
of *compañeros* headed by the new leadership was going to seize the factory,
there were serious incidents in the Welfare office, including an attempted fist-
fight between directors." Troncoso, in a rage that was at once personal and
political, accused Calderón and Lorca of trying "to bring the personnel out on
strike and to leave them without money for the holidays" and tried to provoke
them into a fight. This was bad enough, but it was Troncoso's final flourish
that did him in. At the union meeting the next day, Ramón Vidal testified
that Troncoso had "told him that he was going to look for his revolver and
that he would shoot the first one who tried to seize the industry." The brief
meeting then voted "unanimously to ask for the resignation of the *compañeros*
union directors: José Muñoz and Osvaldo Troncoso."

Amador Yarur still refused to give up the foothold he had on "his" union
leadership, which, as in 1962, might later be used to reverse the tables on
the Left. Hoping to trade a favorable contract for two seats on the union
board, he "petitioned" the new union leaders "not to demand the resignation
of Compañero Osvaldo Troncoso."[58] But when Troncoso took the floor in his
own defense and pleaded that "he had always been honest and always defended
the interests of the workers," Jorge Lorca called him a liar and with a fine
sense of drama pulled out the tape of Yarur's attempt to bribe him, on which
Yarur's messenger had named Troncoso and Muñoz as "his" candidates.[59]
The tactic persuaded the workers that "Troncoso and the other Yellow were
guilty of trying to bribe *compañeros*."[60] Once again, the union assembly asked
the Yellow leaders to resign, and once again they appeared to accede, but
the letter never came. Finally, they were censured and ousted at a January
meeting by a vote of 1300 to 300—the latter the reduced number of blue-
collar loyalists left to Amador Yarur.[61]

When it became clear that honey wouldn't work on the new union leaders, Amador Yarur turned sour. He was still afraid to confront them on an issue that could detonate a strike or a factory seizure, "but he refused to give in on the smaller demands that had to do with everyday problems," related Lorca.[62] Inside the factory, supervisors were instructed to give "the fewest solutions possible to the problems that 'these gentlemen' (as they called us) present," and being "good *apatronados*, they fulfilled Yarur's orders to the centimeter." At the same time, "if an ex-company union leader approached him with a worker request, Don Amador granted it." He had returned to his father's strategy of dealing with an insurgent movement that had won union office over Yarur opposition. "Clearly, what he wanted was that we should appear as inefficient and inefficacious to the masses and that it should seem as if they hadn't gained anything from the change that had taken place; that it was better to have the old Yellow leaders who at least had the right connections and could secure all they wanted."[63]

Amador Yarur also did his best to block the new leadership's efforts to unify the blue-collar workers behind them. "We always called on our *compañeros* not to go around being provocative, not to go around offending the *compañeros* whom we knew were on the boss's side, but rather to converse with them, to let them understand that they should stop fighting for interests that weren't theirs, that were the capitalist's and not the worker's, and that they should take up their rightful place at the side of their *compañeros*," Lorca related.[64] But such efforts to transform the consciousness of the *apatronados* ran aground on the rocks of Amador Yarur's rigid determination to keep the workers divided and a possible reversal of the election results alive. It had happened to every other insurgent movement in the mill's history, and no one could be sure it would not happen again. During the weeks that followed their decisive union defeat, Amador Yarur pumped up his "Unconditionals" with memories of the past and promises that they would soon "make mincemeat of the Reds."[65]

What made these boasts particularly portentous was the new paramilitary appearance of the strong-arm squad and the renewal of threats against the union leaders and their families. Suddenly, members of the strong-arm squad were disappearing from the factory in the afternoons and some for days at a time. They returned with new arms and military bearing, and the leftist leaders received reports that they were being trained by instructors "brought in from Panama" and even sent to Bolivia for special instruction by that country's American-trained Rangers. "Just imagine—*military* training!—about forty guys!" a shocked Raúl Oliva recalled.[66] This transformation of the Yarur strong-arm squad into a virtual paramilitary force may have been done with the goal of guarding against a factory seizure, but the union leaders took personally the heightened threat of physical violence that it represented.[67]

"The same thing happened to four or five of us," Lorca recounted.[68] "A letter was thrown by hand into your mailbox. To me, they sent the threat that they were going to liquidate me . . . just like that, because we were shameless Communists . . . that they would send us to where we belonged. They even sent 'regards' to our mamas." This time, moreover, Yarur loyalists went beyond the threat of violence to the attempt to consummate it, beginning with Lorenzo Calderón's wife. "She realized that she was being followed by an automobile when she went shopping, and they stopped her and told her that if her husband didn't lay off, she was going to 'pay for it'. Then they tried to run her down with the car going very fast, but the *compañera* escaped . . . things like that happened."[69] The same sinister automobile and occupants reportedly also tried to arrange Lorca's murder: "To a lady whom they knew had contact with us and came often to the union, they offered a trip to the United States and a sum of money and a pistol with which to shoot me," the union president charged.[70]

If Amador Yarur's aim was to intimidate the union leaders into submission, he was doomed to disappointment. "None of this worked," affirmed Lorca proudly.[71] If anything, these tactics were counterproductive. To Lorca, "these threats were like a shot in the arm . . . to give a little more passion to my efforts, in order to accelerate things."[72] Even Mora's nervous wife "took courage" and was "much calmer" in the face of these new threats,[73] which also made the union leaders appear heroic in the eyes of the rank and file, who rallied around them in indignation. Moreover, these threats underscored the need for worker unity in the face of Amador Yarur's ruthless attempts to reverse their electoral verdict.

With unity the priority, five of the seven candidates nominated to succeed the censured Yellows resigned in favor of two popular movement leaders—Raúl Oliva and Pablo Rosas—who were elected overwhelmingly on March 5, 1971. "And so just Reds remained," concluded a satisfied movement activist.[74] With Oliva's election, the movement that he had begun little over one year before had lived up to its name: "Union Liberation."

By then its young leaders had transformed the old company union. "After the great victory over the *apatronados* came the struggle to organize the union in order to convert it into a truly representative organ of the working class and in order to give it power as well," its new president, Jorge Lorca, recalled. In the past, the union had been run by "a small group of Yarur's Unconditionals," with minimal rank-and-file participation. Now the new leftist leaders initiated a series of internal reforms calculated to promote popular participation and ensure union democracy. The union statutes were amended to make the censure and recall of officers easier. Union delegates were now elected from each section of each shift in order to give the rank and file a regular channel of communication to their leaders and "so that we should be aware of all the problems that were occurring at the factory floor level," Lorca explained. A full committee structure was also created, and fines were levied for nonattendance at union meetings. Together these measures sought to increase the responsiveness of the union to its members— and the responsibility of the rank and file for their union. "It wasn't difficult," Lorca stressed, "because all the *compañeros* were united and enthusiastic."[75]

Other initiatives swept away the remaining vestiges of the company union era. In order to underscore and consolidate the union's independence from company control, the new leaders decided to acquire their own union hall with the money from the sale of the cemetery mausoleum in which the company leaders had invested their members' dues —a symbolic shift of union concern from the dead to the living. The overpaid union accountant, a friend of the Yarurs, was fired; and Miguel Oyaneder, who had served conscientiously in that capacity during 1962 and 1963, was restored to the post he had held during the previous era of independent unionism at the Yarur mill. For the first time since that unsuccessful movement, moreover, the Yarur union integrated itself into the national labor movement —the CUT and the National Textile Federation (FENATEX)—a linkage forbidden under the old regime. Under their new leftist leaders, the Yarur *obreros* rapidly recast their union in the image of the mainstream of the Chilean labor movement.[76]

Although these measures to ensure union democracy and independence were important steps in the consolidation of the union and its new leftist leadership, in the eyes of many Yarur *obreros* they were less significant than the leaders' successful negotiation of a new contract. If their first effort at collective bargaining was a test of both their leadership capacity and the benefits of an independent union, the new officers passed with flying colors. Within a fortnight of their election, they were able to announce the negotiation of the best contract in Yarur history. Its 45 percent wage raise meant a sizable increase in real incomes, for the previous year's inflation rate had been 36 percent.[77]

The new contract also included concessions that the Yarur *obreros* had long sought: a paid half-hour lunch break and a retirement annuity of seventeen days' pay for each year of service, where no retirement benefits existed before.[78] In addition, the new leaders proudly declared that they had won "permanent permission for the union directors to devote their working hours to their union tasks with full salaries paid for by the enterprise, a pickup truck for the union to be used for the welfare of all its members and for union work," and even "a loan . . . for the purchase of a union hall" outside the mill.[79]

The significance of the contract transcended its provisions. Not only was it the first time that the Yarurs had felt constrained to negotiate in good faith with an insurgent union leadership, but Amador Yarur had also been forced to grant worker demands for which the *obreros* had struggled in vain for decades. No comparable across-the-board increase in real wages had been won before by the Yarur workers, and the paid half-hour lunch was a demand that dated from the introduction of the straight shift in 1966 and was of particular importance to older workers. It was by securing the retirement annuity, however, that the Youngster leaders best repaid the Old-timers for their electoral support. The Yarurs' refusal to grant any retirement benefits had led the Old-timers to strike in 1962, and now that many were approaching retirement age, the issue was urgent for them. Equally significant was Amador Yarur's agreement to allow the leftist union leaders to devote their workdays to their union tasks at the enterprise's expense, for the Yarurs had always tried to undermine the effectiveness of leftist union leaderships in the past. From Amador Yarur's perspective, moreover, a company loan for the acquisition of a union hall outside the industry was adding insult to injury. Since the factory opened, an outside union hall was something that the Yarurs had always fought—let alone financed.

What persuaded Amador Yarur to agree to so heretical a contract was a combination of hope and fear. He hoped to exchange his cooperation on the contract for the leftist leadership's agreement to allow his two loyalists to remain on the union board. An even more powerful motivation was his fear that a refusal to accept such a contract would lead to a legal strike that he could not win and might well provoke the seizure and socialization of the factory—his ultimate nightmare—which seemed imminent to Amador Yarur in the wake of the union elections. Moreover, the contract's wage raise, although substantial, was less than many other industries were granting their workers and thus not a bad deal for the Yarurs under the circumstances.[80]

The Yarur union leaders were aware that the wage increase they had won was modest compared with that of some other enterprises and were convinced that they could have gotten more had they been willing to risk a strike. But they were equally persuaded that a strike was the last thing that they needed a fortnight after having taken over the company union on a platform of benefits without risks. Their initial objective was to consolidate their position and that of the newly independent union by rapidly winning a favorable contract from an enterprise that in the past had always denied leftist union leaders such a plum.[81] So they used the contract negotiations as a way of rallying the rank and file around them and of demonstrating the viability and value of an independent, leftist-led union—and a Popular Unity government. By April 1971, the first independent Yarur blue-collar union in a decade was consolidated. The Youngsters had defeated Don Amador.

8

THE *EMPLEADOS* FORM A UNION

In early 1971, the triumphant *obreros* had company—the first *empleados'* (white-collar)* union in Yarur history. If winning an independent *obrero* (blue-collar) union was difficult, organizing the industry's five hundred salaried *empleados* seemed well-nigh impossible. The blue-collar workers "by class extraction . . . have a much more developed consciousness," explained Ricardo Catalan, one of the employees who led that effort.[1] The *obreros'* upbringing, community, and work experience all reinforced their sense of social solidarity and class identity. By contrast, "the *empleados* were much harder because their first question was what was in it for them—they had neither political clarity nor class consciousness nor any experience of organization, not even a union."

The *empleados'* entire socialization militated against any such class organization or leftist political identification. With few exceptions, they viewed themselves as "middle class," an amorphous social category, which obscured the enormous differences between an ill-paid white-collar worker and a wealthy professional. Most of the Yarur *empleados* were white-collar workers from status-conscious lower-middle-class homes, and those who came from working-class backgrounds were equally anxious to distinguish themselves from the blue-collar workers from whose ranks they had emerged.

It was a self-conscious differentiation that fulfilled the intentions of the framers of the Chilean Labor Code, which created the legal distinction between *obrero* and *empleado* as a barrier to worker unity, establishing a division between manual and "intellectual" labor and reinforcing it with privileges.

---

*Although all *obreros* were blue-collar workers and most *empleados* were white-collar workers, certain categories of skilled blue-collar workers had won *empleado* status by 1970, blurring the original legal distinction between "manual" and "intellectual" work. For a further discussion, see note 2.

Organized in separate unions, enjoying somewhat higher wages and better social benefits, the *empleados* were expected to stress these differences and regard themselves as middle class. Upwardly mobile but economically deprived and socially insecure, the *empleados* were extremely status conscious and resistant to any organization or politics that might stigmatize them as working-class in the eyes of their social superiors.[2]

Yarur *empleados*, moreover, were particularly difficult to organize. Most earned salaries that were often not much greater than the wages of the skilled *obreros*, which made them prize their superior social status all the more highly. In addition, many of them derived their self-esteem from an identification with the Yarurs, basking in the reflected glow of their wealth and power. A high proportion of the Yarur *empleados*, moreover, had been promoted from the ranks of the factory's *obreros* as a reward for their loyalty to their *patrón*, in many cases without the requisite education or talents. As *obreros* they had been *apatronados*, and their fixation on loyalty had been intensified by their experience of the battles between Reds and Yellows and the ruthless repression of blue-collar efforts to organize an independent union. Many of them had been "made" *empleados* by Amador Yarur and tied to him further by the granting of small favors in return for informing on their co-workers, which left them "dependent on Don Amador psychologically," one thoughtful *empleado* stressed.[3] "Here they talked about Don Amador as if he were their owner, as if he were the Lord of us all." As a result, no *empleados'* union existed at Yarur in 1970, and none had been formed during the factory's thirty-four years. There was no organization or tradition for insurgents to draw on.

Yet below "a very suspicious calm" and despite the fear and paternalism, there was a reservoir of resentment that could be turned against the Yarurs—and in favor of a union—if it could be released. The Yarur *empleados* might stress their social superiority over the *obreros*, but they were acutely aware that "they couldn't have a high status because they are paid a miserable salary and very few are able to buy a car or an apartment," the material marks of the middle class. For most *empleados*, moreover, the differentials between their salaries and the wages of the *obreros* were not great, but the gap between their income and that of the upper-level management was enormous. Worse still, the *empleados* at the Yarur bank, the Banco de Crédito e Inversiones, received higher salaries and better benefits as a result of being unionized. The very materialism of the *empleados* argued for a union.[4]

For many employees with professional training, moreover, the personalistic way in which Amador Yarur ran his industry was a source of alienation and frustration. "I never could do my job as I should have," one apolitical accountant complained. "Don Amador was always looking over my shoulder telling me to do it another way or not to get involved here. In the end, I was afraid to do my job right because of what he might say. There was no professional satisfaction in it."[5] It was no accident that the two sections where *empleado* resistance to Amador Yarur first surfaced were IBM (Data Processing) and Industrial Engineering (Production Control and Planning), two of the most modern sections in a highly traditional factory, new sections created during Jorge Yarur's modernization of the preceding decade. The employees in these sections were professionals who owed their positions to their qualifications, not to favoritism. The nature of their work, moreover, entailed a respect for objective norms and ensured a disdain for arbitrary management.

This was particularly notable in IBM, where five employees had been fired in 1966 for staging the first *empleado* work stoppage in S. A. Yarur's history. As a result, a new cohort had been hired from other companies, so that they would have the experience to replace the fired workers. As the new head of Data Processing, Pedro García was frustrated by Amador Yarur's restricting his work "to doing accounts" and "using the computer as a printing press." He was also shocked to discover from his own calculations that the annual reports misrepresented the enterprise's profits.[6] Both García and Catalan, moreover, had worked at firms with strong *empleado* unions and were stunned by what they found at Yarur. "What immediately struck me as strange," García recalled, "is that when I asked where the union was, in order to ask some questions about social benefits, they said to me: 'Never mention the word union here.'"

In addition, most of the IBM employees arrived at Yarur after experiences that had shaped their politics in a leftist mold. For one, it had been a Socialist father; for another, left-wing Christian Democratic students at his university. García had been radicalized by a first job that took him to the coal mines of Lota, where he "was able to see with his own eyes what exploitation is."[7] Their experience at Yarur had reinforced these convictions. It was not just the lack of a union but the entire system of social control. The fifteen IBM employees were alienated at being asked to inform on their co-workers and resentful at the anger and distrust with which their refusal was received by Amador Yarur. To Jorge Iriarte, who had grown up in the countryside, "this industry . . . was run like a rural estate . . . Amador Yarur was like a feudal seigneur."[8]

Industrial engineering exhibited many of the same characteristics. It was also the section where Amador Yarur transferred politically unreliable, but able employees, so as to isolate them where their talents could be utilized without risk of contagion. Several Industrial Engineering employees were Socialist sympathizers, but even the administrative departments had some employees with leftist politics. In general, these employees were members of a younger generation of lower-middle-class *empleados*, with a better education and broader worldview than their parents and less status anxiety and fear of change. They were more sympathetic to the Popular Unity program and felt less threatened by the prospect of a blue-collar revolution.[9]

But, at Yarur, they were the exceptions that proved the rule: Most Yarur *empleados* feared the Left, identified with the Yarurs, and opposed unions. All that existed was the personnel delegate required by law, an old Yarur flunky who "was delegate for life."[10] There had been no real collective bargaining either, although the Labor Code mandated it. "They arranged it all with the personnel delegate and the labor inspectors," Catalan recounted. "I don't know if they bought those functionaries or what, but signed contracts appeared, even though they were illegal because they had been done without consulting us."[11]

In both IBM and Industrial Engineering, a nucleus of "trusted *compañeros*" had discussed organizing a union among themselves, but nothing had come of the idea before 1970 because "to speak of a union was taboo," and the Industrial Engineering group doubted that anyone else would join them.[12] The IBM employees had "had some very veiled conversations" on the athletic field with *empleados* from other sections, but "there were always doubts, fears. They were afraid that the Yarurs would take reprisals against people who were thinking about this subject."[13] Alienated *empleados* and potential activists might exist, but the Yarur system of social control effectively isolated them from each other and prevented any attempt to form an *empleado* union.

It was the Allende campaign that impelled *empleados* with leftist sympathies to reveal—and risk—themselves. Once having crossed that political divide, they began to consider another campaign: forming an *empleados* union at S.A. Yarur. "At the beginning of 1970, when Allende was already a candidate, we began to look into the union question more deeply," Pedro García related.[14] Once again they used the games between *empleado* athletic teams as an opportunity to feel out employees from other sections, focusing on those who had come from firms with unions. "From there were born other conversations with four or five *compañeros*, all of us awaiting the election results, because we knew for sure that, given the way things were in the industry, if Alessandri triumphed—or even Tomic—we could not push the union question here for the real fear of reprisals, in the sense that we all had families who relied upon our work."

It all depended on Allende. His campaign had brought the leftist *empleados* out of the political closet, and it was his election victory that spurred them into action. "We decided that if the election results were positive, the following Monday we would begin to locate the people we needed in order to form a union."[15] They were as good as their word, but only four attended that first meeting. A week later twice that number met at the Socialist party headquarters. They were a mirror of the Popular Unity—a mixture of Socialist, Communist, and MAPU sympathizers, none of them party members. They were acutely conscious of the risk they were taking; but, buoyed up by Allende's victory, they resolved "to make contact with other *compañeros* to obtain their backing now that Allende had won." "Come what may," they decided, they would "embark on the "adventure" of getting together twenty-five employees out of five hundred," the legal minimum for forming a union. [16]

It was a measure of the impact of Allende's election that the insurgents were able to unite a group of twenty-eight *empleados* in less than two weeks, despite the pointed firing during those same days of several supervisors, Communists who had campaigned for Allende. Before September 4, whenever "we added up the numbers of people who would be with us . . . we never arrived at twenty-five, and there were more than five hundred *empleados*," Ricardo Catalan stressed. "But after Allende won the election . . . little by little we made some contacts."[17]

They were also encouraged by contacts made outside the factory, with the CUT and its Textile Workers Federation (FENATEX), with political parties and with the growing Yarur *obreros* movement. Omar Guzmán, one of the Socialist leaders in Industrial Engineering, persuaded Joaquín Santana, a Socialist labor inspector who had not succumbed to Yarur blandishments, to act as the overseeing inspector required by law, and his co-worker Carlos Benavides got his Left Socialist friends from the University of Chile to agree to send a large group of students as witnesses and protection. Orlando Rossi, a Communist leader in Administration, arranged with the editors of the party newspaper *El Siglo* to "wait until we finished voting before closing its morning edition in order to publish the news of the constitution of the union the very next day. Then they couldn't throw us out because we would be elected union officers."[18]

Secrecy was essential to prevent the premature disclosure that would allow Amador Yarur to take countermeasures before their fledgling movement had acquired legal protection. It was a particular problem in an enterprise that was saturated with informers and where they had only a fortnight to identify trusted co-workers. So there was no attempt to generate broad support for their effort, and even the leaders knew only the committed in their section plus the other leaders. But even these measures did not suffice. "It may seem grotesque," recounted Omar Guzmán, a survivor of the 1962 strike, "but by the day on which we were to form the union, Yarur already knew." One of their "trusted" *compañeros* was a Yarur informer. "On September 22," the day before their founding meeting, Guzmán recalled, "[Eugenio] Stark, the personnel chief, called me in to tell me that Amador and Jorge Yarur knew that we were going to form the union and that they suspected me, 'because your friend Joaquín Santana is the inspector. Don

Amador Yarur says that under no conditions is he going to accept it and Don Jorge Yarur doesn't care.'"[19] Their secret was out. Now much depended on what the Yarurs would do in response.

For Stark, a Christian Democrat with a good sense of *empleados'* leanings, it was a mistake to oppose rigidly a union that "was already in the works even before . . . and now with the support of another kind of government wouldn't have any problem."[20] Far better to adjust to the new era and work within it. Yarur loyalists might have the votes to take over the union or to elect some pliant Christian Democrats to its board of directors. It was a position that Jorge Yarur grasped and supported. "On the other hand, Amador Yarur, 'El Chico,' with the paternalism and informing and the cabal that he had mounted, said, 'No!.'"[21] Amador Yarur was used to running "his" industry as a personalistic extension of himself. It was bad enough that he had to confront another *obrero* threat to "his" blue-collar union. To allow "his" *empleados* to have a union of their own was out of the question. Besides, he reasoned, past attempts to form an *empleados* union "had failed, and there was no surety that they would succeed now," nor that Allende would be inaugurated.[22]

Having decided to resist heresy to the last, Amador Yarur pulled out the stops. When Carlos Benavides came to work on September 23 he found that "on Don Amador's orders [Stark] went to offer all the *empleados* . . . everything they needed so that they should torpedo the union."[23] It was at once a test of loyalty and a call to arms. They had mistaken their man in Benavides, but "there were some who played Yarur's game." That day more than 150 employees were released early from work, "and he gave fifty escudos to every three people so that they could take a taxi to the Radical Club, where they were wined and dined. When he had to play the game, Yarur was no miser!" Guzmán admitted.[24]

Guzmán became livid at the thought "that those sons of bitches must have felt very satisfied sitting there paid to defend the rights of the boss,"[25] but he oversimplified the mixed motives of those who had accepted Yarur's invitation to dine and destroy. Some of them were there out of opportunism; some, out of conviction. For some, it was fear of reprisals if they refused to go; for others, the opportunity to get in good with their boss; for still others the prospect of a good meal and some excitement. There were those who gathered at the Radical Club out of anticommunism and those who were there because they feared that the formation of a leftist union would divide and politicize the *empleados*. Among them, too, were Christian Democrats who saw this as an opportunity to form the union that they wanted without antagonizing their boss and to convert it into a Christian Democratic base for the new era of Popular Unity government—a strategy that was attractive to the party's national leadership as well.[26] Their very different purposes were underscored by their fear of a physical confrontation between Reds and Yellows, which had led "the Christian Democratic chiefs . . . to speak with Bernardo Leighton, who at that time was interior minister," whom "they asked for police protection."[27] They knew their boss.

The nature of Amador Yarur's game became clear during the course of the meal. At the Club Radical, Eduardo Ellis and other Yarur loyalists organized their countermove. Once "they ate and drank their fill," the *empleados* assembled there would be taken to the ANEF [National Association of Government Employees] union headquarters, where the insurgent union meeting was to be held. From his informer within their movement, Amador Yarur knew that the insurgents had barely enough *empleados* committed to form a legal union. Perhaps the presence of more than one hundred Yarur loyalists led by his strong-arm squad would intimidate the less resolute into withdrawing. If not, his loyalists would have the numbers to take over the new union and make it a company union.[28]

Forewarned was forearmed. The insurgents were as eager to avoid a confrontation as the Christian Democrats, particularly as the numbers were all on the other side. Forced to alter their plans, "because [Yarur] had found us out,"[29] they improvised, changing the time and place of the meeting two hours before it was supposed to begin, with the crucial aid of the Socialist labor inspector, who would cover the legal niceties at the ministry. The prospective founding members were alerted to the need for a change of scenario, and it was left to Guzmán and Rossi to improvise a new script. It would be a comedy of errors, masquerading as melodrama.

"Rossi and I had to deal with this whole question," Guzmán recounted.[30] They agreed that they had to change the meeting place. Rossi suggested his brother-in-law's house—without asking him. "Now his brother-in-law was a Christian Democrat and Rossi is a Communist," Guzmán underscored, but when they "arrived there, the old man, himself a longtime union leader, boldly said: 'Here there are no Christian Democrats that are on the side of Yarur,' and he offered us his house." Unfortunately, his house was way out in the suburbs and "rather difficult to find," and they spent the next hours rounding up the faithful instead of forming a union.

In the end, the only one they were unable to notify of the change in venue was Carlos Benavides, but he knew from Stark what Yarur was brewing. Benavides had arranged to meet the group of Socialist students at the ANEF headquarters and felt he "had to go there in order to tell the kids not to get involved in the mess because there were fourteen girls there from the School of Sociology." He expected to find his twenty-seven *compañeros* there as well, but instead found himself face-to-face "with the Yarur hordes . . . I was the only one and I confronted more than one hundred Yellows," he recalled without relish.[31]

The Yarur loyalists were well liquored up, and the strong-arm squad was in a boisterous mood. It was just what the Christian Democrats among the *empleados* gathered there had feared, "so they asked for police protection, and they brought in Carabineros with water cannon and made a police cordon in front of the ANEF," separating the strong-arm squad from Carlos Benavides and his coeds. "And there they waited for Joaquín Santana to come and begin the meeting," Guzmán chuckled, "but he was with us in another place" after "escaping from the ANEF crouched on the floor of a taxi so that no one would recognize him."[32]

The new suburban meeting site was "difficult to reach," and the prospective unionists "arrived one by one, which made us all nervous," Ricardo Catalan recalled.[33] One way or another they got twenty-seven *empleados* together, but it was not until eleven at night that they could inform the *El Siglo* editors that the first Yarur *empleados'* union had been formed, with Guzmán as president, Catalan as secretary, and Rossi as treasurer. The drama was over, but their struggle had just begun.

The following morning, each of the "valiant twenty-seven" went to work with a copy of *El Siglo*—whose circulation in the factory was forbidden—visibly in hand, and with "rather serious stomach aches" because "we are all very nervous," Guzmán recalled. The Yarur loyalists had also ended the previous day's festivities with a sense of triumph and entered the industry that morning, proclaiming: "The union failed; they didn't dare," only to be told: "No, we were in another part of town, and we did too form the union" and shown the news in black and white in "that Red sheet," *El Siglo*. "Now we have been had . . . the Reds beat us," one Yarur loyalist lamented loudly, "and that is how we fooled them," Guzmán concluded.[34]

Amador Yarur was not so easily fooled, nor was he willing to accept a "Red union" representing "his" *empleados*.[35] That very day he had his loyalists formally protest the legality of the new union because it was constituted in a different place from the one announced and without the presence of the more than one hundred *empleados* who had gathered at the ANEF headquarters.[36] With this rationale—a legitimate one on the face of it—Amador Yarur could revive his father's old strategy of forming a competing organization dominated by his loyalists. In 1970, in the wake of Allende's election, Amador Yarur wanted "to form a parallel union, like those he was accustomed to . . . because he could not adapt himself to the new epoch."[37]

Yarur's top aides, led by Personnel Chief Eugenio Stark, were completely opposed to this strategy, even men who had helped Juan Yarur fashion his mutual and company union. "I put it to a majority of the department heads, and all of them agreed that in these circumstances it wasn't convenient to form a parallel union," Stark recounted. Even Oscar Zahri, Juan Yarur's confidant and "trusted lawyer," agreed. He "told Amador Yarur that he was just sacrificing his people because they were not going to get anywhere, because the Ministry of Labor controlled by the new government would never recognize such a union's legality and so it would be unable to go forward."[38]

Against all this advice, Amador Yarur insisted that "it was he who commanded here" and that he would not tolerate a "Red union." The result was not the servile obedience that he expected but the first revolt of middle-level managers in the factory's history, something Juan Yarur would never have allowed, but that Amador Yarur "had to abide" in the changed circumstances that followed Allende's election. It was Stark, the fourth employee hired by Juan Yarur back in 1936 and the industry's personnel chief since 1962, who led the rebellion. Like many Yarur managers, he resented Amador Yarur's personalistic administration and regretted the withdrawal of Jorge Yarur, "a real executive," from active involvement in the factory. In this crisis, he realized that his loyalty "was more to the enterprise than to Amador Yarur" and decided that it was up to "the middle-level managers" to save it from El Chico's anachronistic rigidity. He talked not only with the other department heads but with the company controller and general manager as well, and he found that they all agreed with him.[39]

Amador Yarur moved rapidly to defuse this threat to his authority by presenting his aides with a fait accompli. In less than a week, he had his company *empleado* union organized. It was in this situation that his rebellious aides met in a council of war. "The day before there was going to be another union formed here, I spoke with various department heads and we got together in El Caleuche, a neighborhood restaurant. And we were there until one in the morning," recounted Stark. "We arrived at the conclusion that we had to speak with Don Amador the next day in order to convince him to stop promoting employee divisions and the parallel union." The discussion was intense, "and most of us committed ourselves to resign if Don Amador didn't accept our view; but there were two *compañeros* who made us see that they were not in a position to run the risk of losing their jobs. One of them was about to retire, and the other really had no other possibilities." So they decided instead to ask for separate meetings with Jorge and Amador Yarur, hoping to gain the support of the former before confronting the latter.[40]

Amador Yarur was not one to be outmaneuvered by his own aides. "So when he knew that we had asked for an interview with Jorge Yarur, Don Amador anticipated us and saw us an hour before." At nine in the morning, he received his aides in his wood-paneled office with the photographs of his family and heard them out. "From the start, he insisted that he couldn't do it, that he had to respect his group of loyalists and couldn't leave them out in the cold. Afterward, what with all the arguments, the thing became so threatening to him. So in the end he did what he always did: pass the buck. He committed himself in front of all of us that he would not intervene in the problem, but that neither could he go against the wishes of his group. He made it out as if those *compañeros* had asked him to do it, so he said: 'I can't tell them no. You get together with the group and see if you can convince them,'" Stark recounted.[41]

It was a typical Amador Yarur tactic: "passing the buck" to avoid direct conflict, but in such a way as to control the outcome. His "Unconditionals" could be relied on to frustrate his rebellious aides, defusing their revolt and keeping his brother Jorge from contesting his authority anew. Only three of the five people Amador Yarur had named for the meeting showed up. The two Christian Democrats stayed away, and the Stark group "encountered an intransigent position, and there was no way to convince them." El Chico's strategy had worked to perfection, allowing him to place the responsibility for his policy elsewhere and deflect the substantive arguments of his aides with a face of "principle" and an appeal to "democracy." "With this maneuver, Amador Yarur tied our hands," Stark lamented, "because now we could not impose our views as just that of a small group; we had to do it all in the most democratic way possible, and now there was nothing that could be done." So, they "just informed" Jorge Yarur "what had happened" and accepted the inevitable. Their outmaneuvered rebellion had fizzled, and Amador Yarur's parallel union was created with great fanfare on September 30, only one week after El Chico's own attempt to block the formation of an independent *empleado* union had itself been outmaneuvered.[42]

Although the core of Amador Yarur's parallel union were his "Unconditionals," led by Eduardo Ellis and Virgilio Godoy, he was aware that so restricted a group of cronies would lack legitimacy both within and outside the factory. His solution was to include three Christian Democratic leaders on its board and make one of them, Camilo Henriquez, president. "They were all my *compañeros*," Stark lamented, Christian Democrats who "were not of his position, but who accepted out of fear of reprisals." Their independent image was precisely their value. "They were not of those whom they called 'Unconditionals,' but rather people who had some prestige among the other *empleados*."[43]

With the backing of the boss, the fear of reprisals, and the Christian Democratic officers, Amador Yarur's *empleados*' union seemed fairly launched by the start of October. With the founding of two parallel unions, each claiming to represent the Yarur *empleados*, the battle to secure legal recognition and the support of the majority of the industry's five hundred employees began. To make certain that "his" union won this contest, Amador Yarur granted employees who joined the company union the most favorable contract in the firm's history while refusing to deal with the contract demands of the leftist union. The officers of the parallel union were allowed complete freedom to wander around the different departments during working hours whereas the leftist leaders were immobilized and isolated in their own work sections. At the same time, Yarur "let loose a rumor" that all those who refused to join the company union would be fired "later on," after which each *empleado* was "summoned to the office of his department chief and asked to sign up."[44] At the same time, the leaders of the leftist union were subjected to more sinister threats. "The menaces were multiple," Omar Guzmán recalled. "My wife was pregnant at the time, and they called her on the phone; they threatened her, told her that she had better 'be careful' . . . it was a time filled with anguish."[45] Amador Yarur was determined to crush the "Red union," and *empleados* who joined it did so at their peril.

As a consequence, one month after its formation, the leftist union had not grown much beyond its initial 27 members, all of whom were feeling the pressure. The company union, on the other hand, claimed some 380 members. But if numbers were its strong point, depth of commitment was its weakness. Aside from Yarur's Unconditionals, whose numbers did not exceed 100, most *empleados* had joined the company union out of a combination of fear and opportunism. This is what the leaders of the leftist union were counting on. To Ricardo Catalan, "the formation of our union was a first step. We were already at a point where a very different government was about to assume power . . . and the mass of the *empleados* was waiting to see what would happen then."[46] If they could survive until Allende became president, this same opportunism and unease might well produce a rapid reversal of the fortunes of the two unions. Within so difficult a social terrain as Yarur, a leftist *empleados'* union needed the active aid of a leftist government to be able to transform its "adventure" into victory.

In the interim, the fledgling union needed outside help just to survive. Its leaders found such assistance easier to obtain than members—and not only from the Popular Unity. "We covered all the ministries; we bothered half the world," Catalan recalled. "And everyone was worried because Yarur is a strategic enterprise; in other words, everyone knew what was happening here."[47] To the Popular Unity, moreover, Yarur was also emblematic of the old Chile, whose death knell was Allende's election. Amador Yarur's refusal to accept an independent *empleados'* union and his recourse to traditional Yarur divide-and-conquer tactics were emblematic of the Right's refusal to accept Allende's election and their recourse to political deals and military plots to prevent him from coming to power. Yarur might be a local struggle, but it was one with national significance, particularly, as the popular tabloid *Clarín* reminded its many readers, because "the Yarur textile firm is an unusual case within Chilean labor struggles."[48] As a consequence, its embattled *empleados* deserved the support of the entire Left. Other leftist newspapers followed suit, making the Yarur struggle into a public political issue and symbolic class conflict.

The assistance of a Socialist labor inspector and unionists had been central to the formation of the leftist union, and both Labor Ministry functionaries and leftist labor leaders would play crucial roles in helping it survive until Allende's inauguration. "We approached the CUT and the Textile Federation, and the *compañeros* there put us in contact with people who helped us"—including Oscar Ibáñez, a former Yarur worker, now the CUT conflicts secretary, who had advised the 1952 and 1962 *obrero* movements at the mill and understood the Yarur situation.[49] With their help, the inexperienced *empleado* leaders prepared their survival strategy for the national political interregnum.

The five union officers were protected by law from dismissal, but the same was not true for the rest of the members, and if Yarur was able to reduce their numbers below twenty-five, he could liquidate their union. So the officers immediately "presented a formal set of contract demands that was illegal from every point of view." It had not been discussed by a special workers' assembly, nor would Amador Yarur negotiate it, but until it was ruled illegal, "Chilean labor law says . . . you can't fire anyone."[50] With the help of sympathetic functionaries in the Labor Ministry, the *empleado* leaders were able to delay this ruling until Allende's inauguration.

Such assistance would be equally important in the struggle for legal certification, which both sides recognized would ultimately determine the contest between them under Chile's legalistic and statist labor code. It was little wonder that Amador Yarur decided that this was the time to cash in his chips with the Christian Democrats, whose campaigns he had supported generously in the past. His aim was to accelerate one bureaucratic process and slow another, "trying to utilize the members of the outgoing government . . . to obtain legal certification for them before we did," Catalan explained. The implications were clear to all concerned: "If that was the way it came out, his union would win. If we obtained it first, evidently we would win."[51] It all rested on the action—and inaction—of a lame-duck administration. The pressure on Frei's Labor Ministry was tremendous. But despite Yarur's machinations and the pressures from the right wing of their own party, there were Christian Democratic functionaries within the Ministry of Labor who sympathized with the leftist unionists and assisted their progress, while hindering that of the company union until Allende's inauguration.[52]

"It was the sixth of November," Catalan remembered, "that we had our first contact with the new labor minister, José Oyarce," a former CUT officer whose nomination symbolized the new power of organized labor within the state and corroborated Allende's claim that his was a "Workers' Government." "Oyarce had been named minister but he still had not assumed his functions, because Allende had only been in office two days . . . so we went to the headquarters of the Central Committee of the Communist party, and there we talked with the *compañero*. We explained the entire case to him, and the *compañero* called us to the ministry on Monday, November 9. We were the first union that he received, and he promised us that he would set in motion . . . all that had to be done for the decree conceding us legal status." Oyarce was as good as his word. "We obtained legal certification —which normally takes two years—in record time, on November 11, and two days later the decree was signed and published in the *Diario Oficial*. At that point we could rest because now they couldn't throw us overboard," Catalan concluded.[53] The Yarur *empleados'* union might be small, but its struggle was symbolic in the eyes of the Left. It might have only thirty members, but it had priority with the Popular Unity.

If anything, Allende's inauguration was more important to the weak *empleados'* union than to the far stronger *obrero* movement. "That is when we began to grow," one activist recalled, recounting the steps by which the much smaller leftist union—with 30 members to the company union's 380— slowly "reversed the correlation of forces."[54] The combination of the installation of a Popular Unity government with the granting of legal status was a signal to the many *empleados* who had joined Amador Yarur's union out of fear or opportunism. "People began to come over to our side," and the company management "began to feel the external pressures of the labor legislation," Carlos Benavides related.[55] "All this was part of the job of making the other union disintegrate. When we got legal status, it made a very big impact on them because we got it in so short a time. From that point on, they told us that it was 'war to the death,' that one way or another they were going to obtain legal status."

Amador Yarur should have known better. Whoever controlled the state dominated in Chile's system of labor relations. He could—and did—harass employees who joined the leftist union, transferring them to less desirable jobs and threatening them. But when the company union tried to obtain legal certification, the Popular Unity's Labor Ministry dealt their request a bureaucratic death.[56] The powerful state role in labor relations, which had always aided the Yarurs, now worked against them. It was a good example of *la via chilena*'s use of old laws and institutions for new purposes.

The demonstration of Yarur impotence in the New Chile made a powerful impact on wavering *empleados*, who more than anything else wanted to be on the winning side. At the same time, the company union lost support when Amador Yarur failed to fulfill the generous new contract he had given their members in October, "because Yarur had made it 'between *compadres*' [buddies] in order to liquidate us, not to give the guarantees granted there," Catalan explained.[57] Within this newly favorable context, the leftist union "kept moving forward and little by little we began directing an intense organizing drive that enabled us to capture adherents gradually, pointing out all the errors that they made and at the same time doing things well ourselves." By early 1971, an election for personnel delegates demonstrated that the leftist union had almost caught up to the company union in its support. In April 1971, balloting for officers of the *empleados*' sports club was along political lines, and the Popular Unity's four candidates were all elected.[58]

The shifting loyalties of Yarur *empleados* was seen as well in the changing membership lists of the two unions. "When people saw that things were being defined in favor of the Popular Government, they began to resign from the company union, claiming that they had been forced to sign its book . . . and to come over to our union," Ricardo Catalan recounted.[59] "So, one day we received two resignations from the other union, the next day three . . . and on the following day five . . . so that little by little people were leaving them and joining our union." For the Yarur loyalists, it was demoralizing. "These guys were desperate . . . their leaders saw that they didn't have rank-and-file support any longer, that Allende had won, that Amador Yarur didn't know what to do, so they began to let things slide." Several of them were Christian Democrats who had been skeptical of the enterprise from the start and only accepted their posts under pressure from Amador Yarur. Others were Yarur loyalists who had counted on their *patrón*'s omnipotence, only to encounter his seeming impotence instead. For most *empleados*, however, self-interest was more important than ideology, and calculation more evident than commitment. Their choice of unions was less a statement of political consciousness than a manifestation of their anxiety to please the powers that be.[60] Their shifting loyalties reflected the changing political tides in their workplace and their nation. In the end, they linked their fortunes to the side most likely to win.

Gradually, the company union faded away, leaving the leftist union to consolidate its victory. From thirty members in November it grew to almost four hundred in April. It had won a war of attrition in an uphill battle against an intransigent Amador Yarur, who still refused to accept its triumph or recognize its legitimacy. By April, however, it had united the great bulk of the *empleados* under its leftist standard, mirroring the lower-middle-class shift to the Popular Unity in the nation at large. It was another example of the growing support of the Allende government in Chile—and the increasing success of the new leftist workers' movements at the Yarur mill.

9

TOWARD
REVOLUTION?

By April 1971, two leftist unions confronted Amador Yarur where none had existed before. Their leaders, moreover, had initiated a hitherto unheard-of cooperation between the industry's blue- and white-collar workers. By then, the Yarur *obreros* had also fulfilled other historic aspirations—union democracy, collective bargaining, and increased real wages and benefits—and begun to pursue new goals of worker control. Their "conquest" of an independent union proved but the first step in an increasingly radical revolution from below.

Once their goal of a free union was finally achieved, the leftist worker leaders began to look beyond the traditional bread-and-butter demands of Chilean labor to a new, more revolutionary agenda. Increasingly, they refocused their attentions on issues of worker control—not of the union, but of the factory. Their demand that the enterprise change its work contracts to "specify the job . . . that each *obrero* will undertake within a specified section"[1] struck at the company's power to allocate its labor force, a crucial aspect of the Yarur system of work—and social control. Amador Yarur temporized on some of these demands and made excuses on others, but it soon became apparent that although he might give way on wages and benefits, he was unwilling to make more than token concessions where the management of his factory was concerned—unless the workers forced him to do so.

What worried Amador Yarur as much as these formal union demands was the beginning of a social revolution on the factory floor. A fortnight after the union elections, Armando Carrera, the union delegate, led a work stoppage in Conos "in order to get rid of a bad *jefe* . . . one of the biggest slave drivers there was here," Emilio Hernández recounted.[2] Amador Yarur was not accustomed to such job actions in his factory. Yet not only were the workers involved not summarily fired—as they surely would have been be-fore—but Yarur gave in and transferred the offending supervisor. Other job actions followed, including a union demand that Amador Yarur transfer a cafeteria employee "for his bad treatment of, and insults to, his *compañeros*."[3] Once again, the fear of provoking a wider strike and seizure of the mill led Yarur to placate the worker activists where before he would have punished them.

The formation of "Watchdog Committees" in each work section, with the task of overseeing production and stopping "capitalist sabotage," was the next step in the extension of worker control on the factory floor. This was going too far, even for an anxious Amador Yarur. "Nobody tells me how to run my industry," he was reported to have exploded at the news.[4] Con-vinced that his earlier efforts to avoid a confrontation had only encouraged the workers to expand their actions and deepen their demands, Amador Yarur reversed course and returned to his policy of noncooperation.

In response, the union leaders organized a sit-in of union delegates during the February meeting of the Yarur, Inc., Board of Directors "to exact respect for the union leadership."[5] This unprecedented show of strength by the workers' movement persuaded Amador Yarur to resume an outwardly con-ciliatory posture while instructing his subordinates and loyalists to obstruct the movement's efforts to unite the workers and solve the daily problems that arose on the factory floor. As a consequence, by April the most radical of the frustrated leftist leadership of the workers' movement began to talk increasingly about the need to move from the "liberation" of their union to the "liberation" of their factory. "It was there that this movement to take the industry from the Yarurs began," Lorca stressed.[6]

Several factors—national and local—combined to transform a workers' movement to "rescue" their union into a struggle to "liberate" their factory. Allende's campaign speech at the mill planted the seed of socialism in their consciousness. The Popular Unity's electoral promise to nationalize Chile's largest enterprises legitimized their struggle, and sympathetic government officials supported it. The millenarian atmosphere that followed Allende's election and inauguration seemed to make the dream of socialism possible, and the workers' own concrete "conquests" persuaded them that they could become masters of their own destiny. These events, experiences, and aspi-rations brought about a dramatic transformation of consciousness and an inflation of expectations.

The intransigence of Amador Yarur added anger to their motivations and urgency to their plans. Central to the reorientation of the workers' movement from union reform to socialist revolution was their belief that their boss was obstructing "their" revolution and sabotaging the economic policies of "their" government. "From January [1971] on, we began to notice that they were doing some things here against the government, for example shutting down machines by turns, a little here, tomorrow there," explained the blue-collar union president.[7] "We started seeing the problem as one of boycott." It was a perception shared by government advisers in the Ministry of Economics, which reinforced the union leaders in their conviction and resolve to put an end to such "counterrevolutionary sabotage" by rooting out the problem at its source—Yarur's control of the products of their labor.

Other factors were less tangible, but equally important in persuading many workers that they would no longer recognize Amador Yarur as their boss. Although often couching their concern in the legalistic language of Chilean labor relations, at bottom these workers demanded Yarur's recognition of an implicit social contract between them, a set of mutual rights and responsibilities. Amador Yarur's refusal to accept authentic worker representation called into question the legitimacy of his ownership and direction of the factory. In the eyes of the workers, Yarur's rejection of their "reasonable demands" was a justification for rebellion and a rationale for revolution.[8]

The roots of revolution might be present, along with the justification for rebellion, but a precondition for this revolution from below was a dramatic change in the workers' view of themselves, their capacity and power, as well as their perception that for once the state would support them in any showdown between capital and labor. Not until March 1971, after they had won a decisive union victory and comprehended the power and militancy of their movement, did its leaders shift their sights from the control of their unions to the socialization of their factory. Not until then did the altered consciousness of their rank and file permit such a leap into the revolutionary unknown. In the process, the Yarur workers became central protagonists of a revolution from below that changed the course of the Chilean road to socialism.

III

REFORM OR REVOLUTION?

10

SIGNALS FOR
SOCIALISM

On the twenty-fifth of April 1971, the workers at the Yarur cotton mill in Santiago seized control of their factory and demanded "socialism." There had been
strikes before at the Yarur mill—for better wages, for an independent union,
against the Taylor System—but this was different: This was a strike to rule. Three
days later, President Allende reluctantly bowed to their demands and Yarur, Inc.,
became the first Chilean industry to be requisitioned by the Popular Unity government "for the simple fact of being a monopoly."[1]

It was a historical role that took the workers themselves by surprise. All
they had hoped to do was "liberate" themselves from "the yoke of the
Yarurs."[2] All they thought they were doing was fulfilling the Popular Unity
program and redeeming Allende's campaign pledge. But what they did was
enact their own understanding of the Chilean revolution—a model other
workers then followed.

In only five months of Popular Unity government, the workers' movement at
the Yarur mill had fulfilled its historic agenda and gone beyond it to pose questions of worker power that challenged Amador Yarur's control over his own factory. The Yarur workers may have been bywords for political backwardness in the
past, but during the five months of Allende's presidency they had leaped into the
vanguard of an accelerating and deepening revolution from below, one significantly different from Salvador Allende's revolution from above.

A REVOLUTION FROM BELOW?

The Popular Unity program and the authors of its economic strategy envisioned a carefully controlled revolution from above. The structural changes

that would pave the way for socialism were to be carried out legally, using the instruments created by the bourgeoisie and the powers granted the state. At the same time, mandated price controls and wage increases would redistribute income "from the infinitesimal minorities to the overwhelming majority" of Chileans. Together with the Popular Government's vastly expanded social programs, the resultant raised real incomes would "solve the basic needs of the people" and make possible Allende's promised "revolution with meat pies and red wine."[3]

These measures—and successes—were also central to the Popular Unity's political strategy, which was to produce an electoral majority for socialism by the end of Allende's six-year presidential term. It was a strategy that counted on the growing support of Chile's workers, peasants, and *pobladores*, who would be won over by the material benefits that they would receive and persuaded by their experience that socialism was a superior system that was in their own self-interest. But in order to succeed, *la vía chilena* also required the support of a sizable sector of the middle classes, who wanted the benefits of *los cambios* ("the changes") that both Allende and Tomic had proposed, but feared the personal and societal costs of a Marxist-led revolution. Most of them had voted for Tomic and change in 1970 rather than for Alessandri and the status quo, and their support could give the Popular Unity the majority that it sought. The solution was to produce the promised revolution without sacrifice while allaying their fears of a violent or authoritarian revolution in which they might become victims.

This required a carefully controlled and phased revolutionary process, which was also necessary for the successful implementation of the Popular Unity's program of structural change. Here the strategy called for dividing the Chilean bourgeoisie, confronting one sector at a time, and enlisting the cooperation or neutrality of the smaller and medium-sized enterprises by confining leftist attacks to the "monopolies." In this delicately balanced strategy of economic and political change, the role of the "masses"—workers, peasants, and *pobladores*—was to provide political and social support when called on, but otherwise to await patiently the advances and benefits of the revolution from above.

Allende's "popular triumph," however, had a different meaning to his mass base than it had to the politicians and planners of the Popular Unity. To Chile's workers, peasants, and *pobladores*, the election of a "Popular Government" was a signal for them to take the revolution into their own hands and fulfill their historic aspirations through direct action from below. Allende's promise that he would never use the security apparatus of the state against "the people" freed them from fear of governmental repression, and the Popular Unity's commitment to structural change, redistribution of wealth and meeting the basic needs of Chile's poor persuaded many that, in acting for themselves, they were fulfilling the Popular Unity program and advancing the revolutionary process. For them, the underlying meaning of Allende's election was that they were now free to pursue their long postponed dreams.

The result was the unleashing of a revolution from below, which sometimes coincided with or complemented, but increasingly diverged from, the legalistic and modulated revolution from above. More spontaneous, it emerged from the workers, peasants, and *pobladores* themselves, although through a complex process in which certain political groups played an important role. Workers, peasants and *pobladores*, however, were the protagonists of this other revolutionary process, and they infused it with their own concerns, style, and worldview. Their aims tended to be concrete—objectives that responded to problems in their daily lives, but that they equated with advancing "the revolution." It was an uneven process, with varying dynamics, but it was sufficiently powerful to call into question the speed, priorities, and character of the overall revolutionary process. It was never completely autonomous nor totally spontaneous, but from a passive political base the Chilean masses began to transform themselves into active agents of change, the protagonists of their own destiny.[4]

The hallmark of this revolution from below was the *toma* —the seizure of the sites where people lived or worked—or hoped to live or work. Allende's election was followed by a wave of suburban land seizures by homeless urban workers and recent rural migrants desperate for the housing that successive governments had promised to provide but failed to deliver. Led by leftist activists, squatters seized vacant lots on the edge of Chile's cities, raising the national flag, and building cardboard shacks as symbols of legitimacy and signs of possession.[5]

Equally dramatic and even less compatible with Allende's phased revolution from above was the wave of farm seizures that began in the Mapuche Indian areas of the Alpine south and spread rapidly to the rural laborers and poor peasants of the fertile Central Valley, Chile's breadbasket and the economic and political base of Chile's traditional elite. Whether it was "the running of the fences" by Indians to reclaim the lands that European settlers had taken from them during the preceding century or the *toma* of large estates by peasants who had been disappointed by the speed and scope of Frei's agrarian reform, the message was the same. The deprived of Chile had taken Allende's victory as their own and were acting out its meaning in their own direct action. It was at once a sign of faith in the Popular Unity and suspicion of all governmental bureaucracy.[6]

For Chile's industrial workers, Allende's election and inauguration were also a signal: a time to organize, to press for big wage increases, to prepare for the socialization of one's workplace. For the most part, the industrial workers were better organized and better paid, more disciplined and more committed to the Popular Unity than the peasants and *pobladores*. They interpreted the advent of a Popular Government as an opportunity to press for their historic aspiration—higher real wages—an economist orientation ingrained by years of struggle within the legalistic Chilean Labor Code and a politicized labor movement. The workers took the Allende government's wage guidelines—a 36 percent raise, equal to the previous year's inflation—as a starting point for contract negotiations. Taking advantage of their new bargaining leverage—management awareness that government representatives on the tripartite mediation boards would now side with the workers and fear that a labor conflict might lead to a strike that would provoke a factory seizure or government takeover—industrial workers won the largest real wage raises in Chilean history, leading the way to the 30 percent average increase in real incomes that Chilean workers secured for 1971.[7]

For such workers, peasants, and *pobladores*, the meaning of Allende's presidency was the license to fulfill their aspirations and pursue their dreams. Some were conscious of the broader implications of their actions; others, conscious only of the opportunity to realize the goals of a lifetime. Together, their individual actions transformed Allende's narrow electoral victory into a profound revolution from below. It was a social revolution that confirmed the fears of the elite and awoke the anxieties of the middle classes even as it raised the hopes of the most "revolutionary" factions within the Popular Unity and the MIR to its left.

The Popular Unity leaders had banked on the increasing radicalization and support of Chile's workers, peasants, and *pobladores* on their democratic road to socialism, but they had not bargained for a revolution from below. The problem for the Allende government was how to reward the expectations of its mass base while keeping wage increases within noninflationary bounds and land seizures from threatening its political strategy of class coalition.

Although the large raises for 1971 might cause economic problems later on, it was the *tomas* that most worried the Popular Unity leadership. There had been land seizures before the election of Allende, but never on such a scale. The rural revolution from below, in particular, was playing havoc with the Popular Unity's timetable and image of legality and was threatening the governing coalition's political strategy of class coalition by raising the anxieties of small landowners, a central social base of the Radical party.

Still more worrying to many Popular Unity leaders was the prospect of a deepening revolution from below among the industrial working class. Except for those few industries whose owners had abandoned the country, failed to meet payrolls, or shut down plants, factory seizures were conspicuous by their absence before 1971. By March of that year, however, government officials were becoming aware that pressure from below for the socialization of industry was growing.[8] If these pressures could not be contained, the Popular Unity might be forced to choose between its strategy for socialism and its central mass base.

By April 1971, it was becoming clear that Allende's election had set off processes that were calling into question his initial timetable and strategy. A surging revolution from below was threatening to leave the national leaders of the Left behind and to disrupt the Popular Unity's economic and political strategies in the process. Together with the unexpectedly rapid progress of the revolution from above, this unanticipated emergence of a revolution from below was forcing the Popular Unity leaders to reassess the scope, speed, direction, methods, and character of their road to socialism, posing with new urgency the old question: reform or revolution? For an answer, the Chilean Left looked to the April elections.

A MANDATE FOR SOCIALISM?

With the whole world watching, the election of 1653 local alderman on April 4, 1971, became a national test of political strength, with mass mobilization on the scale of a presidential campaign and the intervention of major political figures on behalf of obscure local candidates. For the divided opposition, the municipal elections were a chance to stop the socialist bandwagon. At stake for the Popular Unity was not only a popular verdict on their first five months in office but also a mandate to fulfill the more revolutionary planks of their program.

When the 2.8 million votes were counted, the Popular Unity had won a stunning victory, bettering the combined totals of Right and Center. It was a bare 50 percent majority, but it greatly exceeded both the 36 percent of the vote that Allende had won only seven months before and the expectations of his supporters. To the Chilean Left, their municipal election majority represented a popular mandate to press forward along the democratic road to socialism that Allende had promised in his presidential campaign.

In its wake, the mood of caution among national leaders of the Left that had tempered the elation of Allende's election and inauguration was replaced by a surge of revolutionary euphoria. The old regime seemed to be disintegrating before the mounting tide of revolution, with its political defenders in disarray and a majority of Chileans now prepared to endorse a democratic road to socialism. There would be no other national elections for two years and thus no reason to hold back any longer. The April elections produced a mood of revolutionary opportunism in many Leftists, who argued that the moment had come to force a breakthrough. It was a compelling thesis, but one that threatened to catapult the revolutionary process forward far faster than the Popular Unity had envisioned, with the moderates of November pulled along against their better judgment by the maximalists of April.

The Popular Unity's initial strategy for socialism conceived of Allende's six-year term in office as one in which an electoral majority for socialism would be established gradually. To most of its leaders, the April election returns represented a vindication of that strategy. To some, however, the Left's emerging electoral majority posed the possibility of a more rapid revolutionary breakthrough by means of a national plebiscite that would replace the opposition-controlled Congress with a leftist-dominated "People's Assembly." This would enable the Popular Unity to legislate socialism within Allende's term in office.[9]

Even for the majority of leftist leaders who doubted the wisdom of risking a plebiscite in the near future, the April election victory represented a popular mandate for a major advance toward state control of the economy. Although the opposition majority in Congress was unlikely to approve any attack on the structure of private property in Chile, the Popular Unity seemed confident that the Chilean presidency—a six-year elective monarchy—possessed sufficient powers to gain control of the "commanding heights of the economy" by decree.

The Popular Unity coalition was a diverse blend of Marxists and populists, social democrats and Christian socialists, but even the most moderate among them viewed their April election victory as an opportunity for partisan advantage. With their April electoral majority, the Popular Unity could at last claim a popular mandate for its program of structural change. The "correlation of forces," argued leading leftists, might never be as favorable for initiating the transition toward socialism in the industrial sector. The opposition was divided and in disarray from successive defeats, and the armed forces were still in political shock from the Schneider assassination. In April 1971, Allende seemed a political magician, and his economic policies a salient success. In the eyes of leftist leaders, the Popular Unity was riding a tide of popularity that might well lead on to socialist fortune.[10]

There were fears as well as hopes that argued for a major revolutionary advance in the wake of the April elections. The aging politicians who led the Popular Unity parties were haunted by the Popular Front experience of the 1930s that had been their political school. Allende might believe that all the Popular Front lacked was a Marxist president and proletarian control, but there were growing fears within the Chilean Left that, if they were not careful, the Popular Unity might prove no more socialist than that earlier Center-Left coalition.

By April, such fears had penetrated even the Communist party leadership. Veteran Communists might affirm that, as president, Allende had "performed brilliantly," but even they recognized that he had done little to implement the Popular Unity's program of structural transformation since the nationalization of banks and mines at the start of 1971.[11] The governing coalition had agreed on this moderate pace, in part as an electoral strategy for April, in part out of an awareness of the fragility of their grasp on power. As an electoral strategy, it had been a signal success, but if it continued, the momentum of political victory might be dissipated before the structural transformation was initiated.

Younger Leftists also criticized Allende for being out of touch with "the realities of the people."[12] In their view, his vision was limited by the circle of old friends and aging politicians into which he had retreated and was shaped by a Popular Front experience that was anachronistic in 1971. To them, Allende even seemed unaware of the ferment within his own mass base, which had intensified with each leftist success. The Communist party, generally a moderate voice within the governing coalition, was acutely aware of the expectations and frustration of its working-class supporters and convinced that it might explode into "revolutionary spontaneity" if the Popular Unity did not channel this energy and satisfy these expectations. As one Communist leader who had played a central role in Allende's campaign put it: "The people have voted for something more than the renewal of diplomatic relations with Cuba, and they expect more from us."[13]

Many Popular Unity leaders were afraid that if these expectations were not satisfied, the enthusiasm for "socialism" might give way to an apathy that could be fatal to the hopes of the Left. Others feared that workers and peasants disillusioned with the Popular Unity might be ripe for mobilization by political competitors to the left, such as the Guevarist Revolutionary Left Movement (MIR)—a prospect that particularly worried Communist leaders.[14]

Communist fears were MIR hopes. Although they viewed the Popular Unity as a "reformist" government, the young leadership of the Revolutionary Left Movement increasingly regarded the opening that Allende had created as a unique opportunity for socialist revolution, one that might not come again for decades. The strategy of the MIR was to make up for its weak electoral strength through direct action from below, a strategy that had proved spectacularly successful in the rural areas of southern Chile during the preceding months. By early 1971, the MIR was organizing its Revolutionary Workers Front (FTR) in the mines and factories of Chile, pressing for "worker seizures of the means of production" as the best way to ensure their rapid socialization.[15]

This revolutionary vision of the MIR had strong support within the governing coalition itself, particularly among the left wing of the Socialist party, who saw such direct revolutionary action by the workers as a way of raising their consciousness and radicalizing the revolutionary process. By

April 1971, a revolutionary definition of *el proceso chileno* had become an obsession with the Left Socialists, whose domination of their party—the Popular Unity's largest—had been confirmed at the recent party congress. Allende might be "the best political operator in Chile"—but it was less clear to his party comrades that he was the man to lead a socialist revolution.[16] To such critics, Allende seemed more concerned "to assuage opposition fears and political passions" than to set out on the road to socialism.[17] For them the April elections represented a great divide, which would define the Popular Unity and the revolutionary process it led.

Political hopes and fears within the Chilean Left combined to persuade its leaders that the April election victory was an opportunity to be seized or perhaps lost forever. The Marxist political parties that dominated the governing coalition might differ in their ideological vision and political strategy, but they were agreed in April 1971 that the moment had come to take a giant step along the road to socialism.

The logical next step was the creation of a "social property area" under state control, which would serve as the nucleus of the future socialist economy. The banking and mining sectors were already largely government run. Industry, however, remained in private hands, and its nationalization would both deprive the Left's political enemies of their economic base and satisfy the aspirations of the Popular Unity's own central mass base, the industrial working class. The creation of such a "social property area," moreover, would advance the Popular Unity's long-term political strategy of winning an electoral majority for socialism by 1976, a strategy that depended for its success on the increasing unity of Chilean workers behind its leftist banner. The positive experience of socialism in their own workplace, along with the radicalizing experience of participating in a revolutionary transformation, was expected to bring large numbers of Christian Democratic and independent workers into the Popular Unity camp.

Popular Unity economic strategists such as Pedro Vuskovic, a political independent, shared this perspective, although for somewhat different reasons. In their view, the April elections created a political opportunity for economic advance that might not last long. Officials at Vuskovic's Ministry of Economy, which would be responsible for planning these structural changes and organizing the new public sector, were aware that the political Right was in disarray, but warned that the "economic Right" was still intact. Moreover, its leaders had assumed direction of the resistance to *la via chilena*, "and as they had been learning from the struggle, they began to make demands, to cry out, to sabotage, to use the courts, the Congress, and all of the weapons that they have to defend their interests."[18]

Although the private sector had reaped large profits from the "festival of consumption" generated by the Allende government's populist economic policies, little of this capital had been reinvested, even by the smaller businesses that the Popular Unity did not plan to nationalize. In several cases, production had declined in the face of increased demand. This reluctance of Chilean capitalists to invest on the road to socialism might seem natural, but Allende's economic team was convinced that their noncooperation was considered and coordinated, amounting to a deliberate campaign to "sabotage" the success of Allende's economic policy as a way of stopping the nationalization of their property and undermining the political stability of the government.[19]

There were other economic motives as well for a more rapid socialization of industry in Chile. In view of the drop in private investment, a swift state takeover of the major industries might be the best way to increase employment and production. Vuskovic's economic strategy, moreover, called for large-scale social spending in the interests of economic recovery and political popularity, expenditures that the profits of the social property area were supposed to finance.[20]

The rapid socialization of industry, therefore, was both an economic necessity and a political priority. Significantly, the Ministry of Economy report on the Yarur cotton mill, documenting charges of economic sabotage and justifying state intervention in the management of the textile company, was dated April 6, 1971—only two days after the municipal elections.[21] Within the Allende government, the powerful Economy Ministry was persuaded that the mandate secured at the polls should be translated into a revolutionary advance in the industrial arena.[22]

Although economic and electoral concerns loomed large in their reasoning, the Ministry of Economy experts were also more aware than other government officials of the ferment within the industrial working class—and more impressed by the surging revolution from below. The least politically experienced of Allende's senior cabinet appointments, they were more open to learning from the workers and to modifying their policies in that light. For months, they had been in regular contact with the local union leaders from the major industries, gathering information from them on any "sabotage of production" and monitoring the state of worker opinion and expectation. Textile workers, long among the most exploited in Chile, were now among the most expectant. In March, Deputy Minister Garretón had personally traveled to Quillota, outside Santiago, to persuade the workers of the Said rayon mill not to seize their factory. Garretón's plea for time "to prepare" for the socialization of the textile industry had won a reprieve from the workers, but they could not be held back much longer.[23]

The growing pressure for "socialism" at the Yarur mill was typical. To the leaders of the Yarur workers' movement, the implications of the April election returns were clear. "Until April we were consolidating the union, accumulating data, and talking—with the Ministry of Economy, with the parties, with the FENATEX [National Textile Union], with the CUT [United Workers Confederation]—and all of them asking us to wait . . . to have patience," recalled one Socialist union officer.[24] "But after the triumph of April," we thought: "Why wait any longer . . . the hour has come . . . to go forward. We have to take the factory away from Amador Yarur and do it now."

Among the worker leaders, moreover, there was a sense that their movement "was at a crossroads in which we had to advance further or risk losing our dynamism. In the first instance, it was us, the leaders, who pushed it within the rank and file, but afterwards it was all a process that we could not stop," stressed one of the most reflective of the *empleado* leaders.[25] Among the rank and file, the message of April was less explicit, but its direction was equally evident. "We were all waiting for something to happen," one young weaver, a political independent, recalled. "We had arrived at a point where we had to go forward, or else El Chico might defeat us as usual . . . and then the municipal elections came and what with everyone waiting for something to happen . . . it was like a signal."[26]

If the April elections were a signal, it was one that the leaders of the workers' movement were predisposed to see. "Already in March we had begun to talk about the requisition with the Ministry of Economy," confided Jorge Lorca, "and we thought that the issue was already decided because the nationalization of monopolies figured within the plans of the Popular Unity government." For Lorca, "by the time the municipal elections arrived, the thing was ready. This victory was a green light to go forward."[27]

In early 1971, the Allende government was not ready—either politically or administratively—for "the expropriation of the national bourgeoisie" and the creation of a social property area. The Ministry of Economy, however, was too conscious of economic, social, and political realities within the industrial sector to retain its original six-year timetable. Although the socialization of the textile industry had yet to secure the approval of President Allende or his governing coalition, ministry experts speeded up their preparations for this decisive step. The electoral success of the Popular Unity may have accelerated the revolutionary process in Chile's factories, but these local revolutionary situations, in turn, had begun to force a radicalization of the Chilean revolution nationally.

It was a paradoxical outcome. In order to prevent the revolutionary process that they led from escaping their control, the moderates who dominated the Allende government and the Popular Unity coalition would be forced to radicalize their revolution from above. Although some government and party leaders favored an acceleration of the revolutionary process and others were reluctantly convinced of its necessity, almost all were swept along by the force of this revolution from below and constrained to deal with its consequences—earlier than they had anticipated and before they were ready. In a reversal of conventional wisdom, revolution from below had become a catalyst for revolution from above.

Although the struggle at the Yarur mill reflected a long local history and the conjuncture of specific circumstances, it was emblematic of a more general revolution from below. Yarur was the initial battleground in the undeclared civil war between capital and labor. The fact of being first lent to the contest at the Yarur mill a special significance and drama, one heightened by the factory's long history of repression and resistance. In the process, Yarur came to symbolize both the demise of the old regime and the new socialist order struggling to be born.

11

WHY YARUR?

At first glance, the Yarur mill was a surprising choice for so crucial a revolutionary battleground. The workers' movement at the mill was young and inexperienced, without strong party affiliations or organizational infrastructure. In April 1971, the workers of the Yarur mill had only just recaptured their union from company control, negotiated their first contract through authentic collective bargaining, and begun to discuss politics without fear. In beginning with Yarur, Inc., moreover, the Popular Unity was taking on a family with extensive economic resources and powerful political connections.

The importance of the Yarur mill and its owners, however, could also be viewed as arguments for its selection as the symbolic first "monopoly" to be requisitioned and incorporated into the social property area. The strategic role of the Yarur factory within an industry producing goods of prime necessity took on added significance in the light of the policies pursued by its management during the months following Allende's election. Local suppliers and creditors had not been paid, imported spare parts and raw materials had not been replaced, and both production and product stocks had declined. The Yarur mill seemed to be one of the clearest cases of the economic "sabotage" that the Left was accusing Chile's capitalists of engaging in to the detriment of the Popular Unity program and the Chilean national interest.[1]

Yarur, Inc. was also one of the enterprises whose questionable practices in the pursuit of profit—from phantom distributors and dummy corporations to tax evasion and currency violations—was most extensively documented. The mounting pile of copies of internal company documents obtained with the aid of the workers' movement gave the Allende government a strong legal case against the Yarurs, buttressed further by the discovery of allegedly fraudulent practices at the Yarur Banco de Crédito e Inversiones, some of them involving S.A. Yarur.[2]

On the Chilean road to socialism, such legal considerations were important because they made Yarur a good test case for the use of the government's emergency decree powers to requisition the industries slated for incorporation into the social property area. The legal basis for this rarely invoked authority was a decree placed on the books by the brief Socialist Republic of 1932, empowering the executive to intervene in the management of a private industry if the production of basic necessities was threatened by its financial situation or business practices. Originally intended to keep factories from closing during the Great Depression, this 1932 decree had been resurrected in 1971 to serve new political purposes. The first legal test of so sweeping a use of this old decree would be a crucial one, and the Allende government wanted to select its best possible case.[3]

The Yarur mill would not be the first industry requisitioned and socialized by the Popular Unity government. The coal and steel industries had preceded it into the social property area, as had Teófilo Yarur's Bellavista Tomé woolen mill and Ralston Purina's Chilean subsidiary. But as Deputy Minister Garretón stressed, these had all been special cases.

> The steel industry had already been nationalized, but had then been returned to the private sector. Coal was a losing business that was already financed by the state. Ralston Purina was beset by a serious labor conflict and besides was a Yankee enterprise, not a domestic enterprise. In the case of Bellavista Tomé, the industry had been paralyzed and abandoned by its owners . . . no one defended Bellavista when we requisitioned it. In the case of Yarur it wasn't like that. Here it was clear. [4]

What was "clear" was that the socialization of Yarur, Inc. involved other issues and principles, which made it a new departure of great significance, as Allende's Deputy Minister of Economy was well aware.[5]

> Yarur was the first time that the government didn't nationalize an enterprise because it was inefficient or because it had committed some offense or for being a foreign enterprise, but did it for the simple fact that it was a monopoly and that the government was disposed to act with extreme severity against monopolies . . . and because in addition it had produced consumer shortages that permitted its requisition.

If the Allende government was seeking a "monopoly" to expropriate, Yarur was a classic case. The rapid nationalization of the family's flagship factory, together with the recent government takeover of the Yarur banks and woolen mills, would undermine the economic power of one of Chile's major capitalist "clans."[6] The socialization of the Yarur mill, therefore, was both a symbolic and efficient way of beginning the decisive phase of the

Popular Unity's campaign "to gain control of the commanding heights of the economy."

The Yarurs, moreover, were widely perceived in Chile as using their overweening economic power ruthlessly to advance their own interests. During the preceding decades, the Yarur mill had become a watchword for economic exploitation and industrial oppression in Chile, one that the exponents of a "progressive capitalism" were hard put to defend.

Businessmen as well as workers felt victimized by the Yarurs. A trail of entrepreneurial resentment from lesser figures whom the Yarurs had used or crushed during their climb to wealth remained in the wake of their economic success. The meteoric rise of the Yarurs was also resented by sectors of the traditional Chilean upper class, both for the methods the Yarurs had employed and for their unwanted intrusion into the upper reaches of Chilean society.

Government officials even believed that a significant sector of the Chilean upper class would not be unhappy to see "the Turks" get their comeuppance. "The textile sector was racially closed," stressed Garretón, "and . . . the Chilean bourgeoisie has its racist elements as well. I even remember talking here with important Chilean rightists who affirmed that they would never go to battle for the *turco* textile entrepreneurs . . . Besides, they were not affiliated with the big Chilean entrepreneurial organizations such as the SOFOFA (National Association of Manufacturers)."[7] Given this prejudice against the Yarurs on the part of other Chilean elites, the socialization of the Yarur mill might well divide the national bourgeoisie and elicit a weaker response in defense of private property than a similar step elsewhere in the industrial sector.

There was an element of racism as well in popular resentment of the *turco* millionaires, which the Popular Unity was not averse to utilizing against them. Leftist media caricaturized the Yarurs as Oriental potentates forcing Chilean workers to do their bidding, running their factory like the feudal domain of an Arab sheik, complete with harems of women workers. Moreover, neither Juan Yarur nor his youngest sons had ever become Chilean citizens and the Chase Manhattan Trust Company Ltd. (Bahamas) was the largest shareholder in S.A. Yarur. The government believed that an attack on the Yarurs would enjoy more popular support than state intervention in enterprises with Chilean owners. The choice of Yarur would also focus attention on a case that underscored the Left's charges of the "antinational" character of the country's "dependent capitalism," with its ties to "Yankee imperialism," reliance on foreign technology, and illegal profit remittances. The Popular Unity could clothe a step toward socialism in the colors of Chilean nationalism.[8]

A complex of political reasons reinforced this Popular Unity selection of

Yarur, Inc., as the first "monopoly" to be requisitioned by the Allende government. One was the multifaceted involvement of the Yarurs in opposition politics. The Yarurs had long financed a host of right-wing politicians. They were also close to ex-President Frei and the conservative wing of the Christian Democratic party, to which they wanted to transfer Radio Balmaceda, the Yarur station. Yarur influence in the Chilean media remained strong, the result of years of well-placed advertising, and their privileged access to the Chilean Congress reflected an equally shrewd pattern of campaign contributions. In addition, there was reported Yarur involvement in the rightist plots that followed Allende's election and rumored Yarur financial support for the fledgling neo-Fascist movement, Patria y Libertad (Fatherland and Liberty).[9] The Yarurs had used their political influence ruthlessly to advance their economic interests and to damage those of their workers. In political as well as economic terms, the Yarurs symbolized the overweening concentration of power and dominance of Chile by special interests that the Popular Unity had promised to destroy.

The character and evolution of the workers' movement at the Yarur mill offered complementary political arguments in favor of its choice as the first "monopoly" to be incorporated into the social property area. The unity and authenticity of the worker leadership and the representation of three major Popular Unity parties in its ranks made Yarur a perfect socialist symbol within the governing coalition. "Clearly the *compañeros* became enthusiastic, because a strategic textile enterprise in which there were ten union leaders, all of the Left and all willing to help, was extraordinary and a great assistance," one of these union officers recalled.[10]

The Yarur leaders, moreover, were united in a common cause rather than divided by the differences between white- and blue-collar workers that had undermined working-class unity elsewhere. This was all the more impressive in view of the diverse party affiliations of the Yarur leadership, which was also conspicuously free of the sectarian politics that too often plagued the Popular Unity and the Chilean labor movement. Although the explanation of this worker unity was rooted in the recent emergence of the Yarur movement, its initially nonpartisan character, and continuing struggle against a powerful and intransigent *patrón*, the result was a local labor movement that projected an ideal image of working-class solidarity in support of the revolutionary process.

Within this context of unity, moreover, the Yarur workers' movement offered three major Popular Unity parties a prominent role and a promising political base. Although the initial clandestine movement at the mill had been nonpartisan in character, an intensely competitive recruitment drive meant that, by April 1971, the Communists, Socialists, and MAPU were all represented within its leadership and had begun to win support among the rank and file. The Yarur mill was thus a showcase both for the Popular Unity and its central political parties.[11] Few textile factories could satisfy these conditions.

The Communists had played little part in the early workers' movement, but the Yarur mill was the first choice of its party and labor leaders. In part, this reflected the party's long association with worker struggles at the mill. The socialization of the Yarur mill by the democratically elected Popular Unity government would aptly symbolize the peaceful triumph of the workers that the Communists had prophesied and championed. At the same time, it would represent the personal triumph of the Communist party over one of its most bitter enemies. In addition, the Communist cell at Yarur was the largest and most advanced within the textile industry. Four of the five blue-collar union officers were Communists by April 1971, and three of them were among the most popular leaders of the workers' movement. Equally important was the rare lack of anticommunism within the *empleado* leadership, one of whose key officers was a trusted militant.[12]

The position of the Communists within the workers' movement, moreover, was enhanced by the presence of Pepé Muñoz—the leader of the 1962 Yarur strike—as labor secretary of the district party committee. Muñoz's influence had been crucial in recruiting Jorge Lorca and Héctor Mora, two of the most important *obrero* leaders, to the party standard; and he could be relied on to advise, monitor and shape the Yarur movement in the future —along with Oscar Ibáñez, another former Yarur labor leader, who had counseled the 1953 and 1962 movements at the mill and was now strategically situated as the CUT officer in charge of labor conflicts. Shortly after the municipal elections, the Communist party instructed its local leaders to prepare for the socialization of the Yarur mill.[13]

The MAPU (United Popular Action Movement), the youngest and smallest of the three coalition partners, enjoyed an expanding support among the employees and the dedicated allegiance of the most able and charismatic white-collar leader, the red-bearded union secretary, Ricardo Catalan. Moreover, the involvement of Guillermo Garreton, the MAPU deputy minister of economy, as the high government official in closest contact with the Yarur leaders, ensured the MAPU an influence that transcended party lines and its limited support within the mill. For the MAPU, a fledgling party with proletarian pretensions but a largely peasant and middle-class base, Yarur offered an opportunity to alter its image and expand its working-class constituency.[14]

The Yarur mill was equally attractive political terrain for the Socialist party, which enjoyed a rough parity of representation within the union leadership. Omar Guzmán, the popular president of the employees' union, was a Socialist, as was Raúl Oliva, the blue-collar movement's mastermind and dominating personality. In addition, the Socialists could count on the loyalty of several dynamic blue-collar workers who had played central roles in the clandestine movement and were likely to win leadership positions in the socialized factory. From the outset, moreover, the Yarur workers' movement had been advised by Socialist labor leaders and assisted by Socialist student groups. The central Socialist role in the underground struggle against the Yarurs had created a fund of goodwill and a base for organization. To the Socialists, the Yarur movement "was [their] baby," and they were prepared both to promote and profit from it.[15]

There were ideological reasons as well for the enthusiasm with which the Socialists, along with the MIR, regarded the Yarur workers' movement. It was a movement whose authenticity was beyond doubt and whose politics were not yet ritualized. It was directed by the natural leaders who had emerged from the ranks, not by labor politicians imposed from above. The Yarur leaders—*"even* the Communists," admitted one anti-Communist Socialist[16]—were young and dynamic, nonsectarian and responsive to their mass base. Both the leaders and the rank and file, moreover, had been radicalized by their initial experience of the Chilean road to socialism, making the Yarur movement emblematic of the revolutionary potential of the Chilean working class.

Lastly, party and government leaders close to the Yarur situation were well aware that the dynamic of revolution in the factory left the Popular Unity little choice but to make a virtue of necessity. If the Popular Unity would not select the mill for socialism, the Yarur workers were likely to take matters into their own hands and choose it for themselves.

IV

THE WORKERS
LIBERATE
THEIR FACTORY

12

SETTING
THE STAGE

By the April elections, the leaders of the workers' movement at the Yarur mill were ready for the socialization of their factory. They had themselves laid the legal groundwork for its requisition. At great personal risk, they had assembled compromising documents attesting to the "sabotage of production" so that "the government should be able to act with ease."[1] Aware that the requisition of Yarur, Inc., would be a test of the Popular Unity's strategy of socialization by decree, the Yarur leaders had gone out of their way to give the government the strongest possible case. "The procedure in our case was requisition . . . and we gradually proved all the things that we had claimed and prepared a file that is the most complete of its kind," affirmed one influential white-collar leader.[2] "So we thought that we were handing them the weapons with which to socialize this enterprise," Jorge Lorca stressed.[3] In return for these efforts, the Yarur leaders expected the government to act quickly, and they were unlikely to be patient with further delays.

The situation within the factory, moreover, had reached a point where a decisive confrontation between the workers and the Yarurs seemed imminent. The union leaders were increasingly ignored and their authority challenged; the decline in production and stocks was deepening. The military preparations of the Yarur strong-arm squad against a seizure of the factory intensified. What made these management measures more ominous to the Left was the altered attitude of Yarur loyalists among the workers, who had seemed vanquished once and for all in the December elections. "As time passed, the *apatronados* recovered their cool," Lorca explained with a laugh, adding that by April they "were once again beating their own drum."[4]

At the same time, the rumor spread through the mill that Amador

Yarur, in an effort to defuse the movement and reassert his authority, "was planning to dismiss two hundred *compañeros* at one go, arguing that there was an excess of personnel."[5] The truth of this rumor—and Yarur's personnel chief denied it[6]—mattered less than that it was widely believed. The Yarurs had a history of ruthless response to labor unrest, and it was natural for the workers to believe that "El Chico" would attempt some preemptive strike against them.

These reports and rumors strengthened the hand of those within the workers' movement who argued for the acceleration of plans to seize the mill. "We had them cornered, but after a while those scabs began all over again, so we had to give them another blow," was the way one Socialist leader put it.[7] In this social war, the first blow might well prove the decisive one. By appearing to prepare an attack, Amador Yarur gave leftist leaders a weapon with which to unite the workers behind an offensive strategy. By mid-April, the tensions at the Yarur cotton mill had reached a boiling point.

The Ministry of Economy, however, was not ready to move. They had amassed sufficient production data at Yarur to be convinced that its owners were engaged in a conscious campaign of economic sabotage that would soon lead to shortages of consumer goods and industrial yarns. The requisition of an enterprise as important as Yarur, Inc., however, was as much a political as an economic decision, and the governing coalition had yet to pronounce itself on the subject. Waiting for a political decision, the Ministry of Economy vacillated between the workers' desire for immediate action and its own fear of complications and consequences.[8]

For the Yarur leaders, it was an experience in frustration—and disillusionment with revolution from above. "We had meetings with those officials of the Ministry of Economy all the time . . . meetings in the morning, meetings in the afternoon," recalled a disgusted Raúl Oliva, "but there was no agreement . . . instead we encountered tremendous bureaucratic obstacles: that there was no agreement over this and that . . . that it wasn't convenient to seize it at this moment, that we are fearful . . . all these obstacles, with us demanding that we go forward in spite of everything and them saying that we can't go forward, that the position of the government wasn't decided." To Raúl Oliva, these interminable meetings and the bureaucratic waffling reflected "a lack of experience in exercising power . . . as the class had never been in power, it didn't know how to wield it well at the higher levels . . . so we were confronted by this indecision and bureaucracy."[9]

In the end, they all agreed that the Marxist parties should be brought into their plans, but in a way that circumvented the official decision-making processes within the governing coalition. It was feared that the social democratic parties within the Popular Unity—the Radicals, the Social Democrats, and the A.P.I. (Independent Popular Action)—would oppose the Yarur requisition, and that Allende himself might object to their timing and tactics. As a consequence, the political decision to socialize Yarur, Inc., was handled informally by the three Marxist parties—the Communists, the Socialists, and the MAPU—in concert with a powerful ministry, but at the margins of the rest of the governing coalition and cabinet. The formal authority of Allende and the Popular Unity was circumvented, and the Chilean president and his coalition government presented with a fait accompli for them to ratify.

A week after the April elections, the Yarur leaders were summoned to the Ministry of Economy for a meeting that for the first time included "high-level party *compañeros*," including "Compañero 'Chino' Díaz, the deputy secretary general of the Communist party," and members of the Socialist and MAPU central committees. "We had to tell the whole story all over again," Jorge Lorca recalled, "showing them all the data that we had collected and explaining to the *compañeros* the dramatic situation that we were living in the factory."[10] Then the ministry officials presented their evidence of economic sabotage. The party leaders listened carefully and asked searching questions, but did not commit themselves. Only later, Deputy Minister Garretón informed the Yarur workers that they had been "given the green light" to go ahead with their preparations although not with the requisition itself. However ambiguously it may have been intended, this "green light" was all that the workers needed to force the issue or that the Economy Ministry required to press forward with their plans.

Within the ministry, a special task force was created to direct the Yarur socialization. It was headed by Garretón, but included Socialists and Communists, "all of whom were enthusiastic" about the projected requisition of Yarur, Inc., and committed to carrying it through in the face of anticipated objections from other sectors of the government and the coalition.[11] The autonomy granted the Ministry of Economy by Popular Unity politicians with little understanding of economics would make possible an economic initiative with far-reaching political consequences. By the time other government officials and political leaders became aware of what was afoot and tried to put a stop to the roller coaster for requisition at the Yarur mill, it would be too late.

The daily meetings with Yarur leaders at the Economy Ministry turned into strategy sessions, with discussions of contingency plans and tactics whose offensive thrust was rapidly reflected in political action within the mill. From the start, the relationship between the two levels of the revolutionary process had been a reciprocal one; during the denouement at the Yarur mill, it was to be mutually reinforcing as well. Pressure from below had enabled government officials favoring a revolutionary advance at Yarur to argue for its necessity. Now the approval from above of their local initiative enabled the

Yarur leaders to overcome hesitations and ready the workers for the final act
in their revolutionary drama—the seizure of their factory and expulsion of
their *patrón*.

The movement leaders may have known of the plan to socialize the
factory, but most Yarur workers did not. They needed time to prepare their
workers for an action that represented so large a leap into the revolutionary
unknown. "When we had everything ready," recalled Armando Carrera,[12]
"we began to work hard among the rank and file, arguing that we had to
take away the factory because now we had the complete support of the
government." And on saying "we have the support of the government," the
people began to feel more secure. It reassured workers who shared their
leaders' goal but feared that they themselves were not powerful enough to
prevail over the *patrón*. But it did not persuade those who thought that so
drastic a step was neither legitimate nor necessary.

These workers found an advocate in Alvaro Bulnes, the least political of
the white-collar leaders. Bulnes had been an officer of the employees' union
from the start of its struggle with Amador Yarur, but he "began to exhibit
cold feet" as the prospect of a confrontation approached.[13] Although Bulnes
had fought the union's early battles and "participated in the initial conversations at the Ministry of Economy," after the April elections "we began to
view him with suspicion" because "the *compañero* always went around trying
to hold things back, saying that we should instead talk things over with
Amador Yarur, that we had to enter into a dialogue with him so that things
could be normalized," explained the blue-collar union president.[14]

As the momentum grew for actions that would utterly transform that
"normality," so did Bulnes's reservations, and the other union officers began
"to leave him on the sidelines." They were not certain that Bulnes had sold
out to Amador Yarur—although several suspected as much—but they were
persuaded that he could not be trusted. "The *compañero* had a very developed
sense of opportunism. He was very shifty—*muy chamullero*, as we say here
in Chile."[15] Bulnes might maintain that his position was an honest one and
reflected the feeling of many Yarur employees, but the other union officers
were taking no chances. The Yarurs had too long a history of destroying
worker movements by buying the loyalty of their leaders.

Placing Bulnes on the sidelines might protect their plans against premature disclosure to Amador Yarur and eliminate from their councils a voice
arguing against confrontation, but it did not solve the problem that Bulnes
represented. His claim to speak for a "silent majority" of Yarur workers in
opposing socialization of the factory might be exaggerated, but his hesitations
and doubts reflected the views of many at the mill, as the movement leaders
themselves were well aware: "Because the Old-timers told us—'Bueno, you
have already won the union. Why do you want more? The *patrón* has always

been the *patrón*. Why are you going to throw him out now?'"[16] In the face of such rank-and-file resistance, the movement leaders began an intensive educational effort aimed at convincing their followers that the socialization of the factory was possible, necessary, and legitimate. "We began to struggle more consciously and linked up more directly to the political parties," recalled a Socialist leader. "By making them see the nature of the question . . . we began to win the people here."[17]

Consciousness-raising, however, is a slow process and time was of the essence. The leaders needed a strategy that would require a radical break, one certain to provoke a confrontation that the workers would regard as legitimate and that would justify the requisition of the mill. "We had to have a work stoppage to get state intervention," one *obrero* activist explained.[18] "The government could intervene once there was a halt to production." The result was a strategy of confronting Amador Yarur with a list of impossible demands that the workers would regard as reasonable, but that the Yarurs would never accept. Management intransigence would provide the pretext for the decisive confrontation.

They were obvious demands for the movement leaders, reflecting problems that had been festering without resolution for months. "None of them had anything to do with economic questions," Lorca stressed. "They were purely political measures . . . such as the creation of Production Watchdog Committees (Comités de Vigilancia de la Producción) and the transfer of Daniel 'The Vest' Rojas and other members of the Yarur strong-arm squad because they were really bothering people. We also insisted on respect for the union officers and the setting of dates for meetings with Amador Yarur," and "for company recognition of the union delegates in each work section because they weren't being taken seriously and were being persecuted, questions like that . . ."[19]

Declining production and employment, harassment by Yarur loyalists and management interference with their elected representatives were resonant issues that prompted many workers to respond: "When is Yarur going to approve these just petitions?"[20] There were similar worker reactions to union demands that "Yarur return to their old posts the supervisors whom he had persecuted and demoted . . . such as the five *compañeros* who had been caught campaigning for Allende" and remove his loyalists from these posts.[21] In addition, the union leaders included in their list of demands old worker goals, such as the easing of work norms, which were likely to attract the less political to their cause.[22]

On April 14, the union officers presented these demands orally to Amador Yarur, "who didn't want to respond immediately"[23] and so asked for a few days "in which to study" their proposals. They agreed to give him six days' grace, "but on that occasion we went to receive his reply together with all the union delegates," recounted Lorca.[24] Once again Yarur put them off "because according to him he had too much work," but this time the workers refused to accept his excuses. Instead, the directors of both unions put their demands in writing. On Wednesday, April 21, they presented a formal ten-point petition to Amador Yarur, which incorporated the specific demands made orally the week before, but included as well some more general worker concerns, such as the illegality of worker contracts that did not specify the position for which they were hired.[25] There was little new in the petition; What was unprecedented for Yarur, Inc., was the embodiment of these grievances in a formal ultimatum and its joint presentation by blue- and white-collar unions.

Under the Chilean Labor Code, the rejection of such a "petition" could serve as a legal justification for a strike—unless the government ruled otherwise. Significantly, it was prefaced by a statement relating the workers' local grievances to the national concerns of the Allende government. "This note," it began, "contains the succinct exposition of a series of problems that affect us, some of which directly influence our output, which we would like to be as high as possible, according to the plans for the increase in production of the Workers' Government."[26] In fact, only one of the worker demands was related to increasing production, whereas several other demands, such as the relaxation of work norms, were likely to have the opposite effect. "We raised questions of *control*, not economic issues," stressed one of the most lucid worker leaders.[27] The political preamble emphasized and the list of demands underscored that this was not a typical grievance petition.

"That very day all the union officers signed the document and demanded a reply in writing on Friday the twenty-third, by five o'clock in the afternoon," Ricardo Catalan recalled.[28] Amador Yarur agreed to respond by Friday, but there was little doubt what his reply would be. "We were asking Yarur for *impossible* things," one Socialist leader stressed, "things that he could never accept."[29] At the same time, the formal petition represented the throwing down of the gauntlet. Amador Yarur was well aware that the movement leaders were talking strike to the rank and file and that his denial of their demands might well trigger the requisition that he hoped to avoid. Before rejecting their ultimatum, Yarur did his best to shore up his defenses, preparing his supporters for the coming confrontation and employing his political influence within the Popular Unity government to avert the threat of a worker seizure of his factory.[30]

Amador Yarur did not cut a particularly elegant public figure. But he knew how to play the Chilean political game and had prepared the ground for his effort to defuse the workers' movement—from above. Amador Yarur was an old acquaintance of Salvador Allende. To the disgust of his brother Jorge, Amador had even contributed —a modest sum—to Allende's campaign chest in the belief that this timely donation might yet avert the socialization of his cotton mill. These personal and financial connections allowed him to hope in April 1971 that a deal could still be worked out with the Popular Unity government that would leave him in control of his factory. Later he would claim that Allende had promised him that the factory would not be requisitioned so soon and that it would be transformed into "a mixed enterprise," combining public and private ownership, rather than into a state enterprise.[31]

Now, with two days in which to respond to the worker ultimatum, Amador Yarur took his case to "Pepé" Toha, the Socialist minister of interior and Allende's closest confidant within the cabinet. There he recalled these promises, "advancing a series of considerations that confused the *compañeros* of that ministry," lamented one worker leader.[32] The Interior Ministry was not only the most important cabinet office politically but also the one with the greatest concern for *la vía chilena*'s image of order. Amador Yarur went away from his meeting with a promise that the union leaders would be called into the ministry the following day and asked to postpone any action until a decision had been taken by President Allende and the governing coalition. If there were to be a change in the factory's status, it would come from above and in a controlled fashion, not via a revolution from below. With this assurance, Amador Yarur could stonewall the workers with the flat rejection of their ultimatum. If all went well, they would be humiliated and discredited, along with their strategy of confrontation and goal of socialism. Amador Yarur might not know it at the time, but he had shot the truest arrow in his political quiver. No other would come so near to the Popular Unity mark nor so close to saving his textile mill from socialization.[33]

But the union officers had also been active politically, taking their case to the government and party leaders. "When Yarur refused to accept our demands" on Wednesday, April 21, "we went to the Ministry of Economy and there talked" with Vuskovic, Garretón, and Jaime Riesco" [a leading Communist official], Lorca related. "We told them that we had presented the petition to Yarur and that the union delegates had been very firm: We gave him one more delay [until Friday the twenty-third] and [we told him that] if he didn't respond in satisfactory form, then we were going to stop work because this is the one weapon that we, the workers, have."[34] The ministry officials heard the workers out and raised no objections.

The worker leaders left the Ministry of Economy convinced that their plan enjoyed both governmental and party support. As Jorge Lorca later affirmed: "Afterwards, they [Vuskovic, Garretón, and Riesco] surely talked of this at the level of the government and the Popular Unity, so that both were already informed. They are the same thing, the government and the Popular Unity, but at this point they divided—government functionaries and the party functionaries of the Popular Unity," he added.[35] It was a difficult duality for the Yarur workers to grasp, but they were confident that they had covered all their political bases. The movement leaders had met with party leaders in early April and received their tacit approval, In addition, each of the union officers—who between them represented the major Popular Unity parties—had been in contact with his own party hierarchy.

The dominant left wing of the Socialist Party fully supported the workers' argument that "if it was the government that determined when the industry was going to pass into the power of the workers, the workers were going to lose their 'spirit of struggle' because that was handing the revolution on a platter to *compañeros* who had done nothing for it." Socialist leaders even confided to their most trusted worker cadres that they would prefer to see Yarur fall from below, because "if the government comes and says, 'OK, from this day forth there won't be any Yarur here,' the people would merely interpret it as a change of bosses. If, on the other hand, we seized the enterprise ourselves and it was the workers who demanded that Yarur should never return, that is very different because then we would feel like participants in this revolutionary process."[36]

In the eyes of local Socialist leaders, the MAPU had also "committed itself completely" to the factory's seizure, but the role of the Communist party had been more equivocal: "because until the end the Communist party was never willing to say: 'We will do it; let's do it already,' but rather 'we have to think about it; first we have to study it; first we have to see about the consequences.'"[37] As Raúl Oliva was well aware, the workers' strategy of "we seize the factory and then we hand it over to the government" was the opposite of the Popular Unity strategy "that the government is going to determine when the industry passes into the power of the workers" and "that influenced Allende and a lot of Communists as well."[38]

This Communist reticence was deceptive. In its deliberate and bureaucratic style, the "party of Recabarren and Lenin" was moving toward a decision to support the requisition of the mill. Throughout the month of April, Jorge Lorca was in constant contact with his party, both through labor leaders at the FENATEX (National Federation of Textile Workers) and the CUT (United Workers Confederation) and more directly through Pepé Muñoz and José Cademártori, a leading Communist congressman and economist. Deputy Party Chief Victor Díaz's "green light" at the meeting in the Ministry of Economy had been crucial for the decision to proceed with the preparations for the nationalization of Yarur, Inc., and the Communist party's support for the requisition of the textile mill was equally crucial now.[39]

On Friday, April 23, the day on which Amador Yarur had promised to reply to the worker ultimatum, the Communists broke their silence: A powerful article published in *Puro Chile*, the popular tabloid that often voiced Communist views that were not yet for official attribution, stressed worker complaints that the Yarurs were "boycotting production" and "sabotaging machinery" and highlighted reports of threats made by the Yarur strong-arm squads. It went on to support the worker petition, calling particular attention to the demand for the reinstatement of the five (Communist) supervisors removed from their posts because they had campaigned for Allende. Between the lines could be read a telltale characterization of Amador Yarur as an unreconstructed *momio* (mummy), a reactionary capitalist unwilling to accept "the changes" for which the Chilean people had voted, an obstacle to both the reasonable aspirations of his workers and the democratic road to socialism.

The importance of this political gesture became clear to the union leaders during the course of the day. Early that Friday morning, they received a summons to the presidential palace. "They came here to look for us in an ultrafast microbus, followed by a car to take us to the presidential palace," recalled Raúl Oliva,[40] "because Allende was extremely worried. He had had vague news . . . that we were planning to seize the enterprise and with that to create problems for his government." To the union officers, the hand of Amador Yarur was evident in this presidential summons: "Yarur knew," one movement leader insisted.[41] "He knew that Sunday we were going to seize the enterprise. It was already communicated. That was why they sent a car for us to go speak with "El Chicho" [Allende]."

In the end, Allende was "too busy" to meet with them. Instead, they were received in the Ministry of the Interior by Daniel Vergara, the Communist deputy minister who "looked like Dracula" and had a reputation for bureaucratic toughness, and Haroldo Martínez, Allende's labor aide and an old Socialist comrade. "They wanted to know from us if we really had a work stoppage in mind because the thing transcended the factory gates," one Socialist officer recalled.[42] "We told them no . . . but there was no doubt that we were thinking about it because here again we had to put pressure on the government. The workers had to demand it because the conditions were ripe. Later would not do." So "we told them that there was a meeting on Sunday and that there . . . the *compañeros* would decide."[43]

Such sophistry and protestations of innocence were unlikely to convince such hard-nosed politicians as Vergara and Martínez. Vergara warned the union officers that "the government would not permit the workers to seize the enterprise because of the problem this would create."[44] The lines of conflict between revolution from above and below were clearly drawn. Speaking for Allende, whose concern he stressed, Martínez then "asked us to stop this thing and to play along with Yarur until next Tuesday."[45] The union leaders had won over the workers, but Amador Yarur had triumphed where they least expected him to prevail—within the Workers' Government.

This was a governmental veto that took the worker leaders by surprise, a presidential request that they were neither able nor willing to honor: "We had already done our work in the mass base, and now the people would not permit us to wait until Tuesday because the process was already in motion . . . and could not be stopped."[46] To the union officers, it was a bewildering betrayal, an unanticipated stab in the back. They had gone out of their way to secure the approval of the Popular Unity parties and the government. Now, despite the promises they had received, here were two top officials, a Communist and a Socialist—one speaking for the government, the other in the name of *el compañero presidente*—both telling them to call off their plans, await orders from above, and allow Amador Yarur to humiliate them.

Their autonomy of action was denied, and their local concerns subordinated to the dictates of national politics, with the workers' movement and its leaders sacrificed on the altar of political expediency. "I don't know what in the devil had happened," exploded one blue-collar leader at the memory of that disturbing meeting, "but it seems there was a great conspiracy to distort the facts."[47] Raúl Oliva's angry response to the meeting with Martínez and Vergara was shared by the other union officers, making their meek acceptance of the presidential command unlikely. "We were all ready to press forward with it and at the last minute it seemed as if Amador Yarur still continued to have the power to say to the government—'wait until Tuesday'—something that as union leaders we could not accept . . . Because we were already far along with the thing and could not stop it. It was impossible, it would have meant the liquidation of the entire process of [revolutionary] advance."[48]

Angry and confused, the Yarur leaders took their case across the square to the Ministry of Economy, where they met with a very different reception. Garretón was both sympathetic and supportive. He was aware of the position taken by the Interior Ministry, which he ascribed to a combination of misinformation and bureaucratic politics. Interior had heard that a labor dispute at Yarur, a strategic factory, was about to explode with political ramifications, and their bureaucratic reaction was to stop it before it "threatened law and order." Although Garretón insisted that Vergara and Martínez were good leftists, he confessed "that is what happens to *compañeros* when they get into such posts."[49]

To the Yarur leaders, Garretón's analysis of bureaucratic politics was less important than his declaration of support. After explaining the growing resistance to their revolution from below within the Popular Unity government, Garretón took off his bureaucratic hat and put on the red cap of revolution, promising to put his political career on the line for them.[50]

> Garretón told us: "Bueno, I have been with you since January . . . I am a member of a Popular Unity party. This [socialization] is set forth in the government's program. Perhaps we have been a bit premature, but conditions have forced us to be premature. And I will resign my post if this [promise] is not fulfilled."

It was not just a matter of revolutionary credibility but also a question of whether the Chilean revolutionary process was *of* and *by* the workers or merely *for* the workers.

Garretón had cast his lot with the workers. It remained to be seen whether the powerful economy minister, Pedro Vuskovic, a political independent with broad support, would be willing to stand with them as well. While they were talking with Garretón, Vuskovic arrived. "Fortunately, Vuskovic was of the same opinion as Garretón," one union leader recalled with relief.[51] "He said to [Garretón], we have acted here as a duo, and so let's go forward together. I will also threaten to resign." More than one worker leader confessed to being "moved" by this demonstration of "revolutionary solidarity."[52] On leaving, they told "Compañero Garretón to tell Compañero Allende that the union directors were going to consult with their rank and file, but that they believed that it was not going to be possible [to wait any longer]."[53] The die was cast, and both the Allende government and the Popular Unity seemed rent in two. Government, coalition, and parties all appeared to be divided against themselves, with the presidency and the Ministry of Economy on opposite sides.

The splits within the Popular Unity over the Yarur question became clearer to the worker leaders during the course of the day. Suddenly, the Socialist union officers, Raúl Oliva and Omar Guzmán, received an invitation to lunch with José Toha, a leading Socialist, an Allende confidant, and the minister of interior. Toha was the man who had promised Amador Yarur that the workers would be controlled and whose subordinates had ordered the Yarur workers to halt their revolutionary process only hours before. His unexpected luncheon invitation was but one more surprise in a day filled with surprises.

"We went to talk with him" recalled Raúl Oliva, "and us thinking that naturally we have to convince him, because the government had told us that we could not take the factory and we already had all the people prepared to seize the enterprise that Sunday, and he was the guy just below Allende." "But then, that guy told us: 'Bueno, the position of the party was not exactly the same as the position of the government.' Imagine that!" Oliva exclaimed. "'*Compañeros*'," he said, 'the position of the party is not exactly the position of the government, because the government includes the Social Democratic party, the Radical party, the API (Independent Popular Action) . . . all of them social democrats in the end.'"[54] It was apparent that José Toha was talking to them not as minister of interior nor as Allende's friend nor as a Popular Unity representative, but rather as a national leader of the Socialist party. For "then he said to us: '*Compañeros*, the party is just one member of the Popular Unity, but here we are concerned with it as a political party and the Socialist party [says] press forward! Sunday, the workers seize the enterprise, and that's the end of it. From there we will see.'"[55]

Although Toha's patrician rhetoric might have lost something in Oliva's proletarian translation, his meaning was at once clear and confusing. The division between government and party seemed to extend to the individual— even one as highly placed in both as José Toha. His top aides had conveyed one message to the Yarur leaders in the morning, and Toha instructed them in a contrary one at lunch. It was not just the strategy and tactics of the Yarur nationalization that seemed unresolved, but the central questions of revolutionary leadership and political authority as well.

For the Yarur leaders, however, the contradictory instructions canceled each other out, leaving them free to proceed as they saw fit. So "we continued moving the thing forward," Oliva observed.[56] In the absence of a clear and unitary political direction from above, the Yarur workers were free to pursue their revolution from below, pulling the reluctant politicians and bureaucrats of the Popular Unity behind them. "At bottom, we took the factory because we wanted to," one worker activist later maintained.[57] But the movement leaders also believed that they had no choice—"because we had already committed ourselves," Lorca stressed. "As we approached the day of the strike, it was something that even we could not stop."[58]

On Friday, April 23, confident that the Allende government would rein in the workers' movement, Amador Yarur formally rejected all their demands. "To all the things that we had asked Amador Yarur said no," one Socialist leader recounted.[59] In some cases, he gave excuses—because the incentive system was equitable or because "he could not remove his own people." Amador Yarur's response to other demands, however, was couched in language that made clear he believed that what was at stake was his control over his own factory: "Yarur . . . said that he knew nothing about the Watchdog Committees . . . and didn't want to know anything about them, that no one was going to come to his factory and watch over what he produced."[60] This time *Yarur* had thrown down the gauntlet. "He gave us a response in writing that was negative across the board and threw the decision to the union assembly on Sunday."[61]

The next day, "Saturday, was a very tranquil day," one union leader recalled,[62] but it was the calm before the storm. Relying on Allende's assurances, Amador Yarur did little in preparation for the Sunday union meetings except make certain that some of his trusted people would be at the meeting and be able to keep him informed.[63] Meanwhile, Salvador Allende was taking steps to live up to his side of the bargain—and to make sure that the Yarur workers obeyed his injunctions.

Allende was an experienced Socialist politician who knew well that in a tense situation a mass meeting can yield unforeseen results. As a consequence, he ordered Jorge Varas, a veteran Socialist labor leader and national CUT officer, to attend the Yarur meeting as the representative of the Chilean labor confederation. His mission was to make sure "that things do not get out of control," and Varas's instructions were that "this question could not go forward yet." The Yarur workers must wait until the government was ready for the requisition of their textile mill. Varas was to make sure that the Yarur workers did nothing to overturn Allende's carefully calibrated strategy of revolution from above.[64]

For the leaders of the workers' movement, that Saturday was not a day of rest. On the contrary, faced with Yarur's intransigence and Allende's opposition, they redoubled their efforts to firm up support within the rank and file. "With even more reason now we pressed our propaganda campaign within the mass base so that on April 25 there would be the largest number of people possible at the meeting," recalled one Socialist activist who acted as the link between the union officers and the workers of his spinning section. "So we asked all the *compañeros* to demonstrate their consciousness by not working that Sunday—because people were accustomed to work overtime on Sundays—and explained that we wanted everyone at the assembly."[65]

It was to be the most fateful union meeting in Yarur history. The only warning that most Chileans had that something unusual was afoot at the Yarur mill was the screening of a television special on Saturday, a retrospective documentary about the workers' movement at the Yarur factory, including the history of past labor struggles and their ruthless repression by the Yarurs. The journalist behind the production, Victor Vió, was a Communist Youth leader who had been vice president of Allende's election campaign. Vió's aim was obvious: to put together a program that would justify the socialization of the factory in the eyes of the average television viewer.[66]

The program appealed to the emotions as much as to intellect and did not omit the sensational aspects of the story. There were descriptions of the oaths of loyalty to the Yarurs that workers had been forced to take before a skull and crucifix in order to get hired and also accounts of the "harem" of women workers that the "Oriental" owners had imposed on their women workers. One interview was with a woman worker who claimed that her breast was torn off by a member of a Yarur strong-arm squad, while another woman worker testified that she had been run down by and shot from the car driven by the factory's "welfare manager" during the strike of 1962. The program concluded with an account of the "sabotage of production" at the Yarur mill in the wake of Allende's inauguration—the decline in employment and output, the depletion of raw material stocks and spare part and product inventories, the nonpayment of creditors. Implicit in this portrait of the Yarurs was the message that the workers' cause was just and the conclusion that the Yarur textile mill should be socialized. "The following day," Vió underscored, "the conflict erupted."[67]

13

"WE TAKE
THE FACTORY"

April 25 was a lazy Sunday in mid-autumn for most of Santiago, but the streets around the Yarur mill were filled with workers hurrying to their union assembly. The blue-collar union had moved its meetings out of the factory, where Amador Yarur had controlled its deliberations, but still did not have a home of its own. As a consequence, the most historic of Yarur union meetings was held in the borrowed union hall of the CIC metallurgical workers, "located in a little alley near the Yarur industry," a big concrete and corrugated iron warehouse building, with folding chairs and a table at the front for the union officers. Security was tight: "You had to show your union card to enter . . . many people remained outside," Varas recalled.[1]

The union leaders had spent a restless night—excited, expectant, yet fearful of some unforeseen disaster. By 9 A.M., when the meeting began, it was clear that they had done their work well. From the front of the hall, they looked out on "a sea of faces" and congratulated each other: "We had filled the hall."[2] Ninety percent of the union's 1700 members were present, although to a visiting CUT official, the crowd of workers packed into "the barnlike building" seemed far larger and the atmosphere as "filled with tension and expectation as the hall was with people."[3]

The assembly began deceptively, like any regular monthly union meeting, with the ritual reading of the minutes from the previous assembly and then proceeded through the reading of letters received and a routine discussion of leftover business.[4] Meanwhile, the tension was mounting. More than one worker later confessed: "I couldn't concentrate on all this, knowing what was to come."[5]

Only after all the regular business had been disposed of did the presiding officer, Jorge Lorca, turn to the issue that had brought them there, even then introducing it as if it were just another ordinary piece of union business. "The Directors inform [the members] that in the light of the various problems that the Enterprise has not solved, we went together with the delegates to converse with Amador Yarur. He didn't want to receive this delegation" and so "the Directors . . . drew up a petition with the problems that are affecting the workers."[6]

The petition was read out, with each demand punctuated by applause. Then the movement leaders "began to stir up the Assembly." It was the union president who began: "The management response to this memorandum was overwhelmingly negative. Faced with this rejection, the Directors insist that it is not possible to continue putting up with these anomalies . . . It is time to take serious steps."[7] It was all carefully orchestrated—except for the deafening applause and shouts of approval that greeted Lorca's opening salvo. "As usual in that period we had prepared the meeting in advance. Lorca was going to speak of one thing, another person was going to talk about something else . . . the speakers were already designated, those who spoke best, so that people could understand the situation better because one can have a lot of good ideas, but not know how to develop them in a public meeting."[8]

What followed, however, was very different from what the movement leaders had anticipated—a spontaneous outpouring of worker militancy and anger that both overwhelmed their script and rendered it redundant. It was a rank-and-file response that surprised the workers themselves. "For the first time, I was a little surprised at a union meeting," confessed one generally cynical young weaver. "Normally in meetings most *compañeros* never ask for the floor; and when they do, it is with a certain prudence—trying not to attack the company . . . But in the meeting where the strike was declared, I was amazed at the courage of many *compañeros* shouting out to demand the floor. They told the union president, Compañero Lorca, that he had to go on strike, that once and for all they had to fix the wagon of these Turkish thieves. And many *compañeros* who normally never speak valiantly asked for the floor to say these things."[9]

It was Allende's emissary, Jorge Varas, who best defined the outburst of worker militancy that swept the meeting hall that Sunday. As a CUT functionary, Varas was a veteran of thousands of union meetings, but he confessed: "I have never in my life seen anything like this . . . When the union officers told them that the company didn't want to receive them and had denied all their petitions, the people stopped them and began to cry: 'Socialization! Socialization!' It was incredible. It was *revolution*! Two thousand workers standing and shouting: 'We want socialization!' And the women calling out: 'No more exploitation!' They were in a state of euphoria."[10]

Varas was jarred out of his astonishment by the sudden request that he address the workers as the representative of the CUT. "They asked me to take the floor . . . because they wanted to hear the opinion of the CUT . . . and I didn't know what to say because I had to get up and speak before two thousand workers all demanding 'socialization' . . . and Allende had told me no." Varas realized that he had no choice. It was the workers who were leading here, and the CUT and *el compañero presidente* had little alternative but to make a virtue of necessity. "So, the only thing that I could do was to go and instruct the *compañeros* on how they should proceed," Varas recounted.[11] It was a speech that he would replay in his mind during the days that followed.

"So I said: '*¡Compañeros!* You have decided that this [enterprise] should pass to the social property area. My duty is to demand this of the government.' There was a round of applause; then an Old-timer banged his fist on the table and cried: 'And right now, *compañeros!* We are going on strike and we won't go back to work with those octopuses inside!' And all the Old-timers shouting their approval. It was overwhelming." Jorge Varas decided that he had no choice except to follow their lead. "Well, *compañeros*," he continued, exuding a confidence that he no longer felt, "if you resolve to go on strike immediately, we have to see what is the best way to do it . . . " "By seizing the industry!" one Old-timer shouted out from down below. "*No, compañero!* Varas replied, "we are not discussing a factory seizure. Yes, we will take the industry, but from *outside*. You have to guard the strategic spots of the enterprise, so that no one enters, while we propose this to the president of the Republic. And I know that he will have to accept your position."[12]

It may have seemed a minor point to the workers, but the veteran CUT official was aware that the difference between a factory occupation and cordoning off the mill from outside was a legal distinction of major political significance. If all went well, the Yarur action could be passed off as a strike, not a seizure. The government's position would be protected and Allende's anger mollified.[13]

Jorge Varas may have been overly optimistic where Allende's approval was concerned, but his endorsement of the strike action in the name of the CUT was all the Yarur leaders needed to complete their scenario. "By this time it was ten in the morning and as we had the assembly sufficiently excited we decided to move the strike question," Armando Carrera recalled.[14] It carried by acclamation, with "everybody shouting: *¡Viva la huelga!* [Long live the strike!] Down with Yarur!—even the Old-timers." The union minutes were more controlled but equally definitive: "Compañero Manuel Alemán proposes that we have to go out on strike until they solve these problems. The *compañero*'s proposal is accepted and approved unanimously, bringing the meeting to an end."[15]

This unanimity was deceptive, hiding a multiplicity of meanings and motivations. In part, it was a matter of perspective. As a Socialist labor leader, Jorge Varas saw it as a question of capitalist inhumanity and intransigence. To him, the situation of the workers was intolerable, their demands reasonable, and management's intransigence the trigger for worker insistence on the socialization of their mill. However, as a union bureaucrat, Varas viewed this worker response as understandable but ill-considered, even naive. It had been up to him, as a veteran organizer, to channel their spontaneous outburst into more controlled channels.[16]

The Yarur union leaders understood the vote in still different terms. They had spent the preceding weeks "preparing the terrain"—"talking with the Old-timers," "arguing with the *apatronados*," "responding to the fears of the women," "proposing socialization as the solution to the problems that the workers were facing."[17] The April 25 meeting crowned their efforts with success even if their preparations had been overtaken by the wave of revolutionary fervor that swept the hall. This spontaneous rank-and-file reaction, they believed, reflected the work that they had done "in the mass base . . . relying on the Youngsters" but directed mostly at convincing the Old-timers that they could and should force a confrontation with Amador Yarur.[18]

Although many of the Old-timers shared the leaders' revolutionary fervor, most were survivors who had escaped the Yarur purges by "going along." They were not Yarur loyalists, but in their experience strikes always ended in defeat and disaster, with management victories and worker purges. On April 25, they had voted to strike against their better judgment, swayed by the emotional drama of the mass meeting, by the bandwagon effect of rank-and-file militancy, or by their fears of the consequences of nonconformity "because they say to themselves: 'Bueno, if we don't go with them and they notice, we may end up losing our jobs,'" Raúl Oliva explained.[19]

What made it easier for many workers to take this leap was their belief that "all we were voting for was a strike."[20] The real aim of the work stoppage may have been the requisition of the factory, but the ostensible goal of the strike was to force Amador Yarur to compromise on the union demands. This ambiguity, a formal fiction to the leaders, was an important reality to many rank-and-file workers, and the union officers were reluctant to puncture the myth. Ricardo Catalan admitted[21] that "not everybody knew that we were going to seize the factory," but argued that "they were disposed to do it because they had borne the systematic oppression [of the Yarurs] for a long time." Once Allende was elected, many said: 'Bueno, Amador will leave tomorrow . . . there was a predisposition and a desire to get involved in something like this'"—but not necessarily to force the mill's requisition on a reluctant *compañero presidente*.

As Omar Guzmán confessed: "Those of us who had had conversations with the Ministry of Economy had a clear view. Many thought that the work stoppage was just to solve the problems we had discussed . . . and not a strike to provoke the requisition of the factory."[22] Guzmán was close to the mark. Workers who were close to the movement leaders were well aware that, in voting for the strike, they were voting to socialize the factory, although their rationalizations ranged from "the factory was producing less than it should"[23] to "they didn't want to accept our demands . . . not even a quarter of our demands!"[24]

Far more numerous were those workers who were astonished to find that, in voting to strike that Sunday, they had voted for socialism at their mill. "We didn't know anything," complained one Old-timer, whose politics was survival. "And they called the strike just like that. I don't know what meetings they must have had where they proposed these things, but we didn't know what they were doing."[25] Even leftist workers who were active in the workers' movement confessed that they were surprised by the turn of events. "I didn't even think about seizing the factory [that day] because it wasn't in our plans," one woman worker, a MAPU sympathizer, declared. "I think that the moment we won the union, we all thought that something had to come sometime in the future, but in voting to strike I had no idea that we were [provoking] government intervention in the factory."[26]

In the end, Raúl Oliva, the "worker intellectual," probably summed it up best. "It is difficult to measure," he concluded. "The spirit and spontaneity of the moment were very powerful. Many people didn't know what they wanted, nor where they were going. The thing was against Yarur, and there was a hatred of Yarur. So they said: 'Let's go forward!' . . . It was difficult for those who were not already politically committed to have a clear picture of the situation. For them, for the Old-timers, it was a question of 'Let's go forward!' but without understanding what that meant."[27]

The union leaders were well aware, moreover, that the unanimity of the vote was artificial. "The great majority were with us," noted Jorge Lorca, "but, naturally, those [*apatronados*] who had not voted for us in the [December] union elections were not with us in April either."[28] The Yarur loyalists may have lacked the courage to speak out at the emotionally charged meeting or vote against the strike in the face of its approval by acclamation, but they remained unconvinced. It was for this reason that the union leader took no chances. "Because we saw that there were a lot of Yarur loyalists in the assembly, we said: '*Bueno, compañeros*, so that no one should leave here, we are going to lock the doors of the hall,' one Socialist activist recalled with a smile. Then we said: 'O.K., now we have to wait for the conclusion of the discussion by the *empleados*' union.'"[29]

A few blocks away, the *empleados* had been meeting "in a parallel assembly . . . because we were practically walking hand in hand in the same negotiations, and there was a consensus that we had to stop this thing with a strike," explained Omar Guzmán, the *empleado* union president.[30] The parallelism extended well beyond the timing and business of the two meetings. In both cases, the union leaders had worked hard to prepare their rank and file. In both unions, however, the militancy of the membership made manipulation unnecessary and caution unworkable.

"In reality, we had the thing well prepared, but in the assembly the curious thing was that it came out spontaneously," confessed Ricardo Catalan.[31] "Clearly, some spoke and said we couldn't continue putting up with this situation, and we said . . . that [Yarur's] response was negative to all that we asked and that it was up to the assembly to decide . . . but at that point the whole thing took off spontaneously." The thrust of this response from the floor, moreover, was far more radical than the union officers themselves had hoped. "The rank and file said: 'We stop work and don't begin again until this thing is settled,'" recalled Guzmán.[32] As with the blue-collar workers, the decision of the employees to call their first strike in the history of Yarur, Inc., passed by acclamation, with only one person opposing it.[33] The Yarur mill was on strike.

As in the nation at large, the revolutionary movement at Yarur was based on a social alliance of working and middle classes, but the central mass base was blue-collar workers. On the eve of the April strike, the overwhelming majority of blue-collar workers supported the leftist leadership, but the leftist *empleados* still represented only a significant minority—perhaps 40 percent—of the white-collar workers. "The others still retained a great decision-making power," one leftist leader underscored.[34] Few of the Yarur loyalists among the white-collar workers had come to the crucial Sunday meeting, and those who did held their peace. But the employee officers were under no illusion that they commanded the same mandate as their blue-collar *compañeros*.

As a consequence, the employees added an important leaven of expertise and education, but depended on the machine operators for dynamism and critical mass. It was the blue-collar workers who would define the revolution at Yarur. By noon on Sunday, April 25, however, these distinctions were submerged in the columns of high-spirited strikers that flowed out of the union halls and into the streets surrounding the factory, a visible symbol of the revolution that Salvador Allende had loosed but could no longer control.

The union meetings had lasted most of the morning, ending in an outburst of rhetorical militancy that remained to be translated into concrete action. Guided by Jorge Varas, whose concerns were legal and political, "we finally decided to have a parade. The two thousand workers marched out of the union hall and paraded all around the Yarur neighborhood."[35] It was the first of many such processions by workers intent on the seizure of their enterprises that Santiago would witness during the months to come. To a middle-class housewife who witnessed the spectacle cautiously "from her window," it was at once "an emotional and fearful thing . . . thousands of workers shouting: 'Down with Yarur! Down with exploitation! We want socialization! We want liberation!' I was moved, but afraid of what might follow."[36]

The long column of blue-collar workers met and fused with the smaller, but equally euphoric group of white-collar workers at the factory gates. Like Joshua's army at Jericho, they marched around the walls of Yarur shouting their demands, filled with a faith in the righteousness of their cause, convinced that they enjoyed the support of higher powers and confident that their weapons would suffice to breach those walls and make them masters of the world within. The measures that the Yarur workers took, however, reflected Chile's legalistic labor tradition rather than a revolutionary apocalypse. "It was about midday that we arrived at the factory . . . told the gatekeepers what was happening, and had them put padlocks on the gates . . . We let the *compañeros* who were inside the factory leave, but no one was allowed to enter . . . because we were assuming control of the industry, and if Amador Yarur's people sabotaged it, we would be held responsible."[37]

There had been some workers inside the factory when the strikers arrived, ostensibly working an overtime shift, "but these were our *compañeros*, who were only there to keep an eye on things, so when their shift was over they left. But from that point, no one entered, and no one left." The eight guards doing the rounds of the factory were all Yarur loyalists, and "they had to remain locked up inside for three days. We didn't let them leave, nor did we permit them to be relieved."[38]

With the factory secured, the workers proceeded to the organization of their strike, complete with traditional rituals and legal niceties. "We installed ourselves here in front [of the factory gates]," one worker activist recalled. "We held a little meeting . . . informing all the people, informing the press. We formed the necessary 'commands'—the strike command, the fund-raising command, the food command [for the *compañeros* that would be standing guard], and the other commands."[39] The setting up of a "command post" outside the factory gates "meant that this wasn't a *toma* [seizure] because we weren't inside," Catalan underscored.[40] "We were very careful about this," he explained, "because if it had been a *toma*, the law could have taken the leaders prisoner and liquidated the entire process. But as it was a strike declared by the union assemblies, our position was legally more defensible." Jorge Varas began to breathe a sigh of relief. The workers were following his lead and channeling their outrage into a disciplined strike along traditional lines—but with dramatically new goals.[41]

By afternoon, the strike was a reality. The young leaders of the workers' movement were understandably jubilant at their success, but uneasy about the uncertain dangers ahead. "None of us had ever participated in a labor conflict before. We were all young and hadn't any experience or anything," Ricardo Catalan recalled. Fortunately, the leaders were no longer alone. "Really, it was the people that helped us a lot. They formed picket lines all around the factory," as much for security as for political effect. "This factory is very badly constructed from the logistical point of view," Catalan explained. "There are boilers two meters from the street, for example. The electric plant and gas tank can be destroyed very easily from outside. There is a water plant only centimeters from the fence, the cotton storerooms are only a further three meters away and they can be set on fire easily. All these things we began to consider and to guard against"—even "sending people to the Yarur warehouse near Cerrillos to ensure that no merchandise would be removed from it."[42]

Beyond these concrete tasks lay the mystique of the strike and the sense of heroism and importance that the workers felt. The workers thought of it as a battle in an ongoing social war. "We seized the factory, locked it with chains, and set up our guards," was the way one white-collar worker remembered it.[43] As they had throughout the preceding months, the union leaders "relied on the Youngsters," who shared their generation's worldview and regarded the strike as the culmination of their struggle and the reward for their efforts.[44] "One felt oneself at the center of the world," was the way that a young weaver expressed his heady feelings during those days.[45]

For many of the older workers, however, the strike had even greater resonances. A few Old-timers came out of fear: "I presented myself at the gate so that they noted it down, so that they saw that I came and was in agreement with them."[46] But they were in the minority. For most, it meant liberation from a lifetime of public submission. "I came every day," proudly affirmed one ailing woman worker, "even when the delegates told me: 'Look, *compañera*, you don't have to stand guard here. You can go home. There are young people here' . . . but I came every day, talked a little bit here, gossiped a little bit there, and then went home. The next day I did the same thing— until we won."[47]

For those who had taken part in the long, unsuccessful 1962 strike, the "seizure from outside" of 1971 was less a strike than the fulfillment of a dream. As one middle-aged woman put it: "I didn't consider it a strike, I considered it a fiesta, a carnival. I considered it the most marvelous day in the world because, I said: 'At last, people have opened their eyes and realized what is happening here.' And with that I felt happy."[48]

Young and old, skilled and unskilled, blue- and white-collar, male and female, the workers of Yarur occupied the streets surrounding the factory. It was a heady experience, which imbued the mostly mundane tasks that they had to perform with significance and satisfaction. "Standing guard those nights, I felt that what I was doing was the most important thing in the world. I didn't even mind the cold," one young blue-collar worker from the finishing plant remembered.[49] It was a sentiment shared by the women workers whose task was to keep the cold from getting to the men doing night duty: "There were temporary kiosks to shelter those guarding the gates where we made coffee. I used to run from side to side . . . I just about woke up each morning serving coffee, serving them and caring for them and this and that, worried about everything," one woman worker recalled. "But I felt happy, I felt fulfilled, because I said to myself: 'Now we have won this struggle.'"[50]

14

THE *COMPAÑEROS*
CONFRONT THEIR
COMPAÑERO PRESIDENTE

The euphoria of the Yarur workers was understandable, but it was premature. Their revolutionary fiesta was blind to the political implications of their actions, particularly where Salvador Allende and the Popular Unity were concerned. Jorge Varas was only too well aware of these problems, as was Oscar Ibáñez, the veteran Communist labor leader who had joined him at the factory as unofficial CUT adviser to the Yarur strike, his role in 1962 as well. Varas, in particular, was acutely conscious of what lay ahead of him—confronting President Allende with the news that events at Yarur had gone against his wishes and in the very direction that Varas had been instructed to prevent.

Accompanied by Ibáñez, he left the Yarur mill and "tried to get an interview with the president." While he was doing this, Communist labor leaders Victor Díaz and Mireya Baltra arrived, along with Haroldo Martínez, "a Socialist comrade who was cabinet chief in the Ministry of Interior . . . So we explained the situation to them, and we agreed to hold a meeting with the two unions . . . to see how we were going to present the thing to "Chicho" [Allende] . . . Haroldo Martínez got us an interview with Allende immediately for five o'clock . . . In the meantime, Compañero Haroldo had called "Slim" Altamirano and "Lucho" Corvalán to come to the meeting."[1] The summoning of the heads of the Socialist and Communist parties to an urgent Sunday night meeting with the Chilean president underscored the transcendent political importance of the workers' seizure of the Yarur mill.

Partly to prepare the Chilean president for the bad news, Haroldo Martínez was sent ahead to brief him on what had happened. As Martínez had been the presidential emissary who had instructed the Yarur leaders not to take any steps until a government decision was made, he was hardly a disinterested messenger. To Varas's chagrin, his "friend Haroldo" gave the president "distorted information," telling him "that the union officers had convinced the people to strike and that we had seized the enterprise." By the time Varas arrived at the meeting, Allende was in a rage. "He bawled me out for half an hour," Varas recounted with chagrin:[2]

> "I told you that this could not be," Allende fumed.
>
> "What would *you* say to two thousand workers who are all on their feet demanding socialization . . . demanding that the president fulfill his promises," Varas replied. "What would you say? 'No, that you can't.' They would throw me out of there feet first."
>
> "He began to realize that the question was not as simple as he had been told it was and said: 'You are right, but Haroldo . . .'"
>
> "Haroldo," I told him, "arrived there when it was all over, when we were just seeing how we could keep the people tranquil and secure the strategic points of the enterprise."

At that point, Allende "pushed the buzzer and in came Toha, Millas,* Corvalán, and Altamirano." Then he began "to spout pure nonsense," according to Varas. "'I am the one who commands here, and I do not agree that Yarur should be incorporated into the social property area right now,'" the Chilean president asserted. "There was a big argument that lasted more than an hour," with Allende becoming more and more agitated as time went on, and it became clear that the party leaders had known in advance that the Yarur workers were likely to seize their factory and demand its requisition.[3]

"I don't know anything!" Allende cried indignantly, dressing down his chief aides and political collaborators. Once again, Varas had to tell the whole story, arguing that he had done what he could but that "what made the glass overflow was the negative response to all their demands" and that it was not a planned strike engineered by the union leaders but rather a spontaneous reaction of the rank and file." The Chilean president seemed reluctant to accept this explanation or to curb his anger. Even his old friend and party comrade Pepé Toha could not calm him. "He even called *Toha* a liar!" Varas recalled incredulously.[4]

In the end, it was Luis Corvalán who assumed the voice of reason, proposing a plan that would satisfy worker expectations, while maintaining

---

* Orlando Millas was a Communist deputy, Politburo member, and a leading ideologue and economic adviser.

both the legal forms and the facade of governmental control of the socialization process. "We have to make the workers understand that this is going to be a legal action, which will mean a delay of four or five days, but that the enterprise is going to pass to the socialized sector," the Communist party chief proposed. Allende, however, refused to be mollified or to agree to so radical a new departure in what he saw as the wrong direction. It was not just personal pique—although there was some of that in his reaction—but the implications of governmental ratification of the workers' seizure of the Yarur mill that troubled him. "If I give the OK to this," he prophesied, "there is going to be another and another and another . . . just because one was already gotten out of me."[5]

Allende might have been correct, but he was arguing against history. The others were aware that it was too late to turn back. The consequences of repressing the Yarur workers or of denying their demands seemed far worse than the risks of accepting their revolution from below and making a virtue out of necessity. Varas tried again to make Allende see this—and to get himself off the hook of presidential displeasure: "You should talk to the union officers, *compañero* . . . They have a proposal dictated by the union assembly, and you have to receive them. You know, *compañero*, the history of Yarur, how these people have suffered, the persecution, how they have been treated—and you tell them 'No!' *compañero?*"[6]

Allende's reply was laced with rage and irony. "Don't try to raise *my* consciousness, *compañero*, or to convince *me* with words," he snapped. "It's your fault. Why did you have them form picket lines at once?" "And what do you want, *compañero?*" Varas replied. "That the guys occupy the factory? That they seize the industry?" Allende finally began to calm down and "committed himself to make a study of the economic and legal situation of the enterprise because there were various questions that were in bad shape: arrears of taxes, unpaid welfare benefits, a thousand and one legal questions." In the end, Allende said: "We will do this study, and then we will see."[7] The meeting was over, but the struggle over the socialization of the Yarur mill had just begun.

By early evening Salvador Allende was ready to talk to the union leaders. In the interim, he had done some investigations of his own to resolve the conflicting reports on what was happening at the Yarur mill. As the workers were setting up their assignments for night guard duty, "A member of the GAP, the personal guard of *el compañero presidente*, arrived. He was sent to see what was happening here, whether it was a strike or a seizure," Armando Carrera recalled.[8]

In the meantime, Amador Yarur had also been active. He may have been surprised that the government had failed to stop the shutdown of his plant, but he took immediate steps to reverse the situation. "Of course, Yarur knew at once that something had happened at the factory, and he began to mobilize his forces. He gave out a press release that misrepresented what had happened," one activist complained, "because he told the press that we had taken the factory, and really it wasn't a factory seizure, only a strike."[9] As a result, the workers faced a battery of hostile reporters and were soon aware that "in the reactionary media they were saying that the Communists had seized the factory . . . and a lot of things like that . . . all lies."[10]

By the time Jorge Varas arrived at the besieged factory to take the union leaders to the presidential palace, they had heard that their celebration was premature and that "a few little problems had arisen."[11] "I had to go there," Varas recalled," to tell them that they had to go and talk with *el compañero presidente*, and all of them scared to death at the prospect."[12]

If the Yarur worker leaders were feeling uneasy about confronting their president, Allende's greeting did nothing to allay their fears. "Who are those people that you have brought here?" he barked as they entered the room. "Are you the union officers? You are. Well, you had better tell me what happened there."[13] "So we began to tell the whole story all over again. We explained the pressures that we were submitted to daily and the drop in production and the repression in the industry . . . and how we had drawn up the ten-point petition . . . and how Yarur had rejected all of them and that we had left it up to the assembly to decide . . . and that the *compañeros* had demanded that we go on strike."[14]

Allende heard them out, but then countered sarcastically: "You are not going to convince *me* that the whole thing was spontaneous. There was work behind the scenes in this." "What do you mean behind the scenes?" asked one of the union officers. "An effort to motivate the people to react in this way," Allende replied, "because they wouldn't react that way by themselves." "But *compañero*, the people reacted violently because of the way in which the enterprise had responded to our petition."[15]

Allende was not convinced. He had been a Socialist leader too long to believe in worker spontaneity. It was not just a question of who was telling the truth, nor was it just the truth of the matter that was worrying him. He explained to the Yarur leaders that their revolution from below raised central questions of revolutionary direction and threatened the success of the revolutionary process that he led.[16] "After scolding us a bit more, Allende began to lecture us in serious tones. 'Successful revolutionary processes are directed by a firm guiding hand, consciously, deliberately—not by chance,' " he stressed. " 'The masses can not go beyond their leaders, because the leaders had an obligation to direct the process and not to leave it to be directed by the masses.' "[17] The conflict between revolution from above and revolution from below was all too clear—as was Allende's view of it: "*I am the president, and it is I who give the orders here!*" he concluded imperiously.[18]

The lecture on revolutionary leadership finished, Allende returned to the matter at hand. "And this thing we are going to have to study. You have created a difficult situation by bringing all the people out on strike. Come back here on Wednesday and see if I have an answer for you."[19] Allende had had his say, but the Yarur leaders were left in an impossible position. So the president of the union, Jorge Lorca, said to him: "What assurance can you give us that the industry will be socialized?" "None at all," Allende replied. "Because we will have to see what the general situation of the enterprise is." "But can I at least tell the people that there are possibilities?" pressed Lorca, desperate for at least something that could permit him to place a hopeful interpretation on this disastrous first encounter with his *compañero presidente.* "You can tell them whatever you want," responded Allende curtly, "but we are going to have to see what the situation is before making a decision."[20] Then, in saying good-bye, he softened his stand a little and assured them that "we are going to have to look at the legal situation, and if we are permitted to act, we will act rapidly."[21] It was an ambiguous parting shot, but it was the most hopeful thing that the Yarur leaders had heard.

As the workers left the room, Allende called Varas back. " '*You* come here!' he said to me, and made me go back inside where he continued the tongue lashing," Varas recalled. 'I now realize what it means when I hear that you have gone to a workers' assembly at RCA or Sumar; it means that I am going to have to dedicate my time purely to signing requisition decrees that you bring me!'" Allende raged. Jorge Varas was in the presidential doghouse, and there was little that he could do about it except object lamely that he "had to go to these meetings as a CUT officer." Finally, Allende calmed down and got down to business. "You, Compañero Millas," he said to the Communist deputy and chief economic spokesperson, "are in charge of getting me all the background information and data by Tuesday at the latest. We are going to go over them in a meeting with Vuskovic and the union officers." "I left La Moneda at eight in the evening," Varas recalled. It had been a long and difficult day for him, and the exhausted labor leader went home for a badly needed rest.[22]

But for the crestfallen Yarur leaders, the night was far from over. No sooner had they returned to the euphoria of the picket lines than they "were summoned to the Ministry of Economy. Vuskovic and Garretón were there ... It was Sunday night, and there we were conversing about the strike, discussing everything," Lorca recalled. In the Ministry of Economy, however, the union officers were preaching to the converted and could drop their mask of innocence and "declare the real purpose of the strike . . . that it was the right conjuncture for requisition." After a "long discussion" in which "everyone took an active part . . . the Ministry of Economy declared that it would make the requisition . . . and we returned to our strike and *compañeros*."[23]

At the factory, the heady sense of a world turned upside down continued. Buoyed by their meeting at the Ministry of Economy, the union leaders did not share with the rank and file the substance of their interview with Allende. Under the circumstances, it seemed both unwise and unnecessary: unwise because it might confuse and demoralize the workers; unnecessary because both the parties and the CUT seemed prepared to support their demands and the Economy Ministry was proceeding with plans to requisition the mill.[24]

The following morning, a Monday, the confidence of the Yarur leaders was shattered. Once again, they were called into the Ministry of Economy, "but this time they told us that there were some problems, and it wasn't possible to requisition [the enterprise], that it wasn't yet within the time period that the government had fixed to take those steps. And it was there that we began to see that the question was becoming a difficult one," Lorca recalled. What had happened became clear in the course of their conversation: "Vuskovic and Garretón told us that it was becoming a mess because Allende was determined that the thing should not proceed."[25]

The desertion of their strongest allies within the government was a heavy blow to the Yarur leaders, but they had gone too far to draw back now. Without the support of the Ministry of Economy, they had no chance of forcing the requisition of their factory, so they played their last card—revolutionary solidarity—in an effort to persuade Vuskovic and Garretón to reverse their decision to bow to Allende's wishes. "We explained to them that they knew better than ourselves what the origins of the process were because they had participated with us since the beginning . . . and from there we kept on insisting that they commit themselves all the way and try to convince Allende somehow."[26]

It was an appeal that neither Vuskovic nor Garretón could resist, but now it was the Yarur leaders who took the initiative and the government officials who were following their lead. With the Ministry of Economy once more behind them, the Yarur officers proceeded to build their political alliance, lining up solid support from labor to offset Allende's presidential power. "We went to the CUT as well," Ricardo Catalan related. "There the *compañeros* designated Victor Díaz, deputy secretary-general of the Communist party, who carries a lot of political weight and has a great deal of influence in the government agencies, to handle the matter."[27] "Chino" Díaz had been present at the meeting in the Ministry of Economy in the wake of the April elections where he and other party leaders had given them "a green light," and "he headed the conversations at a ministerial level." The Yarur leaders impressed on him that "it was really impossible to turn back at this point" and persuaded one of Chile's most hardheaded and powerful Communist leaders to plead their case.[28]

In the process, the leaders of the Yarur workers' movement were transformed from local cadres into political protagonists on the national stage. They were newcomers to this role, but they mobilized their supporters, rallied their troops, and built their alliances with a skill that matched that of their adversary—the ultimate Chilean political pro, Salvador Allende. The contest between the workers of Yarur and their president was Allende's first conflict with his central mass base, which he viewed as a crucial precedent that he had to win.[29]

This became clear to the Yarur leaders later that same Monday, when two Socialist union officers were summoned to the presidential residence for another interview with Allende. "He summoned us to give us a warning . . . and in very harsh terms," Raúl Oliva recounted. "We went to his house in Tómas Moro . . . the day after the *toma* . . . and well, he warned us that we had gotten out of control and that either we marched in step with the government or we didn't march at all." To the Socialist worker leaders, Allende's words were as resolute and ominous as before, but there was also a sense of déjà vu. "It was practically the same as the other day . . . except that we had already heard that conversation. We didn't come to any resolution [of the problem], and in the end he threw us out of the house." To Oliva, however, Allende seemed "a changed guy . . . because he saw that he was dancing on a tight rope in those moments."[30]

It was a perceptive comment, but only Allende was aware of all that it implied. In part, he was trying to avoid short-term political problems. Amador Yarur was mobilizing a campaign of protest against the seizure and possible socialization of his factory in the media, in the Congress, and even among Arab diplomatic missions. He was also pressuring Allende directly, reminding him of his promise of the week before and demanding government intervention, but on *Yarur's* behalf. "Toha told us that Yarur had called and wanted to know when the government would order an end to the work stoppage," Omar Guzmán recalled ruefully. All the Socialist interior minister could do was put Yarur off with the reply that "he could give him no assurances until there was a political agreement within the Popular Unity."[31]

Allende, however, had more profound reasons for concern. A seizure of the Yarur textile factory threatened to undermine both his political strategy and his authority to pursue it. The Chilean road to socialism, he knew, "was a difficult road, with many enemies and little room for maneuver." Allende's strategy was to fight on one front at a time in order to discourage his adversaries from uniting to block his program of structural transformation.

He had already challenged "the financial oligarchy" by pushing the nationalization of the banking sector and the "Yankee imperialists" by pressing the expropriation of their copper mines. Moreover, Allende had been forced by peasant land seizures to accelerate the agrarian reform, antagonizing the rural aristocracy and jeopardizing his strategy of alliance with the middle classes. Adding the "industrial bourgeoisie" to his list of enemies at this juncture might be fatal to his economic plans and political hopes. Allende was determined to postpone that decisive confrontation until he had won the battles that were already in progress. His image as "a man you can do business with" depended on his ability to keep his promises—and keep the revolution from their door. Controlled change, with a disciplined mass base and a clear hierarchy of command, was central to his strategy. The revolution from below at the Yarur mill threatened this delicate edifice, and Allende was determined to save it before it was too late.[32]

Omar Guzmán did not know it when Allende shooed him out of his house, but there was worse to come. Later that same day Allende tried to call in the other Yarur union officers. A military aide came to tell them to communicate [with Allende] by telephone."[33] It was Lorca, the Communist head of the blue-collar union, whom he was looking for, but it was Guzmán, the Socialist president of the *empleado* union, that he found. Omar Guzmán had already had one unpleasant conversation with *el compañero presidente* that day, and he was not eager to have another, but he was the only one there, and "duty is duty. So . . . I went to my house," he recalled, "and we looked up the number in the phone book and a *compañero* handed me the telephone."[34]

It was a conversation that even a year later, Guzmán found painful to recall and difficult to recount. "I had the bitter experience to have had to talk with Allende at two in the morning, two days into the strike," he began. "I said: 'Who is it?' and he responded, 'Salvador Allende.' We must have spoken some ten to fifteen minutes. He spoke more than I. I gave him explanations, told him how things were, etc. . . . He was very forceful and *very* annoyed. He said that we, the workers, could not be boycotting production with this type of strike and that tomorrow he was going to order the renewal of production . . . But he told me a whole lot of things . . . that they were ready to take Radio Balmaceda away from the Yarurs . . . and so Allende would seem to be persecuting the clan if he took their textile mill away as well . . . Therefore, he told me, it wasn't opportune."[35]

For a Socialist sympathizer like Guzmán, who had risked his job to campaign for Allende, his conversation with *el compañero presidente* "was a shock . . . even mortifying." "Naturally, if the president, who has the last word, tells me that it isn't opportune for very powerful reasons according to him, well . . . what can you do?" The president of the *empleados'* union, however, was equally convinced that the Yarur movement had passed the point of no return, so he resolved to make one last effort to persuade Allende to change his mind. "So when he said that it wasn't opportune, I told him: 'On the contrary it was *the* opportunity because the workers had already thrown themselves into it, and when workers are frustrated, *compañero presidente*, it is a terrible thing, and we, as leaders, don't want that to happen.' Here too we had to demand [socialization] from the government because conditions were ripe. 'Later would be of no use to us,' " Guzmán told Allende.[36]

Guzmán even tried to manipulate Allende with a bit of amateur psychology: "Salvador Allende was very annoyed when I told him:[37]

> *Compañero presidente*, here is a problem that you don't know anything about, and you have to hear it from the mouth of the union leaders. Amador Yarur is a very clever man, a real fox. To the rank and file, he says that he is very friendly with Salvador Allende and that the government is going to make him the head of the entire textile industry . . . and always when we have meetings with him, he threatens us with meetings with high executives of the government. So all these things are chipping away at your rank-and-file support.

And he said to me: "Comrade. I have thirty-odd years of an irreproachable political life, and I am not going to accept that Yarur can place doubts in the minds of the workers." "So I said that:

> I had the moral obligation to inform the president of what was happening here because the problem that is asphyxiating us here perhaps didn't even exist for him, the president of the Republic, who has much bigger problems. But that Yarur, with great ability, was destroying the image of our president and . . . we were not going to accept that the moral stature of Allende was stained by a son of a bitch like Yarur just because he was a millionaire several times over. The leader may have a clear understanding of what's going on, but it was equally important that the rank and file also have it, and that is why I had to inform the president of the danger.

Guzmán may have been laying it on thick, but Salvador Allende had been around too long to be taken in by such an obvious ploy. "The upshot was that he told me a lot of things . . . and at the end declared: 'Tomorrow I am going to order the resumption of work.'"[38]

To an Old-timer like Guzmán, this was 1962 all over again, only now the president threatening to break the Yarur strike was not the capitalist Alessandri, but the Socialist Allende. In desperation, Guzmán tried one last gambit: "I told him that the FENATEX (National Federation of Textile Workers) and the CUT agreed with us and that . . . " Allende cut him off before Guzmán could conjure up the rest of the political alliance that the Yarur leaders had assembled and said curtly: "Tomorrow I want to have a talk with *you—and* with the *compañeros* of the FENATEX and the CUT." And with that, Allende hung up, leaving a shaken Guzmán to inform his fellow union officers that not only was the requisition of the factory still in doubt, but that Allende was threatening to break their strike, possibly the very next day. Not surprisingly, Guzmán "spent a horrible night, filled with sleepiness but without sleep," tossing and turning, wondering and fearing what the morning would bring.[39]

Bad news travels fast. Word began to circulate among the strikers that something had gone wrong. "We had been out too long in the cold, and with the union leaders disappearing all the time running from one secret meeting to another," one young weaver explained, "something had to be wrong."[40] As a result, early Tuesday morning the union officers called a meeting, "because we hadn't given any account of our conversations to the rank and file . . . there was an uneasiness, an anxiety to know how things were going."[41] The officers tried to reassure their members, but their own nervousness was evident. They had the support of labor and the parties. "The only thing that we didn't have yet was the approval of the government."[42]

On Tuesday morning, however, it began to appear as if they would never obtain it. "At nine in the morning," Catalan recalled, "Garretón was sent to look for us because President Allende had made a decision. We had to be present there, but they were going to help, Garretón assured us." On the surface, their chances did not look very good. "First Garretón came and then Vuskovic as well, and they informed us that Compañero Allende has continued insisting that it was impossible [to requisition the factory] and that he was going to take a serious administrative measure. And we were all asking ourselves: What could it be?"[43]

The meeting with Allende had been enlarged to include all the labor, party, and governmental actors in the Yarur drama, itself a sign that the denouement was near. Garretón had been summoned to a private interview with Allende before the meeting began, so the Yarur leaders made their "last pleas and arguments" to him, with the request that he "present them to *el compañero presidente*."[44]

The Yarur leaders waited with growing anxiety for Garretón's return. Finally, "at eleven in the morning . . . Garretón arrived and informed us that the President was going to receive us, that he [Garretón] had presented to him the history of the whole process, and that as all the antecedents were already known, there would not be much discussion, but rather a decision."[45] Garretón was in a grim mood. He had explained the central role of the Ministry of Economy in the genesis and evolution of the Yarur movement, and Allende "had dressed him down" for his pains.[46] The Yarur union officers—the "Famous Ten" to their worker supporters —were in no better shape as they arrived at the presidential palace for what they knew would be a decisive meeting. Jorge Lorca found himself thinking that it had always been his "dream to be at La Moneda with *el compañero presidente*, but that now it was like a nightmare."[47]

The eighteenth-century presidential palace was a strange setting for a fundamental debate over the direction of a socialist revolution, stranger still to the Yarur workers, who mounted the ornamental staircase of La Moneda, passing the paneled rococo rooms "to talk with our comrade president."[48] In the end, they were asked to wait in an anteroom while the Popular Unity leaders deliberated with Allende over whether to give the factory to its workers or return it to the Yarurs.

The worker leaders could hear from the room next door that "a hot discussion" was in progress. "It seems as if there really was a debate because we waited a long time," growing increasingly anxious with each rising cadence and passing minute.[49] Finally, the doors opened, and the Yarur leaders were ushered in. Lorca recalled that "el Compañero Minister Vuskovic was there, and el Compañero Deputy Minister Garretón. El Compañero 'Chino' Díaz was there for the CUT, and the FENATEX was represented by an officer, Boabadilla, who is a Communist. There was also a *compañero* representing the Socialist party and the MAPU and Compañero Minister Toha, who is a Socialist, and Compañero Millas, a Communist."[50]

Despite the presence of all these political notables, the meeting from the start was a contest between Salvador Allende and the Yarur leaders. As Ricardo Catalan put it: "We had a duel with *el compañero presidente*." Allende landed the first blow:[51]

> Straight out Compañero Allende said that there would be no requisition. Then he really blasted our eardrums. He said that the workers by themselves could not take decisions. That if he had been elected president, it was to plan in conjunction with them, but not to leave him on the sidelines of the decisions that the government should take. That if what they wanted was to have a government that would play the role of a figurehead, then he would resign his post, and they could elect another president.

The Yarur leaders responded with the arguments that they knew by heart and with which Allende himself was by now all too familiar:[52]

> That he knew how they did things here [at Yarur], that he had been to the factory and . . . knew how much exploitation there was at Yarur and that he had said so himself in some of his speeches. That at one time he

was a friend of the Yarurs... and therefore Amador Yarur was taking advantage of this and said: "I am an intimate friend of the president, and he is not going to abandon me"... that he was flaunting it in front of us.

Although the union officers thought that "we had won him over," Allende was unmoved by these appeals to his revolutionary conscience "because he approached it from the side that we had many good arguments, but that he had the authority." Worse, *el compañero presidente* became patronizing. "As he saw that we were all young, he said: 'I am the one who commands here because I am the oldest' and then he gave us an enormous dressing down, with curses and everything."[53]

Allende was moving inexorably toward a negative decision. Then, at the last minute, Vuskovic and Garretón intervened. Declaring "that they were with the workers," they threatened to resign if the Yarur mill was not requisitioned.[54] Stunned and furious at this dramatic gesture by his top economic advisers, Allende broke off the meeting and stalked out of the room, leaving Toha to interpret his behavior to the surprised and worried Yarur leaders. "Compañero Toha told us: '¡*Bueno!* The president has made a decision that you will have a [government] intervenor this afternoon with orders to start up the production lines.'"[55] It was as bad as they had feared and worse than they had expected. "This was to throw the whole process overboard," Catalan explained, "because to bring in an intervenor was to deny the authority of the union leaders and to say to our people that we were good for nothing."[56]

"It was then that Jorge Lorca became melodramatic," Guzmán recalled.[57] The *obrero* union head was a bit embarrassed at this description, but he had a clear memory of what he had said:[58]

> It was at this point that I intervened and told Compañero Toha that our movement was not a movement that was made with an economist spirit. If we asked for the requisition of the industry, it wasn't as if we were doing it thinking that we were going to gain a better salary and that we were going to line our pockets with silver, but rather that we were asking because the situation here had become unbearable, that we couldn't take it anymore, and that we were asking because we were conscious that we were doing it in the interest of the people and the government itself. The only thing that we had asked as representatives of the workers was that they [the government] should grant us this demand that was, besides, within the plans of the government, and that the Yarur workers would demonstrate thereafter with actions that they [the government] had not committed an error in granting us this right and taking this opportunity to requisition the industry.

"Compañero Toha listened intently, took notes, and even got a journalist who was there to record part of it."[59] After hearing Lorca out, "Toha told us that he would stand up to the president during lunch."[60]

If anyone could persuade Allende to change his mind, it was his old friend and comrade Pepe Toha. Still, the Yarur leaders reacted with shocked dismay to what was, in effect, a dismissal: "Because Toha, although very serious, but half laughing to himself, said: '*Bueno*, you have to go now.' And all of us stood up and told him that this could not be." "I was prepared to do something so that this shouldn't happen," recalled Catalan, "when in that very moment a waiter came in carrying a luncheon invitation for the cabinet ministers that were there . . . for Toha, Vuskovic, and Garretón," and then "they called for Compañero 'Chino' Díaz, and they all went inside" after "wishing us good luck."[61]

The Yarur leaders had become protagonists of their own destiny and movers of national politics only to see the power of decision once again taken out of their hands. The course of their revolution from below suddenly depended on the outcome of a luncheon debate within the Allende government, with the workers and their leaders relegated to the sidelines. It was an outcome for which they were unprepared and that left them anxious that Allende would carry out his threat to break their strike without their being able to say any further words in their defense.

It was a heavy burden to take back to the expectant strikers around the Yarur mill. "We returned to the industry a little demoralized and a little worried," Lorca recalled, "because we really thought that they weren't going to requisition the industry just when our desire for it was greatest. We mixed with the people, but didn't tell them anything. We didn't want to let them know what had happened at the meeting. So we just went on with the strike. That's all."[62]

In retrospect, it was an unduly pessimistic perspective. There were powerful forces on the side of the Yarur workers, including their own authenticity, eloquence, and sense of urgency. In addition, major leftist parties and labor organizations had promised their support. Before going in to lunch at the presidential palace, Victor Díaz, at once a Communist labor and party leader, told Jorge Lorca:[63]

> That he was going to talk with Compañero Allende. He had been spending nights in meetings at the Ministry of Economy when he should have been resting, and he would not go on sacrificing important party tasks just so that afterward nothing should be done. Either they respected his party as they should . . . or he would not participate ever again in anything.

Díaz's remark reflected more than personal pique. The issue of revolutionary leadership that the Chilean president had raised with such irritation also involved a contest between the Popular Unity parties and the Allende government. As a consequence, the Yarur workers could count on the support of major Popular Unity parties even if they had jumped the gun and demanded the requisition of the textile industry before Allende's strategy called for it.

They could also depend on the loyalty of one of the most important, powerful, and autonomous ministries within the government, the Ministry of Economy. It was a support that transcended party lines and personalities, rooted as it was in a common vision of the revolutionary process and shared experience of the struggle at the Yarur mill. When Vuskovic and Garretón threw their resignations onto the scales, it was no idle threat, but one that would have to weigh heavily in Allende's calculation, raising the costs of not requisitioning the Yarur mill to the level of a major government crisis, involving his central economic advisers, the architects of his initial economic success, the base of the Popular Unity's political progress.

At the decisive lunch, therefore, Allende was surrounded by party, labor, and governmental leaders who were all committed to the requisition of the Yarur mill. It was a tough debate, but "a very fraternal one," fought on the issues. The luncheon meeting lasted until 4 P.M., but by then Garretón could call a fellow MAPU leader with an optimistic report. "The problem is solved," he told Catalan. "I didn't have to resign, and neither did Vuskovic."[64] In the end, Allende would choose to maintain the unity of the Left—his political life's work—at the risk of increasing conflict with his economic, social, and political opponents.

The debate over the socialization of Yarur had not ended with lunch. Discussions continued with a changing cast of characters, but with the Ministry of Economy at the center. By evening, they had progressed to a point where Vuskovic felt justified in giving Jorge Lorca some good news. "That night, Compañero Vuskovic called me by telephone," Lorca recalled," and said that he wanted to tell me unofficially that Allende's opposition to the requisition was weakening, that we should wait calmly until the following day." The economy minister explained to the blue-collar union president that the problem was that "the government was only recently established . . . and first had to consolidate its bases so that afterward it could begin to take appropriate measures. What we were asking for anticipated their plans but [Vuskovic] concluded with the assurance that one way or another we were going to press forward."[65] It was the news that the Yarur workers had been waiting for. Lorca rushed to tell the other union leaders, and soon the news had spread to the workers standing night guard around the walls of the Yarur mill.

Once again, euphoria swept the benumbed strikers, banishing the cold of an autumnal April night. "The union officers didn't sleep that night,"

Lorca recalled. Instead, "we remained with the *compañeros* making the rounds with them of the factory walls. Here it was really a fiesta; it didn't even seem like a strike. The workers were all happy, everybody content with what they were doing. We were receiving mutual aid from other workers, congressmen visited us, the Mexican press came, and also the French television, all of them expecting the industry to be requisitioned and interviewing the *compañeros* . . ."[66]

From the outset, the Yarur strike had exuded a sense of excitement and newfound power. Now a sense of expectation and self-importance were added, stimulated and underscored by the presence of political notables and media journalists. The morning press spoke in veiled terms of the probability that the Yarur mill would be requisitioned while the union leaders, halfway between elation and exhaustion, began to believe themselves that "the requisition was imminent . . . We had finally won!"[67]

15

"DAY OF
LIBERATION"

Wednesday, April 28, 1971, was the "day that would live on in the memory" of Yarur workers as "the day of liberation."[1] In time it would become the founding myth of Ex-Yarur. All day the workers' sense of expectation kept building. Finally, "at about 4:30 in the afternoon, Garretón phoned us once again and said: 'Come immediately to the Ministry.'"[2] It was the call that the union leaders had been waiting for, and they responded with alacrity "although all of us were hung over from lack of sleep."[3] "One last time we went over there," Catalan recounted. "We arrived at about five and they told us that the government and the Popular Unity had agreed to intervene in the industry . . . Garretón himself showed us the requisition decree with the names of the *compañeros* who would be coming [as government managers]."[4]

The union leaders had been meeting informally with the Ministry of Economy officials for months. This final meeting was formal, even ceremonial in character. It symbolized the legalism of the Popular Unity's revolution from above rather than the spontaneity of the worker revolution from below that had forced the government's hand. "The director of DIRINCO [the National Supply and Price Control Agency], Compañero Martínez, got up and said: "The Ministry of Economy, through DIRINCO, has resolved to requisition this enterprise for legal infractions and because of the fall in production" while the flashbulbs popped and the workers applauded.[5]

It was left to Garretón, who had been with the workers from the start and risked his job for them in the end, to articulate the reasoning that lay behind the government's action and its remaining ambiguity. "The Popular Unity program is very clear," he said. It aimed:

to put an end to monopolies. And in the textile industry, Yarur is an example of the concentration of power. But we are announcing the requisition now because there is a conflict between the entrepreneurs and the workers, which is causing problems of shortages. We have full legal powers to ensure that the enterprise operates from now on under state control. The requisition will last as long as there are no guarantees that production will be normal.[6]

There was no ambiguity, however, for the Yarur workers themselves. A few hours before, in front of the factory gates, a Socialist activist had spoken for his fellow workers when he told reporters: "What we want here is to not see Yarur anymore inside the factory. To say Yarur is to say intrigue and paternalism, and by now we are fed up with all this. It would be like a liberation if the state were to take part in the industry. We are all for this, and we will make ourselves responsible for producing more, including with voluntary work to raise production."[7]

Later that day they got their wish. The union officers were introduced to the government interventors who would "participate in the management of the industry" on behalf of the state. Two of them, the Yarur leaders already knew, although not equally well. They had met Andrés Van Lancker the night of the *toma*. The young Belgian textile engineer had married into a family of Chilean Socialists and thrown in his lot with their revolution. Van Lancker, tall and bearded, spoke fluent Spanish with a Flemish accent and had many years of experience in Latin America as a textile expert for the United Nations and the Chilean Development Corporation. In naming Andrés van Lancker, their only experienced textile engineer, as general manager of the Yarur mill, the Popular Unity was underscoring the importance of the enterprise's experiment in socialism. The Yarur factory had become a symbol of the Chilean revolutionary process, and the Left could not risk failure there.

The second government *interventor*, Oscar Ibáñez, was much better known to the Yarur leaders and was well qualified for the post of labor relations manager. A veteran Communist labor leader, with a round mustachioed face, hawk nose, and sharp tongue, Ibáñez was a former worker at the Yarur mill who had been fired for trying to organize its workers and returned to advise the unsuccessful strike of 1962. A reputation for independence and a talent for troubleshooting had won him the post of conflicts secretary for the CUT. If Van Lancker symbolized the recent radical thrust of the Socialist party that had brought the Left to power in Chile and attracted many intellectuals to its democratic road to socialism, Ibáñez represented the continuity of the Popular Unity's revolutionary process with the "decades of struggle" in the factories and mines that had been the workers' experience and the Communist standard.

It was the first time that the Yarur leaders had met the third government manager, Juan Francisco Sánchez, who would be in charge of the industry's finances. Young and personable, Sánchez was a recent university graduate with training in economics and accounting, but little practical experience. His education, social background, and political affiliation represented the third element in the political coalition that had brought Allende the presidency—the radicalized Chilean middle class, who had voted for Frei and reform in 1964, but were pushed by their disillusionment with that experience toward Allende and revolution in 1970. Sánchez's party, the MAPU (United Popular Action Movement), had begun as a Christian Democratic splinter group but had evolved in the direction of Marxism since then.

The meeting at the Ministry of Economy lasted about two hours. After the forms were observed and the introductions made, the participants got down to business, discussing "what had to be done first, how we were going to inform the *compañeros* of the decision, all of this."[8] It was after six in the evening when the Yarur leaders left the ministry in Constitution Square to return to the factory. This time, however, they did not make the journey alone. "Compañero Jaime Suárez [Allende's Cabinet Secretary] came with us to be the 'judge' for the intervention," Jorge Lorca recalled, "and the interventors came, as did all the party representatives, and behind us as well came all the reporters—and we didn't understand why."[9]

The Yarur leaders were still only dimly aware that their every action and word were now a matter of national interest and political import. Their movement, begun clandestinely by a few frightened workers little over a year before, had come to symbolize the revolutionary process as a whole in the popular imagination. It was a transformation of situations that the worker leaders found difficult to fathom and even harder to handle. Nothing in their experience had prepared them for so central a revolutionary role or so intense a public scrutiny.

"When we entered the door of the Ministry of Economy that Wednesday afternoon, there was a large number of reporters . . . who wanted to ask us some questions, but we were being very cautious and told them that we had nothing to tell them and that we were going to talk with the compañero minister who had summoned us, and then when we returned, we could talk with them," Lorca explained. "But when we left they were still there, and they had been joined by more reporters—some twenty or thirty more!— and there they were waiting for us to come out, and on leaving the only thing that we said was that if they wanted news they should follow us back to the industry because the only place that we were going to give them the news was here [at the factory]."[10]

It was a crazy caravan that wound its way through the streets of downtown Santiago from the ministry to the factory, but the "good news" had traveled faster. Their reception heralded the triumph that they had come to announce. As one of the movement activists who had remained on guard at the Yarur mill recalled: "It was about seven in the evening that the news reached here that they [the government] had requisitioned the factory, that they had named interventors, and that they were all on the road back to the factory. With that the people began to sing and dance in the streets surrounding the factory . . . and then we began to call all the people together in the Plaza Yarur alongside the factory gates . . . and at about eight at night they all arrived . . . the three interventors arrived . . . along with Compañero Garretón, and they called an assembly."[11]

From all sides, Yarur workers, their wives, and children, converged on the factory, along with the well-wishers and the curious. In the company housing project a few blocks from the plant, one woman recalled, "Suddenly the little kid from next door came running up shouting: 'We've won! We've won! They're coming to requisition the industry' . . . and all of us began to run toward the factory."[12] Some workers were further afield when they heard the news, but their reaction was similar. "I was in school . . . in the Tecnico [State Technical University]," a white-collar worker recounted, "when one of the guys who was listening to a transistor radio called out to me: 'Listen, they have requisitioned the factory. They are just arriving there now' . . . So I got out of there like a shot and came back here at once . . . to see what would happen . . . and I remember that Garretón was there . . . and Vuskovic . . . and many more . . . what a day!"[13]

The Plaza Juan Yarur, dominated by the marble statue of the founder of the firm, was transformed into a stage set, whose backdrop was the factory walls, placarded with slogans and drawings befitting the revolutionary theater in which they were all participants: "YARUR! Don't Boycott the Government!" "We Want Socialization!" Others lampooned Amador Yarur or proclaimed the workers' desire for "an end to exploitation."[14]

As the procession of union officers and government officials entered the little square, it was engulfed by throngs of euphoric workers. "The joy was really indescribable . . . something very difficult to translate into words successfully," explained Jorge Lorca, making a valiant effort to evoke the experience:[15]

> It was a very special moment . . . all joy and happiness, as at last we had achieved something that had cost so much, for which moreover we had struggled so hard and so long, something for which so many had been

In this worker cartoon a defeated Amador Yarur, peering into the factory over a wall on which LIBERATION has been painted, says sadly to himself: "And to think that all of this . . . (sniff) was . . . (sniff) mine."

fired and remained without work . . . I tell you that there were Old-timers there who remembered all this, and when I entered with the compañero minister [Vuskovic] and some of these *compañeros* approached us to embrace me and greet me, it was with tears in their eyes. They also embraced the compañero minister. Many of the women workers kissed him and . . . it was very special, you understand. It was the kind of thing that remains in your mind forever . . . At bottom there was a sense of . . . *liberation.*

The union leaders were overwhelmed by the reception. "There was a great explosion of joy as we entered," Omar Guzmán recalled with a sentimental smile. "The Old-timers dancing, shouting . . . it was a day to remember."[16]

Still, this was Chile, and the forms had to be observed, beginning with the ritual mass meeting. "Garretón and Vuskovic called together all the *compañeros*, and we had an assembly right here in the Plaza Yarur . . . we set up a platform, and from that platform we informed the *compañeros* that the industry had been requisitioned."[17] Garretón spoke for the government, and then Lorca spoke on behalf of the workers. Then the interventors were introduced and said a few words. What struck one labor veteran was that the words uttered seemed totally inadequate to express the emotions surging around them. When "they announced that the enterprise was requisitioned," Jorge Varas recalled, "there were women crying with joy, Old-timers embracing each other. They embraced each other crying: 'The yoke is lifted!' It was really moving."[18]

Even to a high government official like Guillermo Garretón, for whom requisitions would soon become commonplace, "the requisition of Yarur was very special. For someone like myself . . . from the middle class and the university, it was thrilling," the deputy minister and future MAPU head affirmed. "In the square between those two huge factory buildings, there were workers singing, dancing, crying . . . I have talked thousands of times about "the Chilean revolution," but this was the first time that I really understood what it was."[19]

The speeches over, the crowd of workers surged toward the gates of the factory, whose opening would mark their liberation, just as closing them three days before had symbolized their rebellion. "Garretón and I . . . were the first to enter the factory with the decree of requisition," Omar Guzmán recalled, "and I had to go and look for the person in charge of the gates so that they could be unlocked." The guard, however, was a Yarur loyalist who "told me no," but "I was accompanied by a government inspector who showed him the decree so he could see that the requisition was official."[20]

At last the wrought-iron gates swung open. "We entered the industry running. The workers brought some sackcloth and covered the Juan Yarur monument," Varas recounted. "The Old-timers applauded . . . some wanted to overturn the statue, but we stopped them, leaving it standing but covered."[21] With his proud marble head shrouded in penitential burlap, Juan Yarur would not have to witness what "his workers" were doing to "his industry." For the workers, however, the symbolism was different: In covering his statue, they were freeing themselves from his gaze and liberating their factory from his sons.

With Garretón leading the way, other workers surged into the administration building to take possession of what had formerly been a private management preserve. "We ran up the marble staircase to the second floor and into Yarur's wood-paneled office," the MAPU leader recalled, "and there many blue-collar workers saw for the first time the offices of the enterprise's managers. I remember them standing there in amazement. It reminded me a lot of that photograph of the Russian Revolution . . . of a Russian soldier standing in the throne room looking up . . . the same expression of incredulity . . . of not being able to imagine the life-style and luxury that took place there . . . or their own conquest of such heights."[22]

Few Yarur workers possessed Garretón's ability to articulate what they felt. "I had my doubts," confessed one Old-timer, who had supported "an independent union" but could not understand "why they wanted to kick out the *patrón.*" However, "that day changed the picture . . . I cried and shouted with the rest . . . and in the moment that I entered the factory where I had worked so many years . . . I felt like a new man . . . and everybody else did as well."[23]

The requisition of their factory may have "liberated . . . the workers from the yoke of the Yarurs,"[24] but it also thrust on them new responsibilities, which they were quick to assume. "Afterward, they all offered to do what they could to start up the factory . . . although the machinery wasn't affected by the strike because when we stopped work, we took care to send in teams of workers to relieve the pressure on the bearings," Omar Guzmán explained.[25] Blue-collar and white-collar, male and female, young and old, the workers of Yarur were ready to demonstrate that "high sense of responsibility" that their leaders had promised Allende they would display.[26] "That same afternoon," one administrative employee recalled, "the IBM people entered and began to work in order to prepare the [pay] envelopes for the blue-collar workers, because it was Wednesday and therefore Data Processing had only two days to make sure that the *obreros* received their pay as usual . . . That same night the boiler personnel also began to work so that the boilers could be ready for production the following morning."[27]

For most Yarur workers, however, that "unforgettable night" was "a night of fiesta," a celebration such as the streets around the factory had never known. "Everyone was dancing. There was one group here in front of the gate and another group at the corner and other groups distributed around the industry," Lorca recalled. "Each group . . . had a party right there in the streets. Each one had a guitar—dancing and drink and fireworks too . . . And, *bueno*, one couldn't allow oneself the luxury of going around to all the groups, because all the union officers would have ended up drunk because as soon as the *compañeros* saw us, they passed a bottle of pisco [liquor], a bottle of this . . . they passed us everything they had . . . it was a *great* party!"[28]

"And I will tell you one thing," Lorca hastened to add. "That night we said to the *compañeros* who had to work the first shift the next morning to go home, but they didn't obey us. They just stayed there dancing, and drinking . . . but the next morning, sleepless and hung over, they went to work just the same. The following day *no one* was absent! Sometimes the same group that had been doing guard duty together partied together and then went inside to work together at 7:30 the next morning. They worked their eight hours and afterward just continued celebrating."[29] Their labor, moreover, had been transformed by their liberation. "I remember that day well," said one woman worker. "We entered the factory singing the national anthem . . . I worked eight hours and didn't stop singing . . . "[30]

Still, it was not a day of joy for everyone. Yarur loyalists, who had staked their future on the omnipotence of their *patrón*, often serving as informers on their fellow workers to demonstrate their unconditional loyalty to Amador Yarur, were now worried that "the Reds would take this opportunity to get their revenge."[31] Those who occupied administrative or supervisory positions felt particularly vulnerable to the uncertainties of the new order at the Yarur mill.[32]

Many Old-timers, whose consciousness had not kept pace with the rapid march of events at the Yarur factory, could not comprehend what the new order would look like or how it could possibly operate without Amador Yarur. A year later, José Lagos, a peasant's son who had been at the factory since its founding, remembered his feelings on that night:[33]

> That we should have an independent union, which the *patrón* had to listen to, had to respect—agreed. That was something we had fought for all those years, something we all believed in, all knew was right. But that there should be *no patrón*! That *we*, the workers, should be our own *patrón*! . . . How was this possible? Who would run the industry? That was something that I could not understand at all.

Only experience would answer his question, but that experience would require the active collaboration of the technical and supervisory personnel, few of whom had taken part in the worker struggle and most of whom owed their appointments and careers to Amador Yarur. For them April 29 was a day of decision and self-definition. Amador Yarur had been active behind the scenes, phoning key personnel and telling them not to show up for work. If they followed these instructions, they risked being fired by the new managers of the enterprise; but if the Yarurs recovered their industry, any disloyalty would be repaid in kind. Most of these employees were essentially apolitical, but they were accustomed to conforming to the demands of authority rather than to exercising their own judgment and initiative. Now that the lines of command were unclear, each was required to make a fateful personal decision.

In the end, it was Luis Bono, the head of the maintenance division, who took the lead, and most of the others followed. For Bono, who had come up the hard way, out of the ranks of the blue-collar workers that he had entered some twenty-five years before, the requisition was a moment of truth.

It led him to realize that his "loyalty was to the factory" in which he had spent his adult life and "not to the boss." On the Sunday that the workers took the factory, Bono had received a phone call from Amador Yarur "in which he ordered me not to show up [for work] . . . because he knew that if I showed up, all the others would run as well; and as I knew the factory, at least the technical part, it would cost them . . . but when the kids from the union came looking for me and told me that there were problems here, I came like a shot." Yarur's ordering him to stay away from work, even though he knew that the machinery might be ruined as a result, made Bono, an apolitical man of integrity, realize that Don Amador "cared only about the monetary aspect of the industry . . . not about the human aspect." It was a realization that freed Bono from his sense of obligation to Juan Yarur's sons.[34]

Bono was both a respected figure among the factory staff and one of the few accustomed to taking initiatives in Amador Yarur's personalistic system of management. As a consequence, most of the technical and supervisory personnel followed his lead, some against their better judgment and many with fears, doubts, and misgivings—virtually all with a wait-and-see attitude: "Let's see how the technical part goes" or "What about the disciplinary aspect?"[35] In the end, only a few refused "to work with the Reds" and didn't show up for work. Moreover, although there were a few suspicious incidents—a fire in the merchandise warehouse, for example—there was no serious sabotage by Yarur loyalists, as many had feared.[36] Amador Yarur was legally entitled to return to his office in the "temporarily" intervened factory, but after one of his intimates was barred at the gate, he decided not to risk his dignity. So long as "his mill" was was under worker control, he would disappear from their view, pursued as well by a warrant for his arrest for alleged fraud. "We took the factory and the boss left and never came back," was the way one weaver put it.[37]

By Friday, April 30, the "liberated" Yarur cotton mill was functioning normally and producing at full capacity, under the management of a committee composed of government and worker representatives with a large worker majority. One era had come to an end at the Yarur factory, and another had begun. The old regime had fallen. It remained to be seen whether the workers could construct their new order on firmer and more just foundations. The shrouded statue of Juan Yarur would bear silent witness to their efforts to create an "Ex-Yarur: Territory Free of Exploitation."

V

AFTERMATH

16

EX-YARUR: SOCIALISM FROM BELOW

The seizure and socialization of the Yarur mill marked the end of one historical era for its workers and the beginning of another.[1] The change was symbolized by the banner, hung above its entrance, made of factory cloth dyed in the national colors and bearing the proud message—"Ex-Yarur: Territory Free of Exploitation." It signified the end of capitalism in one of its most repressive redoubts and signaled the start of a transition toward socialism at the Yarur mill.

The workers of Ex-Yarur had only seventeen months in which to create a socialism of their own before national events overtook their efforts, circumscribing their autonomy and foreclosing their future. Between May 1971 and October 1972, they were relatively free to shape their own revolutionary road. During this brief space of time, they tried to pioneer a new kind of socialism —a participatory socialism, a socialism from below. They had few models and no experience, many obstacles to overcome and minimal resources to call on. They made mistakes and encountered problems, transcending some, failing to resolve others. Yet the balance was positive, and through a process of trial and error, which drew on the talents and commitment of its workers, Ex-Yarur increasingly advanced toward its goal.

Perhaps the proudest achievement of Ex-Yarur's workers was becoming their own managers, the first industry in Chile to inaugurate a system of worker participation. "This was the first industry to have a council, the first to have a coordinating committee, the first to hold a general assembly . . . we have been first in everything," boasted one Ex-Yarur leader.[2] Pioneers of Chilean economic democracy, the workers of Ex-Yarur adapted the CUT-

Factory entrance with sign reading: EX-YARUR TERRITORY FREE OF
EXPLOITATION.

government accord on comanagement to their local conditions and own
revolutionary vision, making worker participation at Ex-Yarur more democratic, responsive, and powerful than in the national guidelines.[3]

By mid–1972, a comprehensive system of comanagement stretched from
the production committees on the factory floor elected by each work section
to the enterprise's Council of Administration, a "socialist board of directors,"
half of whose members were directly elected by all the workers of Ex-Yarur
in annual secret balloting. At both the section and enterprise level, periodic
worker assemblies afforded the rank-and-file the opportunity to hear reports
on the industry's progress and problems, call their representatives to account,
and voice their concerns. In addition, a coordinating committee, composed
of delegates from each production committee, the worker councillors, and
the union officers, functioned as a fortnightly forum and communications
bridge between the work sections and the enterprise managers. There rank-
and-file concerns were articulated, worker initiatives and industry problems
were discussed, and recommendations were made for the worker represen-

tatives to carry to the Council of Administration, Ex-Yarur's executive body. At the latter's weekly meetings, blue-collar workers, with the cotton dust still in their hair, sat in Amador Yarur's wood-paneled boardroom, together with government delegates, deciding how their industry would be run.[4]

The first year of comanagement at Ex-Yarur was "a learning experience for *all* of us"—leaders, rank-and-file, and government representatives alike— stressed one councillor; "because we had no idea at all of the picture . . . we have had to learn about *everything*," one sectional coordinator added.[5] Indeed, Emilio Hernández confessed to feeling "like a little six-year-old child entering the classroom for the first time" on taking up his seat on the Council of Administration.[6] Yet most learned their new roles rapidly and soon were playing them well.

Still, even at the year's end, there were production committees that did not function well, a "liberation hero" who "wasn't very effective as a councillor," and Coordinating Committee delegates who did not report back to their constituents out of "stage fright" at "standing before them" and "addressing a meeting of their *compañeros*."[7] There were tensions between the different groups of delegates who claimed a mandate to speak for the workers, tensions between those who favored a system of representative democracy and those who pressed for direct participatory democracy, tensions between advocates of worker participation and partisans of worker power. Yet, despite these failings and tensions, the balance of that first year of comanagement was positive.

Although worker participation and performance were uneven, on balance, both outside observers and the workers themselves considered the new system of comanagement a success, a new source of worker pride and power, but also the agency of worker involvement in, and identification with, their socialized enterprise. "An impressive quantity of leaders have been created, *compañeros* who . . . have transcended their limitations in incredible ways . . . acting as leaders, as actors in the process and not passively," attested Andrés Van Lancker, Ex-Yarur's first government interventor and later head of the socialized textile sector. Equally striking for him was the "gaining of consciousness by the mass of the workers . . . not in a partisan sense . . . but a coming to consciousness of the problems and the workers beginning to have a response to those problems."[8]

The transformation of workers into managers may well have been Ex-Yarur's most important accomplishment, but equally striking was its ability to carry out this transition from an authoritarian capitalism to a democratic socialism without any significant drop in production or decline in the quality of the mill's output. Had they done nothing else, that would have been a major achievement. But Ex-Yarur had done much more during its first seventeen months.

Maestranza, the factory's maintenance shop, was a model section of Ex-Yarur. It was converted by its workers into a "factory" for making within the mill the spare parts that the enterprise used to import. Here its workers go about their tasks under a sign that boasts: MAESTRANZA OF EX-YARUR SAVES THE COUNTRY DOLLARS.

The workers of Ex-Yarur had taken over a declining enterprise, with antiquated machinery, falling productivity, depleted inventories, a weak financial position, and an inefficient personalistic system of management—and had turned it around. During this year and a half, they had won "the battle of production," reversing the decline in output since 1968.[9] They had accomplished this without significantly increasing the labor force and, moreover, had done it despite inferior raw materials and homemade spare parts, adaptations made necessary by the United States' "invisible blockade" of Allende's Chile.[10] In response, the mill's maintenance division had "widened the aisles" of its repair shop and transformed it into a "spare parts factory" that was producing more than three-quarters of the previously imported spare parts by September 1972.[11] By then, Ex-Yarur was being held up nationally as an example of how socialism could lessen Chile's dependence on foreign capital and technology.[12]

Its improvised spare parts factory also exemplified another Ex-Yarur success story: innovation from below. Worker participation had released the creativity that Amador Yarur had discouraged, and the result was worker initiatives that ranged from ways to improve the production process to a more rational accounting system to the design and construction of a ventilation system that removed 80 percent of the cotton dust from the air.[13]

The new ventilators reflected as well the new concern for worker welfare at Ex-Yarur. Working conditions were improved, too, by the elimination of Amador Yarur's repressive overseer discipline and by the easing of the Taylor System's "inhuman" work norms by 10 percent, although many workers continued to work at the old rhythm in return for an increased production bonus.[14]

The workers of Ex-Yarur also received enhanced material rewards. On the second anniversary of Allende's election, they could look back on an average real wage gain of more than 50 percent during the twenty-two months of Popular Government, although these gains were eroded by inflation during 1972.[15] They had also won comparable increases in fringe benefits, including a retirement annuity of one month's pay for every year of service, a goal of the 1962 strike, "which Amador Yarur *never* would have given us," stressed Blanca Bascuñan, an Old-timer who was "content because . . . now I can retire in peace."[16] In addition, workers benefited collectively from larger company expenditures on housing, medical care, education, and recreation, as well as from the introduction of a full hour for lunch and the establishment of a model day-care center and nursery school for their children.[17] Workers also gained from Ex-Yarur's new promotion policies, which replaced Amador Yarur's elevation of unqualified loyalists with merit promotions through open competitions. At the same time, a conscious effort was made to utilize technical and supervisory personnel more effectively and creatively.

These new personnel policies were part of a general restructuring of the industry's administration along more rational and more revolutionary lines. Integrity was restored to financial and marketing practices, decision making and planning were institutionalized, and a start was made on the introduction of mathematical programming. At the same time, the workers decided "that we should not produce for the rich anymore," recounted Emilio Hernández, "that we should dedicate ourselves to produce purely 'popular' fabrics."[18] This "democratization of production" was complemented by a policy of "compensatory distribution." Faced with an increased consumer "demand superior to our capacity to produce," Ex-Yarur gave priority to those who had been "the most deprived." As a consequence, boasted Sales Chief Francisco Navarro, "for the first time in history the Chilean peasant is sleeping on sheets."[19] By September 1972, the workers of Ex-Yarur had fulfilled their pledge to place their enterprise "at the service of the people of Chile."[20]

There had been economic setbacks as well as successes, and productivity and absenteeism were a problem in several work sections. The enterprise's financial losses deepened, following the failure of an experiment in "socialist accounting," in which the profits of other mills producing luxury lines were supposed to balance the programmed losses of factories such as Ex-Yarur, which would concentrate on "popular" fabrics at subsidized prices. Ex-Yarur's high production figures, moreover, reflected its focus on these simpler textiles, and "the democratization of distribution" did not resolve the growing shortages of Yarur products in Chilean markets. Still, even Ex-Yarur workers who criticized policy decisions and stressed the mistakes that had been made agreed that the balance of the economic ledger was positive, particularly in view of the constraints and handicaps under which the socialized mill was operating.

What made these economic accomplishments especially impressive was that they were achieved while carrying out a far-reaching social revolution within the Yarur mill. More difficult to quantify than Ex-Yarur's economic achievements, these changes were equally important to its workers.

Although individual workers valued aspects of this social revolution differently, most stressed Ex-Yarur's progress in advancing toward the French Revolution's goals of liberty, equality, and fraternity. Seventeen months after its socialization, much had been done to transform a hierarchical workplace notorious for its lack of liberty into an egalitarian industrial community with substantial freedom for all. By then, the apparatus of repression through which the Yarurs had controlled their work force had been dismantled. "Now there is no longer any strong-arm squad, nor Pool, nor informing. Now you can say what you wish," stressed Emilio Hernández.[21] Equally striking was the change of atmosphere on the factory floor. "Before, they went around with little less than a pistol. Now the people work with more liberty," attested one apolitical Old-timer. "They don't have the pressure that we had before. They are working more tranquilly."[22]

This new feeling of "tranquillity" reflected not only Ex-Yarur's "freedom from fear," easing of work discipline, and ending of authoritarian management, but also the leveling of hierarchies. The advent of a more democratic structure of power compelled supervisory personnel to treat workers with equity and respect. Equality was the cutting edge of the social revolution at Ex-Yarur, one with many facets—work relations and social relations, status and income, power and privilege—and the changes in some were more dramatic than in others. But, by October 1972, social distance had been eroded, special privileges diminished, and income differentials narrowed, while the significance of the distinction between *empleado* and *obrero* had been decreased by the merging of athletic facilities, cultural clubs, and unions. The old social hierarchy gave way to a more open and fluid social order in which status reflected consciousness and *compañerismo*, productivity and participation.

The increasing equality of social relations was symbolized by the replacement of *señor* by *compañero* as a form of address, a verbal assertion as well of an organic relationship and common purpose among the workers of Ex-Yarur. This shift in rhetoric was accompanied by an increase in *compañerismo*—in social solidarity and interaction—in the daily life of the industry and the social life of its workers. "There is more *compañerismo* now because there is more trust," one Old-timer explained.[23]

In the process, the factory became a community, and workmates became friends who now socialized outside the mill as well. There was also a range of activities and institutions—meetings and committees, athletic teams and cultural groups—which drew Ex-Yarur workers back to the industry in their idle hours and enabled them to fraternize as well with workers from other sections. In addition, the entire factory came together at special events — union meetings and general assemblies, drama and song festivals—and shared celebrations, the most important of which was the anniversary of their Day of Liberation, where the workers of each section, with their families, ate and drank, sang and danced together. Rituals of community, these periodic events and celebrations were at once creators, consolidators, and symbols of the new fraternity at Ex-Yarur.

Social revolution, however, cuts two ways. Equality was a double-edged sword, which many supervisors perceived as striking at their authority. Many lower-middle- class *empleados* resented attempts to redefine them as working class, resisted the merger of the unions, and were reluctant to subsume their superior status in an egalitarian industrial community. Yarur loyalists felt both less free to express their views in the socialized mill and excluded from the new proletarian fraternity. "Liberation" did not end social conflict at the Yarur mill; it merely changed its terms. Still, a majority of the workers applauded the social revolution that shifted power from foreman to machine operators on the factory floor and from *empleados* to *obreros* in the enterprise, and many in the minority who lost as well as gained from this revolution recognized its justice.

The social revolution at Ex-Yarur also promoted a goal of the American Revolution—the pursuit of happiness. For many workers, whose possibilities had been limited by Chile's rigid class society, the revolutionary process was their promised land of opportunity. Some of their aspirations were material, and the revolutionary process in the factory and nationally had enabled Ex-Yarur workers to satisfy their families' basic needs and even to acquire some of the luxuries that they had always coveted, but never been able to afford—

from the "popular televisions" available through the factory at a subsidized price to inexpensive seaside vacations at a "popular resort" built for workers who may never have seen the ocean.

Equally important for many workers were the new opportunities for vocational and educational advancement for themselves and their children. At Ex-Yarur, internal promotion and open competitions for all staff vacancies enabled ambitious workers to aspire to posts with greater power and prestige, responsibility and remuneration. "God willing, I am going to make supervisor next year, when I have enough years here to qualify," affirmed one mechanic, and another stressed that "now the Production Committees concern themselves about people with merit and promote them."[24] Although some accused the new factory managers of employing political criteria for promotions and posts within the mill, one opposition leader affirmed: "I would have been worse off under another system—and believe me I have known that system."[25]

In addition, several worker leaders had been chosen for important positions outside the mill: Orlando Rossi had become a government interventor in another textile mill; Jorge Lorca, a candidate for congress; Ricardo Catalan, a FENATEX councillor; and Raúl Oliva, a participation troubleshooter for the CORFO. Although all four had been union leaders, underscoring the political character of such "revolutionary mobility," the altered expectations of the rank and file were seen in the growing number of workers taking special courses to qualify for such roles.

Seventeen months after the socialization of their factory, many Ex-Yarur workers were as concerned about values and intellectual limitations as they were about material needs and vocational aspirations. The revolutionary process had proved a powerful transformer of worldviews as well as of structures. It was not just their external conditions that had changed, but their inner lives as well—their self-image, their job satisfaction, their consciousness. These changes were harder to detect and more difficult to define, but no less important.

One such change was the increase in self-esteem summed up in the word "dignity," which reflected their transformation from "Don Amador's people" into "Ex-Yarur workers," masters of their own lives. Another was the altered feelings of many Ex-Yarur workers about their jobs; they seemed to have transcended much of the alienation that had been a central feature of their work experience under the old regime. There were machine operators who no longer felt exploited because "now we are working for Chile," mechanics who felt a new sense of job satisfaction because "now we can work with tranquillity," technical employees who talked of "feeling realized" because "now we can apply our own initiative" and "develop ourselves professionally."[26] Few Ex-Yarur workers experienced an "end to alienation," but

On a Sunday of voluntary labor in mid-1972, the factory was festooned with Chilean flags, underscoring the point that the workers of Ex-Yarur were now "working for Chile and not so that the boss would become even more of a millionaire."

changed feelings about their jobs were among the most important benefits many workers had derived from "socialism." As one Old-timer, a former Yarur loyalist, put it: "The biggest part of one's life is one's work, and if one's work is bitter, then we spend most of our lives embittered. To work now is to realize oneself."[27]

This new self-image and attitude toward work were part of a larger transformation of consciousness that most Yarur workers had experienced during the two years that followed Allende's 1970 election. Not all workers had undergone so dramatic a change in worldview as José Lagos—the skeptical old *apatronado* of April 1971, who one year later was convinced that "workers can run their own industries . . . and ministries too"[28]—but most workers experienced a significant shift in mindset and many a veritable transformation of consciousness.

By September 1972, it was clear that a significant radicalization of worldview had occurred at Ex-Yarur. In the process, *apatronados* had been transformed into populists, populists into radical reformers, and radical reformers into revolutionaries.[29] So dramatic a transformation of consciousness was not universal. Many Yarur loyalists remained firm in their *apatronado* worldview, and other workers moved only to a centrist, communitarian mind-set. Changes in mentality, moreover, were often incomplete, leaving workers holding seemingly inconsistent views. Still, the transformation of consciousness at Ex-Yarur was striking, and to a former teacher like Vicente Poblete, its second general manager, these changes were Ex-Yarur's "most important achievement":

> "If one asks the *compañeros* who are leaders or rank and file: 'Did you think the same way or see things the same way in October [1971] as now?' they say: 'No.' They are aware that now they see the destiny of the country another way and see the progress here more clearly, that they are more conscious of where we are heading. Well, that is what is called 'forming the New Man,' because socialism has to be constructed not only in things, but in people, in our own consciousness," the Socialist Interventor underscored.

"And it is important for the *compañeros* to understand that when they go away from the factory, they remember that there, too, they are participating," he concluded.[30]

The changes in consciousness of Ex-Yarur workers were reflected in altered patterns of political participation and partisanship, both inside the factory and beyond its gates. Within the Yarur mill, there was a dramatic increase in the extent of participation, whether measured by voting, meeting attendance, or committee membership. At the same time, there was a transformation in the quality of political life at the Yarur mill, including a marked radicalization of both the language of politics and the issues debated. Union meetings were tumultuous affairs, with workers shouting out from the floor, applauding and decrying speakers, and behaving with a political intensity that their elected leaders often found difficult to control. At factory general assemblies, even the government managers were challenged and their reports rejected because they weren't "clear and concise, so that all the workers can understand."[31] At Ex-Yarur, the politics of deference had given way to a participatory democracy.

A comparable qualitative change was evident in the election of representatives. When elections for provincial and national CUT officers and delegates were held in May–June 1972, six slates associated with political

Froilan González, who was fired after the 1962 strike and rehired after the requisition a decade later, is singing and beating out on his drum a *"cueca of liberation"* at a political demonstration in downtown Santiago. Behind him are massed Ex-Yarur workers holding a banner inscribed: EX-YARUR: FIRMLY WITH ITS GOVERNMENT.

parties from Left to Right ran candidates and engaged in open campaigns characterized by competing manifestos and partisan debates. Equally striking was the shift in rhetoric and concerns. Although "Reds" and "Yellows," the terms that had dominated the mill's politics in 1970, were still heard in mid–1972, they no longer shaped the language of politics or the agenda of public debate. Now the issues were more complex, the debates more sophisticated, with the problems of revolutionary transformation and socialist transition replacing the politics of liberation on the mill's political agenda.

More visible to the nation than these changes inside the mill walls was the intensified participation of Ex-Yarur workers in political activity beyond the factory gates. Although the extent and quality of this political partici-

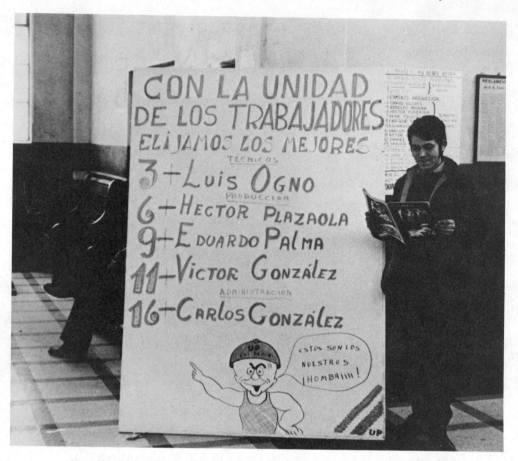

A worker reads *Ramona*, a new leftist youth magazine, near a campaign poster advertising the Popular Unity (UP) slate for the Council of Administration in the August 1972 elections. The cartoon figure at the bottom, waring a hardhat inscribed UP EX-YARUR, points to the list of candidates and says: "These are ours, man!"

pation varied with the immediacy and character of the issue and the degree of difficulty of the activity, what was striking was the dramatic increase in the intensity and scope of worker political participation during the year and a half that followed the socialization of the Yarur mill. During this time, the workers of Ex-Yarur demonstrated that they were now prepared to vote, to speak their mind in public, to sign petitions, to join demonstrations, and to organize the physical defense of the factory when they perceived that their vital interests were at stake. In mid–1972, almost all Ex-Yarur workers appeared ready to defend the socialization of "their" industry, most were

Election day at Ex-Yarur. A union leader checks an *empleado*'s identification during the August 1972 balloting for workers' councillors, while poll watchers look on and another worker heads for the voting booth.

willing to act in support of "their" president, and many were prepared to participate in active efforts to advance "their" revolution from below. "If things go badly, we are the first to be in the streets," boasted Omar Guzmán, "so one sees that here there is more consciousness," a judgment shared by national leaders such as Guillermo Garretón, who placed the Ex-Yarur workers "in the vanguard of Chilean society."[32] The Yarur workers' movement had come a long way from its first fearful attempts at a clandestine politics aimed at nothing more revolutionary than union democracy.

Equally striking was the development of political parties and partisanship at Ex-Yarur, where none had existed before. By September 1972, there were five fully articulated party organizations at Ex-Yarur—Communist, Socialist,

Christian Democrat, MAPU, and MIR (FTR)—which reflected in their structure, statutes, style, ideology, and policies those of their national parent organizations. By then, each party had identified, trained, and tested a group of worker leaders, who had been recruited for that role or had emerged from the ranks by dint of their ability and dedication and matured rapidly in the refining fire of the revolutionary process. The parties had also enrolled and formed a core of cadres who could be relied on to follow party orders and to carry on party activities among their friends and co-workers. Many more Ex-Yarur workers had become party "sympathizers." In addition, the major parties had begun to gain the support of political independents, whose preferences were expressed at the ballot box in the periodic elections that punctuated politics at the Yarur mill between December 1971 and August 1972.

Although all political parties grew in strength and support at Ex-Yarur, not all expanded equally or enjoyed the same power and influence. The politics of liberation at Ex-Yarur was also a process of radicalization, in which the parties of the Left were the greatest gainers. By September 1972, the political ascendancy of the Popular Unity parties was both clear and consolidated. The August 1972 balloting for worker councillors confirmed what the CUT elections had suggested two months before: Christian Democratic support was sizable (about 27 percent), but the Popular Unity majority [which averaged 58 percent] was both unchallengeable and unchanging.[33] Moreover, if the FTR (MIR) ballots were added to the Popular Unity totals, the leftist majority approached three-quarters of the valid ballots cast. By the second anniversary of Allende's election, the process of competitive political mobilization was essentially complete at the Yarur mill, and a leftist hegemony was assured.

If anything, these voting statistics understated the disparity in political power at the Yarur mill in mid–1972. In terms of organizational strength, membership, patronage, and decision-making power within the industry, the dominance of the Popular Unity was far more complete. The superiority of leftist party organizations at Ex-Yarur also reflected the deeper commitment of large numbers of leftists to the party of their choice. Most Christian Democratic voters were "just sympathizers," affirmed one opposition leader, a former Yarur loyalist, adding that few "had party cards" because "we do not want to get involved too deeply" in party politics.[34] By September 1972, however, more than five hundred Ex-Yarur workers were formally inscribed in the rolls of leftist parties and movements.[35]

This leftist political hegemony was both reflected and reinforced by the Left's monopoly of power and patronage at the enterprise level. The Christian Democrats might represent more than one-quarter of the work force, but they were shut out of positions of political influence at the mill. The Popular

Unity had a monopoly in the Council of Administration and the union board of directors and undisputed control of the coordinating committee. If the political battle in mid–1972 was still between "Reds" and "Yellows," it seemed as if the "Reds" had finally won a definitive victory.

Not that all workers at Ex-Yarur shared so positive a view of these political developments. Even Leftist workers criticized the intrusion of sectarian criteria into mill politics and looked back nostalgically to the days where workers "voted for the best *compañero*," not for the party. Christian Democratic leaders, for their part, complained of being denied an influence and patronage commensurate with their support among the rank and file. At the same time, the triumph of the Popular Unity was not absolute either. The mill's politics had polarized with one-quarter of the workers still supporting the Christian Democrats. The increasing unification of the working class around the banner of socialism called for in the Popular Unity's political strategy seemed to have peaked short of its goal—even at a vanguard factory such as Ex-Yarur. Still, by September 1972, even an FTR (MIR) leader at the mill was forced to admit:: "Neither the MIR nor any other movement is going to best the Popular Unity because it is there that the great mass of workers are concentrated."[36]

Seventeen months after its requisition, Ex-Yarur seemed a managerial, economic, social, and political success. It was not a total success, or the only success story within Chile's social property area, but it was one of the enterprises most frequently cited as demonstrating the achievements and possibilities of a Chilean democratic socialism. It was a showing that Ex-Yarur's first general manager attributed to "the fund of goodwill from being first" and that other knowledgeable observers ascribed to Ex-Yarur's "good fortune" in its government managers and worker leaders, but that the most perceptive of those leaders himself ascribed to the fact that Ex-Yarur's workers had had to struggle for the socialization of their factory and thus valued it more highly and identified more with its performance.[37]

But Ex-Yarur's general success did not mean that there were no problems. "Do we have problems?" Interventor Vicente Poblete asked rhetorically. "We have all kinds of problems."[38] Many were "inevitable problems of an era of transition," one CUT observer underscored, "the product of a revolutionary process *a la chilena*—without adequate preparation or planning."[39] Some of these —such as the limited participation of many workers and the uneven performance of their representatives in the new system of comanagement—reflected the inexperience of Ex-Yarur workers in their new managerial roles, along with the old regime's legacy of worker passivity. The same was true for the "lack of communication" between the "top managers" and "the rank and file," which left the latter "without the information they needed."[40] In other cases, the shortcomings of "*compañeros* who do not participate as they should,"[41] stemmed from their unsuitability for the posts to which they had been elected as heroes of the "liberation." Other transitional problems, such as lax work discipline and uneven labor productivity, reflected unrealistic worker expectations of what "liberation" would mean.

These were the transitional problems of a new and untested system, which might be solved in time because the awareness of the difficulty and the will to transcend it were present at Ex-Yarur. Where the difficulties stemmed from a lack of experience, inadequate preparation, or too narrow a worldview, Ex-Yarur was a "school for socialism" in which progress was marked and further advances could be expected. Where the problem was unsuitable or uninterested representatives, it was solved by replacing them with better-qualified and more committed workers. By September 1972, there was a better fit between personnel and posts and representatives and responsibilities at Ex-Yarur, while education and experience were remedying misunderstood priorities and inadequate communication.

But not all of the problems encountered at Ex-Yarur were problems of learning and transition to a new order. Some were embedded in the structure of the new system of comanagement, and others reflected tensions within the revolutionary process as a whole—profound problems that were far more difficult to solve. The vague boundaries between the authority and functions of the various organs of worker participation and the representatives elected to them led to overlapping pretensions, competition, and tensions between worker councillors, coordinators, and union officers. Political differences within the Left over revolutionary strategy and tactics, along with a competition for support and struggle for ascendancy, fed rivalries at once partisan and personal. As the national parties imposed themselves on what had been a nonsectarian workers movement, they introduced into Ex-Yarur the political problems that plagued the Popular Unity nationally, particularly *sectarismo*—sectarian politics—the Left's Achilles' heel.

At Ex-Yarur, moreover, continuing tensions between the revolution from above and the revolution from below were clear not only in rank-and-file pressures to eliminate the Taylor System, fire the Yarur loyalists, secure larger wage increases, and win more rapid internal promotions, but in the *obrero* drive for equality and fraternity as well. The push from below to level social differences and create an egalitarian industrial community conflicted with the Popular Unity's central political strategy of allying with the middle class in order to create an electoral majority for socialism. Most *empleados* resented their loss of power, privilege, and status. Confronted with a blue-collar revolution from below, they clung to their middle-class self-image and identified increasingly with the opposition Christian Democrats as "the party of the middle class." Nor was the Popular Unity's objective of unifying the working class in favor of socialism advanced by local activists who pressed a partisan definition of that goal on the many Ex-Yarur *obreros* who were loyal Christian Democrats. These difficulties represented tensions and contradictions in the revolutionary process at Ex-Yarur, which reflected the specific history of the Yarur mill, but also revealed problems plaguing the Popular Unity's democratic road to socialism nationally.

Yet even where these less tractable problems were concerned, progress was made at Ex-Yarur although the advance was slower and less uniform. There were both "good and bad" sections in each division of the enterprise, Poblete stressed. In one Acabados shift, he boasted, "they have solved these problems in an impressive manner." The Finishing section's productivity, efficiency, and innovation were among the highest in the factory, as were its levels of social interaction and sense of community. It had no problems with absenteeism or discipline, no conflicts between *obreros* and *empleados*, and no problems with sectarian politics. Significantly, Poblete stressed, it was also one of the sections where worker "participation is fullest and has worked best . . . in which the criticism and self-criticism among the *jefes*, the production committee, and the workers are done in a constructive manner."[42] Acabados was so successful in solving, through effective worker participation, the problems that plagued other Ex-Yarur production sections that by mid–1972 it was being projected as a model for other sections to follow.[43]

There were some problems, however, that even raised worker consciousness and perfected participation could not solve. The workers of Ex-Yarur might democratize their production and maximize their output, but they could still never satisfy a demand that exceeded the mill's installed capacity. They could close the factory outlet store, decrease deliveries to merchants suspected of speculating, and increase direct distribution of Yarur products to lower-class consumers, but they could not prevent a black market in the factory's scarce goods. They could increase their efficiency and save on spare parts and raw materials, but with a 75 percent increase in their costs and no rise in their prices, they still could not balance their books. They could save dollars and decrease dependency by innovating from below, but with foreign exchange scarce and the American credit blockade, they still could not purchase the imported machinery that alone could enable Ex-Yarur to meet this consumer demand and undermine the black market.

Together with the social and political problems that reflected the unresolved tensions within the Popular Unity and the revolutionary process that it led, these problems might have local manifestations, but they required national solutions. The workers of Ex-Yarur realized this by mid–1972, and their delegates to the July 1972 Textile Encounter of the socialized textile sector were among those who took the lead in recommending national remedies for these problems and in demanding that the Allende government take steps to resolve them.

In September 1972, Ex-Yarur's workers and government managers were aware of mistakes they had made and problems that remained to be solved, but they were also proud of their achievements and optimistic about the future course of their socialist road. By then, workers had become managers, the mill was producing at close to capacity, and innovations from below had transformed working conditions in the plant and the maintenance shop into a spare-parts factory. Along the way, the workers had won higher wages and benefits, increased liberty and equality, created a new sense of solidarity and community, and secured greater opportunities for themselves and their children. They had also undergone profound internal changes, emerging with more dignity, less alienation, and transformed worldviews. These changes both reflected and generated a new politics at the mill, one characterized by greater popular participation and solid Popular Unity support, but troubled by sectarian tensions, social conflict, and personal rivalries.

Above all, Ex-Yarur had demonstrated the viability and creativity of a new kind of socialism —a participatory socialism. It was this model that the socialized textile sector endorsed at its July 1972 Encounter and that an enthusiastic Pedro Vuskovic, now head of the social property area, projected as an example for the other socialized sectors to emulate.[44] In September 1972, the Ex-Yarur workers seemed to be in the forefront of a pioneering effort to forge a uniquely Chilean economic democracy, one that differed from the initial ideas of the Popular Unity's politicians and planners, but was beginning to reshape even their visions of the New Chile in a more representative and responsive mold.

On a September afternoon in 1972, Armando Carrera sat in the deserted cafeteria talking about "the revolutionary process" at Ex-Yarur. They had come "a long way in a short time," but they "had only just begun to construct socialism," the Socialist councillor stressed. Still, he remained optimistic that they would reach their goal. "Just give us time," Carrera concluded.[45]

But time was precisely what the workers of Ex-Yarur would not be granted. Beyond their factory gates, the forces opposed to their revolution were gathering to block their path, reverse their gains, and turn their dreams into nightmares.

17

THE END
OF THE DEMOCRATIC
ROAD

What made the achievements of Ex-Yarur particularly impressive was that its workers had made so much progress toward their goals within an increasingly problematic national context.[1] During the seventeen months between the requisition of the Yarur mill and the declaration of the October Strike, the issue was not only whether the workers could create socialism in their factory but also whether the Popular Unity could advance toward socialism in the nation. Their revolution from below might enjoy substantial autonomy, but it was part of a larger revolutionary process whose progress and problems increasingly shaped their own.

During 1971 the progress of the revolutionary process obscured the problems, but as 1972 advanced, they grew in magnitude, intensity, and visibility. Advances along the democratic road to socialism slowed to a crawl. By October 1972, economic dislocations, class conflict, and political polarization had become so severe that it was not clear whether Chile was advancing toward socialism—or social war.

TOWARD SOCIALISM?

On November 4, 1971, Salvador Allende celebrated "the first year of Popular Government" with a speech whose theme was "fulfilling the program." "We are here to signal that we have advanced in the creation of the social property area, the base of the economic program, the cornerstone of power for the people," *el compañero presidente* told a packed national football stadium. "We control 90 percent of what were the private banks . . . more than seventy

227

strategic and monopolistic enterprises have been expropriated, intervened, requisitioned or acquired by the state. We are *owners!*" he announced to the cheering crowd, which included many Ex-Yarur workers. "We are able to say: *our* copper, *our* coal, *our* iron, *our* nitrates, *our* steel; the fundamental bases of heavy industry today belong to Chile and the Chileans."[2]

To this impressive record of structural change, Salvador Allende added still other accomplishments: the participation of workers and peasants in the management of their workplaces, as at Ex-Yarur; the massive redistribution of income; the diminution of both inflation and unemployment; the expanded housing, health, and education programs; the extension of social security; and the reform of the legal system. It was an extraordinary set of achievements, one unequaled by any previous Chilean president, let alone in his very first year in office. Taken together, these advances seemed ample justification for Allende's optimism that Chile was well launched on his democratic road to socialism.[3]

Between the requisition of the Yarur mill and the first anniversary, the Chilean revolution had taken a great leap forward. As a result of this revolutionary advance, the socialized sector included twenty of the twenty-three largest private corporations in Chile a year before. The newly socialized enterprises were concentrated in a few industrial sectors, where they accounted for a major share of output and many of the largest firms, with textiles leading the way.[4] The Yarur workers had not only "liberated" their own mill but had also inaugurated a new phase of the revolutionary process.

Like S.A. Yarur, two-thirds of the firms socialized during 1971 had been taken over using emergency decree powers to requisition private firms. Most had yet to be incorporated definitively into the social property area, but with a government interventor managing the company and militant workers insisting on socialism and wage increases that threatened the profitability of the enterprise, the Allende government expected the old owners to sell to the state at a reasonable price.

The relationship between the revolution from above and the revolution from below might seem complementary and free of conflict. But the fact that less than a quarter of the enterprises that had come under state control were on the government's list for incorporation into the social property area revealed that it was the workers who were leading the way, shaping the social property area according to their own revolutionary vision and priorities. Pressure from below had also been largely responsible for the inauguration of worker participation in the management of 40 enterprises of the social property area employing 71,000 workers—with Ex-Yarur again the pioneer.[5] The impact of the revolution from below was equally evident in the countryside, where peasant land seizures were responsible for accelerating and radicalizing the agrarian reform.[6] Pressure from below also led to record real-wage increases and housing starts, along with a shift of some 10 percent of the national income from capital to labor, fulfilling Allende's six-year income distribution goal in one year. Both income redistribution and housing programs were central to Allende government economic, social, and political strategies; but without this pressure, the increases in personal incomes and social programs would have been slower in pace and smaller in scope.[7]

On the first anniversary of Allende's inauguration, it appeared as if he had delivered on his campaign promise of a revolution without sacrifice—and the revolution from below could take substantial credit for his success.[8] But it was also largely responsible for problems that had begun to appear on the horizon by November 1971 and would assume serious proportions during the year that followed.

The principal economic problems that emerged to confront Allende and to confound his image of success were price inflation and government deficits, consumer shortages and scarce dollars. Although their causes were complex, the revolution from below played a significant role in their generation or exacerbation. The recrudescence of inflation, Chile's old nemesis, which would quadruple during 1972, was an early warning sign of coming economic crisis. It was fed by budget deficits, which reflected the enlarged public sector and outsize wage increases that the revolution from below pressed on a reluctant Allende government, as well as the refusal of the opposition-controlled Congress to vote new taxes. Although in Popular Unity theory, the socialized enterprises were supposed to finance government programs with their profits, as at Ex-Yarur, the combination of greatly increased costs with controlled prices spelled losses that were covered by the government, through an expansionist monetary policy, which more than doubled the money supply in one year.[9]

Another major source of inflationary pressures was the growing scarcity of certain consumer goods. Although the Left blamed capitalist sabotage and hoarding and the Right attributed it to socialist inefficiency and corruption, at bottom, the emergence of consumer shortages reflected an excess of demand over supply, the consequence of the explosion of consumer purchasing power that followed the 30 percent average increase in real wages during 1971, and far outstripped the productive capacity of Chile's semi-developed economy.[10]

Allende government efforts to satisfy this excess consumer demand with increased imports exhausted Chile's foreign reserves by late 1971. Together with the 25 percent fall in international copper prices, the rise in import prices, and the United States' "invisible credit blockade," this Allende effort to protect consumer living standards generated balance-of-payments difficulties that forced currency devaluations that further exacerbated the inflationary spiral. Moreover, as Ex-Yarur workers were only too well aware, the shortage of foreign exchange made it difficult to import the spare parts, raw materials, fuels, and machinery needed to maintain and expand the industrial and agricultural production that might satisfy the greatly enlarged consumer demand that the very "success" of the revolution from below had generated.[11]

Many of the economic problems that the revolution from below had helped create—such as accelerating inflation and consumer shortages—were also corrosive socially and costly politically. By mid–1972, it was clear that the Allende government was not only faced with growing economic dislocations, but with rising class conflict and political opposition as well. The accelerated revolutionary advance impelled by the revolution from below united disparate forces, under the leadership of the national bourgeoisie, in opposition to its radical transformation of Chilean society.

Initially, Chile's capitalists were divided on how to deal with the Popular Unity government. Many businessmen believed they could strike a deal with Allende, as they had with his reforming predecessors; Amador Yarur himself sought to negotiate the transformation of his factory into a mixed ownership enterprise.[12] The drive for the establishment of the social property area that began with the seizure of the Yarur mill ended elite illusions that a deal with Allende was possible and brought the different sectors of the national bourgeoisie into concerted opposition to both the Popular Unity and its structural reforms. The government's determined efforts to "put an end to the large landed estate"(*latifundio*) elicited a similar response from the agrarian bourgeoisie. By the end of 1971, the elite business associations (*gremios*) had united their efforts behind a general defense of private property and begun to draw the small business *gremios* into their campaign, playing on the latter's anxieties over the wave of *tomas* that followed the seizure and socialization of the Yarur mill and included smaller enterprises not on the Popular Unity's list of "monopolies" to be expropriated.[13] The revolution from below helped push anxious small business and farm owners into this capitalist alliance, even where their own economic interests had not been directly attacked and although many had profited from the Allende boom.[14]

This capitalist resistance took varied forms, ranging from the spontaneous to the premeditated and from the individual to the organized. The 17 percent drop in private investment during 1971 mostly reflected the natural reluctance of capitalists to invest during eras of uncertainty, particularly where they felt unsure about the future status of private property itself. The profit motive provided insufficient incentive to secure reinvestment on the road to socialism, yet enough to cause speculation in scarce goods for which the Allende government had fixed low prices, as the black market in Yarur textiles demonstrated.

Other elite economic resistance was more considered and concerted.

Although some capitalists agreed to sell their enterprises, most refused and instead fought Allende's socialization by decree with all the weapons at their command. The Yarurs were the first to resist, a model that other capitalists followed. When their cotton mill was requisitioned, the Yarurs used their influence to secure press and congressional opposition to the measure and even prevailed on the Jordanian ambassador to lodge a diplomatic protest—although their "Arab" enterprise was Chilean and both Amador and Jorge Yarur were Peruvian citizens. When these measures failed to reverse the Allende government's requisition of the mill, the Yarurs took their case first to the *Controlaría** and then to the courts, challenging the constitutionality of the decree and "keeping [their] legal claim alive."[15] Other entrepreneurs followed their example, urged on by their business associations and the opposition media. By mid–1972, few capitalists were willing to sell their enterprises to the state, and such individual responses to the expropriation of their assets had become part of a comprehensive elite strategy to block Allende's road to socialism.

By then, the United States government and copper corporations had joined these efforts to stop Allende's structural changes, undermine the success of his economic policies, and weaken the appeal of his socialist ideology. Although the Nixon administration's hostility to a socialist Chile probably would have ensured U.S. involvement in any case, Allende's decision not to compensate Anaconda and Kennecott for their expropriated copper mines because of past "excess profits" justified an expanded United States covert campaign to destabilize the Allende government by supporting its domestic opponents, blocking international loans for Chile, and making contacts with potential coup plotters in the Chilean armed forces.[16]

What Allende feared most had come to pass. The seizure and socialization of the Yarur mill had set off a revolution from below that had escaped control, disrupted his economic strategy, accelerated his program of structural change, and radicalized the revolutionary process. As a consequence, the Chilean revolution he led had been propelled prematurely into a decisive confrontation with the national bourgeoisie. Allende now had to confront "the power of Chilean capitalism and Yankee imperialism" simultaneously and do so within a context of growing economic dislocation, political opposition, and social conflict.[17]

By October 1972, Chile faced the most intense and widespread class conflict in its history, a reflection of the challenge of the revolution from below to Chile's class structure and social relations. Its threat to capitalist ownership, demand for a redistribution of the national income, and insistence

---

* The Controlaría was an autonomous administrative body with quasi-judicial powers to rule on the legality of executive acts.

on worker oversight in private firms posed this challenge in its starkest form; but its threat to established status was equally conflictual. Upper-class Chileans felt threatened by the surge in working-class power and assertiveness, as deference gave way to a social revolution that threatened to turn their hierarchical world upside down. Typical was the comment of one upper-class matron watching the Ex-Yarur workers parading up the Alameda that "what most annoyed" her was that "the *rotos* ["broken ones"]—the elite's disdainful term for the lower class—were "taking over" Chile.

Significantly, the Chilean middle classes seemed as threatened by this social revolution from below as the elite they emulated. Even members of the lower middle class who had little or no property to lose shared elite concern about "worker power," which appeared to jeopardize their own precarious social position. As the example of Ex-Yarur's white-collar employees demonstrated, the result of the surge in working-class power and consciousness was escalating class conflict.

As 1972 advanced, it became increasingly clear that these growing social tensions carried political consequences as well. The revolution from below not only alienated the middle class from the Popular Unity cause, but it also helped push them into the ranks of the Christian Democrats, "the party of the middle class," undermining the Popular Unity's political strategy of social alliance in the process. Their loss was clear in opposition victories in congressional by-elections during the year that followed the seizure of the Yarur mill, triumphs that enabled the opposition to seize the political initiative by 1972.[18]

By then, the centrist Christian Democrats were allied with the rightist Nationalists. Some of the reasons for this Christian Democratic embrace of the Right were purely political, including the Popular Unity's majority in the April 1971 municipal elections and refusal to consider an alliance with the Christian Democrats in its wake. Equally important was the Center party's shocked disapproval of the speed, scope, and tactics of the revolutionary advance of 1971 in general and the revolution from below in particular. Rejected by the Left and resistant to its socialist vision, the Christian Democrats accepted the overtures of the Right, a more natural alliance for its anti-Communist and procapitalist right wing, which had regained its traditional ascendancy within the Center party. The secession of the *tercerista* left wing, which left the party in August 1971 to protest this embrace of the Right, consolidated this trend. During the months that followed, the initial Christian Democratic stance of "loyal opposition and occasional collaboration" was replaced by an increasingly obstructive opposition.[19] As the year advanced, it became clear that the social and political center—the balance wheel of Chilean politics—had turned right, against Allende and his democratic road to socialism.

The Popular Unity's insistence on a partisan definition of working-class unity was also problematic, ignoring long-standing social and ideological divisions, making more difficult the unification of Chile's workers around a common program. As the experience of Ex-Yarur demonstrated, instead of unifying the working class, as called for in the Left's political strategy, sectarian politics and "vanguardism" exacerbated preexisting social, ideological, and partisan cleavages. The Left's failure was clear in the ability of the Christian Democrats to win more than one-quarter of the vote in nationwide union balloting for CUT officers in mid–1972.

The Left's inability to unite the working class behind its banners and win the support of the lower middle class called into question the Popular Unity's political strategy for securing an electoral majority for socialism. By mid–1972, resources for further populist policies of redistribution were exhausted, and intensifying class conflict and political polarization made future electoral inroads at the expense of the Christian Democrats unlikely. The democratic road to socialism seemed blocked.

By then, the viability of the Allende government's original economic strategy was also open to question. The first phases of the revolutionary process had been completed far ahead of schedule, with substantial success in the major areas of structural reform and the redistribution of income. The economic costs of these gains, however, had only begun to be paid. Inflation was accelerating, budget deficits were multiplying, foreign reserves were exhausted, and consumer shortages were emerging. One year after the requisition of the Yarur mill, leftist optimism had given way to pessimism, and the success of *la vía chilena* itself now seemed in doubt.

In June 1972, the leaders of the Popular Unity met at Lo Curro, near Santiago, to devise a strategy that would revive the Left's sagging political fortunes, correct the economic errors of the first phases of the revolutionary process, and steer a safe course through the economic shoals ahead. There were two competing strategies at the Lo Curro conclave. Allende and the Communists argued for a policy of economic consolidation, social conciliation, and political compromise. At bottom, it represented an attempt to save the original Popular Unity political strategy of class alliance. Pedro Vuskovic and the Socialists advocated pressing forward, relying on the growing militancy of the working class and its allies among the peasants and *pobladores*. In essence, they proposed that the Popular Unity scrap its original strategy, place itself at the head of the revolution from below, and rely on its creativity and dynamism to see the revolutionary process through the coming crisis. Beneath the seemingly theological debate over whether to *avanzar consolidando* ("advance by consolidating") or *consolidar avanzando* ("consolidate by advancing") lay a dispute over diametrically opposed economic, political, and social strategies.

Given the parliamentary pasts of most Popular Unity leaders and the disarray of the economy, it was not surprising that the Communist-*allendista* position triumphed at Lo Curro. The forward economic policy was halted, and negotiations were begun with the Christian Democrats on a compromise accord that would legalize most of the structural changes while sacrificing some and giving others a communitarian flavor. In the process, a potential constitutional clash between executive and legislature would be averted over a Christian Democratic amendment prohibiting takeovers of private enterprises by decree and giving Congress control over the creation of the social property area. As part of the package, property seizures would be stopped and the "ultra-Left" MIR neutralized. The revolution from above and the revolution from below had come to a parting of the ways.

The appeal of the Lo Curro strategy was that it seemed to offer a way to consolidate important advances, defuse the counterrevolution, and buy time in which to rectify past errors and prepare for future advances on firmer foundations. The crux of the strategy was the negotiation of a compromise with the Christian Democrats. Such an accord might have been possible in 1971, when the Popular Unity was ascendant and the Christian Democratic progressives stronger, but by mid–1972 it was too late. By then, class conflict and political polarization had gone too far to be reversed so easily. Although two weeks of intense negotiations between Popular Unity and Christian Democratic moderates produced substantial agreement over fundamental issues and optimism about resolving the few that remained, their compromise accord was vetoed by the Christian Democratic right wing under pressure from the party's middle-class constituency. The opportunity was lost to reverse the political polarization and constitutional clash threatening both the Popular Unity's socialist road and Chile's democracy. A turning point in the Chilean tragedy had been reached.[20]

The failure of compromise in July 1972 and the advent of confrontation politics one month later were indications that the opposition was not going to give the Lo Curro strategy the opportunity to succeed. Thrown on the defensive, the Popular Unity wrestled with putting its own economic and political house in order, but in increasingly straitened circumstances. This flurry of activity obscured the exhaustion of the revolution from above, but failed to achieve either a revolutionary breakthrough or a centrist consolidation—or to halt the drift toward political confrontation that was evident by August 1972.[21]

By then, rightist paramilitary squads—with rumored Yarur financing —were fighting pitched battles with leftist youths and blocking traffic with burning barricades in downtown Santiago, stoning stores and shoppers who refused to join opposition business stoppages. In the halls of Congress, conservative politicians blocked all attempts at compromise and hinted at the need to oust Allende instead. The newly conflictual political atmosphere was even felt within the walls of Ex-Yarur, where anonymous leaflets began to appear warning that the Yarurs would return, along with reports of meetings of Yarur loyalists in Don Jorge's Vitacura mansion. While leftist newspapers warned darkly of a "September Plan" to overthrow the Allende government, Jorge Yarur himself stressed that he would never recover his factory so long as Allende was president, but was equally skeptical that a Christian Democratic government would take so dramatic a step in the face of worker resistance. "Only a [military] regime of force, closely tied to the [right wing] National party " would serve that purpose, he affirmed, and he implied that such a scenario was in the wings.[22]

TOWARD COUNTERREVOLUTION?

On September 4, 1972, behind proud banners proclaiming "Ex-Yarur: Firmly Behind Its Government," some twelve hundred workers marched down the broad boulevard of the Alameda, together with hundreds of thousands of chanting Popular Unity supporters, in one of the biggest demonstrations in Chilean history. But the second anniversary of Allende's "Popular Triumph" signified the end of the constructive period of the Chilean revolution and the beginning of its struggle for survival against a counterrevolution of growing strength.

One month later, a work stoppage by a small group of truck owners in distant Aysén, in the far south of Chile, triggered a national walkout and lockout by merchants and manufacturers, professionals and shopkeepers, that rapidly engulfed Chile in a virtual class war, complete with paramilitary attacks and terrorist bombings. At bottom, the *Paro de Octubre* (October Strike) was a "general strike" of the bourgeoisie, intended to demonstrate their power as a class, stop the advance toward socialism, and create the conditions within which Allende could be ousted—by military coup or congressional impeachment.[23]

The October Strike represented the culmination of more than a year of planning, organization, and orchestration by Chile's economic elites, during which they had drawn the social and political center into their strategy for bringing Allende's socialist road to an end. It was the business interest groups that led the October Strike, with the middle class *gremios* as the visible vanguard.[24] This gave the strike broader appeal and greater legitimacy, as well as a stronger claim on the backing of the Christian Democrats, whose ranks included many who preferred compromise to confrontation. The opposition parties, however, were reduced to a supporting role, competing with each other in endorsing the strike while privately worrying about their

During the final struggle for power that began with the October Strike, terrorist attacks by rightist paramilitary groups increased and leftist political demonstrations took on a darker tone. Here an Ex-Yarur truck, damaged by a bomb and adorned with a sign reading HERE IS THE WORK OF FASCISM, is juxtaposed against a truck bearing women workers adorned with fabrics designed and manufactured at Ex-Yarur. The latter sign reads: HERE IS THE WORK OF THE WORKERS, representing an effort to teach the public a political lesson.

loss of control. In the end, they embraced the business associations' non-negotiable "Demands of Chile," an ultimatum to the Allende government to reverse its revolutionary course, abandon its socialist goals, and surrender its political project.

Although it had faced periodic military plots during the preceding two years, the October Strike was the most serious challenge that the Allende government had yet confronted. It forced the Popular Unity to transcend its internal divisions, postpone promising reforms, mobilize its remaining resources, and loose the revolution from below in order to contain the counterrevolutionary threat. From the start, the government based its defense on three pillars: its executive powers, the armed forces, and the organized working class. Using its emergency powers under the Constitution, the Allende government commandeered media networks, requisitioned trucks, and arrested roadblocking strikers. By declaring a "state of emergency" in affected provinces, Allende was able to involve the armed forces in the restoration of order. From the outset, the CUT played a major role in mobilizing working-class support for governmental efforts to maintain the production and distribution of essential goods. But the revolution from above remained on the defensive, always a step behind its antagonists, parrying opposition thrusts but unable to contain the spreading strike or mobilize a counteroffensive that could transform the crisis into a revolutionary breakthrough.

It was the revolution from below that took up the torch, interpreting the CUT's call for vigilance as a license for direct revolutionary action. In the face of enormous obstacles, the comanaged factories maintained their production levels while organizing their own defense against rightist paramilitary attacks. They also mobilized manpower, transport, and other resources for the national effort to defeat the "Bosses' Strike." When the government agencies alone proved incapable of ensuring neighborhood defense and direct distribution of essential goods and services, the workers and their grass-roots organizations filled the breach.

The experience of Ex-Yarur was a case in point. At Ex-Yarur, organization reached a new level with the formation of self-defense brigades, whose worth was proved by the mobilization in minutes of one thousand workers armed with pointed staves to repel an attempted assault on the industry in mid-October.[25] Within the factory, Ex-Yarur gave priority to the national effort to combat the strike, retooling its machine shop for the assembly of trucks, turning the industry garage over to the maintenance of requisitioned vehicles, and using the enterprise's walled-in grounds as safe parking for other government trucks. At the same time, production levels were maintained although distribution was made more difficult by the loan of Ex-Yarur trucks—and drivers—to the Ministry of Economy. An angry workers' assembly voted to erase the names of striking merchants from their list of clients and to distribute their quotas directly to *pobladores* and peasants instead. Many workers volunteered for after-hours labor in the nearby Central Railway Station, loading and unloading goods.

For the first time, moreover, the Ex-Yarur workers placed their resources at the disposition of other workers and residents in the surrounding area. They were one of the principal founders and largest industry of the Cordon O'Higgins, one of Santiago's four major *cordones industriales*, which united workers within the same industrial belt or zone into local organizations [councils] under their direct control. Within that context, Ex-Yarur workers helped organize several of the small clothing factories and played an important part in the seizure and socialization of the Salinas y Fabres machine shop, a large industrial garage with the capacity to repair the sabotaged trucks and other heavy vehicles needed to maintain distribution networks in the face of the transport strike. Within the broad territory of the Cordon O'Higgins, Ex-Yarur coordinated the distribution of essential goods and helped in neighborhood defense, dispatching a group of workers to drive off an attack by a rightist paramilitary squad on the headquarters of a local Popular Unity Committee (CUP). In response to the October Strike and the *cordon industrial*, the workers of Ex-Yarur were extending their revolution into the surrounding community and leading workers in other factories, large and small, toward socialism.

The experience of Ex-Yarur was typical. Throughout Chile, the October Strike was the hour of the *cordones industriales*. They proliferated rapidly throughout the industrial zones of Chile, uniting workers of diverse factories and backgrounds and generating the dynamism, organization, and will to stalemate the counterrevolutionary offensive and transform it into an opportunity for revolutionary advance. The *cordones* organized the seizure of private sector enterprises where workers had been locked out or distribution sabotaged, and they incorporated workers in plants and shops that were too small to be legally unionized by the CUT. Joining together workers of differing sectors, crafts, statuses, and politics, the *cordones* were able to transcend at the grass-roots level the limitations that the Chilean Labor Code had placed on labor organization. In essence, the *cordon industrial* represented the successful response of the Chilean working class to the "bourgeois strike."

The October Strike was also a pressure cooker of consciousness. It was the most naked and intense class conflict that Chile had ever seen. In that refining fire, the mind-set of many workers was transformed, generally in a more "revolutionary" direction. In the process, the ambivalent became committed, the aloof involved, and the sectarian united. The class character of the October Strike made it possible to mobilize a working-class opposition to the "Bosses' Strike" that transcended party lines. At Ex-Yarur and elsewhere, even Christian Democratic *obreros* felt the pull of class solidarity to be greater than that of political partisanship, and few joined the strike that their party supported.

This quantum jump in working-class organization and consciousness, mobilization and militancy, unity and activity was an unintended consequence of the October Strike. In order to counter the *paro patronal* (Bosses' Strike), Chile's workers created more representative, responsive, and powerful class institutions. The question was what use the Popular Unity government would make of this revolutionary leap by its central mass base.

Allende's decision to end the October Strike by incorporating the military chiefs into the cabinet dictated the answer. The status quo ante conditions of the "truce of November," guaranteed by the participation of the armed forces in the government, precluded seizing the opportunity and using the mobilized working class to force a revolutionary breakthrough. The preference of President Allende and the Communist party for controlled change, class coalitions, and the familiar arena of electoral politics also militated against scrapping the original Popular Unity strategy for a more confrontational revolutionary route.

On the other side, the Christian Democrats were uneasy at their loss of control over opposition politics and their own social base. They viewed the October Strike as an electoral strategy for creating the conditions for an opposition landslide in the March 1973 legislative balloting, which would make it possible to impeach Allende. By late October, moreover, even the Nationalists and the *gremios*, who had hoped that the strike would create the chaos and conflict that would justify military intervention, were sobered by the social stalemate and the refusal of the armed forces to oust Allende. The result was an electoral truce, with the military supervising the cooling of social tensions. Both government and opposition settled down to campaigning for congressional elections "as usual," although in an atmosphere of economic crisis, social conflict, and political polarization that gave the March 1973 balloting a plebiscitary air.

The election returns allowed both sides to claim victory. The opposition alliance, with 54 percent of the vote to the Popular Unity's 44 percent, had won a clear majority, but fallen far short of its own predictions or the two-thirds needed to impeach Allende. The Popular Unity had gained 8 percent over its 1970 showing, increasing its support among workers, peasants, and *pobladores*; but it had lost strength in middle-class districts since April 1971 and failed to win the majority that it needed to legislate socialism. From the elated perspective of the presidential palace, however, the Popular Unity had won a great victory, and the political wisdom of Allende and his strategy had once again been demonstrated. With no major elections scheduled before the 1976 presidential balloting, Allende seemed confirmed in power for another three years.[26]

Appearances were deceiving. The March elections may have been a triumph for Allende and his democratic road, but they were a Pyrrhic victory. The confirmation of the civilian stalemate decided the Christian Democrats in favor of a military coup and probably made up Washington's mind as well. Despite Allende's efforts to open a dialogue, the Christian Democrats replaced their moderate leadership with a right wing "coup team" in May. The possibility of political accommodation was now discounted, and the final confrontation became inevitable.

Increasingly open expressions of political opposition by military officers now became common as well. The armed forces, the last institution capable of keeping the social peace, were being politicized and encouraged by opposition politicians to cast off their constitutional neutrality.[27] In late June, the *tancazo*, a rebellion by a Santiago armored regiment, revealed that only a handful of senior officers still supported Commander in Chief General Carlos Prats' constitutionalist stance.[28] During the weeks that followed, their position was undermined, and Prats himself was forced to resign in late August. General Augusto Pinochet replaced him, and a fortnight later the coup took place.[29]

Allende's decision after October 1972 to rely on the pacifying power of the army, instead of on the revolutionary potential of the mobilized working class, would prove fatal to the Chilean revolution.[30] In the process, the Left lost an opportunity for working-class unity and a revolutionary breakthrough that never occurred again. The channeling of working-class militancy into an election campaign restored the primacy of political identification in Christian Democratic workers who had begun to give priority to class solidarity without transforming the conditions that were confining the revolutionary process. The *cordones industriales* were demobilized, and the Left never regained its October momentum. The revolution from above, its political ingenuity, legal levers, and economic resources exhausted, proved incapable of effective leadership and creative response to the succeeding months of deepening crisis and renewed confrontation. Salvador Allende had relied too heavily on his considerable political skills and those of General Prats, realizing too late that class conflict in Chile had reached a level of intensity that transcended even their capacity to conciliate or conjure away.

One result of the Popular Unity's decision to cling to the strategy of 1972 in the very different conditions of 1973 was increasing disunity within the governing coalition. Although both personal and sectarian rivalries played a role in this deepening division within the revolution from above, at bottom it represented a renewed struggle over revolutionary strategy, with the Communist-led majority backing Allende's policy of dialogue with the Christian Democrats and revolutionary restraint whereas the Socialist-led minority argued for mobilizing the revolution from below and preparing for the military confrontation that they now regarded as inevitable. In the gathering crisis, Allende rejected Socialist advice to "mobilize the masses," with the bitterly sardonic retort: "How many masses equals one tank."[31] In a nation increasingly divided by class conflict and political polarization, Allende's desperate efforts to pursue conciliation with the Christian Democrats while mollifying his own left wing failed on both counts, leaving a paralysis which was replicated elsewhere within the revolution from above.[32]

This failure of national leadership was shared by the CUT, which should have served as a bridge between the revolution from above and the revolution from below. Instead, the CUT viewed the latter with increasing antagonism and alarm, regarding the *cordones industriales* in particular as rivals and threats. From the "vanguard of the working class," the CUT was transformed into the national supervisor of productivity and the watchdog of the workers, whose function was to keep labor on a leash. As a consequence, the Chilean working class became confused, divided, and demoralized —even at a vanguard factory such as Ex-Yarur.[33]

Since the October Strike, Ex-Yarur's workers had soldiered on, struggling with national economic dislocations that forced them to close the factory for "collective vacations" in January 1973 for lack of cotton and to barter their cloth for potatoes in August for lack of food. During these months, the revolutionary process struggled to survive, and the autonomy and resources that had allowed Ex-Yarur to experiment with its own socialist path disappeared. After October 1972, the experience of Ex-Yarur merged with that of the nation at large.

Within this increasingly constrained context, there was little opportunity for mistakes to be corrected or innovations pursued. Instead, the revolutionary process at Ex-Yarur was shaped by the social and political conflict swirling around its walls, and the desires of its workers for a deepened revolution and visions of a participatory socialism were sacrificed on the altar of an undeclared civil war that they did not want and could not win.

With its own advance toward socialism at risk, Ex-Yarur was now no longer in the vanguard of the revolution from below, but rather a bastion of worker support for Allende's more cautious revolution from above. It was a shift symbolized by Salvador Allende's decision to celebrate the second anniversary of his inauguration at the Yarur mill, where he thanked the cheering workers for their support and appealed to them to channel "the commitment demonstrated during the October Strike" into the election campaign and "the battle for production." Ex-Yarur's social politics were shared by most Chilean workers, who looked to their president, party, and union leaders for guidance; loyally contributed their labor and support; and continued to hope for a peaceful and democratic road to socialism.

At Ex-Yarur, this was clear in the April 1973 union elections, which revealed that although a quarter of the workers supported the "revolutionary" line of the Left Socialists, MAPU and MIR, about half of Ex-Yarur workers, the largest bloc by far, endorsed candidates pledged to the moderate Popular Unity line of President Allende and the Communists. The same vote showed that although the polarization within the Left had grown and the moderates had won the contest for support, in other ways little had changed from the year before. The Left still represented almost three-quarters of the Ex-Yarur workers and the Christian Democrats more than one-quarter. Allende's "democratic road to socialism" still seemed viable to most Ex-Yarur workers, justifying a MIR militant's lament that "for the majority here, the Popular Unity's policies continue to command support, and they don't see it as reformism."[34]

During the months that followed the April union elections, the workers of Ex-Yarur shared the national experience of division and paralysis. Inside the mill, sectarian rivalries between Socialists and Communists took their toll. Within the Cordon O'Higgins, the opposition of Ex-Yarur's Communists to "parallel" organizations outside the CUT restricted Ex-Yarur's role. The local cordon became weak and inactive as a consequence, despite the commitment of a sizable group of workers led by the Left Socialist union officer Armando Carrera.

At the same time, Ex-Yarur supported Allende's pursuit of the vanishing center by allowing the Christian Democrats to elect a union director in April 1973. Significantly, in the wake of the *tancazo*, this leftist tolerance was replaced by a demand for Christian Democratic workers to place social solidarity over political partisanship, as in October 1972. When Juan Fuentes, the Christian Democratic union director, refused to break with his party's position of nonsupport for the Allende government's request for emergency powers to deal with the crisis of civil rule, he was denounced by Carrera at a public meeting and forced to resign, and a Christian Democratic supervisor was fired for making a strongly antigovernment speech outside the factory. Tolerance of dissent at Ex-Yarur had fallen victim to the intensified political conflict raging outside its gates. The only question that seemed to matter after the *tancazo* was: Which side are you on? But this demand divided the workers, doomed the Ex-Yarur dialogue between Left and Center, and precluded a unified response to the August 1973 replay of the "bourgeois strike."

Ex-Yarur continued to meet its production quotas, extend direct distribution, and aid in the national effort to contain the strike; but continued opposition to involvement in the Cordon O'Higgins by Ex-Yarur's Communists limited its ability to prepare the "defense" of its area against the threat of military searches or the danger of a military coup. Not until September 10, on the very eve of the coup, did the Communists decide—"in view of the dangerous situation"—to "integrate" their supporters into the *cordon*.[35]

By then it was too late, despite the renewed dynamism of other *cordones*, which mobilized their workers during the *tancazo* to defend the government and seize hundreds of private-sector enterprises. During the weeks of deepening crisis that followed, the *cordones* united in regional committees and stepped up their preparations for the defense of their "territories" against military attack; their mass mobilization and direct distribution of goods and services largely stalemated the August "bourgeois strike." Had they faced a purely civilian counterrevolution, as in October 1972, the *cordones'* efforts might well have succeeded, but blocking a military coup required a national leadership, legitimacy and resources that only the revolution from above could provide. Its leaders, however, distrusted the *cordones* and viewed their strategy of armed popular resistance as a dangerous illusion, pursuing instead the elusive political compromise with the Christian Democrats. Although it is unlikely that even an armed and united working class could have successfully resisted an undivided armed forces willing to use its superior firepower against its own civilian population, the divisions within the revolutionary camp dashed any remaining hopes of effective resistance to the coup. [36]

Yet even the most "revolutionary" workers shared with Salvador Allende a "military" strategy that assumed that a portion of the armed forces would remain loyal to the government and "fight alongside the people." The Cordon O'Higgins, a zone of military barracks and training areas, responded to rumors of a coup with plans to fraternize with the troops on the nearby parade ground and hang political posters inside their factories urging soldiers not to fire on "their brothers and sisters."[37] Underscoring the Chilean workers' preference for democratic process and passive resistance, Héctor Mora, one of the most militant Ex-Yarur workers, a hero of the "liberation," confessed that if he had "thought that Allende was going to lead us into civil war, [he] would never have voted for him."[38]

On September 4, 1973, the mass organizations of the Left mobilized the largest political demonstration in Chilean history in militant commemoration of the third anniversary of Allende's election victory and as a gesture of their continued support for their *compañero presidente*. The workers of Ex-Yarur were among the estimated one million Chileans who paraded past a subdued and drawn Allende, chanting: "¡Allende! ¡Allende! ¡El pueblo te defiende! —"Allende! Allende! The people will defend you!"

It no longer mattered. The support of a mobilized working class could no longer deter the military coup, nor could Allende's own desperate efforts

On September 4, 1973, the Popular Unity Committee (CUP) of Ex-Yarur mobilized its workers to march in the parade celebrating the third anniversary of President Allende's election. Here a Socialist union leader stands before a truck carrying women workers, who hold pom-poms (decorated in the national colors) and Communist party banners. It would be Ex-Yarur's last political demonstration. One week later the Allende government was overthrown by a military coup.

to arrange a national plebiscite during the week that followed. He had even decided to break with his Socialist party over the issue and planned to announce the plebiscite on the night of September 10, but postponed his radio address twenty-four hours in order to polish his remarks, resolve some legal issues, and wait for the assent of the Christian Democrats. It was a fateful decision, which symbolized the failed strategy of the revolution from above and underscored the center party's complicity in the tragedy that followed.[39]

Tomorrow would be too late. Twenty-four hours later, Allende would be dead, the most prominent victim of the military coup that brought his democratic road to socialism—and Ex-Yarur's revolution from below— to a violent end.

18

THE DEATH
OF A DREAM

The coup began with the navy in Valparaíso at dawn on Tuesday, September 11, 1973, but soon spread to the army and the air force.[1] By 10 A.M. the Carabineros had joined the military rebellion, and President Allende was faced with an ultimatum from his united armed forces that he would not accept, yet could not successfully resist. Determined to deny the rebel military Junta legitimacy and to set a revolutionary example, Allende rejected their ultimatum and chose martyrdom instead, prophesying that "the future will belong to the workers." He was joined in this suicidal resistance at the presidential palace by some of his closest friends and aides, seconded in the government buildings surrounding the Plaza of the Constitution by militant members of the Socialist Youth. By 2 P.M. the presidential palace was in flames, and Salvador Allende was dead, a machine gun in his hands, dying the revolutionary that he had always claimed to be, yet rarely seemed.

By then, the battle was over at Ex-Yarur as well although there the workers made a very different decision than did their *compañero presidente*. The workers of Ex-Yarur had begun their day shift as usual and only become aware that "something was happening" when planes and helicopters began to fly overhead. Radios soon informed them of the military coup, and in midmorning an agent from Investigaciones, the Chilean FBI, arrived to confirm that the presidential palace was besieged, the city center under rebel control, and his the only loyal service left.

At 10 A.M. the order was given to stop the machines for a special meeting. It would be the last Workers' Assembly at Ex-Yarur. Although some argued for armed resistance, there were no arms at the factory with which to resist, and there were flammable or explosive stocks of cotton and chemicals within the industry and an artillery regiment across the road. Nor was there widespread enthusiasm for an armed defense of the mill. The workers of Ex-Yarur were ready to repel an attack by rightist terrorists or Yarur thugs, with pointed sticks if necessary, but they were unprepared to confront the Chilean army. They had neither the weapons and training nor the mind-set and will for so unequal an armed struggle. The Communists had opposed such preparations as provocative, and the Socialists and the MIR proved themselves "just theoreticians, not practical revolutionaries," who failed to prepare for the military coup that they themselves had predicted.[2] By early afternoon, news reached Ex-Yarur that the military situation was desperate. The workers decided that resistance was pointless, and anyone who wished could go home while it was still possible. It was the last act of worker participation at Ex-Yarur.

By midafternoon, only a handful of the most "revolutionary" workers remained at the mill, maintaining a symbolic "defense."[3] The following morning, they jumped over the south wall to escape capture by the troops approaching from the north to take control of the factory, leaving only the proud banner—"Ex-Yarur: Territory Free of Exploitation"—to oppose their entry.

Other Santiago factories did resist, particularly those in the more militant *cordones industriales*, such as Cordon Cerrillos and Cordon Vicuña Mackenna. The Battle of Santiago raged for five days, but it was an unequal contest, in which the workers had to oppose with improvised weapons the overwhelming firepower of a ruthless modern military. The armed forces reduced the resisting industrial belts and residential barrios one by one, calling in tanks and helicopter gunships where needed, waging their first war in a century—against their own people. Within a week, the illusion of "popular power" had been destroyed, leftist fantasies of a division in the military or a popular rising dispelled, and a military dictatorship consolidated. The fighting was over, but the killing had just begun.

During the weeks that followed, some 25,000 Chileans were killed by their own armed forces—the equivalent of more than 500,000 people in a country the size of the United States. Many were killed by soldiers who shot first and asked questions later; other were executed in sports stadiums and military barracks, often after barbarous tortures. Those whose tragic fate was featured in the media and protested abroad were all prominent people—political, cultural, or labor leaders. But most of the victims of this terror were unsung and unknown—young, male workers from the shantytowns and working-class *poblaciones* that ringed Chile's cities, like the workers of Ex-Yarur, several of whom disappeared during this massacre. Although this official violence often seemed arbitrary, the policy that loosed it was calculated: an attack on the working class, the military's chief antagonist and the one group from which it feared a popular rebellion or effective resistance movement might emerge. The scope and intensity of the repression reflected the extent and depth of popular mobilization in Chile by September 1973. It was an ironic tribute to the success of the revolution from below.

Leftist activists fortunate enough to survive the initial massacre were victimized in other ways. Thousands were arrested as a result of arbitrary searches and seizures or the anonymous denunciations of neighbors or co-workers. All were interrogated, most were tortured, and many disappeared into the Junta's prisons and concentration camps, located in the burning deserts of the north or the frozen islands of the south. They were arrested without warrants, held without charges, or else brought before kangaroo military courts and accused of acts that often were not crimes when allegedly committed. An estimated 100,000 leftists—10 to 20 percent of the work force in the socialized industries—were purged from their jobs because of their politics and then blacklisted so that they remained unemployed.[4]

By the close of 1973, a Chilean army officer could "reassure" a foreign observer that the military had moved from "massacre to selective slaughter"[5] —a computerized repression focused on local cadres who could lead a resistance movement. Soon it would be directed by the DINA, the Junta's dread secret police, who institutionalized torture as an interrogation technique, pressured an estimated one of every ten Chileans into informing on their neighbors and friends, colleagues and co-workers, and made Chile an international byword for the denial of human rights. Although this multi-faceted repression affected Chileans of all classes and vocations, once again it was workers who suffered most of all from the military's efforts to "extirpate the Marxist cancer"[6] and consolidate their dictatorship. Not only were the *cordones industriales* liquidated and the socialized factories occupied by soldiers. The national and regional trade unions were also proscribed, and their leftist leaders were killed, imprisoned, or driven underground.

The repression of the organized working class did not stop with the decapitation of its national and regional leadership. Within enterprises, worker participation came to an end, along with union democracy and collective bargaining. All local union elections were prohibited, with gerontocracy replacing democracy as the principle of selection. Vacancies for union office were now to be filled by the oldest worker in the enterprise, and the unions themselves were reduced to formal ciphers, barred from actively defending the interests of their members or protesting the abuses committed against them.

Democracy was another casualty of the coup. The Junta imposed martial law, closed the Congress, and suspended the Constitution. The Christian Democrats expected to inherit the power that they had been instrumental in wresting from the Popular Unity, but they were sorely mistaken. All political activities were proscribed: the leftist parties banned, the others suspended indefinitely. Elections of any kind were prohibited, even for the officers of neighborhood associations, social clubs, and women's groups—all of which were subject to military intervention and "restructuring." Civil liberties were violated routinely, and freedom of expression disappeared. More than half of the nation's newspapers were banned or suspended, and the media that survived were subject to heavy government censorship. Book burnings were carried out in public squares and libraries, and the very possession of "subversive literature" became grounds for arrest. The staffs, students, and curricula of universities and schools were also systematically purged as part of what military officers candidly described as a *limpieza de cabezas*—brainwashing. By the close of 1973, nothing was left of Chile's vaunted democracy or traditional pluralism. On the surface, five decades of mass politics had been erased in less than five months.

By then, it was clear that the military regime had also embarked upon a far-reaching economic counterrevolution, which would reverse not only the "irreversible changes" of the Allende era but the strong state economic role, protected industrialization, and welfare policies established during the preceding decades of reform as well. Its aim was to restore the laissez-faire capitalism advocated by "Los Chicago Boys," the Junta's American-trained economic advisers, and supported by substantial aid from the United States, whose complicity in the coup and its aftermath was officially denied but widely reported.[7]

The austerity program they implemented was so harsh and regressive that it required a ruthless and massive repression to implement. Price controls and subsidies for basic consumer goods —Chilean features since the 1930s— were now eliminated, wages were frozen, and both strikes and collective bargaining were prohibited. The result was an increase of 1000 percent in the price of bread, a quadruple-digit inflation, and a halving of real wages during the six months that followed the coup. In the process, labor's share of the national income, which had risen to 66 percent in 1972, fell by almost half. To this regressive economic policy was added a far-reaching restoration of private ownership, beginning with enterprises—such as S.A. Yarur—that had been taken over, but not purchased, by the Allende government.

When the Yarur workers returned to their jobs on September 20, 1973, they found their mill occupied by soldiers and run by the army. In the office from which the old CUT leader, Oscar Ibáñez, had handled labor relations, Captain Luis Zanelly, the military security chief, now held court. During the days that followed, Zanelly interrogated each of the workers in turn, pressing them all to inform on their co-workers, holding their destinies hostage to the denunciations he required.

If the presence and practices of Captain Zanelly signified the end of liberty at the Yarur mill and the start of a new era of military repression, the choice of Colonel Armando Baeza as Government Delegate symbolized the counterrevolution that he was expected to implement. Colonel Baeza was no stranger to the Yarur mill. As government interventor in the wake of the 1962 strike, he had broken that earlier workers' movement, purged the mill of "Marxists," and restored "discipline and order." Now Baeza was called on to perform a strikingly similar task in the very different conditions of September 1973. Colonel Baeza was there to turn the clock back—to a time before worker participation, a socialized enterprise, or an independent union existed at the Yarur mill.

During the weeks that followed, military intelligence purged the labor force of activists, and many of the union leaders and councillors were arrested, tortured, and imprisoned. The entire structure of worker participation vanished, along with many of the committee delegates, democracy on the production floor, equality in social relations, and the sense of community. Hierarchy, alienation, repression, and fear returned, accompanied by mass firings and starvation wages. Behind the bayonets of the Chilean army, an industrial discipline even more authoritarian and oppressive than the old order was imposed on the Yarur mill.

Yet both production and productivity remained high, and what one supervisor termed "the restoration of work discipline"[8] was only a partial explanation. During the first three months of military management, the Yarur workers applied themselves with the same extra effort they had displayed during the final months of worker participation. "We were all putting our shoulder to the wheel to convince the military not to return the factory," explained one weaver.[9] It was a final expression of the spirit of Ex-Yarur, bringing the workers together in a united action calculated to preserve what little remained of their "liberation."They were even willing to accept a rapid and massive reversal in their factory and lives, one that deprived them of most of their achievements and dashed almost all their aspirations provided that "El Chico [Amador Yarur] did not return."[10] It was a point on which all but the small number of Yarur loyalists agreed and with a determination that transcended politics and status.

By the end of November, they believed that they had proved their point and gotten their message across. Some speculated that the solution might be a tripartite management of the mill, in which the company would regain formal control, but a worker-government-management council would run it; others envisioned an indefinite military administration of the enterprise. Both groups shared the expectation that the Junta would not restore the Yarurs to direct management of the mill—and that "El Chico" would not dare return to run it.

All their efforts were in vain. The Yarur workers had not grasped the alliance between Chile's military and capitalists that underlay the new regime or understood the extreme private enterprise ideology motivating its economic advisers. The Junta might promise to "protect the social and economic conquests of the workers,"[11] and Colonel Baeza might talk vaguely of a possible "statute of guarantees" ensuring the workers some form of "real participation," but his public statements indicated that the Yarur mill would be restored to its "legitimate owners."[12] His job was to prepare the ground for the return of the old order by restoring production and work discipline, social control and political passivity. By December, that task was accomplished.

On Friday morning, December 7, Baeza told the department heads that Amador Yarur would soon return to take personal charge of his mill. That same afternoon the workers got the news from their supervisors in special meetings. Their initial reaction was shock, followed by a wave of desperation that swept through the factory, uniting the workers for the last time in a common cause. Over the weekend, they talked of "getting up a petition" or of "making some kind of protest."[13] But when they arrived at work on Monday, they found armed soldiers patrolling each work section, and "everyone became frightened, thinking about what had happened elsewhere."[14] This renewed demonstration of the military's willingness to use brute force intimidated the workers into passivity. The return of the troops was followed by a new wave of dismissals, a second political purge calculated to denude the industry of workers who might emerge as leaders of a movement opposing the return of Amador Yarur. Although the workers tried to maintain their dignity, increasingly their determination gave way to despair; and their unity, to division.

On January 24, 1974, Amador Yarur returned to take charge of his family's cotton mill, while a watchful military kept guard over his workers, symbolizing the alliance of armed force and capitalism that had put an end to their "territory free of exploitation." "Ex"-Yarur was no more, alive only in the memories of its workers and the pages of this history.

By the end of the month, "Don Amador" was once again running "his" industry from a wood-paneled office in the marble-corridored administration building. There he talked of his plans for restoring the toppled statue of Juan Yarur to its "rightful place" in front of the factory that his father had founded.[15] By February 1974, the counterrevolution at the Yarur mill was complete.

By then, most of the workers who had led the movement to seize and socialize the industry were missing from his restored mill. Some of them were dead or had "disappeared"; others were imprisoned or had gone underground. Raúl Oliva was missing, Jorge Lorca was in a desert concentration camp, and Ricardo Catalan was in the clandestine resistance. Pablo Rosas had been picked up four times, savagely tortured four times, and then released to see if his movements would lead the secret police to underground Communist comrades. By then, some two hundred activists were also gone, fired for their political beliefs, swelling the ranks of the unemployed. Branded as "Marxists," they would find it difficult to get another job, particularly in an economy already plunging toward depression. With Amador Yarur's return, the workers who remained were convinced that the purges they had survived were but a harbinger of more to come.

The leaders of Ex-Yarur had paid a heavy price for their role in the workers' movement, but the rank-and-file Yarur workers had not fared much better. Many had lost friends or relatives in the repression that followed the coup. In addition to the two hundred already purged for their politics, many more would lose their posts in the years that followed, victims of Amador Yarur's repressive social politics and General Pinochet's regressive monetarist economics. Even those who retained their jobs found their real wages cut in half and their families reduced to "a diet of bread, onions, and tea."[16] Those who had lost their livelihood were forced to depend on the charity of relatives, friends, or the Church. Yet, as bad as these physical losses and material deprivations was the psychological trauma that they suffered. The Yarur workers paid a heavy price for their temerity in believing that they had become the masters of their own destiny.

Berta Castillo was well aware of the price that she had paid. Barely thirty, she looked old, with stooped shoulders and prematurely graying hair. At Ex-Yarur, she had been one of the most fervent of the faithful, a model worker, an active participant, and a popular *compañera*. In less than five months, she had lost her job, her home, and her husband to the coup and counterrevolution. "But worst of all," she concluded sorrowfully, "they have killed my dream . . . It was such a beautiful dream."[17]

EPILOGUE

A decade later, the Yarur mill was moribund as well, forced to the edge of bankruptcy by the economic policies of the military regime that the Yarurs had helped bring to power. The economic "shock treatment" recommended by General Pinochet's "Chicago Boys" advisers depressed the internal market and eliminated industrial protection, plunging Chile—and its textile industry—into a deep economic crisis in 1975–76. The government then promised renewed protection for the textile industry if its owners would modernize their mills with an eye to competing in Latin American export markets. But S.A. Yarur's efforts to replace its mill's antiquated machinery with sophisticated imported technology deepened the enterprise's indebtedness without enabling it to compete with cheaper textiles abroad or more modern competitors within Chile.

In order to save the family firm, the Yarurs engineered a merger with two other textile enterprises. But, as in the decade before the coup, they could not free themselves of their traditional mentality in a situation that required bold entrepreneurship and vision. In 1981 the conglomerate collapsed under the weight of its combined debts and in the face of an internal market limited by foreign competition and renewed recession. Juan Yarur's descendants proved incapable of saving the enterprise that he had founded and shaped into the leading cotton textile industry in Chile.

The Yarur conglomerate was on the verge of declaring bankruptcy when the government intervened and transformed it into an "economic unit" under state control. The state assumed the conglomerate's debt, in return for which the enterprise froze employment and production levels. In 1985 the Yarur mill was operating at half its installed capacity. A decade after returning the mill to the Yarurs, the Pinochet government was once more in control of the factory, unable to find private buyers for the bankrupt enterprise. By 1985 all but one of Chile's large textile enterprises were back in the hands of a state that, ironically, had set out in 1973 to return the economy to the private sector.

The Yarur workers did not remain passive in the face of these adversities. Although the authoritarian state had replaced the paternalistic boss as the arbiter of their working conditions and the enforcer of social control, they tried to protect their interests, drawing on the legacy of Ex-Yarur. Using their weakened union, they demanded job security in the face of massive dismissals of workers in the name of modernization. In 1979 they opposed the formation of the conglomerate, which meant yet a further reduction in the mill's labor force. When the Yarur conglomerate collapsed in 1981, it was the workers who pressed the government to declare it an "economic unit" and keep the mill running under state control.

Despite these efforts, a decade after the return of the factory to the Yarurs, the work force had been halved, and those fortunate enough to have jobs labored for real wages so reduced that they could barely support themselves. In 1985 the remaining Yarur workers clung desperately to the ill-paid and tenuous jobs that separated them from the unemployed, who comprised a third of Chile's labor force.

By then a new generation of workers had grown up in the poverty and repression of Pinochet's Chile, and a different labor movement had emerged. During the decade that followed the coup, the military regime permitted the rebirth of a sanitized union movement—but only under new statutes calculated to weaken and depoliticize it. The laws of the market replaced collective bargaining and individual interest superseded group welfare as the guiding principle of labor relations. Government decrees encouraged the formation of parallel unions, barred pre-coup activists from office, and undermined the right to strike, while restricting the role of labor federations and prohibiting union involvement in politics. The result was a divided and debilitated labor movement, with inexperienced leaders and a defensive stance. This weakened union movement, moreover, had to contend with political repression, an economic crisis, massive unemployment, and a reduced membership.

Yet despite these obstacles, a relatively strong labor movement had reemerged by 1985, with a structure and leadership profile similar to the pre-coup era and an ideological stance that called into question the military regime's model for a brave new Chile. At the local level, beleaguered unions fought a courageous battle for job security, adequate wages, and decent working conditions. At the regional and national levels, several confederations replaced the CUT. Reflecting differing political orientations, they joined together in demanding the restoration of democracy, the recovery of social rights, and the reconstruction of the economy.

If the military regime had hoped to create competing apolitical unions sympathetic to the government's objectives and subject to its influence, it had failed utterly. The new labor movement might be more autonomous from political parties than in the past, but democracy was its watchword and the resolution of Chile's grave economic and social crisis was its demand.

This new workers' movement was part of a broad-based "convergence" of the Left and Center, which united those too young to remember the Allende era with those too old to forget. It was a movement that included Chileans of all classes and parties: workers and capitalists, partisans of the Popular Unity and protagonists in its overthrow. They remained divided over strategy and tactics, ideology and leadership. But they all agreed that the Pinochet dictatorship had to be ousted and democracy restored.

Behind the escalating "national protests" that began in 1983—bringing hundreds of thousands of Chileans into the streets and Chile to a standstill— lay a rejection of the military's political project and economic model. During the decade that followed the coup of 1973, General Pinochet had transformed an institutional civil government into a personal military dictatorship, and a democracy known for its respect for civil liberties into a police state notorious for its deprivation of human rights. All Chile now seemed like the pre-Allende Yarur mill: a closed-off world with oppressive social control and repression of political dissent.

By 1985 General Pinochet's military autocracy had become intolerable even to former civilian supporters, who were alienated as well by the failure of his regime's economic model. A decade after his seizure of power, the Chilean economy was mired in the deepest depression of the century, and Chile's industrial fabric was in tatters. Neither the "magic of the market" nor the decrees of the dictatorship could make Chile's dependent capitalism dynamic or cure the country's chronic economic ills.

Under the regime's free-market policies, speculators made millions, while industries went bankrupt and ordinary Chileans paid the bill: In 1985 Chile had the highest per capita foreign debt of any country in Latin America, and poverty had become a way of life for most of its citizens. By 1983 the empty pots that middle-class housewives had beaten for Allende's ouster a decade earlier were sounding for Pinochet's removal—and nostalgia for the martyred president was growing.

At the same time, in the desperately poor shantytowns surrounding Chile's cities, a more militant and violent movement was emerging. Its protagonists were young, destitute, and angry. Most were unemployed, and many had never held a job and had little prospect of finding one. They had little to lose but their lives, and they risked those in increasingly violent protests against a regime they felt had pauperized their present and foreclosed their future. Their confrontations with government security forces provided the masses and martyrs that fueled the political opposition's demand for an end to Pinochet's dictatorship. But, although their leftist sympathies were clear, the slum dwellers' militant activism was largely spontaneous and autonomous, controlled by neither the old political parties nor the new labor unions. On the contrary, the *poblador* movement had its own organization and leadership, and far more radical tactics and goals.

This new movement represented an embryonic revolution from below. Though very different from the Yarur workers' movement of the previous decade, it was heir to the former's legacy of direct social action—and was centered in some of the same shantytowns where Ex-Yarur workers had lived. Their 1971 chants for "socialism now" resonated in the new cries for "democracy now," although much had changed in the interim. "I have been waiting ten years for this," affirmed one middle-aged activist[1].

Like the Yarur Youngsters of 1970, this new generation had taken up the standard of struggle from their defeated parents. Like those earlier Youngsters, moreover, they believed in the need for action from below. "Democracy can not be negotiated like bread," explained one young shantytown militant[2]—and this new generation of Youngsters wanted both bread *and* democracy. They took to the streets because they had neither, and "because there is nothing else to do but protest,"[3] "to express our feelings about the government, and to mobilize other people."[4] It was a mobilization of the desperate and the destitute, with neither a democratic road to follow nor a Salvador Allende to lead them. The Christian Democratic head of the opposition political alliance confessed that neither he nor the political parties could control these Youngsters. "Their explosion is coming," he warned.[5]

General Pinochet may have repressed the revolutionary process of the 1970s, but like the Yarurs before him, his policies only served to provoke the revolutionary fervor he feared. Pinochet's grip on Chile still seemed strong in 1985, but so had Amador Yarur's control over his factory in 1969. By 1985 only the continued support of an army fearful of being called to account for its killings and corruption sustained Pinochet in the arbitrary power that he had exercised so ruthlessly—and ruinously—for so long. As in 1973, he lived by the sword, begetting popular violence through his own increasingly violent response to peaceful protest.

A new cycle in the history of Chile had begun.

NOTES

INTRODUCTION

1. An insightful typology and analysis of the extensive literature on the Chilean revolutionary process can be found in Arturo and J. Samuel Valenzuela, "Visions of Chile," *Latin American Research Review*, 10:3 (Fall 1975), 155–76. Although their review essay was written over a decade ago, in most respects its typology and judgments are still valid today. The Valenzuelas divide the literature into interpretations of the Maximalist Left, the Gradualist Left, the Center, and the Right, with foreigners as prone as Chileans to write from political perspectives. In partisan terms, the Maximalist Left corresponds to the MIR and the left wing of the Popular Unity (the Left Socialists, the MAPU, and part of the Christian Left). Two of the best Chilean and foreign examples of these accounts are Gabriel Smirnow, *The Revolution Disarmed: Chile, 1970–1973* (New York, 1979), and Ian Roxborough, Philip O'Brien, and Jackie Roddick, *Chile: The State and Revolution* (New York, 1977). The Gradualist Left refers principally to the right wing of the Popular Unity, particularly the Communists, the moderate Socialists (including Salvador Allende), the MAPU Obrero y Campesino, and the moderate wing of the Christian Left. Two of the most thoughtful of these analyses are by Allende's political adviser, Joan Garcés, *Allende y la experiencia chilena: Las armas de la política* (Barcelona, 1976), and his economic adviser, Sergio Bitar, *Transición, socialismo y democracia: La experiencia chilena* (Mexico City, 1979). The Center mostly means the Christian Democrats, whereas the Right includes the National Party, the neo-Fascist Patria y Libertad, and the military Junta and its foreign apologists. Analytically, however, the similarity between Center and Right critiques of the Chilean revolution is striking as are their common lack of self-criticism. The best Right Christian Democratic account is Genaro Arriagada Herrera, *De "la vía chilena" a "la vía insurreccional"* (Santiago, 1974), with Paul Sigmund, *The Overthrow of Allende and the Politics of Chile, 1964–1976* (Pittsburgh, Pa., 1977), offering an American academic version of this stance. They should be compared to such Rightist accounts as Hernán Millas and Emilio Gilippi, *Chile 1970–1973: crónica de una experiencia* (Santiago, 1974), and Robert Moss, *Chile's Marxist Experiment* (Abbot Devon, Eng., 1973), and to the Junta's *Libro blanco del cambio de gobierno en Chile* (Santiago, 1974). Left Christian Democratic views, such as those expressed by Radomiro Tomic in symposia and interviews, come the closest to striving for a balanced perspective, but they, too, have their biases. In general, a decade after the coup, opinions remain as politically polarized as they were in 1973. A salient exception

to this rule is Arturo Valenzuela's *The Breakdown of Democratic Regimes: Chile* (Baltimore, Md., 1978), which offers a brief, but balanced, interpretation. A variety of partisan perspectives, with a stress on the Center and the Gradualist Left, can be found in Federico Gil, Ricardo Lagos, and Henry Landsberger, eds., *Chile at the Turning Point: Lessons of the Socialist Years, 1970–1973* (Philadelphia, 1979).

2. For a convenient summary of the literature as of a decade ago, see Alan Angell, *Politics and the Labour Movement in Chile* (London, 1972). A more critical evaluation of the state of research was given by Kenneth Ericson, Patrick Peppe, and Hobart A. Spalding, Jr., "Research on the Urban Working Class and Organized Labor in Argentina, Brazil and Chile: What Is Left to Be Done?" *Latin American Research Review*, 9:2 (Summer 1974), 115–42. More recent assessments include Peter Winn, "The Urban Working Class and Social Protest in Latin America," *International Labor and Working Class History*, 14–15 (Spring 1979), 61–64, and Eugene Sofer, "Recent Trends in Latin American Labor Historiography," *Latin American Research Review*, 15:1 (Spring 1980), pp. 167–76; see also the exchange immediately following between Sofer, on the one hand, and Ericson, Peppe, and Spalding, pp. 177–182.

3. For a liberal anti-Communist interpretation of this kind. See, for example, the works of Moisés Poblete Troncoso, of which his volume with Ben Burnett, *The Rise of the Latin American Labor Movement* (New Haven, 1960), is the most accessible. Other surveys in this genre are Robert J. Alexander, *Organized Labor in Latin America* (New York, 1965), and Victor Alba, *Politics and the Labor Movement in Latin America* (Stanford, Calif., 1969). Interpretive surveys from a Socialist perspective are offered by Jorge Barría Serón in several works, the most recent and comprehensive of which is his *El movimiento obrero en Chile* (Santiago, 1971). A Communist view of the nineteenth century, Hernán Ramírez Necochea's *Historia del movimiento obrero en Chile* (Santiago, 1956) is useful, as are Barría's *Los movimientos sociales de Chile desde 1910 hasta 1926* (Santiago, 1963), *Trayectoria y estructura del movimiento sindical chileno, 1946–1962* (Santiago, 1963), and *Historia de la CUT* (Santiago, 1971). Also interesting are the Marxist interpretive essays of Marcelo Segall, *Desarrollo del capitalismo en Chile* (Santiago, 1953) and Julio César Jobet, *Ensayo crítico del desarrollo económico-social de Chile* (Santiago, 1955). Mention should also be made of Enrique Reyes's work on the early nitrate industry, *El desarrollo de la conciencia proletaria en Chile: el ciclo salitrero* (Santiago, 1970). Although there is some promising work by a younger generation of American and Chilean researchers, most of it has yet to appear. An exception is the pioneering study of Peter De Shazo on the anarchist-led labor movement, summarized in his *Urban Workers and Labor Unions in Chile, 1902–1927* (Madison, Wis., 1983). The history of rural labor organization is well traced in Brian Loveman, *Struggle in the Countryside: Politics and Rural Labor in Chile, 1919–1973* (Bloomington, Ind., 1976).

4. For wages and prices, see Peter Gregory, *Industrial Wages in Chile* (New York, 1967); Markos Mamalakis and Clark Reynolds, *Essays in the Chilean Economy* (Homewood, Ill., 1965); Markos Mamalakis, *The Growth and Structure of the Chilean Economy from Independence to Allende* (New Haven, Conn., 1976) and *Historical Statistics of Chile: Demography and Labor Force* (Westport, Conn., 1980); and Ricardo Ffrench-Davis, *Políticas económicas en Chile, 1952–1970* (Santiago, 1973). For a discussion of income distribution by class, see Barbara Stallings, *Class Conflict and Economic Development in Chile, 1958–1973* (Stanford, Calif., 1978). The best analysis of strike patterns is Manuel Barrera, "Perspectiva histórica de la huelga obrera en Chile," *Cuadernos de la Realidad Nacional* [Santiago], No. 9 (September 1971), 119–55. Voting behavior of Chilean workers is discussed in James Petras and Maurice Zeitlin, *El radicalismo político de la clase trabajadora chilena* (Buenos Aires, 1969), and in several more conservative studies, which are summarized in James Prothro and Patricio Chaparro, "Public

Opinion and the Movement of the Chilean Government to the Left, 1952–1972," *Journal of Politics*, 36 (1974), 2–43.

5. There is a large body of literature on labor relations. See, for example, James Morris, *Elites, Intellectuals and Consensus* (Ithaca, N.Y., 1966); J. Samuel Valenzuela, "The Chilean Labor Movement: The Institutionalization of Conflict," in *Chile: Politics and Society*, ed., Arturo and J. Samuel Valenzuela (New Brunswick, N.J., 1976); and Manuel Barrera, *El sindicato industrial como instrumento de lucha de la clase obrera chilena* (Santiago, 1971). For labor and political parties, see James Petras, *Politics and Social Forces in Chilean Development* (Berkeley, Calif., 1960), and Angell, *Politics and the Labor Movement in Chile*, in addition to the works cited in notes 3 and 5. J. Samuel Valenzuela, "Labor Movement Formation and Politics: The Chilean and French Cases in Comparative Perspective, 1850–1950," (Ph.D. diss., Columbia University, 1979), takes a broad view and offers an original vision of these issues from the perspective of historical sociology. James W. Wilson, "Freedom and Control: Workers' Participation in Management in Chile, 1967–1975," 3 vols. (Ph.D. diss., Cornell University, 1979), provides an extensive study of worker participation in Chile from a labor relations viewpoint.

6. The most illuminating biographies are Julio César Jobet's broadly conceived *Recabarren y los orígenes del movimiento obrero y socialismo* (Santiago, 1955) and the autobiography of Elías Lafertte, *Vida de un comunista*, 2d ed. (Santiago, 1971).

7. Some of the most interesting analyses based on survey research are Juan Guillermo Espinosa and Andrew Zimbalist, *Economic Democracy: Workers' Participation in Chilean Industry, 1970–1973* (New York, 1978); Patrick V. Peppe, "Working-Class Politics in Chile" (Ph.D. diss., Columbia University, 1971); and Henry Landsberger, Manuel Barrera, and Abel Toro, "The Chilean Labor Leader: A Preliminary Report on His Background and Attitudes," *Industrial and Labor Relations Review*, no. 17 (April 1964), 399–420.

8. For a description of my approach to oral history, see Peter Winn, "Oral History and the Factory Study: New Approaches to Labor History," *Latin American Research Review*, 14:2 (Summer 1979), 137–39.

CHAPTER 1

1. Nicolás Yarur (Santiago), January 1974; Jorge Yarur (Santiago), August 1972. [Oral history interviews will be cited in this form throughout: Name of source (place of interview), date of interview.] *Diccionario biográfico de Chile*, 9th ed. (Santiago, 1953–55), pp. 1372–73.

2. Nicolás Yarur (Santiago), January 1974.

3. Ibid.; Jorge Yarur (Santiago), August 1972; Salvador Abugatas (Arequipa), July 1973.

4. Nicolás Yarur (Santiago), January 1974; Jorge Yarur (Santiago), August 1972; Hortensia Paz y Basurco (Arequipa), July 1973. His wife, Olombí Banna, had lost several babies in Oruro. Jorge Yarur Banna was born in Arequipa in 1918; and Amador, two years later. (Arequipa, Parroquia del Sagrario, *Libro de Bautismos*, Vol. 142, p. 483, and Vol. 145, p. 37). Carlos, the couple's oldest son, had been born in Bethlehem and raised there during the war by his grandmother and aunt (Nicolas Yarur [Santiago], January 1974.)

5. Domingo Said (La Paz), July 1973; Guillermo Atanasio (Arequipa), July 1973; *Guía de Oro de Arequipa*, ed. Adela Pardo Gómez (Arequipa, 1944), p. 267.

6. Guillermo Atanasio (Arequipa), July 1973; Domingo Said (La Paz), July 1973; Salvador Abugatas (Arequipa), July 1973.

7. Domingo Said (La Paz), July 1973; Nicolás Yarur (Santiago), January 1974. Juan and

Nicolas Yarur were joined in Bolivia by their youngest brother, Sabá, who had remained in Palestine during World War I.

8. Nicolás Yarur (Santiago), January 1974; Domingo Said (La Paz), July 1973; Guillermo Atanasio (Arequipa), July 1973; Abraham Jeada (Arequipa), July 1973; Rosemary Thorpe and Geoffrey Bertram, *Peru, 1890–1977: Growth and Policy in an Open Economy*, (New York, 1978), pp. 54–62, 121–24, 129–31. Their Bolivian concession included tariff protection and exemption from taxes and import duties. (*El Diario* [La Paz], 28 November 1926, p.3).

9. Domingo Said (La Paz), July 1973; Nicolás Yarur (Santiago), January 1974; Hernán Mauricio (La Paz), July 1973; Leticia Sucre (La Paz), July 1973; René Ballivián (La Paz), July 1973; William McGowan, president, Comisión Fiscal Permanente, to Ministro de Hacienda, La Paz (6 May 1931), "Re: Fábrica Nacional de Tejidos de Algodón 'Said & Yarur'," *Archivo Histórico de la Universidad Mayor de San Andrés de La Paz*, Bolivia, Ministerio de Hacienda, *Informes, Comercio e Industria*, 3 (1931), no. 173.

10. Hernán Mauricio (La Paz), July 1973.

11. *El Diario* (La Paz), 21 July 1929, Sunday Supplement; Nicolás Yarur (Santiago), January 1974; Legrand Smith, Director, American Institute (La Paz), July 1973; Leticia Sucre (La Paz), July 1973; Domingo Said (La Paz), July 1973.

12. Nicolás Yarur (Santiago), January 1974.

13. *La Reforma/Al-Islah*, (Santiago), 6 May 1933, p. 2.

14. P. T. Ellsworth, *Chile: An Economy in Transition* (New York, 1945), pp. 7–22; Paul W. Drake, *Socialism and Populism in Chile, 1932–52* (Urbana, Ill., 1978), pp. 60–62, 70–72.

15. Drake, *Socialism and Populism*, pp. 63–98, 113–25.

16. *La Reforma*, 10 March 1934, p. 2, and 4 August 1934, p. 3.

17. Nicolás Yarur (Santiago), January 1974. For the congressional debate over the Yarur concession, see Chile, *Diario de la Camara de Diputados*, Sesiones Extraordinarias [hereafter Ses. Extra.] (1933–34), 62d Session (5 February 1934), vol. 3, p. 2931; (1934–35), 26th Sess. (5 December 1934), vol 2, pp. 1186–1206; and (1934–35), 9th Sess. (7 November 1934), pp. 480–81; and Sesiones Ordinarias [hereafter, Sess. Ords.] (1934), 5th Sess. (30 May 1934), vol 1, p. 235, and 6th Sess. (4 June 1934), vol. 1, pp. 288–32; *El Mercurio* [Santiago], 2 July 1934, pp. 3 and 26.

18. Domingo Said (La Paz), July 1973. See also, chapter 16 in Thomas R. Navin, *The Whitin Machine Works Since 1831* (Cambridge, Mass., 1950).

19. "Retiro de Socios y modificacion de sociedad: Salvador Said y otros y 'Yarur Hermanos,' " Santiago (23 December 1936), *Archivo del Notario Jorge Gaete Rojas*, Santiago (December 1936), vol. 2, Documento No. 319: fols. 701–4; "Cesion. Juan Yarur y otros a Said e Hijos," Santiago (23 December 1936), *Archivo del Notario Javier Echeverria Vial*, Santiago (December 1936), vol 2, Documento No. 384: fols.802v–5; Nicolas Yarur (Santiago), January 1974; Jorge Yarur (Santiago), August 1972; Domingo Said (La Paz), July 1973; Eric Neumann (Santiago), June 1972; Yarur Hermanos, Libro de Inventario, Inventario No. 2 (31 December 1936), *Archivo S. A. Yarur, Manufacturas Chilenas de Algodón*, Santiago [hereafter, *SAYMCHA/ STGO*]. Juan Yarur held 40 percent of the firm's $1.8 million registered capital.

20. Liliana Torres (Santiago), June 1972. Torres was one of the few residents of the area near the factory when the mill was built. Juan Yarur purchased the land in his own name, paying only $27,000 for a 174,000 square-meter tract. ("Compraventa. Antonia Pizarro v. de Espejo a Juan Yarur Lolas," Santiago [9 March 1935], Santiago, *Archivo de Notario Abraham del Rio* [March 1935], vol 2, Documento no. 46: fols. 126–30.)

21. Nicolás Yarur (Santiago), January 1974; Jorge Yarur (Santiago), August 1972.

22. Santiago, S. A. Yarur, *Correspondencia Exterior*, Said & Yarur to Guaranty Trust, Santiago (19 December 1936); S. Linderson, Guaranty Trust, J. Yarur, New York (15 April 1942; Yarur Hermanos, *Libro de Caja* (15 March 1937, 14 and 26 May 1937), *SAYMCHA/STGO*; Jorge Yarur (Santiago), August 1972. The Newburgher Company of Memphis became the Yarur cotton brokers, and Whitin, Draper, and Saco-Lowell supplied most of the mill's machinery through Austin Baldwin of New York, who became the firm's exporters.

23. Yarur Hermanos, *Libro Central*, vol. 1 (January–April 1937) and "Contrato de compraventa entre Yarur Hnos. y S. A. C. Saavedra Benard," Santiago (31 December 1939), *SAYMCHA/STGO*; S. A. C. Saavedra Benard, *Memorias*, no. 14 (1936–37), Chile, Superintendencia de Compañías de Seguros, Sociedades Anónimas y Bolsas de Comercio [hereafter *SCSSABC*], Departamento de Sociedades Anónimas [hereafter *DSA*], Santiago, Rol 486, Carpeta 1; Departamento de Sociedades Anónimas, "Informe sobre la Sociedad Comercial Saavedra Benard y Cia., S. A. C., Santiago (October 1937), *SCSSABC/DSA*. Saavedra Benard became their exclusive distributors and remained so for many years. (Jorge Yarur [Santiago], August 1972.)

24. From then on, the general manager of the Banco de Chile was always vice-president of Yarur, Inc. Other members of that first Board of Directors included Luis Kappes, manager of Chile's largest insurance group and linked to two of the nation's most powerful financial clans; Arturo Alessandri, a skilled corporation lawyer and son of the former president, who was linked to both the political Right and another major economic group; and Roberto Wacholtz, a powerful figure in the governing Radical party, who was both finance minister in the Center-Left Popular Front government of 1938–41 and the first head of the new state Development Corporation (CORFO) it created and would remain an important intermediary between the worlds of business and politics (*Diccionario Biográfico de Chile*, 9th ed. [Santiago, 1953–55], pp. 27, 549–50, 1347–48; *Diccionario Político de Chile, 1810–1966* (ed.), Jordi Fuentes and Lia Cortes [Santiago, 1967], pp. 24–27, 523; Jorge Yarur [Santiago], August 1972; Marcelo Cavarozzi, " "The Government and the Industrial Bourgeoisie in Chile: 1938–1964" [Ph.D. diss., University of California, Berkeley, 1976], pp. 117, 158–59).

25. "S. A. Yarur, Manufacturas Chilenas de Algodón" was registered on August 19, 1941, with a capital of eighty million pesos divided into 1.6 million shares, and began to function on October 1. ("Prospecto de la Sociedad Anónima en formación "Manufacturas Chilenas de Algodón, S.A.," Santiago [5 August 1941]; *SCSSABC/DSA*, Rol 882, Carpeta 2-Y-1; "S. A. Yarur, Manufacturas Chilenas de Algodón" [hereafter SAYMCHA], Archivo Legal; "Constitución de sociedad Anónima y Estatutos: Manufacturas Chilenas de Algodón, S.A.," Santiago (19 August 1941), *SCSSABC/DSA*, Rol 882, Carpeta 2-Y-1; Departamento de Sociedades Anónimas, Superintendencia de Compañías de Seguros, Sociedades Anónimas y Bolsas de Comercio to Ministro de Hacienda, no. 525, Santiago [25 August 1941], in *SCSSABC/DSA*, Rol 882, Carpeta 2-Y-1; S.A. Yarur, Manufacturas Chilenas de Algodón, "Memorias del Directorio presentada a las Accionistas [hereafter *Memorias*], no. 25 [1965], *SAYMCHA/STGO*). Juan Yarur received 600,000 shares in the new limited liability company, his brother Nicolás got 525,000 shares, and Sabá only 375,000—a proportional division of the unequal partnership's seventy-one million peso assets that partly explained its dissolution (Yarur Hermanos, *Libro de Inventario*, Inventario no. 7 [29 November 1941], *SAYMCHA/STGO*; "Constitutución de Sociedad Anónima").

26. Nicolás Yarur (Santiago), January 1974; Jorge Yarur (Santiago), August 1972.

27. Oscar Muñoz, *Crecimiento industrial de Chile, 1914–1965*, 2d ed. (Santiago, 1971), pp. 43–49; Markos J. Mamalakis, *The Growth and Structure of the Chilean Economy from*

Independence to Allende (New Haven, Conn., 1976), p. 163. During the war years, industrial production grew at the rapid annual rate of 9.3 percent and industry's share of the national income jumped by one-third, to 22.4 percent.

28. Mamalakis, *Growth and Structure*, pp. 163–64; Muñoz, *Crecimiento industrial*, pp. 79–89; Ellsworth, *Chile*, pp. 49–105. The Corporación de Fomento (CORFO), the state development corporation established by the Popular Front in 1939 with the ambivalent participation of Chilean business, emerged during the war decade as the handmaiden of the private sector and the key state agency in the promotion of industrialization. By lending large sums of money at low real interest rates, purchasing stocks or bonds of private enterprises, and giving technical and financial aid, the CORFO promoted a wide variety of industries, from basic metals and machine tools to construction and consumer goods (Cavarozzi, "The Government and the Industrial Bourgeoisie," pp. 115–150; Ellsworth, *Chile*, pp. 85–91).

29. Luis Carrillo, "Consumo de algodón en las últimas 22 años," (1952), W. R. Grace, Unpublished Statistics. I am indebted to Carrillo, former manager of Tejidos Caupolican, S.A., then a Grace subsidiary, for making these data available to me. British Chamber of Commerce of Chile, *Bulletin* (Santiago), 8:86 (November 1949), 35–36; SAYMCHA, *Memorias* (1941–44); *SAYMCHA/STGO*; Andrés Sanfuentes, "La influencia de los árabes en el desarrollo económico de Chile" (Memoria de Licenciado, Universidad de Chile, Santiago, 1964), p. 140; Jorge Yarur (Santiago), August 1972; Luis Carrillo (Santiago), December 1973. These profit rates would have been far higher had it not been for Yarur's 50 percent watering of stock and extensive capitalization of revalued assets. Nor do they include Yarur's rumored unreported profits on illegal foreign exchange transactions, using subsidized dollars granted the firm for cotton imports.

30. SAYMCHA, *Memorias* (1944–45); Jorge Yarur (Santiago), August 1972.

31. Miguel Hirmas (Santiago), January 1974.

32. Reinaldo Jara (Santiago), December 1973.

33. Miguel Hirmas (Santiago), January 1974; Luis Carrillo (Santiago), January 1974. The centrality of political access to entrepreneurial activity in Chile was underscored by Yarur's Arab rival, Salomón Sumar, who in 1952 contributed to all the presidential candidates, from the Conservative Arturo Matte (his business partner) to the Socialist Salvador Allende because "capitalists are obliged to be on good terms with everyone." (Donald Bray, "The Political Emergence of Arab-Chileans," *Journal of Inter-American Studies*, 4:4 [Oct. 1962], 588).

34. Fernando Morales (Santiago), January 1974. Morales was the deputy minister of labor at the time.

35. Although he claimed that W. R. Grace was unwilling to stoop to such manipulations, its manager recalled that "the more powerful Arab industrialists had no such qualms . . . and the most powerful was Yarur." (Luis Carrillo [Santiago], January 1974). The rising economic importance of political influence and the growing political power of the Arab-Chileans under Ibáñez were reasons why Grace made a decision in the mid-1950's to "leave the cotton textile industry to the *turcos* [Turks]" (*ibid.*).

36. Luis Carrillo (Santiago), January 1974.

37. *La Reforma*, 20 April 1940, p. 1; *Boletín Arabe* (Santiago), April 1944, p. 5; 15 and 31 August 1946, p. 1; 31 May 1947, p.1; Jorge Yarur (Santiago), August 1972; Miguel Hirmas (Santiago), January 1974; Sanfuentes, "Los árabes," p. 145.

38. Eugenio Stark (Santiago), June 1972.

39. Muñoz, *Crecimiento industrial*, p. 93; André Gunder Frank, "La política económica en Chile—Del Frente Popular a la Unidad Popular," *Punto Final* [Santiago], No. 153 (14 March 1972), Supplement, p. 5.

40. Luis Carrillo, "Comparative Profits in Pesos of 1940: Caupolican, Yarur, Textil Viña,

Sumar," Tejidos Caupolican, S.A. unpublished statistics (1955); SAYMCHA, *Memorias*, (1954–58).

41. Jorge Yarur (Santiago), August 1972; Juan Carvajal (Santiago), August 1972. Jorge Yarur became president of Yarur, Inc., with his younger brother, Amador, as managing director. Juan Yarur's eldest son, Carlos, a poor businessman long estranged from his father, was given his share of the inheritance, a seat on the board, and the title of general administrator, but was excluded from executive power.

42. Jorge Yarur (Santiago), August 1972. Jorge Yarur confessed that his father was a hard man to break in under and that his apprenticeship at the factory had been "a frustrating experience" that had come to a sudden end when his father rescinded his appointment as manager and sent him to work in the family bank.

43. Ibid.; Juan Corvo (Santiago), August 1972; Eugenio Stark (Santiago), June 1972; Miguel Hirmas (Santiago), January 1974.

44. Juan Corvo (Santiago), August 1972; Jorge Yarur (Santiago), August 1972; Price Waterhouse Peat & Co. to Amador Yarur, Santiago (17 May and 6 December 1962), *SAYMCHA/STGO*.

45. Jorge Yarur (Santiago), August 1972; Juan Corvo (Santiago), August 1972; Eugenio Stark (Santiago), August 1972.

46. Jorge Yarur (Santiago), August 1972; Juan Corvo (Santiago), August 1972; Leicester Warren, vice-president, Burlington Industries (telephone interview), July 1981; C.W. Bendigo, director, International Services, Burlington Industries, to Jorge Yarur, Santiago (8 July 1962); Alex S. Brown, chief industrial engineer, Burlington Industries, to Jorge Yarur, Greensboro, North Carolina (8 November 1962), *SAYMCHA/STGO*.

47. Jorge Yarur (Santiago), August 1972; Juan Corvo (Santiago), August 1972; SAYMCHA, *Memorias*, nos. 25–26 (1965–66); Ex-Yarur, Departamento Terminación de Géneros, Sección Acabados, "Producción de Géneros Buenos y Fallados, 1959–1971," *SAYMCHA/STGO*. In 1966, the factory's first full year of production under the Taylor System, the 1,667 remaining blue-collar workers produced 13 percent more cloth than 3800 workers had manufactured in 1959.

48. Juan Corvo (Santiago), August 1972.

49. Eugenio Stark (Santiago), June 1972.

50. Ibid.; Juan Corvo (Santiago), August 1972; Jorge Yarur (Santiago), August 1972.

51. Eugenio Stark (Santiago), June 1972.

52. Ibid.; Juan Corvo (Santiago), August 1972.

53. Eugenio Stark (Santiago), June 1972.

54. Juan Corvo (Santiago), August 1972.

55. Jorge Yarur to Sociedad de Fomento Fabril, Santiago (25 April 1963), *SAYMCHA/STGO*: "We have an expansion program underway, with an eye to produce articles for export to ALALC [Latin American Free Trade Association], as well as to meet the growing domestic demand," Jorge Yarur informed the SOFOFA. He estimated its cost at 3 million U.S. dollars in machinery and 2.5 million escudos in construction.

56. SAYMCHA, Sesiones del Consejo Directivo, *Actas* (24 April 1963), *SAYMCHA/STGO*; Jorge Yarur (Santiago), August 1972.

57. That same year, more S.A. Yarur funds were invested in acquiring control of Química Industrial, an aging Santiago polyester plant, which was projected as a supplier of synthetic fibers for the new Yarur Caupolican mills, but would also prove a major drain on the family fortune. Carlos Yarur became head of Química Industrial (SAYMCHA, Sesiones del Consejo Directivo, *Actas* [15 May 1963], *SAYMCHA/STGO*).

58. SAYMCHA, *Memorias*, Nos. 23–30 (1963–70); Juan Corvo (Santiago), August 1972;

La Nación (Santiago), 1 April 1967, p. 4.; Carlos Benavides (Santiago), June 1972; Aldo Manzanares (Santiago), September 1972. Benavides and Manzanares were administrative employees in the S.A. Yarur financial department.

59. SAYMCHA, *Memorias*, nos. 24–30 (1964–70); Chile, Ministerio de Economía, Comisión Investigadora Especializada [hereafter, C.I.E.], "Investigación Informe de Yarur S.A.," Santiago (April 6, 1971), p. 4.

60. C.I.E., "Informe de Yarur S. A.," p. 4. The government investigators who compiled this report were unaware of a further 1.4 million U.S. dollars in loans from German and United States banks, which were company obligations yet never entered in its books and which were contracted in apparent violation of Chilean regulations (Patricio Taulis [Santiago], August 1972. Taulis was financial manager of Yarur after its requisition.)

61. SAYMCHA, *Memorias*, nos. 24–30 (1964–70); Instituto Textil de Chile [hereafter INCHITEX], *Memorias* (1967), p. 16; Algodones Hirmas, S.A., *Memorias* (1964–70). Their business association, the Instituto Textil de Chile, stressed as well the negative impact of Chile's periodic currency devaluations on an industry "that imports an important percentage of its raw materials, spare parts, and other inputs." (INCHITEX, *Memorias*, [1967]).

62. Luis Carrillo (Santiago), January 1974; *Las Noticias de la Ultima Hora* [Santiago], 24 March 1966, p. 16. *El Siglo* (Santiago), 24 March 1966, p. 3; Raúl Alvarez, president, Asociación Industriales de Cautín, to Julio del Rio, president, Sociedad de Fomento Fabril, "Confidential," Temuco (11 January 1963), *SAYMCHA/STGO*. Popular skepticism was fueled by revelations that similar data had been falsified by the textile industry during the previous decade and by reports that the Yarurs were getting around price controls by altering their product lines and diminishing the production of "popular fabrics." Yarur efforts to evade government price controls are documented in the minutes of its Board of Directors (SAYMCHA, Sesiones de Consejo Directivo, *Actas* [22 June 1966], *SAYMCHA/STGO*; See also, *Ahora* [Santiago], August 1971, p. 7).

63. C.I.E.,"Informe de Yarur S. A.," pp. 4–5.

64. Victor Valencia (Santiago), August 1972. Valencia, an accounting employee charged with an internal audit, was stunned by Amador Yarur's vetoing his auditing the shareholder lists.

65. Pedro García (Santiago), September 1972. Another source of S.A. Yarur's declining profits was the sizable S.A. Yarur capital sunk unproductively in 6.6 million Tejidos Caupolican shares. In fact, Caupolican proved a financial drain, forcing S.A. Yarur to draw on its own credit in order to advance that troubled family enterprise considerable sums (some 1.6 million escudos) "as financial aid" (SAYMCHA, Sesiones de Consejo Directivo, *Actas* [24 August 1966], *SAYMCHA/STGO*).

66. Pedro García (Santiago), September 1972; Eugenio Stark (Santiago), June 1972; Juan Corvo (Santiago), August 1972. Luis Bono (Santiago), July 1973; Hernán López (Santiago), September 1972 and January 1974. Stark was Personnel Chief under Amador Yarur; Corvo, head of Industrial Engineering; Bono, chief of Maintenance; García, head of Data Processing; and López, a production section technical supervisor.

67. Yarur had implemented almost all the recommendations on improved productivity and efficiency made to the Chilean textile industry by government studies long before they were published in 1968–69, yet had failed to replace its antiquated machinery or respect "rational business administration" (Chile, Corporación de Fomento de la Producción [CORFO], "Informe de la misión chilena al área andina" [Santiago, 1968]; CORFO, Departamento de Industrias de Consumo Corriente, Grupo Textil, "Estudio provisiorio de una política textil nacional" [Santiago, 1969]. See also, Consultores en Ingenería y Administración de Empresas [CADE], *Situación actual y proyecciones futuras de la industria textil chilena*, 8 vols. [Santiago, 1968–69]).

68. Sanfuentes, "Los árabes," p. 139.

69. SAYMCHA, Sesiones del Consejo Directivo, *Actas* (24 April and 15 May 1963); *SAYMCHA/STGO*.

70. Empresas Juan Yarur, S.A.C., *Memorias* (1957–70), and "Análisis del fondos de fluctuación de valores" (1965), *SCSSABC/DSA*. Empresas Juan Yarur was a private corporation whose shares were almost entirely owned by Yarur Banna family members. It had only one employee, Francisco Navarro, an accountant who had an office in the S.A. Yarur administration building (Francisco Navarro [Santiago], August 1972). Its major function was as an agency of family capital formation that avoided income taxes by rarely distributing profits. Sanfuentes characterized it as a "legal fiction" (Sanfuentes, "Los árabes," p. 146).

71. Ricardo Lagos, *La concentración del poder económico* (Santiago, 1960); Roger Burbach, "The Chilean Industrial Bourgeoisie and Foreign Capital, 1920–1970," (Ph.D. diss., Indiana University, 1975), pp. 134–38.

72. Jorge Yarur (Santiago), August 1972.

73. Although the concentration of a bank's advances within its controlling group was typical in a Chilean economy where runaway inflation converted seemingly usurious loans into negative interest rates, the Yarurs were an extreme case. In 1960, the Superintendencia de Bancos levied one of the stiffest penalties in Chilean banking history on Jorge Yarur for kiting checks among his many branches on a scale that reduced his bank's reserves below legal margins and increased its loans to one individual (himself) above legal limits. Government investigators claimed in 1972 to have found evidence that he had used the Banco de Crédito to help other Yarur enterprises evade taxes and to violate exchange regulations by overvaluing imports (Héctor Espinoza, Government Interventor, Banco de Crédito e Inversiones [Santiago], July 1972). By 1970, the arrears of interest alone on advances to Yarur enterprises amounted to almost $1.5 million (ibid.; Chile, Ministerio de Economía, C.I.E., "Investigación Informe: Tejidos Caupolican, S.A.," Santiago [10 May 1971]).

74. Heraldo Pérez (Santiago), August 1972.

75. Fernando Dahse, *Mapa de la extrema riqueza. Los grupos económicos y el proceso de concentración de capitales*, (Santiago, 1979), pp. 22–23, 69–71; Lagos, *La concentración del poder económico*, passim; Oscar Guillermo Garretón and Jaime Cisternas, "Algunas características del proceso de toma de decisiones en la gran empresa: la dinámica de la concentración,"(mimeographed; Santiago, Servicio de Cooperación Técnica, 1970), pp. 27–37; Sanfuentes, "Los árabes," pp. 137–56. The Yarurs also owned a major radio station and extensive real estate (Sanfuentes, "Los árabes," pp. 149–51).

76. Sanfuentes, "Los árabes," pp. 145–50; Héctor Espinoza (Santiago), July 1972; Empresas Juan Yarur, S.A.C., "Análisis del fondos y fluctuación de valores" (1964–70), *SCSSABC/DSA*, Rol 1717. In addition, they could count on the collaboration of the Banco Continental, controlled by the Yarur Kazakias (the children of Nicolás Yarur), especially where the family's textile enterprises were concerned. Through Tejidos Caupolican, moreover, they were also linked to the Banco Edwards, the Banco de Chile, and the Banco del Pacífico, all of which owned sizable blocs of its shares—and through these banks to the Chilean economic elites who controlled them, some of whom also were linked to the Banco de Crédito by shareholdings or seats on its board of directors (Sanfuentes, "Los árabes," pp. 146–50, 159–66; Burbach, "The Chilean Industrial Bourgeoisie," pp. 135–37).

77. Miguel Hirmas (Santiago), January 1974; Dahse, *Mapa de la extrema riqueza*, pp. 22–23, 69–71; Sanfuentes, *Los árabes*, pp. 137–41, 151–52; Francisco Navarro (Santiago), August 1972.

78. Nicolás Yarur (Santiago), January 1974; Sanfuentes, "Los árabes," pp. 137–65.

79. Calculated from information in annual reports deposited in the Superintendencia de Companías de Seguros, Sociedades Anónimas y Bolsas de Comercio, Departamento de So-

ciedades Anónimas. See also Sanfuentes, "Los árabes," pp. 137–67, and Burbach, "Chilean Industrial Bourgeoisie," pp. 192–202.

80. Victor Valech (Santiago), December 1973; Jorge Yarur (Santiago), August 1972; Marcelo Cavarozzi, "Government and Industrial Bourgeoisie," pp. 393–94. Valech was co-founder of INCHITEX and its president in 1973.

81. Garretón and Cisternas, "Algunas características," pp. 27–30.

82. Fernando Sanhueza, quoted in *Las Noticias de la Ultima Hora*, 24 March 1966, p. 16.

83. Sanfuentes, "Los árabes," p. 137.

84. Victor Vió (Santiago), May 1972. A broadcast journalist, Vió investigated Yarur activities for a 1971 television special.

85. Luis Ballasteros (Santiago), April 1972.

CHAPTER 2

1. Most had been screened first, however, by Personnel Chief Daniel Fuenzalida, a tough former army officer.

2. Laura Murillo (Santiago), August 1972.

3. Eugenio Stark (Santiago), June 1972. Stark worked in the Personnel Department from the factory's founding and became its head in 1962.

4. María López (Santiago), August 1972.

5. Eugenio Stark (Santiago), June 1972.

6. Ibid.; Mario Leníz (Santiago), September 1972. Leníz was a Yarur loyalist leader and company union president.

7. Alicia Navarrete (Santiago), August 1972; Blanca Bascuñan (Santiago), August 1972.

8. Luis Carrillo, Chile, Corporación de Fomento, Comité Textil, (Santiago), January 1974.

9. Rosa Ramos (Santiago), July 1972.

10. Blanca Bascuñan (Santiago), August 1972.

11. Rosa Ramos (Santiago), August 1972.

12. Blanca Bascuñan (Santiago), August 1972.

13. Alicia Navarrete (Santiago), August 1972.

14. Blanca Bascuñan (Santiago), August 1972.

15. Eugenio Stark (Santiago), June 1972. Mario Leníz (Santiago), September 1972.

16. Eugenio Stark (Santiago), June 1972.

17. Ibid.

18. José Lagos (Santiago), April 1972. These small gifts and and loans were cited frequently by Yarur loyalists as examples of "Don Juan's benevolence" that justified their loyalty.

19. Mario Leníz (Santiago), September 1972.

20. Ibid.; The legal distinction between *obreros* and *empleados* corresponded roughly to a division between blue- and white-collar workers. For an extended discussion, see Alan Angell, *Politics and the Labour Movement in Chile* (London, 1972), pp. 66–68.

21. Eugenio Stark (Santiago), June 1972.

22. María López (Santiago), August 1972; Inés Latorre (Santiago), June 1972; Blanca Calvo (Santiago), September 1972. Before Jorge and Amador Yarur married, some of these women even entertained the fantasy that Don Juan's son might fall in love with them and carry them off to the altar, as in the pulp fiction romances of the day (Inés Latorre (Santiago), June 1972).

23. Elena Toro (Santiago), September 1972.

24. Eugenio Stark (Santiago), June 1972.

25. Eduardo Ellis, president, Sindicato Industrial S.A. Yarur, quoted in *El Mercurio*, 14 March 1946, p. 23.

26. José Lagos (Santiago), April 1972.

27. Alicia Navarrete (Santiago), August 1972.

28. Ibid.

29. Luz Castro (Santiago), August 1972.

30. Ibid.

31. Blanca Bascuñan (Santiago), August 1972.

32. Eugenio Stark (Santiago), June 1972.

33. Alicia Navarrete (Santiago), August 1972.

34. Isabél Torres (Santiago), September 1972.

35. Reinaldo Jara (Santiago), January 1974.

36. Laura Coruña (Santiago), September 1972.

37. Reinaldo Jara (Santiago), January 1974.

38. María López (Santiago), August 1972; Eugenio Stark (Santiago), June 1972; Mario Leníz (Santiago), September 1972.

39. Laura Coruña (Santiago), September 1972. Fuenzalida, a former military officer, served as the industry's personnel and "welfare" chief for twenty-five years. Hiring a military man as personnel chief was a common practice in Chilean industry at the time, the theory being that they knew how to handle lower-class youths. (Eugenio Stark [Santiago], June 1972).

40. Mario Leníz (Santiago), September 1972.

41. Ibid.

42. Alicia Navarrete (Santiago), August 1972.

43. Reinaldo Jara (Santiago), January 1974.

44. A government survey of 1942 found that: "[a] sizable percentage of workers lack housing or live in unhealthy rooms lacking in the most minimal hygienic conditions; our worker is badly fed; infant mortality in his family is one of the highest in the world; their scant salaries do not permit them to dress decently; they do not have the means to provide their families with healthy entertainments; alcohol is the escape in which their lives of misery and humiliation are summed up" (quoted in Victor Reuly Guzmán, "Condiciones económicas-sociales de los obreros textiles, 1938–49," Memorias de Licenciatura, Derecho de Trabajo, Facultad de Ciencias Jurídicas y Sociales, Universidad de Chile, vol. 24 (Santiago, 1950), p. 167]. Textile workers, whose average wage was below the national average, lived no better than most, Reuly's study concluded; even the better paid *obreros*, such as the mechanics, lived in housing that was only slightly better and expended most of their income on food (ibid., pp. 173, 179–83, 191–92, 195–205).

45. Reinaldo Jara (Santiago), January 1974.

46. María López (Santiago), August 1972.

47. Beginning with the social laws of 1924 and the Labor Code of 1931, a series of laws and decrees made the state the arbiter of labor relations and the watchdog of union democracy. State recognition became the touchstone of union legitimacy; state labor inspectors supervised union affairs and state mediation boards—there was a separate Junta de Conciliación for the Santiago textile industry—now dealt with deadlocked conflicts between labor and management. The right to strike was equally subject to state regulation, with state officials granting or witholding the right to hold a union vote on a "legal" strike and reserving the right to break "illegal" strikes by executive order. Conceived as a solution to the "social question" posed

by labor militancy, the Chilean system offered labor legal recognition in return for state regulation while exchanging coercion for co-optation as an elite strategy of social control. After a decade of resistance—and repression—most of the labor movement accepted the trade-off implicit in the labor laws and began to work within it during the Popular Front government of 1938–41. (For the system's origins, see James O. Morris, *Elites, Intellectuals and Consensus* [Ithaca, N.Y., 1966].)

48. Blanca Bascuañan (Santiago), August 1972.

49. Sindicato Industrial "Yarur Hermanos," *Libro de Actas* (February–December 1939); Brigada Ibañista de Yarur, "¡Camaradas Adelante!" (undated pamphlet of December 1952); "Obreros de S.A. Yarur" to Jorge Yarur, Santiago (19 December 1952), *SAYMCHA/STGO*.

50. Roberto Bugueño, president, Sindicato Industrial "Yarur Hermanos," quoted in *Frente Popular* [Santiago], 27 February 1939, p.9.

51. Ibid..

52. Eugenio Stark (Santiago), June 1972.

53. Ibid.; Mario Leníz (Santiago), September 1972.

54. The 1939 movement is chronicled in the contemporary press and in the union minutes. (See *Frente Popular* [Santiago] and *La Crítica* [Santiago], and Sindicato Industrial "Yarur Hermanos," *Actas* [1939].) Although some Old-timers had clear memories of its most dramatic moments, origins, and lessons, few remembered its entire course. The best source I encountered for the 1947 movement, on the other hand, was its leader, Reinaldo Jara, although *El Siglo* (Santiago) and the records of the Ministry of Labor (and, in particular, those of the Junta de Conciliación for the Santiago textile industry) were valuable.

55. Javier Altamirano (Santiago), January 1974; Reinaldo Jara (Santiago), January 1974; María López (Santiago), August 1972.Altamirano was a veteran state labor inspector who stressed low government salaries as the explanation for corrupt officials.

56. Fernando Morales (Santiago), January 1974. Morales was Almeyda's Deputy Minister.

57. José Lagos (Santiago), September 1972.

58. Inés Latorre (Santiago), August 1972.

59. Alicia Navarrete (Santiago), August 1972.

60. Juana Garrido (Santiago), August 1972.

61. Alicia Navarrete (Santiago), August 1972.

62. Juana Garrido (Santiago), August 1972.

63. Personnel records for this period were said to have perished in the fire of 1964, but the average age of the blue-collar work force in 1961 was about forty, and many workers had been hired in the interim, almost all of them far younger (Eugenio Stark [Santiago], June 1972).

64. In 1962 there were still three hundred illiterates working as *obreros*, a number probably reduced from the number in 1954 by attrition and by Jorge Yarur's encouraging them to learn how to read and making it clear that if they couldn't, their future at the mill was bleak. (The number of illiterates was calculated by counting the workers who signed the union rolls with thumb prints at the end of 1961. (Sindicato Industrial S. A. Yarur, "Lista de Socios" [December 1961], Chile, Ministerio de Trabajo, Dirección General de Trabajo, Departamento de Organizaciones Sociales, [hereafter *DGT/DOS*] Carpeta 83). A Communist labor expert who followed the Yarur situation for the CUT ascribed the failure of the 1953 movement to "the veneration of Juan Yarur" by a majority of his workers (Luis Campos [Santiago], January 1974).

65. The *apatronado* mind-set and role in his system of social control was typified by the anonymous "friend" who warned "Don Juan" about a group of mechanics who applauded and shouted, "Yarur is an octopus!" after drinking at a local restaurant: "On several occasions,"

he wrote, "I have had the occasion to observe disorders and cries against you, despite your stature, which should lead them to be appreciative of the job that they have in your industry" ("Su Amigo" to Juan Yarur, Santiago [13 May 1954], *SAYMCHA/STGO*).

66. Jorge Yarur (Santiago), August 1972.

67. Mario Leníz (Santiago), September 1972; Eugenio Stark (Santiago), June 1972. In the wake of the 1953 movement, he expanded the benevolent side of his paternalism and reportedly toyed with the idea of giving the workers shares in Yarur, Inc., through a profit-sharing plan that he called "popular capitalism."

68. Jorge Yarur (Santiago), August 1972.

69. Eugenio Stark (Santiago), June 1972; Mario Leníz (Santiago), September 1972; Alma Gallegos (Santiago), August 1972.

70. Mario Leníz (Santiago), September 1972; Eugenio Stark (Santiago), September 1972. Still, the union remained company controlled, with managed elections from which insurgents were excluded and choreographed contract negotiations. The uniformed company police force, headed by the hated Arturo Hoffmann, whom even Leníz considered "a crazy guy," remained in charge of internal security. Supervisors continued to exercise arbitrary power over their workers, and Daniel Fuenzalida was still the feared personnel chief who hired and fired at his whim or will. Nor did the practice of informing cease with Juan Yarur's death. Dissident workers, therefore, viewed Jorge Yarur's changes as purely cosmetic and Juan Yarur's system of social control as essentially intact (Luis Campos [Santiago], January 1974).

71. Even his own company union head admitted that "Don Jorge was very despotic" and, while claiming that "at bottom he was a good person," conceded that "he had an arrogant style that made one afraid to talk to him" (Mario Leníz [Santiago], September 1972).

72. Javier Altamirano (Santiago), December 1973.

73. Jorge Yarur (Santiago), August 1972. By 1962, only one thousand women worked at the Yarur mill, and, by 1970, women formed only 10 percent of the Yarur labor force (Sindicato Industrial S. A. Yarur, "Lista de Socios" [December 1961 and December 1969], *DGT/DOS*, Carpeta 83).

74. Eugenio Stark (Santiago), June 1972; Juan Corvo (Santiago), August 1972. New blue collar workers entering the mill were now required to have a primary education.

75. Jorge Yarur (Santiago), August 1972; Juan Corvo (Santiago), August 1972. Social security increases under Ibáñez had more than doubled the cost of labor, Jorge Yarur maintained.

76. Leicester Warren, vice-president, Burlington Industries (telephone interview), July 1981; Eugenio Stark (Santiago), June 1972; Jorge Yarur (Santiago), August 1972.

77. Juan Corvo (Santiago), August 1972. Corvo, who became head of the new Industrial Engineering Department, was the Yarur employee assigned to work with the Burlington advisory team. Although *taylorismo* was the label Chileans used to describe the system and one popular magazine (*Vistazo* [Santiago], 31 July 1962, p. 10) seemed to blame "Mr. Taylor" personally for the resulting unemployment of Yarur workers, the system implemented at the Yarur mill was really a modification of Taylor's ideas. For the original source, see Frederick Winslow Taylor, *The Principles of Scientific Management*, (New York, 1911).

78. One veteran spinner confessed: "At times I cried right there among the machines, seeing that I wasn't capable of doing as much work as they gave us each day" (Alma Gallegos [Santiago], August 1972).

79. Blanca Bascuñan (Santiago), August 1972.

80. Rosa Bermúdez (Santiago), August 1972.

81. Lidia Chelén (Santiago), August 1972.

82. Jorge Yarur (Santiago), August 1972.

83. Alma Gallegos (Santiago), August 1972.

84. María López (Santiago), August 1972.

85. Marta Vilas (Santiago), August 1972.

86. José Lagos (Santiago), September 1972.

87. Blanca Bascuñan (Santiago), August 1972.

88. Enrique Ortega (Santiago), August 1972.

89. Julio Lagos (Santiago), August 1972.

90. Rosa Ramos (Santiago), September 1972.

91. Mario Lemus (Santiago), September 1972.

92. Alma Gallegos (Santiago), August 1972.

93. Luis Campos (Santiago), January 1974.

94. Lidia Chelén (Santiago), August 1972.

95. Miguel Concha (Santiago), September 1973.

96. Armando Guerra (Santiago), September 1972.

97. Luis Campos (Santiago), January 1974.

98. Ibid.

99. Jorge Barría, *Historia de la CUT* (Santiago, 1971), pp. 104–5.

100. *El Siglo*, January–June 1962, *passim.*

101. See Chile, Camara de Diputados, *Diario de Sesiones*, Ses. Ords., 26th Sess. (31 July 1962), vol. 3, pp. 2648–49.

102. Luis Campos (Santiago), January 1974.

103. Luz Castro (Santiago), August 1972.

104. Eugenio Stark (Santiago), June 1972. The mass firings were possible, he stressed, because "in that time there was no job security law for blue-collar workers."

105. Jorge Yarur (Santiago), August 1972. From the viewpoint of production, however, the pattern of the purge was not so "helpful" to the Yarurs. "Everywhere in the factory, the Reds were the best workers," stressed the chief of Industrial Engineering, who was in charge of installing the Taylor System. But despite the pleas of the Burlington experts, they were fired, and less productive Yarur loyalists were retained, proof that politics, not productivity, was the Yarur guiding principle here (Juan Corvo [Santiago], August 1972).

106. Luis Campos (Santiago), January 1974.

107. Eugenio Stark (Santiago), June 1972.

108. Juan Corvo (Santiago), August 1972.

109. Eugenio Stark (Santiago), June 1972.

110. Luis Campos (Santiago), January 1974.

111. Daniel Gómez (Santiago), September 1972.

112. Juan Galo (Santiago), August 1972.

113. Yolanda Gajardo (Santiago), August 1972.

114. Iris Valenzuela (Santiago), August 1972.

115. Luz Castro (Santiago), August 1972.

116. Laura Coruña (Santiago), August 1972.

117. Iris Valenzuela (Santiago), August 1972.

118. Enrique Osorio in Chile, Camara de Diputados, *Diario de Sesiones*, Ses. Ords., 28th Sess. (1 August 1962), vol. 3, p. 2761.

CHAPTER 3

1. In writing this chapter, I have drawn heavily on my own oral history interviews, including a series of twenty-two interviews with political leaders, and on my research in

contemporary newspapers, periodicals, statistical materials, and published reports. I have also consulted a large number of published and unpublished writings about Chile from 1940–1970 by participants, observers, and scholars. Except where noted otherwise, I have relied mostly on the following works: Paul Drake, *Socialism and Populism in Chile, 1932–52* (Urbana, Ill., 1978); Ricardo Ffrench-Davis, *Políticas económicas en Chile, 1952–1970* (Santiago, 1973); Sergio Bitar, *Transición, socialismo y democracia: la experiencia chilena* (Mexico City, 1979); Marcelo Cavarozzi, "The Government and the Industrial Bourgeoisie in Chile: 1938–1964" (Ph.D. diss., University of California, Berkeley, Calif., 1976); Alan Angell, *Politics and the Labour Movement in Chile* (London, 1972); James Petras, *Politics and Social Forces in Chilean Development* (Berkeley, Calif., 1969); Brian Loveman, *Struggle in the Countryside: Politics and Rural Labor in Chile, 1919–1973* (Bloomington, Ind., 1976); Barbara Stallings, *Class Conflict and Economic Development in Chile, 1958–1973* (Stanford, Calif., 1978); Arturo Valenzuela, *The Breakdown of Democratic Regimes: Chile* (Baltimore, Md., 1978); Joan E. Garcés, *Chile: el camino político hacia el socialismo* (Barcelona, 1972); Genaro Arriagada Herrera, *De la vía chilena a la vía insurreccional* (Santiago, 1974); *The Chilean Road to Socialism*, ed. J. Ann Zammit (Brighton, Eng., 1973); and Aníbal Pinto Santa Cruz, *Chile: Un caso del desarrollo frustrado*, 2d ed. (Santiago, 1962), and *Chile, hoy* (Mexico City, 1970).

2. Adonis Sepúlveda (Santiago), June 1972. Sepúlveda was a Socialist senator and long-time party leader.

3. Salvador Allende (Santiago), July 1972.

4. Ibid.

5. Ibid.

6. Volodia Teitelboim (Santiago), April 1972. In 1972, Teitelboim was a Communist senator, a politburo member, and a leading party theoretician.

7. Salvador Allende (Santiago), July 1972.

8. Ibid.

9. Ibid.

10. Volodia Teitelboim (Santiago), April 1972.

11. Fernando Morales (Santiago), January 1974.

12. Salvador Allende (Santiago), July 1972.

13. Chile, Dirección de Registro Electoral, "Variación porcentual de los partidos políticos, 1957–1971," (unpublished statistics); Drake, *Socialism and Populism*, pp. 51–52, 97–99, 303–04.

14. The Chilean Communist party has yet to find its historian although it counts several eminent historians in its ranks and has published many internal documents and speeches. I have relied for this account on my reading of the party newspaper, *El Siglo* (1941–1973), and journal, *Principios* [Santiago], 1946–1973, and on my oral history interviews with Volodia Teitelboim (Santiago), April-June 1972; Enrique Kirberg (New York), October-December 1979; Victor Vió (Santiago), May-June 1972. Kirberg was rector of the State Technical University and a longtime central committee member and campaign fixture; Vió, a Communist Youth leader, journalist, and Allende campaign manager. The party's early history is chronicled in Hernán Ramírez Necochea, *Orígen y formación del Partido Comunista de Chile* (Santiago, 1965). Two views of its history through the eyes of former party chiefs are presented in Elias Lafertte's autobiography, *Vida de un comunista*, 2d ed. (Santiago, 1971), and Eduardo Labarca's *Corvalán: 27 horas* (Santiago, 1972).

15. In addition to Drake's prize-winning study *Socialism and Populism*, there have been several important books published by Chilean Socialists on their party's history. See, for example, Julio César Jobet, *Historia del Partido Socialista*, 2 vols. (Santiago, 1971); Fernando Casanueva and Manuel Fernández, *El Partido Socialista y la lucha de clases en Chile* (Santiago,

1973); and the document collection edited by Jobet and Alejandro Chelén, *Pensamiento teórico y político del Partido Socialista de Chile* (Santiago, 1972).

16. Prior to this reform, each party printed its own ballots for voters to deposit in the urn, which led to widespread bribery and intimidation of lower-class voters, particularly in rural areas where peasants were dependent on the favor of their *patrón*. Some scholars have traced the subsequent demise of Chilean democracy to this electoral reform and the resultant political mobilization either because they view the concession to the Right of a secure rural base as the precondition of Chilean political stability or because they view the intense competitive mobilization that followed and continued through the Allende period as too rapid and massive for Chile's political system to absorb (See Loveman, *Struggle in the Countryside*, pp. 201–220, for the former argument and Henry Landsberger and Tim McDaniel, "Hypermobilization in Chile, 1970–1973," *World Politics*, 28 (July 1976), 502–41 for the latter. For a reply to both, see A. Valenzuela, *Chile*, pp. 25–33).

17. Angell, *Politics and the Labour Movement*, pp. 43–56; Jorge Barría, *Historia de la CUT* (Santiago, 1971), pp. 127–30; A. Valenzuela, *Chile*, p. 28, Table 7. Valenzuela's calculation, the most sophisticated, yields 437,000 nonagricultural workers, to which the 137,000 workers in peasant unions should be added. These calculations, however, understate the size of organized labor in Chile as they restrict themselves to official statistics on legal unions, which could only be formed in the small minority of enterprises with more than twenty-five workers.

18. Chile, Dirección del Registro Electoral, "Variación"; Valenzuela, *Chile*, p. 35, Table 10. The frontier between Left and Center was occupied by small parties, such as the National Democrats (PADENA), remnants of earlier reform parties, who were often allied with the Left but could equally be regarded as Center parties. For a minimum bound calculation that excludes all but the Socialist and Communists from the Left's totals, yielding a 28.1 percent total for 1969 but a similar doubling of its support since 1953, see Valenzuela, *Chile*, p. 6, Table 2. For an opposed analysis, based on fragmentary survey data confined to the Santiago area, see James W. Prothro and Patricio E. Chaparro, "Public Opinion and the Movement of Chilean Government to the Left, 1952–1972," *Journal of Politics*, 36 (1974), 2–32.

19. An adequate history of the Radical party remains to be written. In addition to the works cited in the first footnote to this chapter, I have drawn on Peter Snow, *Chilean Radicalism: The History and Doctrine of the Radical Party* (Iowa City, Iowa, 1971); Luis Palma Zuñiga, *Historia del Partido Radical* (Santiago, 1967); Gérman Urzúa Valenzuela, *El Partido Radical: Su evolución política* (Santiago, 1961); and John R. Stevenson, *The Chilean Popular Front* (Philadelphia, 1942).

20. See, for example, Leonard Gross, *The Last Best Hope: Eduardo Frei and Chilean Christian Democracy* (New York, 1967); David E. Mutchler, *The Church as a Factor in Latin America* (New York, 1971); Brian Smith, *The Church and Politics in Chile* (Princeton, N.J., 1982). The Senate Intelligence Committee concluded that "the United States was involved on a massive scale in the 1964 presidential election in Chile," contributing $3 million to $4 million covertly to the effort "to prevent the election of a Socialist or Communist candidate" —the equivalent of $60 million to $80 million in a country the size of the United States (United States Senate, Select Committee to Study Governmental Operations with Respect to Intelligence Activities, Staff Report, "Covert Action in Chile, 1963–1973" [Washington, D.C., 1975]). Former U.S. Ambassador Edward Korry later charged that even this was an understatement and that "tens of millions of dollars of 1960 Chilean earthquake relief funds were diverted into the Jesuit-led Catholic groups for domestic political activity in Chile" (*Sunday News Journal* [Wilmington, Del.] 28 November 1976, p. 1).

21. For the Christian Democrats, in addition to the works already cited, see George

Grayson; *El Partido Demócrata Cristiano Chileno* (Santiago, 1968); Jaime Castillo Velasco, *Las fuentes de la Democracia Cristiana*, 3d ed. (Santiago, 1972); and the chronicle of Arturo Olavarría Bravo, *Chile bajo la Democracia Cristiana*, 5 vols. (Santiago, 1965–69). For a representative collection of Frei's early thought, see Eduardo Frei, *Pensamiento y acción* (Santiago, 1958). For a view from Frei's cabinet, see Sergio Molina, *El proceso de cambio en Chile: La experiencia 1965– 1970* (Santiago, 1972).

22. On the agrarian reform, see also Robert Kaufman, *The Politics of Land Reform in Chile, 1950–1970* (Cambridge, Mass., 1972), and David Alaluf, Solon Barraclough, et al., *Reforma agraria chilena: Seis ensayos de interpretación* (Santiago, 1970).

23. On the Chileanization of copper, see also Theodore Moran, *Multinational Corporations and the Politics of Dependence: Copper in Chile* (Princeton, N.J., 1974).

24. See Roger Burbach, "Chilean Industrial Bourgeoisie and Foreign Capital, 1920–1970," (Ph.D. diss., Indiana University, 1975), pp. 149–167; Oscar Guillermo Garretón and Jaime Cisternas, "Algunas características del proceso de toma de decisiones en la gran empresa: la dinámica de la concentración" (mimeographed; Santiago: Servicio de Cooperación Téchnica, 1970); [MAPU], *El Libro de las 91: Las empresas monopólicas y el area social de la economía chilena* (Santiago, 1972); and Fernando Dahse, *Mapa de la extrema riqueza* (Santiago, 1979). As a consequence, by 1970, foreign interests controlled forty-two of Chile's one hundred largest enterprises.

25. The best summary of statistics for this period is ODEPLAN, *Plan de la economía nacional: Antecedentes sobre el desarrollo chileno 1960–70* (Santiago, 1971). There are no national unemployment statistics for this period. Unless otherwise noted, the figures quoted are for Greater Santiago, the standard Chilean measure.

26. Chile, Dirección del Registro Electoral, "Variación porcentual de los partidos políticos, 1957–1971."

27. Rafael Gumucio (Santiago), June 1972; Jacques Chonchol (Santiago), May 1972; Luis Maira (Santiago), June 1972; Jaime Gazmuri (Santiago), May 1972; Ignacio Palma (Santiago), July 1972; Plan Chonchol, "Proposiciones para una acción política de una via no capitalista de desarrollo," *PEC* [Santiago], no. 239 (28 July 1967), pp. i–xx; and Julio Silva Solar and Jacques Chonchol, *Desarrollo de la nueva sociedad en América Latina*, 2d ed. (Santiago, 1969). Gumucio was a Christian Democratic senator, a party founder, and past president; Maira was a deputy; and Chonchol and Silva Solar, leading party theoreticians. Gazmuri would become head of the MAPU in 1972.

28. "The Programme of Unidad Popular" (17 December 1969), in *Chile's Road to Socialism*, ed. Joan Garcés (London, 1973), pp. 23–24, 26–27, 37–38. My analysis draws heavily on the Popular Unity program and *El pensamiento eonómico del gobierno de Allende*, ed. Gonzalo Martner (Santiago, 1971), in addition to the works cited earlier.

29. Ibid., p. 37.

30. Ibid., p. 34.

31. Ibid., p. 31.

32. Ibid., p. 41. A final focus of the Popular Unity program was foreign policy, promising a combination of nonalignment, Third World nationalism, and socialist internationalism.

33. A. Valenzuela, *Chile*, p. 43, Table 13; Volodia Teitelboím (Santiago), April 1972.

34. Isabél Torres (Santiago), June 1972.

35. For a good journalistic account of the nomination process, see Eduardo Labarca Goddard, *Chile al rojo: Reportaje a una revolución que nace* (Santiago, 1971), pp. 177–253.

36. Adonis Sepúlveda (Santiago), June 1972; Joan Garcés (Santiago), June 1972. Garcés, a Catalan political scientist, was Allende's top political adviser and campaign strategist.

37. Rafael Tarud (Santiago), July 1972; Rafael Gumucio (Santiago), June 1972; Volodia Teitelboim (Santiago), April 1972. Tarud was the head of a small populist party, the A.P.I., and its candidate for the Popular Unity presidential nomination.

38. Volodia Teitelboim (Santiago), April 1972.

39. Salvador Allende (Santiago), July 1972.

40. Volodia Teitelboím (Santiago), April 1972.

41. In addition to the sources already cited, I have drawn on two evocative descriptions of the 1970 election campaign: Richard Feinberg, *The Triumph of Allende* (New York, 1972), and Labarca, *Chile al rojo*.

42. Joan Garcés (Santiago), June 1972. For a detailed exposition of this Allende strategy, see Garcés, *1970: La pugna por la presidencia en Chile* (Santiago, 1971).

43. One year before the election, opinion polls gave Alessandri 46 percent of the vote to 23 percent for Tomic, 18 percent for Allende, and 15 percent undecided. (Joan Garcés [Santiago], June 1972).

44. Salvador Allende (Santiago), July 1972; Joan Garcés (Santiago), June 1972; Victor Vió (Santiago), May 1972.

CHAPTER 4

1. Alma Gallegos (Santiago), August 1972.

2. Bernardo Lara (Talca), April 1972. My translation in brackets.

3. Jaime Riscal (Santiago), August 1972.

4. Enrique Ortuzar, quoted in *Los Angeles Times*, 7 September, 1970.

5. CIA Director Richard Helms's notes on meeting of 15 September 1970, quoted in U.S. Senate, Select Committee to Study Governmental Operations with Respect to Intelligence Activities, Interim Report. *Alleged Assassination Plots Involving Foreign Leaders* (Washington, D.C., 1975), p. 227.

6. U.S. Senate, Select Committee on Intelligence, Staff Report. *Covert Action in Chile, 1963–1973* (Washington, D.C., 1975), pp. 23–26. See also, Seymour M. Hersh, *The Price of Power: Kissinger in the Nixon White House* (New York, 1983), pp. 271–79. President Eduardo Frei was approached and told that if he secured his party's support for this strategy, Alessandri would then resign and back Frei in a special election. He was assured that funds were available with which to bribe reluctant members of Congress.

7. U.S. Senate, Select Committee on Intelligence, *Covert Action*, pp. 25–26; *Assassination Plots*, pp. 227–28, 233–46; Hersh, *Price of Power*, pp. 276–93.

8. Helms, Notes on Meeting of 15 September, 1970, quoted in U.S. Senate, Select Committee on Intelligence, *Assassination Plots*, pp. 227, 234; *Covert Action*, p. 25.

9. Ambassador Edward Korry, quoted in H. Hendrix and R. Berrellez to E. J. Gerrity, vice–president, International Telephone and Telegraph Corporation, Santiago (17 September 1970); reprinted in bilingual facsimile edition entitled *Documentos secretos de la ITT* (Santiago, 1972), p. 12. One of several compromising internal ITT documents released by columnist Jack Anderson, it reveals that corporation's active efforts to involve the United States government and other American corporations in plots to prevent Allende from becoming president. Part of this document was also quoted in the *Washington Post* (27 March 1972).

10. Thomas Karamessines, deputy director for plans, Central Intelligence Agency, "Memorandum for the Record/Minutes of the Meeting of the 40 Committee" (14 October 1970), quoted in U.S. Senate, Select Committee on Intelligence, *Assassination Plots*, p. 250.

11. U.S., Central Intelligence Agency, Chile Station to Headquarters, Cable 495, Santiago (9 October 1970), quoted in *Assassination Plots*, p. 246.

12. *Washington Post* (4 November 1970).

13. Ignacio Palma (Santiago), July 1972. Palma, a Christian Democrat, succeeded Allende as president of the Senate.

14. Volodia Teitelboim (Santiago), May 1972.

CHAPTER 5

1. Hernán López (Santiago), January 1974.

2. Juan Corvo (Santiago), August 1972.

3. Eugenio Stark (Santiago), June 1972.

4. Ibid.

5. Ibid.; Juan Corvo (Santiago), August 1972.

6. María López (Santiago), August 1972. The full impact of the Taylor System did not hit the mill until 1966, when the traditional split shift (four hours on, four off, four on) was replaced by a straight eight-hour shift for the 1600 *obreros* remaining at the factory. When the straight shift was introduced, Amador Yarur refused to allow a lunch break. For the Old-timers in particular, the combination of the Taylor System with the straight shift and no lunch break was "very exhausting" (María López). From a management perspective, however, the introduction of the Taylor System, with its rigid regulation of productivity, made the split shift unnecessary as a means of boosting productivity (Eugenio Negrón [Santiago], September 1972. Negrón was a senior administrative employee).

7. Héctor Mora (Santiago), July 1972.

8. In some ways, Amador Yarur was even more involved with personnel management than his father, for he never permitted Fuenzalida's successor as personnel chief, Eugenio Stark, to be welfare chief as well or to exercise the same authority. In general, Amador Yarur "did not allow intermediate bureaucracies to handle what he could do himself," concluded Dr. Patrick Peppe from his interviews at the Yarur mill (Patrick Peppe, "Notes on a Visit to the Yarur Mill" [8 August 1968]. I am grateful to Dr. Peppe for sharing his research notes with me.)

9. Horacio Cárdenas (Santiago), February 1972.

10. Julio Solar (Santiago), August 1972.

11. Guillermo Jordan (Santiago), September 1972.

12. David Manuel (Santiago), September 1972.

13. Eugenio Stark (Santiago), August 1968. Cited in Peppe, "Notes."

14. Ibid..

15. Héctor Mora (Santiago), August 1972.

16. Ibid.; Armando Carrera (Santiago), June 1972; Jorge Lorca (Santiago), July 1972.

17. Heraldo Romo (Santiago), August 1972.

18. Peppe, "Notes."

19. Eugenio Stark (Santiago), June 1972.

20. Raúl Guerra (Santiago), September 1972.

21. Daniél Juantorena (Santiago), September 1972.

22. Jorge Giusti, "La formación de las poblaciones en Santiago," *Revista Latinoamericana de Ciencias Políticas* (Santiago), 2:2 (1971), 370–85.

23. Froilán Garrido (Santiago), September 1972.

24. Héctor Mora (Santiago), July 1972.

25. Jacobo Valenzuela (Santiago), September 1972.

26. Carlos Macera (Santiago), July 1972.

27. Ricardo Berro (Santiago), August 1972.

28. For an account of the limited impact and changing role of the Church within the working class, see Brian H. Smith, *The Church and Politics in Chile* (Princeton, N.J., 1982), pp. 98–100, 106–61.

29. Juan Lazo (Santiago), September 1972.

30. The transformation of the Communist party into a mass party after its legalization in 1958 spurred the growth of the Communist Youth in the years that followed (Volodia Teitelboim [Santiago], May 1972.) The Socialist Youth played a similar role in areas of Socialist strength, but was smaller in size, more middle class in membership, and weaker within the Chilean working class as a whole. Still, the Juventud Socialista was where such future Yarur leaders as Emilio Hernández were formed politically. (Emilio Hernández [Santiago], June 1972).

31. Raúl Oliva (Santiago), June 1972.

32. This is an upper bound. Even at their Allende era height, their memberships were probably closer to 100,000. Reliable statistics are lacking, and party claims are probably exaggerated.

33. Juan Lazo (Santiago), September 1972; Jorge Lorca (Santiago), July 1972.

34. Manuel Fernández (Santiago), August 1972.

35. Julio Menéndez (Santiago), August 1972.

36. For the postwar changes in the countryside, see Cristóbal Kay, *El sistema señorial europeo y la hacienda latinoamericana* (Mexico City, 1980), pp. 77–93 and, "Comparative Development of the European Manorial System and the Latin American Hacienda System" (Ph.D. diss., University of Sussex, Eng., 1971), pp. 107–60; Almino Affonso et al., *Movimiento campesino chileno*, 2 vols. (Santiago, 1970); Brian Loveman, *Struggle in the Countryside*, (Bloomington, Ind., 1976), pp. 180–220.

37. Jorge Lorca (Santiago), July 1972.

38. Ibid. The Taylor System's requirements meant that the rural migrants hired at Yarur had to be at least semieducated. The quality and character of this education varied, but as the experience of Jorge Lorca demonstrated, it often afforded these young migrants a different perspective from their parents although the classroom was not always the decisive experience.

39. Ibid.

40. Joaquín Duque and Ernesto Pastrana, "La movilización de los sectores populares en Chile, 1954–1972," *Revista Latinoamericana de Ciencias Sociales* (Santiago), 4 (December 1972), 262–63.

41. Héctor Mora (Santiago), July 1972.

42. Antonio Barragán (Santiago), September 1972.

43. Emilio Hernández (Santiago), June 1972.

44. Héctor Mora (Santiago), July 1972.

45. Raúl Guerra (Santiago), August 1972.

46. Armando Carrera (Santiago), June 1972.

47. Raúl Guerra (Santiago), August 1972.

48. Jorge Lorca (Santiago), July 1972.

49. Raúl Oliva (Santiago), June 1972.

50. Manuel Fernández (Santiago), September 1972.

51. Emilio Hernández (Santiago), August 1972.

52. Armando Carrera (Santiago), June 1972.

CHAPTER 6

1. The American Institute for Free Labor Development (AIFLD) is a joint venture of the AFL-CIO and a corporate business association, the Council of the Americas, with rumored CIA participation as well. (See Fred Hirsch, *An Analysis of Our AFL-CIO Role in Latin America* [San Jose, Calif., 1974].) The purpose of its Chilean operation was to identify promising labor leaders and train them in "apolitical," anti-Communist unionism on the AFL-CIO model, with the goal of undermining leftist control of the Chilean labor movement. Ironically, Duarte was taught at AIFLD's Santiago school by Reinaldo Jara, the former Communist leader of the 1947 insurgent movement at Yarur, now a virulent anti-Communist with close ties to the American embassy (Reinaldo Jara [Santiago], December 1973).

2. Peppe, "Notes"; Sindicato Industrial Yarur S. A., *Actas*, (1964–1970), *passim*.

3. Emilio Hernández (Santiago), August 1972.

4. Ibid.

5. Raúl Oliva (Santiago), June 1972.

6. Emilio Hernández (Santiago), August 1972.

7. Raúl Oliva (Santiago), June 1972.

8. Liliana Díaz (Santiago), November 1973. Díaz was a CUT and Socialist Party labor adviser assigned to the Yarur mill.

9. Raúl Oliva (Santiago), June 1972.

10. Héctor Mora (Santiago), August 1972; Eugenio Stark (Santiago), June 1972.

11. Raúl Oliva (Santiago), June 1972.

12. Liliana Díaz (Santiago), November 1973.

13. Ibid. Oliva was married to a woman who was a university student and a political activist. Díaz, who came to know him well, stressed the tensions within him between what she termed the "proletarian" and the "petit bourgeois."

14. Raúl Oliva (Santiago), June 1972.

15. Héctor Mora (Santiago), August 1972.

16. Raúl Oliva (Santiago), June 1972.

17. Ibid.

18. Ibid.

19. Ibid. Oliva also stressed the fact that "the industries had taken the decision to recruit exclusively young people up to thirty years old . . . so the man who was older than thirty had to keep his job, no matter what the cost."

20. Ibid.

21. Héctor Mora (Santiago), August 1972.

22. Ibid.

23. Ibid.

24. Jorge Lorca (Santiago), July 1972. In part, the leading role of the night shift at Yarur reflected its greater *compañerismo* (social solidarity) "due to the fact that it is a permanent [nonrotating] shift" and "the *compañeros* of the night shift talk to each other more" because "the *compañero* leaves work . . . and finds himself in daylight . . . the morning elates him so . . . he forms his little group and they converse." In part, "the night shift always heads anything that means a struggle," Lorca explained, because of the absence of Yarur paternalism after midnight. In addition, many night shift workers were daytime students at the State Technical University (U.T.E.), a leftist stronghold, which became both a meeting place and recruiting ground for the clandestine Yarur movement.

25. Raúl Oliva (Santiago), June 1972; Tito Palestro (Santiago), July 1972.

26. Raúl Oliva (Santiago), June 1972.
27. Ibid.
28. Héctor Mora (Santiago), August 1972.
29. *La Firme* (Santiago), June-August 1970.
30. Jorge Yarur (Santiago), August 1972; Eugenio Stark (Santiago), September 1972.
31. Armando Carrera (Santiago), June 1972.
32. Ibid.
33. Raúl Oliva (Santiago), June 1972.
34. Héctor Mora (Santiago), July 1972.
35. Ibid.
36. María López (Santiago), August 1972.
37. Héctor Mora (Santiago), July 1972.
38. Ibid.
39. Raúl Guerra (Santiago), August 1972. Although this group included Jorge Lorca, the future Communist union president, it was led by Guerra and other MIR sympathizers.
40. Héctor Mora (Santiago), July 1972.
41. Ibid.
42. Ibid.; Raúl Oliva (Santiago), June 1972.
43. Héctor Mora (Santiago), July 1972.
44. Ibid.
45. Raúl Oliva (Santiago), June 1972.
46. Armando Carrera (Santiago), June 1972.
47. María López (Santiago), August 1972.
48. Alicia Navarrete (Santiago), August 1972.
49. Raúl Oliva (Santiago), June 1972.
50. Emilio Hernández (Santiago), August 1972.
51. Ibid.; Armando Carrera (Santiago), June 1972; Jorge Lorca (Santiago), July 1972.
52. Emilio Hernández (Santiago), August 1972.
53. Ibid.
54. Ibid.
55. *La Firme de Yarur* [Santiago], September-November 1970.
56. Emilio Hernández (Santiago), August 1972.
57. I am indebted here to Robert Darnton, *The Literary Underground of the Old Regime* (Cambridge, Mass., 1982). Like the Grub Street *philosophes* of the eighteenth century, whose political pornography helped prepare the ground for the French Revolution, the worker journalists of Yarur undermined their Old Regime with a combination of muckraking and derision that ensured *La Firme* a wide and eager audience for its radical political message.
58. Emilio Hernández (Santiago), August 1972.
59. Raúl Oliva (Santiago), June 1972.
60. Héctor Mora (Santiago), July 1972.
61. Eugenio Stark (Santiago), September 1972.
62. Raúl Oliva (Santiago), June 1972.
63. Armando Carrera (Santiago), June 1972.

CHAPTER 7

1. Héctor Mora (Santiago), August 1972.
2. Raúl Guerra (Santiago), August 1972.

3. Héctor Mora (Santiago), July 1972.

4. Emilio Hernández (Santiago), August 1972.

5. Raúl Oliva (Santiago), June 1972.

6. Ricardo Catalan (Santiago), September 1972.

7. Sindicato Industrial S. A. Yarur, *Actas* (15 November 1970).

8. Ricardo Catalan (Santiago), September 1972.

9. Emilio Hernández (Santiago), August 1972.

10. Ibid.

11. Ricardo Catalan (Santiago), September 1972.

12. Raúl Oliva (Santiago), June 1972. The movement now incorporated even those work sections—such as spinning—where they had had difficulty identifying trustworthy activists. The problem with the militant workers in the large spinning section, in the view of the Union Liberation leaders, was that they were too individualistic to subordinate themselves to a disciplined movement and "proposed anarchist positions" (Emilio Hernández [Santiago], August 1972).

13. Emilio Hernández (Santiago), August 1972.

14. Ibid.

15. Armando Carrera (Santiago), June 1972. Chilean labor law allotted ten votes after only three years at an enterprise.

16. Jorge Lorca (Santiago), July 1972.

17. Armando Carrera (Santiago), June 1972.

18. Emilio Hernández (Santiago), August 1972.

19. Ibid.

20. Armando Carrera (Santiago), June 1972.

21. Emilio Hernández (Santiago), August 1972.

22. Héctor Mora (Santiago), July 1972.

23. Emilio Hernández (Santiago), August 1972.

24. Jorge Lorca (Santiago), July 1972. The messenger was the cafeteria manager.

25. Héctor Mora (Santiago), July 1972.

26. Ibid.

27. Jorge Lorca (Santiago), July 1972.

28. Héctor Mora (Santiago), July 1972.

29. Ibid.

30. Mario Leníz (Santiago), September 1972.

31. Raúl Oliva (Santiago), June 1972.

32. Jorge Lorca (Santiago), July 1972.

33. Ibid.

34. Ibid.

35. Ibid.

36. Ibid.

37. Emilio Hernández (Santiago), August 1972.

38. Armando Carrera (Santiago), June 1972.

39. Héctor Mora (Santiago), July 1972.

40. Emilio Hernández (Santiago), August 1972.

41. Armando Carrera (Santiago), June 1972.

42. Emilio Hernández (Santiago), August 1972.

43. Armando Carrera (Santiago), June 1972.

44. Emilio Hernández (Santiago), August 1972.

45. Ibid.

46. Ibid.

47. Ibid.

48. Héctor Mora (Santiago), July 1972.

49. Ibid.

50. Emilio Hernández (Santiago), August 1972.

51. Héctor Mora (Santiago), July 1972.

52. Ibid.

53. Ricardo Catalan (Santiago), September 1972.

54. Héctor Mora (Santiago), July 1972.

55. Emilio Hernández (Santiago), August 1972.

56. Eugenio Stark (Santiago), June 1972.

57. Sindicato Industrial S. A. Yarur, *Actas* (20 December 1970), pp. 316–17.

58. Ibid. (31 December 1970), p. 319.

59. Ibid.; Jorge Lorca (Santiago), July 1972.

60. Arnaldo Pérez (Santiago), August 1972.

61. Sindicato Industrial S. A. Yarur, *Actas* (10 January 1971), p. 325.

62. Jorge Lorca (Santiago), August 1972.

63. Ibid.

64. Ibid.

65. Daniel Gómez (Santiago), September 1972. Gómez was a longtime Yarur loyalist and a member of the revived strong-arm squad.

66. Raúl Oliva (Santiago), June 1972.

67. Mario Leníz (Santiago), September 1972; Eugenio Stark (Santiago), September 1972.

68. Jorge Lorca (Santiago), August 1972.

69. Ibid.

70. Ibid.

71. Ibid.

72. Héctor Mora (Santiago), July 1972.

73. Jorge Lorca (Santiago), August 1972.

74. Arnaldo Pérez (Santiago), August 1972.

75. Jorge Lorca (Santiago), August 1972.

76. Sindicato Industrial S. A. Yarur, *Actas* (December-March 1971), pp. 321–36; Jorge Lorca (Santiago), August 1972; Roberto Campos (Santiago), January 1974.

77. S. A. Yarur, Manufacturas Chilenas de Algodón, "Acta de Avenimiento" (28 December 1970); Chile, Ministerio de Trabajo, Dirección General de Trabajo, Junta de Conciliación Especial para la Industrial Textil, Departamento de Santiago. The rise in the hourly wage was even greater because of the granting of the paid half-hour lunch.

78. Ibid.

79. Sindicato Industrial S. A. Yarur, *Actas* (27 December 1970 and 10 January 1971), pp. 318–19, 323.

80. Eugenio Stark (Santiago), September 1972. The average wage and salary increase in Chile for 1971 was closer to 63 percent although this figure includes the large raises granted later in the year by socialized enterprises. Still, in view of the Allende government's freeze on textile prices, the contract implied a significant redistribution of S. A. Yarur's revenues from its owners to its workers.

81. Jorge Lorca (Santiago), August 1972.

CHAPTER 8

1. Ricardo Catalan (Santiago), September 1972.
2. For the origins of the labor code and intentions of its framers, see James O. Morris, *Elites, Intellectuals and Consensus* (Ithaca, N.Y., 1966), and Louis Wolf Goodman, "Blue Collar Work and Modernization" (Ph.D. diss., Northwestern University, 1970), pp. 7–9. For a more extended discussion of the *empleado-obrero* distinction and its implications, see Alan Angell, *Politics and the Labor Movement in Chile* (London, 1972), pp. 66–68, 148–69. In time, some skilled blue-collar workers joined white-collar workers in the *empleado* category, a reflection of political pressures and worker aspirations.
3. Ricardo Catalan (Santiago), September 1972.
4. Ibid.
5. Victor Valencia (Santiago), August 1972.
6. Pedro García (Santiago), August 1972.
7. Ibid.
8. Jorge Iriarte (Santiago), August 1972.
9. Arnaldo Pérez (Santiago), August 1972; Omar Guzmán (Santiago), August 1972; Juan Carvajal (Santiago), August 1972; Carlos Benavides (Santiago), September 1972.
10. Omar Guzmán (Santiago), August 1972.
11. Ricardo Catalan (Santiago), September 1972.
12. Omar Guzmán (Santiago), August 1972.
13. Ricardo Catalan (Santiago), September 1972.
14. Pedro García (Santiago), August 1972.
15. Jorge Iriarte (Santiago), August 1972.
16. Ricardo Catalan (Santiago), September 1972.
17. Ibid.
18. Ibid.
19. Omar Guzmán (Santiago), August 1972.
20. Eugenio Stark (Santiago), September 1972.
21. Omar Guzmán (Santiago), August 1972.
22. Eugenio Stark (Santiago), September 1972. Stark's ambiguous warning to Guzmán was intended to dissuade the insurgents from proceeding, but at the same time to warn them that their plans had been discovered and that Amador Yarur was preparing countermeasures— although Jorge Yarur would accept their victory if they succeeded in besting his brother. It reflected his own internal conflict between his Christian Democratic beliefs and his role as Amador Yarur's personnel chief.
23. Carlos Benavides (Santiago), September 1972.
24. Omar Guzmán (Santiago), August 1972.
25. Ibid..
26. Eugenio Stark (Santiago), September 1972; Mario Leníz (Santiago), September 1972; Humberto Lares (Santiago), September 1972. By 1970, the Christian Democrats had abandoned Labor Minister William Thayer's strategy of forming a parallel union movement and were trying instead to increase their strength within the CUT. (For an account of the evolution of Christian Democratic labor policy, see Angell, *Politics and the Labor Movement*, pp. 190–209.)
27. Luis Larrañaga (Santiago), September 1972.
28. Omar Guzmán (Santiago), August 1972; Eugenio Stark (Santiago), September 1972; Humberto Lares (Santiago), September 1972. The ANEF (National Association of Govern-

ment Employees) had long been a stronghold of militant *empleados* unionism. Ellis had led Juan Yarur's takeover of the first *obrero* union back in 1940.

29. Omar Guzmán (Santiago), August 1972.

30. Ibid.

31. Carlos Benavides (Santiago), September 1972.

32. Omar Guzmán (Santiago), August 1972. The impact of Allende's election on leftist labor inspectors is clear in this story. It is unlikely that Santana would have taken such a risk otherwise.

33. Ricardo Catalan (Santiago), September 1972.

34. Omar Guzmán (Santiago), August 1972.

35. Eugenio Stark (Santiago), September 1972.

36. *El Siglo*, 25 September 1970, p. 11.

37. Eugenio Stark (Santiago), September 1972.

38. Ibid.

39. Ibid.

40. Ibid.

41. Ibid.

42. Ibid.

43. Ibid.

44. Ricardo Catalan (Santiago), September 1972.

45. Omar Guzmán (Santiago), August 1972.

46. Ricardo Catalan (Santiago), September 1972.

47. Ibid.

48. *Clarín* (Santiago), 25 September 1970, p. 19.

49. Ricardo Catalan (Santiago), September 1972.

50. Ibid.

51. Ibid.

52. Ibid.

53. Ibid.

54. Carlos Benavides (Santiago), September 1972.

55. Ibid.

56. Ricardo Catalan (Santiago), September 1972.

57. Ibid.

58. Jorge Iriarte (Santiago), August 1972.

59. Ricardo Catalan (Santiago), September 1972.

60. Eugenio Stark (Santiago), September 1972; Mario Leníz (Santiago), September 1972.

CHAPTER 9

1. Sindicato Industrial S. A. Yarur, *Libro de Actas* (20 December 1970), p. 316.

2. Emilio Hernández (Santiago), August 1972.

3. Sindicato Industrial S. A., Yarur, *Actas* (27 January 1971), p. 328.

4. Eugenio Negrón (Santiago), September 1972.

5. Jorge Lorca (Santiago), August 1972.

6. Ibid.

7. Ibid.

8. Ibid.

CHAPTER 10

1. Oscar Guillermo Garretón (Santiago), August 1972.
2. Roberto Soto (Santiago), August 1972.
3. Salvador Allende (Santiago), July 1972.
4. Peter Winn, "Loosing the Chains: Labor and the Chilean Revolutionary Process, 1970–73," *Latin American Perspectives*, 3:1 (Winter 1976), p. 75.
5. Although much commented on and studied, the *poblador* revolution has yet to receive a definitive treatment. A useful overview is provided in Monica Threlfall, "Shantytown Dwellers and People's Power," in *Allende's Chile*, ed. Philip O'Brien (New York, 1976), pp. 167–91. One of the most insightful studies is Manuel Castells, "Movimiento de pobladores y lucha de clases," *Revista Latinoamericana de Estudios Urbano Regionales {hereafter EURE}* [Santiago], 3:7 (April 1973), 9–37. The most systematic study is reported on in Equipo de Estudios Poblacionales del CIDU, "Reivindicación urbana y lucha política: Los campamentos de pobladores en Santiago de Chile," *EURE*, 2:6 (November 1972), 55–82. The number of urban *tomas* in Chile increased almost tenfold during 1970, a rate of land seizures that almost doubled again during the first half of 1971 (Castells, "Movimiento de pobladores," p. 26, Table 5).
6. For an evocative account of this rural revolution from below in Cautín Province, where it began, see Kyle Steenland, *Agrarian Reform Under Allende: Peasant Revolt in the South* (Albuquerque, N.M., 1977). The number of rural land seizures increased threefold during 1970 and then tripled again in 1971 to 1278 *tomas* (Juan Carlos Marín, "Las Tomas [1970–1972]," *Marxismo y revolución*, no. 1 [July-September 1973], 59, Table 1). A provincial breakdown of land seizures for 1967–71 can be found in Manuel Barrera, *Chile 1970–1972: La conflictiva experiencia de los cambios estructurales* (Caracas, 1973, p. 274, Table 11). These *tomas* reflected peasant desires to accelerate or expand the Allende government's expropriations, to make sure that they would be among the beneficiaries, and to ensure that the old owner did not decapitalize the farms before they were expropriated.
7. For an account of the modification of the government's income guidelines under pressure from below, see Instituto de Economía, University of Chile, *La economía chilena en 1971* (Santiago, 1972), pp. 114–30. Its importance is stressed in Sergio Bitar, *Transición, socialismo y democracia*, (Mexico City, 1979), pp. 102–3. The impact of the Allende government on the tripartite panels is underscored in Barbara Stallings, *Class Conflict and Economic Development*, (Stanford, Calif., 1978), pp. 128–30, and an illuminating case study is provided in Lance Compa, "Labor Law and the Legal Way: Collective Bargaining in the Chilean Textile Industry Under the *Unidad Popular*" (Working Paper no. 23, Program in Law and Modernization, Yale Law School, May 1973).
8. Oscar Guillermo Garretón (Santiago), August 1972. Garretón was deputy minister of economy at the time.
9. Volodia Teitelboim (Santiago), April 1972; Salvador Allende (Santiago), July 1972; Rafael Gumucio (Santiago), June 1972; Adonis Sepúlveda (Santiago), June 1972. Gumucio, former head of the Christian Democratic Party, was a MAPU senator in April 1971. Sepúlveda was a senator and leader of the Socialist party; Teitelboím, a Communist senator and leading politburo member.
10. Victor Vió (Santiago), May 1972; Volodia Teitelboím (Santiago), April 1972; Adonis Sepúlveda (Santiago), June 1972.
11. Volodia Teitelboím (Santiago), April 1972.

12. Victor Vió (Santiago), May 1972.

13. Ibid.

14. Ibid.; Volodia Teitelboím (Santiago), April 1972.

15. Raúl Guerra (Santiago), September 1972. Guerra was on the national committee of the FTR.

16. Adonis Sepúlveda (Santiago), June 1972; Jorge Varas (Santiago), January 1974.

17. Victor Vió (Santiago), May 1972.

18. Oscar Guillermo Garretón (Santiago), August 1972.

19. Ibid.

20. Ibid.; Sergio Bitar (Cambridge, Mass.), August 1975. Bitar became minister of mines and a leading Allende economic adviser. As government expenditures were expanding more rapidly than anticipated and the opposition majority in Congress was refusing to vote new revenues, the rapid acquisition of these profitable capitalist enterprises was also a way to help balance the budget.

21. Chile, Ministerio de Economía, Comisión Investigadora Especializada [hereafter, C.I.E.], "Informe S. A. Yarur."

22. Oscar Guillermo Garretón (Santiago), August 1972; Sergio Bitar (Cambridge, Mass.), August 1975.

23. Oscar Guillermo Garretón (Santiago), August 1972

24. Antonio Lora (Santiago), August 1972.

25. Ricardo Catalan (Santiago), September 1972.

26. Manuel Fernández (Santiago), August 1972.

27. Jorge Lorca (Santiago), August 1972.

CHAPTER 11

1. Chile, Ministerio de Economía, Comisión Investigadora Especializada [hereafter C.I.E.], "Informe S. A. Yarur"; Guillermo Garreton (Santiago), August 1972; Ricardo Catalan (Santiago), September 1972; Hernan Labarca (Santiago), August 1972. Labarca was the fiscal (chief legal officer) of DIRINCO, the Economy Ministry agency charged with supervising the production and pricing of basic necessities.

2. C.I.E., "Informe S. A. Yarur"; Hernán Labarca (Santiago), August 1972; Héctor Espinoza (Santiago), July 1972. Espinoza was the government interventor at the Banco de Crédito, which was taken over in March 1971.

3. Oscar Guillermo Garretón (Santiago), August 1972; Hernán Labarca (Santiago), July 1972.

4. Oscar Guillermo Garretón (Santiago), August 1972.

5. Ibid.

6. Ibid. Garretón, a specialist in economic concentration and interest groups, was well aware of the economic importance of the Yarurs. See, Oscar Guillermo Garretón and Jaime Cisternas, "Algunas caracteristicas del proceso de toma de decisiones en la gran empresa la dinamica de la concentración" (mimeographed; Santiago: Servicio de Cooperación Téchnica, 1970).

7. Oscar Guillermo Garretón (Santiago), August 1972. Jorge Yarur had led a walkout of Arab-Chilean entrepreneurs from the SOFOFA in 1963 precisely over their exclusion from power by the traditional Creole elites (see, Marcelo Cavarozzi, "The Government and the Industrial Bourgeoisie in Chile, 1938–1964," [Ph.D. diss., University of California, Berkeley, 1976], pp. 393–94).

8. In 1971, the largest shareholder in S. A. Yarur was the Chase Manhattan Trust Corporation, [Nominee] Ltd. (Bahamas), which the Left often mistakenly interpreted as implying Rockefeller ownership (see, for example, *El Siglo*, [Santiago], 29 April 1971, p. 1). In fact, it represented the end result of twenty-five years of complicated maneuvers, by which Yarur holdings in the family firm were transferred from one *palo blanco* (front) to another. (The process was traced in an undated (1965?) internal memorandum in the S. A. Yarur file in the Superintendencia de Compañías de Seguros, Sociedades Anónimas and Bolsas de Comercio, Departmento de Sociedades Anónimas, Rol 882, Carpeta 3.) The purpose of this "laundering" of their share holdings was to evade taxes and restrictions on the export of Chilean capital (Andrés Sanfuentes, "La influencía de los árabes en el desarollo económics de Chile," (Memoria de Licenciatura, University of Chile, 1964), pp. 141–44). Significantly, the list of major shareholders in S. A. Yarur included a Panamanian "legal fiction," and another Bahamas dummy corporation. (S. A. Yarur, "Lista de accionistas" (28 August 1972); *SAYMCHA/STGO*).

9. See, *El Siglo* [Santiago], 29 September 1970, p. 1; 30 September 1970, pp. 1 and 4; 1 October 1970, p. 5. One Yarur grandson was reported to have fled the country to avoid prosecution on "terrorism" charges.

10. Ricardo Catalan (Santiago), September 1972.

11. The Radical party, the other major coalition partner, which had considerable strength in some white-collar sectors, had little support at the Yarur mill.

12. Victor Vió (Santiago), May 1972; Marcelo Bunuel (Santiago), August 1972. Bunuel, a former labor leader, was the local Communist party political secretary for the Yarur district.

13. Victor Vió (Santiago), May 1972; Luis Larrañaga (Santiago), September 1972.

14. Jaime Gazmuri (Santiago), April 1972; Oscar Guillermo Garretón (Santiago), August 1972; Ricardo Catalan (Santiago), September 1972; Jorge Lorca (Santiago), August 1972. Gazmuri was secretary-general of the MAPU when interviewed.

15. Raúl Oliva (Santiago), June 1972; Tito Palestro (Santiago), July 1972.

16. Raúl Oliva (Santiago), June 1972.

CHAPTER 12

1. Luis Larrañaga (Santiago), September 1972.
2. Ibid..
3. Jorge Lorca (Santiago), August 1972.
4. Ibid.
5. Ibid.
6. Eugenio Stark (Santiago), September 1972.
7. Antonio Lara (Santiago), August 1972.
8. Alfredo Cantor (Santiago), July 1972. Cantor was a member of the Yarur working group within the ministry.
9. Raúl Oliva (Santiago), June 1972.
10. Jorge Lorca (Santiago), August 1972.
11. Oscar Guillermo Garretón (Santiago), August 1972.
12. Armando Carrera (Santiago), June 1972.
13. Antonio Lara (Santiago), August 1972.
14. Jorge Lorca (Santiago), August 1972.
15. Ibid.
16. Armando Carrera (Santiago), June 1972.

17. Ibid.

18. Rolando Cruz (Santiago), June 1972.

19. Jorge Lorca (Santiago), August 1972.

20. Aníbal Caro (Santiago), August 1972.

21. Luis Larrañaga (Santiago), September 1972.

22. Armando Carrera (Santiago), June 1972.

23. Ibid.

24. Jorge Lorca (Santiago), August 1972.

25. Sindicato Industrial S. A. Yarur, *Libro de Actas* (25 April 1971), pp. 342–43.

26. Sindicato Industrial S. A. Yarur and Sindicato Professional S. A. Yarur to Amador Yarur, Santiago (21 April 1971); in Sindicato Industrial S.A. Yarur, *Actas*, pp. 343–44.

27. Ricardo Catalan (Santiago), September 1972.

28. Ibid.

29. Antonio Lara (Santiago), August 1972.

30. Eugenio Negrón (Santiago), September 1972.

31. Jorge Yarur (Santiago), August 1972; Salvador Allende (Santiago), July 1972; Jorge Varas (Santiago), January 1974; Eugenio Stark (Santiago), September 1972.

32. Luis Larrañaga (Santiago), September 1972.

33. Eugenio Stark (Santiago), September 1972; Jorge Yarur (Santiago), August 1972; Jorge Varas (Santiago), January 1974; Oscar Guillermo Garretón (Santiago), August 1972.

34. Jorge Lorca (Santiago), August 1972.

35. Ibid.

36. Raúl Oliva (Santiago), June 1972.

37. Ibid.

38. Ibid.

39. Jorge Lorca (Santiago), August 1972; Oscár Ibáñez (Santiago), May 1972; Victor Vió (Santiago), May 1972.

40. Raúl Oliva (Santiago), June 1972.

41. Antonio Lara (Santiago), August 1972.

42. Ibid.

43. Raúl Oliva (Santiago), June 1972.

44. Ricardo Catalan (Santiago), September 1972.

45. Ibid.

46. Ibid.

47. Raúl Oliva (Santiago), June 1972.

48. Ricardo Catalan (Santiago), September 1972.

49. Oscar Guillermo Garretón (Santiago), August 1972.

50. Ricardo Catalan (Santiago), September 1972.

51. Ibid.

52. Antonio Lara (Santiago), August 1972.

53. Luis Larrañaga (Santiago), September 1972.

54. Raúl Oliva (Santiago), June 1972.

55. *Ibid.*

56. *Ibid.*

57. Rolando Cruz (Santiago), August 1972.

58. Jorge Lorca (Santiago), August 1972.

59. Armando Carrera (Santiago), June 1972.

60. Jorge Lorca (Santiago), August 1972.

61. Ricardo Catalan (Santiago), September 1972.

62. Luis Larrañaga (Santiago), September 1972.

63. Eugenio Negrón (Santiago), September 1972.

64. Jorge Varas (Santiago), January 1974.

65. Armando Carrera (Santiago), June 1972.

66. Victor Vió (Santiago), May 1972.

67. Ibid.

CHAPTER 13

1. Jorge Varas (Santiago), January 1974.

2. Armando Carrera (Santiago), June 1972.

3. Jorge Varas (Santiago), January 1974. At previous meetings, union attendance had averaged about 900 members, so the presence of an estimated 1500 workers reflected both activist efforts and rank-and-file awareness of the meeting's significance. (Sindicato Industrial S. A. Yarur, *Libro de Actas* (January–April 1971).

4. Sindicato Industrial S. A. Yarur, *Actas* (25 April 1971), pp. 342–43.

5. Rolando Cruz (Santiago), June 1972.

6. Sindicato Industrial S. A. Yarur, *Actas* (25 April 1971), p. 343.

7. Armando Carrera (Santiago), June 1972.

8. Emilio Hernández (Santiago), August 1972.

9. Silvio Castillo (Santiago), August 1972.

10. Jorge Varas (Santiago), January 1974.

11. Ibid.

12. Ibid.

13. The strike, however, would still be "illegal" under the Chilean Labor Code, for the union had not gone through the bureaucratic steps and received government permission to hold a strike vote. What underscored that this was a revolutionary situation was that no one, not even Varas, suggested that the workers channel their grievances into that due process.

14. Armando Carrera (Santiago), June 1972.

15. Sindicato Industrial Yarur S. A., *Actas* (25 April 1971), pp. 344–45.

16. Jorge Varas (Santiago), January 1974.

17. Emilio Hernández (Santiago), August 1972; Jorge Lorca (Santiago), August 1972; Héctor Mora (Santiago), July 1972; Armando Carrera (Santiago), June 1972.

18. Raúl Oliva (Santiago), June 1972.

19. Ibid.

20. Blanca Bascuñan (Santiago), August 1972.

21. Ricardo Catalan (Santiago), September 1972.

22. Omar Guzmán (Santiago), August 1972.

23. Jacobo Valenzuela (Santiago), September 1972.

24. Luz Castro (Santiago), August 1972.

25. Luis Bujones (Santiago), August 1972.

26. Laura Coruña (Santiago), August 1972.

27. Raúl Oliva (Santiago), June 1972.

28. Jorge Lorca (Santiago), August 1972.

29. Armando Carrera (Santiago), June 1972.

30. Omar Guzmán (Santiago), August 1972.

31. Ricardo Catalan (Santiago), September 1972.

32. Omar Guzmán (Santiago), August 1972.

33. Luis Larrañaga (Santiago), September 1972.

34. Ricardo Catalan (Santiago), September 1972. Although leftist candidates had recently won symbolic popularity tests in balloting for the officers of the *empleados'* athletics club, Catalan estimated leftist supporters as only two hundred of the enterprise's five hundred employees.

35. Jorge Varas (Santiago), January 1974.

36. Marta Yáñez (Santiago), June 1972.

37. Ricardo Catalan (Santiago), September 1972.

38. Rolando Cruz (Santiago), June 1972.

39. Armando Carrera (Santiago), June 1972.

40. Ricardo Catalan (Santiago), September 1972. It was, however, still an "illegal" strike under Chile's Labor Code, leaving the workers legally vulnerable to dismissal and an executive order to return to work, as had happened in 1962.

41. Jorge Varas (Santiago), January 1974.

42. Ricardo Catalan (Santiago), September 1972; Jorge Varas (Santiago), January 1974.

43. Carlos Benavides (Santiago), September 1972.

44. Raúl Oliva (Santiago), June 1972.

45. Roberto Mayo (Santiago), September 1972.

46. María Frías (Santiago), August 1972.

47. Blanca Bascuñan (Santiago), August 1972.

48. Laura Coruña (Santiago), September 1972.

49. Manuel Vega (Santiago), August 1972.

50. Laura Coruña (Santiago), September 1972.

CHAPTER 14

1. Jorge Varas (Santiago), January 1974. Carlos Altamirano was the secretary-general of the Socialist party and leader of its left wing. Luis Corvalán was the secretary-general of the Communist party.

2. Ibid.

3. Ibid.

4. Ibid.

5. Ibid.; Salvador Allende (Santiago), July 1972.

6. Jorge Varas (Santiago), January 1972.

7. Ibid.

8. Armando Carrera (Santiago), June 1972.

9. Rolando Cruz (Santiago), June 1972.

10. Armando Carrera (Santiago), June 1972.

11. Raúl Oliva (Santiago), June 1972.

12. Jorge Varas (Santiago), January 1974.

13. Ibid.

14. Antonio Lara (Santiago), August 1972.

15. Jorge Varas (Santiago), January 1974.

16. Salvador Allende (Santiago), July 1972.

17. Jorge Lorca (Santiago), August 1972.

18. Jorge Varas (Santiago), January 1974.

19. Ibid.

20. Ibid.; Jorge Lorca (Santiago), August 1972.
21. Raúl Oliva (Santiago), June 1972.
22. Jorge Varas (Santiago), January 1974.
23. Jorge Lorca (Santiago), August 1972.
24. Antonio Lara (Santiago), August 1972.
25. Jorge Lorca (Santiago), August 1972.
26. Ricardo Catalan (Santiago), September 1972.
27. Ibid.
28. Luis Larrañaga (Santiago), September 1972; Jorge Lorca (Santiago), August 1972.
29. Salvador Allende (Santiago), July 1972.
30. Raúl Oliva (Santiago), June 1972.
31. Omar Guzmán (Santiago), August 1972.
32. Salvador Allende (Santiago), July 1972.
33. Jorge Lorca (Santiago), August 1972.
34. Omar Guzmán (Santiago), August 1972.
35. Ibid.
36. Ibid.
37. Ibid.
38. Ibid.
39. Ibid.
40. Rafael Osorno (Santiago), August 1972.
41. Ricardo Catalan (Santiago), September 1972.
42. Ibid.
43. Ibid.
44. Ibid; Jorge Lorca (Santiago), August 1972.
45. Ricardo Catalan (Santiago), September 1972.
46. Ibid.; Oscar Guillermo Garretón (Santiago), August 1972.
47. Jorge Lorca (Santiago), August 1972.
48. Omar Guzmán (Santiago), August 1972.
49. Ricardo Catalan (Santiago), September 1972.
50. Jorge Lorca (Santiago), August 1972.
51. Ricardo Catalan (Santiago), September 1972.
52. Ibid.
53. Ibid.
54. Omar Guzmán (Santiago), August 1972.
55. Ricardo Catalan (Santiago), September 1972.
56. Ibid.
57. Omar Guzmán (Santiago), August 1972.
58. Jorge Lorca (Santiago), August 1972.
59. Ibid.
60. Omar Guzmán (Santiago), August 1972.
61. Ricardo Catalan (Santiago), September 1972; Jorge Lorca (Santiago), August 1972.
62. Jorge Lorca (Santiago), August 1972.
63. Ibid.
64. Ricardo Catalan (Santiago), September 1972.
65. Jorge Lorca (Santiago), August 1972.
66. Ibid.
67. Ricardo Catalan (Santiago), August 1972.

CHAPTER 15

1. Alberto Soto (Santiago), April 1972.
2. Ricardo Catalan (Santiago), September 1972.
3. Jorge Lorca (Santiago), August 1972.
4. Ricardo Catalan (Santiago), September 1972.
5. Omar Guzmán (Santiago), August 1972.
6. Quoted in *Punto Final*, [Santiago], 11 May 1971, p. 5.
7. Ibid.
8. Jorge Lorca (Santiago), August 1972.
9. Ibid.
10. Ibid.
11. Armando Carrera (Santiago), June 1972.
12. Ana Montero (Santiago), April 1972.
13. Carlos Benavides (Santiago), September 1972.
14. Armando Carrera (Santiago), June 1972; Jorge Lorca (Santiago), August 1972; *Punto Final*, 11 May 1971, p. 5.
15. Jorge Lorca (Santiago), August 1972.
16. Omar Guzmán (Santiago), August 1972.
17. Jorge Lorca (Santiago), August 1972.
18. Jorge Varas (Santiago), January 1974.
19. Oscar Guillermo Garretón (Santiago), August 1972.
20. Omar Guzmán (Santiago), August 1972.
21. Jorge Varas (Santiago), January 1972.
22. Oscar Guillermo Garretón (Santiago), August 1972.
23. Roberto Valderrama (Santiago), April 1972.
24. Rolando Cruz (Santiago), April 1972.
25. Omar Guzmán (Santiago), August 1972.
26. Jorge Lorca (Santiago), August 1972.
27. Carlos Benavides (Santiago), September 1972.
28. Jorge Lorca (Santiago), August 1972.
29. Ibid.
30. Marisol Paz (Santiago), August 1972.
31. Daniel Gómez (Santiago), September 1972.
32. Luis Bono (Santiago), July 1972.
33. José Lagos (Santiago), April 1972.
34. Luis Bono (Santiago), July 1972.
35. Ibid.; Juan Corvo (Santiago), August 1972; Eugenio Stark (Santiago), September 1972.
36. Omar Guzmán (Santiago), August 1972.
37. Ricardo Lobo (Santiago), August 1972.

CHAPTER 16

1. This discussion of Ex-Yarur between May 1971 and October 1972, a condensation of a larger manuscript, is based on my own interviews and observations, supplemented by published and unpublished reports, statistics, memoranda, and minutes of Ex-Yarur, except where otherwise noted.

2. Emilio Hernández (Santiago), August 1972. Hernández, a hero of the movement against the Yarurs, was elected to the Council of Administration after the industry was socialized.

3. For the background and genesis of the CUT-government "Basic Norms of Participation," see Juan G. Espinosa and Andrew S. Zimbalist, *Economic Democracy: Worker's Participation in Chilean Industry, 1970–1973* (New York, 1978), pp. 29–53; and Guillermo Campero, "Gestión de la empresa y participación de los trabajadores," *Nueva Economía* [Santiago], no. 2 (January–April 1972), 8–10. This same issue also reprints (pp. 137–55) the "Normas basicas de participación de los trabajadores en la dirección de las empresas de las areas social y mixta," an English translation of which can be found in Michael Raptis, *Revolution and Counter-Revolution in Chile: A Dossier on Workers' Participation in the Revolutionary Process* (London, 1974). For an account of Ex-Yarur's adaptation of the Basic Norms, see Peter Winn, "Workers into Managers: Worker Participation in the Chilean Textile Industry," in *Popular Participation in Social Change*, ed. Jorge Dandler, Nicholas Hopkins, and June Nash (The Hague, 1976), pp. 582–86. For an exhaustive study of the evolution of workers' participation in Chile, see James W. Wilson, "Freedom and Control: Workers' Participation in Management in Chile, 1967–1975," 3 vols. (Ph.D. diss., Cornell University, 1979).

4. For a more extended discussion, see Winn, "Workers into Managers," pp. 586–91.

5. Marcelo Bunuel (Santiago), August 1972; Humberto Albano (Santiago), August 1972.

6. Emilio Hernández (Santiago), August 1972.

7. Francisco Catalan (Santiago), September 1972.

8. Andrés Van Lancker (Santiago), September 1972. A shrewd and committed observer of worker participation, Van Lancker, by then head of the state textile sector, was highly critical of its implementation in other enterprises, stressing that at Ex-Yarur, by contrast, "the process of participation was very solid."

9. Ex-Yarur,Departamento de Terminación de Géneros, Sección Acabados, "Producción de Géneros, 1952–1972" (unpublished statistics). The declining production curve reflected metal fatigue in the mill's antiquated machinery, some dating from the factory's founding. 98 percent of the looms were from twenty-four to thirty-six years old despite a normal life span of twenty years. (Chile Ministerío de Economía, Comisión Investigadora Especializada [hereafter C.I.E.], "Informe Yarur S. A.," p. 2; Carlos Benavides [Santiago], September 1972).

10. Patricio Taulis (Santiago), August 1972; Héctor Olivares (Santiago), September 1972. Taulis was the financial manager; Olivares, an administrative employee. In mid–1972, the biggest worker complaint was the need to utilize inferior Brazilian cotton, which led to machine stoppages, imperfect yarns, and flawed fabrics (Juan Corvo [Santiago], August 1972).

11. Luis Bono (Santiago), July 1972. Bono was head of the Maintenance Division and the originator of the idea, which was so successful that by September 1972, Ex-Yarur was being projected as the model for a national spare parts industry. (Henry Bahna, [Santiago], September 1972.) Bahna was a senior official at the CORFO's Textile Committee, which was responsible for developing the plan.

12. See, for example, *La Nación* [Santiago], 22 June 1972, p. 4.

13. Ex-Yarur, División de Mantenimiento, "Sintesis de los principales trabajos realizados por la División de Mantenimiento desde el 28 de abril de 1971 hasta la fecha" (August 1972); Luis Bono (Santiago), July 1972; Patricio Taulis (Santiago), August 1972; Pedro García (Santiago), August 1972; Victor Valencia (Santiago), August 1972; Hernan López (Santiago), January 1974.

14. Ex-Yarur, Consejo de Administración, *Resoluciones* (17–19 December 1971); Raúl

Guerra (Santiago), September 1972. The incentive system was retained, but in a modified form that was both less punitive and more rewarding for the workers (Juan Corvo [Santiago], August 1972).

15. The accelerating inflation of 1972 makes a monthly average a better measure of worker real wages than an annual average. I have calculated them using the 1970–72 Yarur contracts and the official monthly price index (which better reflected a worker's living costs for this period than the University of Chile index). I am indebted to José Serra for suggesting this approach.

16. Blanca Bascuñan (Santiago), August 1972.

17. Sindicato Unico de los Trabajadores de Ex-Yarur, "Acta de Avenimiento General," (21 February 1972).

18. Emilio Hernández (Santiago), August 1972.

19. Francisco Navarro (Santiago), August 1972.

20. Jorge Lorca (Santiago), September 1972.

21. Emilio Hernández (Santiago), August 1972. Significantly, this was a point on which politically opposed workers concurred.

22. Blanca Bascuñan (Santiago), August 1972.

23. Alicia Navarrete (Santiago), August 1972.

24. Manuel Fernández (Santiago), August 1972; Benjamín Arguello (Santiago), August 1972.

25. Héctor Oviedo (Santiago), September 1972.

26. Manuel Fernández (Santiago), August 1972; Jacobo Valenzuela (Santiago), September 1972; Pedro García (Santiago), August 1972; Juan Corvo (Santiago), August 1972. Corvo, a Christian Democrat, was critical of other aspects of Ex-Yarur.

27. Luis Opazo (Santiago), July 1972. Most machine operators who reported dramatic changes in job satisfaction, however, still found the work itself exhausting and monotonous.

28. José Lagos (Santiago), April 1972.

29. For a more extensive discussion of my methodology, typology, and conclusions on the transformation of consciousness, see Peter Winn, "Oral History and the Factory Study: New Approaches to Labor History," *Latin American Research Review*, 14:2 (1979), 134–39, and "Consciousness and the Chilean Working Class: Creation, Diffusion, Transmission, Transformation" (paper presented at the Shelby Collum Davis Center of Historical Studies, Princeton University, December 1974).

30. Vicente Poblete (Santiago), August 1972.

31. Héctor Mora (Santiago), August 1972.

32. Omar Guzmán (Santiago), August 1972; Oscar Guillermo Garretón (Santiago), August 1972.

33. In these mid–1972 elections, Popular Unity votes averaged 1400 of Ex-Yarur's 2400 workers (calculated from official returns announced by Ex-Yarur Sindicato Unico [June 1972] and Consejo de Administración [August 1972]).

34. Mario Leníz (Santiago), September 1972.

35. Although the Communist party's one-to-three ratio of members to votes was exceptionally high, the proportion of cadres to sympathizers in all of Ex-Yarur's leftist parties was high. This ratio of leftist party members to votes defined Ex-Yarur as a highly mobilized and radicalized work force (Enrique Kirberg [New York], April 1980).

36. Ramón Guerra (Santiago), August 1972.

37. Andrés Van Lancker (Santiago), September 1972; Liliana Díaz (Santiago), November 1973; Guillermo Garretón (Santiago), August 1972; Raúl Oliva (Santiago), June 1972.

38. Vicente Poblete (Santiago), August 1972.

39. Liliana Díaz (Santiago), November 1973.

40. Humberto Albano (Santiago), August 1972. Albano, a laboratory technician elected as his section's coordinating committee delegate in the wake of the requisition, rose to become president of the coordinating committee and then worker councillor in 1972.

41. Ibid.

42. Vicente Poblete (Santiago), August 1972.

43. Delegates from other sections sat in on the Acabados section's production meetings to learn from its experience, and Acabados leaders were brought in as participation "consultants" by more troubled work sections (Manuel Vera [Santiago], August 1972).

44. Oscar Guillermo Garretón (Santiago), August 1972; Andrés Van Lancker (Santiago), September 1972; Henry Bahna (Santiago), September 1972. The accords reached at this meeting were summarized in Central Unica de Trabajadores; Primer Encuentro Nacional de Trabajadores Textiles, *Participación es Poder* (Santiago, 1972).

45. Armando Carrera (Santiago), September 1972.

CHAPTER 17

1. Except where noted otherwise, this chapter is based on my own observations and interviews; reading of the daily press (*El Mercurio, La Prensa, La Tercera, La Nación, El Siglo, Puro Chile, Las Noticias de la Ultima Hora* and *Clarín*) and periodicals (*Ercilla, Mensaje, Chile Hoy, Posición, El Rebelde, De Frente, Punto Final, Ahora, Tarea Urgente, La Tribuna, ¿Qué Pasa?, Tizona, Patria y Libertad* and *Sepa*); and on the following books: Sergio Bitar, *Transición, socialismo y democracia* (Mexico City, 1979); Arturo Valenzuela, *The Breakdown of Democratic Regimes: Chile* (Baltimore, Md., 1978); Stefan de Vylder, *Allende's Chile* (New York, 1976); Genaro Arriagada, *De la vía chilena a la vía insurreccional* (Santiago, 1974); Gabriel Smirnow, *The Revolution Disarmed: Chile, 1970–1973* (New York, 1979); David Cusack, *Revolution and Reaction* (Denver, Colo., 1977); Manuel Barrera, *Chile, 1970–1972* (Caracas, 1973); Joan Garcés, *Allende y la experiencia chilena* (Barcelona, 1976); Brian Loveman, *Struggle in the Countryside* (Bloomington, Ind., 1976); Barbara Stallings, *Class Conflict and Economic Development* (Stanford, Calif., 1978); Ian Roxborough, Philip O'Brien, and Jackie Roddick, *Chile: The State and Revolution* (New York, 1977); Paul Sigmund, *The Overthrow of Allende and the Politics of Chile* (Pittsburgh, Pa., 1977); Patricio García, *Los gremios patronales* (Santiago, 1973); Claudio Orrego V., *El paro nacional: via chilena contra el totalitarismo* (Santiago, 1972); James Petras and Morris Morley, *The United States and Chile: Imperialism and the Overthrow of the Allende Government* (New York, 1975); United States Senate, Select Committee on Intelligence, Staff Report, "Covert Action in Chile" (Washington, D.C., 1975); and the following anthologies: Philip O'Brien, ed., *Allende's Chile* (New York, 1976); Kenneth Medhurst, ed., *Allende's Chile* (New York, 1972); Federico Gil, Ricardo Lagos, and Henry Landsberger, eds., *Chile at the Turning Point: Lessons of the Socialist Years, 1970–1973* (Philadelphia, 1979); J. Ann Zammit, ed., *Chilean Road to Socialism* (Austin, Tex., 1973); Paul Sweezy and Harry Magdoff, eds. *Revolution and Counter-Revolution in Chile* (New York, 1974); Salvador Allende, *Allende: su pensamiento político* (Santiago, 1972); Gonzalo Martner, ed., *El pensamiento económico del gobierno de Allende* (Santiago, 1971); Instituto de Economía, Universidad de Chile, *La economía chilena en 1971* (Santiago, 1972), and *La economía chilena en 1972* (Santiago, 1973); and the annual presidential messages to the Congress, which contain a wealth of statistics, as do the publications of ODEPLAN, the state planning agency.

2. Salvador Allende, "Primer Año del Gobierno Popular," Discurso pronunciado en el Estadio Nacional (4 November 1971), in Allende, *Pensamiento político*, pp. 258–59.

3. Ibid., p. 280.

4. Claes Croner and Oriana Lazo, "El area de propriedad social en la industria," in *La economía chilena en 1971*, pp. 424–26; ODEPLAN, *Informe económico 1971* (Santiago, 1972), p. 135. During this revolutionary advance, the Allende government utilized all the legal powers, instruments, and methods at its command. The giant Anaconda and Kennecott copper mines were expropriated by a special constitutional amendment, which the opposition-controlled Congress passed unanimously. Where legislative approval was unlikely, the Allende government used the power of the CORFO to acquire enterprises by purchase and the power of the executive to requisition private firms where the production of essential commodities was threatened and to intervene in the management of companies where production was paralyzed by labor conflicts. As at Yarur, labor conflicts were easy to provoke and difficult to resolve where "the principal concern of the workers was the transfer of their enterprise to the state sector" (Héctor Benavides, quoted in *La Economía chilena en 1971*, p. 442.) By October 1972, another 116 firms had been taken over by decree (Calculated from data in Instituto de Economía, *La economía chilena en 1972*, pp. 116–20, Appendix 1).

5. *La Economía chilena en 1971*, pp. 423–24.

6. Jacques Chonchol (Santiago), May 1972; Chile, Corporación de la Reforma Agraria (CORA), Departamento de Control y Estadística, "Expropriaciones desde 1965 al 31-III–1972" (mimeographed; Santiago, 1972); Peter Winn and Cristóbal Kay, "Agrarian Reform and Rural Revolution in Allende's Chile," *Journal of Latin American Studies*, 6:1 (May 1974), 140–53. Some 1278 rural properties were seized during 1971, almost three times as many as during 1970 and a virtual ninefold increase over 1969 (Barrera, *Chile, 1970–1972*, p. 258, Table 9).

7. Estimates of income redistribution vary considerably, with Economy Minister Pedro Vuskovic claiming a 9 percent shift from capital to labor in 1971 and other calculations shifts of 11 to 15 percent (see Pedro Vuskovic, "The Economic Policy of the Popular Unity Government," in *Chilean Road to Socialism*, ed. Zammit, p. 53; Barbara Stallings and Andrew Zimbalist, "Political Economy of the Unidad Popular," *Latin American Perspectives*, 2:1 (Spring 1975), 72; and Stallings, *Class Conflict and Economic Development*, p. 216). Record real-wage increases fueled this shift, reflecting both the celebratory raises granted workers in the newly socialized enterprises and labor's new success in a state-regulated collective bargaining system where government representatives on the tripartite mediation boards now tended to side with the workers (see Lance Compa, "Labor Law and the Legal Way: Collective Bargaining in the Chilean Textile Industry Under the *Unidad Popular*," Working Paper no. 23, The Program in Law and Modernization, Yale Law School [New Haven, May 1973]).

8. The success of Vuskovic's economic reactivation was central here. Keynesian pump priming, magnified by pressure from below, produced an 8.5 percent growth rate, Latin America's best in 1971, another Allende success for which the revolution from below was an unwitting handmaiden. Moreover, during 1971, the great increase in wages, consumption, and social spending was achieved while reducing the rate of inflation from 35 percent to 22 percent (*La Economía chilena en 1971*, p. 231; Stallings and Zimbalist, "Political Economy," p. 72).

9. Bitar, *Transición, socialismo y democracia*, pp. 90–103. Significantly, the overwhelming majority of government credits to the industries of the social property area in 1972 (mining excepted) went to finance operating deficits, not for new investment (Chile, Ministerio de Hacienda, Dirección de Presupuestos, Departamento de Empresas, "Autorización y créditos a las empresas de la Area de Propiedad Social y Mixta en el año 1972 (Santiago, n.d.)"; Sergio Bitar [Cambridge, Mass.], August 1975). Both the popularity and the inflationary consequences of the Allende income redistribution were increased by its nonpunitive character.

In keeping with the Popular Unity's political strategy of class coalition, the income distribution was accomplished by "leveling upward," so that only the top 5 percent of income earners suffered a decline in their relative share of the national income from mid–1970 to mid–1972 (José Serra, "Economic Policy and Structural Change in Chile, 1970–1973" [Ph.D. diss., Cornell University, 1976], pp.338–60).

10. The revolution from below did exacerbate production difficulties by forcing an accelerated socialization of enterprises that outpaced the government's capacity to identify and train qualified interventors. The *cuoteo*, the political quota system in administrative appointments that often placed partisan loyalty over governmental responsibility or technical competence, further compounded the managerial problems in the social property area (Sergio Bitar [Cambridge, Mass.], August 1975).

11. Bitar, *Transición, socialismo y democracia*, pp. 104–10, 137–42.

12. Jorge Yarur (Santiago), August 1972.

13. Cusack, *Revolution and Reaction*, pp. 39–44.

14. Guillermo Hirmas (Santiago), July 1972. Hirmas, a well-connected owner of a medium-sized textile mill, himself admitted that he was afraid that his workers might seize it or that a radicalization of the revolutionary process place it on the Popular Unity's expropriation list.

15. Jorge Yarur (Santiago), August 1972; Oscar Guillermo Garretón (Santiago), August 1972; Hernán Labarca, (Santiago), July 1972. During the Allende years, the Controlaría was headed by a member of the right wing Democracia Radical appointed by Frei and was increasingly hostile to Allende's use of decree powers to incorporate enterprises into the social property area.

16. U.S. Senate, Select Committee on Intelligence, *Covert Action in Chile*, pp. 27–28, 33–39; James Petras and Morris Morley, *United States and Chile: Imperialism and the Overthrow of the Allende Government* (New York, 1975), pp. 79–118.

17. Salvador Allende (Santiago), July 1972.

18. Another sign was the March 1972 shift of the PIR, a centrist Radical faction with a small landholder social base, from the government coalition to the opposition alliance, in large part because of the Popular Unity's inability or unwillingness to control the rural revolution from below.

19. Ignacio Palma (Santiago), July 1972; Radomiro Tomic (Princeton, N.J.), March 1975; Sergio Bitar (Cambridge, Mass.), August 1975. See also Tomic, "La Democracia Cristiana y el gobierno de la Unidad Popular," in *Chile, 1970–1973*, pp. 219–20, 233–34, 330–31, and the reply of Julio Silva Solar, "Errores de la Unidad Popular y critica de la Democracia Cristiana," in *Chile, 1970–1973*, pp. 322–27.

20. For a balanced analysis of these pivotal negotiations, see A. Valenzuela, *Chile*, pp. 73–77. Although the left wing of the Popular Unity also opposed the accords, this was a minority position within the governing coalition, as the Lo Curro meeting demonstrated. The right wing Christian Democrats, on the other hand, were the dominant force within their party by mid–1972 and were able to veto the compromise that was within their grasp.

21. By August 1972, most Chileans of all classes believed that "a climate of violence" existed, although they differed on who was responsible (*Ercilla*, 13–19 September 1972, p. 11). Although the opposition blamed the Left for the violence, the bulk of the incidents were provoked by the Right, and most of their victims were supporters of the Left.

22. Jorge Yarur (Santiago), August 1972.

23. The coincidence of the October Strike with efforts by American copper companies to embargo Chilean copper exports by legal actions in Europe persuaded many leftists that they faced a coordinated assault by their domestic and foreign enemies. In addition, CIA funding

of, and involvement in, the *paro* was widely reported although the Senate report stops short of admitting it. (U.S. Senate, Select Committee on Intelligence, *Covert Action in Chile*, pp. 30–32).

24. For the *gremios*, in addition to Cusack, *Revolution and Reaction*, and "Politics of Chilean Private Enterprise Under Christian Democracy (Ph.D. diss., University of Denver, 1970)"; and [Quimantú], *Los gremios patronales*, and Arriagada, *La oligarquía patronal chilena* (Santiago, 1970), see Carmen Barros,"Nuevos actores en la protesta social 1971–72: el movimiento gremial," in Dagmar Raczynski et al., *Los actores de la realidad chilena* (Santiago, 1974). The CIA's covert action campaign pursued similar aims during 1971–72 (U. S. Senate, Select Committee on Intelligence, *Covert Action in Chile*, pp. 28–31).

25. During October, another state-intervened Yarur textile plant at Caupolican Chiguayante was destroyed by a suspicious fire so the threat was a real one.

26. Under the circumstances, it was a remarkable showing for the Left, which confirmed its replacement of the Center as the strongest of Chile's three political blocs, an electoral force that only a coalition of Right and Center could defeat. A comparative analysis of the 1969 and 1973 congressional balloting, however, reveals that the Popular Unity coalition as a whole received exactly the same percentage of the vote in both elections, with the Socialist gains balanced by Radical party losses (see A. Valenzuela, *Chile*, p. 85, Table 27).

27. Other factors in this politicization of the officer corps were the Chilean military's anti-Communist socialization, their disillusioning experience of civilian rule during their months in the government, and the accelerating economic deterioration. Harder to assess is the importance of American influence in this process. The U.S. Senate's Select Committee on Intelligence revealed a concerted and sustained campaign by the CIA to influence the Chilean officer corps against its government, using fabricated "evidence" of Allende's involvement with Cuban Intelligence, as well as expanded assistance and training (U.S. Senate, Select Committee on Intelligence, *Covert Action in Chile*, pp. 36–39).

28. It is not clear whether a purge of the officer corps in the wake of the *tancazo* would have been feasible, but it is evident that this was the last point where a counterattack might have been mounted and the coup dismantled (see General Arrellano Stark's comments in *Miami Herald* [18 February 1974]). For an insider account of the Popular Unity debate and Allende's refusal to take the risk, out of fear of provoking the confrontation that he wished to avert, see Garcés, *Allende*, pp. 304–13.

29. Ironically, Pinochet was Prats's choice—the respected "apolitical" military man who could preserve the constitutional neutrality of the armed forces after Prats's departure. During the *tancazo*, Pinochet reportedly had been so enraged at the mutineers that he had wanted to line them up and shoot them (Orlando Letelier [New York], September 1976).

30. For a passionate argument in favor of adopting the alternative strategy of relying on "popular power" and the politicization of the lower ranks of the armed forces, see Smirnow, *The Revolution Disarmed*. This alternative strategy, however, might have led to an even earlier—and bloodier—military intervention, but that is a counterfactual hypothesis that can not be tested. Allende never seriously entertained it. He shared General Prats's skepticism about the power of the "mobilized masses" and distrust of the revolution from below (see Garcés, *Allende*, pp. 277–84, 300–2, for an exposition of his position.) For analyses that project the *cordones industriales* in particular as potentially "the Soviets of Chile," see Smirnow, *The Revolution Disarmed*, pp. 81–99; Patricia Santa Lucía, "The Industrial Working Class and the Struggle for Power in Chile," in *Allende's Chile*, ed. O'Brien, pp. 128–66; E. Sader et al., *Cordón Cerrillos-Maipú: balance y perspectivas de un embrión de poder popular* (Santiago, 1973). For a more skeptical view of the *cordones*, which stresses their minority support among Chilean

industrial workers and their weak military response to the *tancazo*, see A. Valenzuela, *Chile*, pp. 101, 131 note 58.

31. Sergio Bitar (Cambridge, Mass.), August 1975. Arturo Valenzuela, drawing on Regis Debray, reports this remark as follows: "How many masses does one need to stop a tank?" (*Chile*, p. 94.) The point remains the same, as does its revelation of Allende's pessimism in the wake of the *tancazo*.

32. For a balanced view of this failed dialogue, based on interviews with Christian Democratic leaders, see A. Valenzuela, *Chile*, pp. 96–98.

33. A further source of division and confusion for many workers was the strike by a significant sector of workers at the El Teniente copper mine, which emerged as a national political issue, with the opposition backing the strike and the Left attacking it as counterrevolutionary. Although technical Popular Unity errors in drafting the annual wage readjustment legislation opened the way for the conflict and governmental intransigence magnified it, the strike leaders were trained and advised by AIFLD *gremialistas*, whose purposes were political (Reinaldo Jara [Santiago], December 1973; Sergio Bitar [Cambridge, Mass.], October 1975). See also Bitar, *Transición*, pp. 229–33. Bitar was minister of mining at the time.

34. Alvaro Ordoñez (Santiago), August 1973.

35. Cordon Industrial Bernardo O'Higgins, Meeting of the Executive Committee (10 September 1973)—author's notes.

36. The *tancazo* and its aftermath consolidated the *cordones'* image as the last hope of the revolution, the "popular power" alternative to an exhausted democratic road and a paralyzed government. Increasingly, leftists discontented with the failure of revolutionary leadership from above viewed the *cordones* not only as a revolutionary alternative from below but even as embryonic Chilean "soviets," potential institutions of dual power. We will never know whether these projections were prophetic or illusions, although the coup revealed the *cordones* as more effective politically than militarily. The Left Socialists and the MAPU pushed the *cordones*, while the MIR promoted the *comandos comunales*, which united workers with *pobladores* and peasants in a countywide organization. (See Smirnow, *The Revolution Disarmed*, pp. 81–99; Santa Lucía, "The Industrial Working Class," pp. 128–66; and Sader et al., *Cordón Cerrillos-Maipú*. For a more skeptical view of the *cordones*, which argues that they involved only a minority of Chilean industrial workers, were weak militarily and overrated politically, see Valenzuela, *Chile*, pp. 101, 131 note 58.)

37. Cordon Industrial Bernardo O'Higgins, Meeting of the Executive Committee (10 September 1973).

38. Héctor Mora (Santiago), August 1973.

39. Sergio Bitar (Cambridge, Mass.), August 1975. For an insider's account of that final week by Allende's political adviser, see Garcés, *Allende*, pp. 331–57. The role of the political parties was to legitimate a military coup by declaring the government "illegal," using the constitutional conflict over the social property area as a major excuse. Prats himself held ex-President Eduardo Frei personally responsible for the coup, accusing him of "using the military to get back into power" (see *Washington Post*, 8 March 1977). The leading role of Christian Democratic generals such as Oscár Bonilla and Sergio Arrellano, both former Frei aides, in the coup conspiracy supports his point.

CHAPTER 18

1. Except where otherwise noted, this chapter is based on my own observations and interviews and on my reading of the Chilean and foreign press. I have drawn as well on my

article entitled: "The Economic Consequences of the Chilean Counterrevolution," *Latin American Perspectives*, 2 (Summer 1974), 92–105. In order to protect my sources, I have changed the names of workers interviewed after the coup who were also cited in earlier chapters.

2. Germán Gómez (Santiago), November 1973. The bitterness of this MIR sympathizer at this failure of revolutionary leadership was echoed by many other leftist workers interviewed after the coup.

3. Lorenzo Aguirre (Santiago), October 1973.

4. Richard Pierson, "Chile: Can the Junta Rule?" *Ramparts* (June 1974), pp. 25–28. Church sources later estimated the number of political arrests as 95,000, close to one out of every hundred Chileans (*The New York Times*, 12 May 1975).

5. Major Augusto Laredo (Santiago), December 1973. I have changed the officer's name, as his remarks were not for attribution.

6. General Jorge Gustavo Leigh Guzmán, commander of the Air Force, radio and television broadcast, 11 September 1973.

7. Senate investigators later confirmed United States complicity in the coup while concluding: "There is no hard evidence of direct U.S. assistance to the coup, despite frequent allegations of such aid" (U.S. Senate, Select Committee to Study Governmental Operations with Respect to Intelligence Activities, Staff Report: "Covert Action in Chile, 1963–1973" [Washington, D.C., 1975], p.28).

8. Roberto Caldera (Santiago), November 1973.

9. Fernando Balaguer (Santiago), December 1973.

10. Jaime Costa (Santiago), December 1973.

11. General César Mendoza Durán, commander of the Carabineros, radio and television broadcast, 11 September 1973.

12. *La Tercera* (Santiago), 10 October 1973, p. 7.

13. Diego Solano (Santiago), January 1974.

14. Ibid.

15. Amador Yarur (Santiago), January 1974.

16. Teodoro Castro (Santiago), January 1974.

17. Berta Castillo (Santiago), January 1974.

EPILOGUE

1. Quoted in *The New York Times* (17 August 1983), p. 2.

2. Quoted in the *Boston Globe* (6 September 1983).

3. Quoted in *The New York Times* (17 August 1983), p. 2.

4. Quoted in the *Boston Globe* (9 September 1983), p. 3.

5. Quoted in the *Washington Post* (19 September 1983), p. A15; see also *The New York Times* (6 September 1985), pp. A1, A4.

GLOSSARY

APATRONADO/APATRONADA   the boss's person, a Yarur loyalist

BUENO   well

CAZUELA   a soupy stew containing meat, potatoes and onions

CAMBIOS   changes; structural changes or reforms

COMPADRES   buddies

COMPAÑERO/COMPAÑERA   comrade

COMPAÑERISMO   social solidarity

CONTROLARIA   autonomous executive agency with power to rule on legality of executive
    actions

CORDON INDUSTRIAL   industrial belt (or district) workers council

CUOTEO   political quota system for governmental appointments

EMPLEADO/EMPLEADA   white-collar worker or skilled blue-collar worker

GANAMOS   We won

GREMIALISTA   worker who adheres to "apolitical" unionism advocated by Chilean Right

GREMIO   guild; business association

IMPORT SUBSTITUTION INDUSTRIALIZATION   strategy for industrial development that begins
    with domestic production of previously imported consumer goods

JEFE   chief; foreman; supervisor

JUVENTUD COMUNISTA   Communist Youth

JUVENTUD SOCIALISTA   Socialist Youth

LATIFUNDIO   large landed estate

LIMPIEZA DE CABEZAS   brainwashing

OBRERO/OBRERA   blue-collar worker

PATRÓN   boss, but with a precapitalist, paternalistic connotation

PISCO   Chilean hard liquor

SECTARISMO   sectarian politics

SOCIAL PROPERTY AREA   publicly owned sector of economy

TANCAZO   failed rebellion of armored regiment of 29 June 1973

TOMA   property seizure

UNIDAD POPULAR   Popular Unity; leftist coalition of 1969–73.

VENCEREMOS   We shall win/overcome

VIA CHILENA   Chilean road to socialism; democratic road to socialism

SELECT BIBLIOGRAPHY

Primary Sources

Interviews

Most of my interviews were with workers whose names have been changed in this book in order to protect my sources. There would be little point to listing these fictitious names in a bibliography. They can be found in the relevant footnotes and the index. The interviews with public figures that proved particularly valuable for this book include the following.

Allende, Salvador. Santiago, July 1972.
Bussi de Allende, Hortensia. Santiago, June 1972.
Bahna, Henry. Santiago, September 1972.
Bitar, Sergio. Cambridge, Mass., June–September 1975.
Carrillo, Luis. Santiago, December 1973–January 1974.
Chonchol, Jacques. Santiago, May 1972.
Espinoza, Héctor. Santiago, July–August 1972.
Garcés, Joan. Santiago, June 1972.
Garretón, Oscar Guillermo. Santiago, August 1972.
Gazmuri, Jaime. Santiago, May 1972.
Gumucio, Rafael. Santiago, June 1972.
Hirmas, Miguel. Santiago, January 1974.
Ibáñez, Oscar. Santiago, May 1972.
Jara, Reinaldo. Santiago, December 1973–January 1974.
Kirberg, Enrique. New York, April–May 1980.
Labarca, Hernán. Santiago, August 1972.
Letelier, Orlando. New York, September 1976.
Maira, Luis. Santiago, June 1972.
Morales, Fernando. Santiago, January 1974.
Palestro, Tito. Santiago, July 1972.
Palma, Ignacio. Santiago, July 1972.
Poblete, Vicente. Santiago, February and August 1972.
Said, Domingo. La Paz, July 1973.
Said, Juan. Santiago, July 1972.

300

Said, José. Santiago, July 1972.
Sánchez, Juan Francisco. Santiago, September 1972.
Sepúlveda, Adonis. Santiago, June 1972.
Smith, Legrand. La Paz, July 1973.
Sumar, Fernando. Santiago, January 1974.
Taulis, Patricio. Santiago, August 1972.
Tarud, Rafael. Santiago, July 1972.
Teitelboim, Volodia. Santiago, April–June 1972.
Tomic, Radomiro. Princeton, N.J., April 1975.
Valech, Victor. Santiago, December 1973.
Van Lancker, Andrés. Santiago, September 1972.
Vió, Victor. Santiago, May–June 1972.
Yarur Banna, Jorge. Santiago, August 1972.
Yarur Lolas, Nicolás. Santiago, January 1974.

Archival Sources

Unless otherwise noted, all archives in the following listing are located in Santiago, Chile.

Arequipa. Archivo Departmental. Registro de Escrituras Públicas. Notarial archives, of which the Archivo del Notario dr. Victor Rojas Romero proved the most useful.

Arequipa. Oficina de Registros Públicos. Registro de Propiedad Privada. Distrito de Arequipa. 1906–26.

Arequipa. Archivo de la Municipalidad. Libro de toma de razón de las licencias expedidas por la Inspección de Policía.Tomo I.

Arequipa. Parroquia del Sagrario. Libro de Bautismos. 1918–20.

Central Unica de Trabajadores. Documents in author's possession include copies of the minutes of the Consejo Directivo Nacional for 1953–62, minutes of meetings with textile union delegates in 1953, accounts for 1953–59, and miscellaneous internal reports and memoranda.

Chile. Corporación de la Reforma Agraria. Departamento de Control y Estadística. "Expropiaciones del 1965–31 de marzo de 1972" and other unpublished statistics.

Chile. Dirección de Registro Electoral. "Variación porcentual de los partidos políticos, 1957–1971." Unpublished statistics.

Chile. Ministerio de Economía. Comisión Investigadora Especializada. Internal reports of investigations of S.A. Yarur and Tejidos Caupolican S.A. from 1971.

Chile. Ministerio de Hacienda. Dirección de Presupuestos. Departmento de Empresas. Unpublished statistics and internal memoranda on employment and investment in the social property area for 1971–72.

Chile, Ministerio de Trabajo. Departmento de Conflictos Colectivos, Sueldos y Salarios. Correspondence from 1960–65 and unpublished statistics on wages, salaries, and strikes for 1960–70.

Chile. Ministerio de Trabajo. Departamento Jurídico. Internal correspondence and reports for 1939–65.

Chile. Ministerio de Trabajo. Dirección General de Trabajo. Correspondence and internal reports for 1939–71 regarding the Yarur mill, its working conditions and labor relations, including ùnion petitions and strike reports. Separate files for the Sindicato Industrial S.A. Yarur (1939–71) and the Sindicato Profesional de Empleados Particulares de S.A. Yarur (1970–71) include statutes, election results, accounts, membership lists, and correspondence.

Chile. Ministerio de Trabajo. Junta de Concilación Especial para los Textiles para Santiago. Files include the minute book of the mediation board, contract demands and agreements, and correspondence for 1939–71.

Ex-Yarur. Documents researched include contracts and internal regulations for 1971–72,"Libro de acuerdos y ordenes de los Interventores" for 1971, "Actas del Comité Coordinador" for 1971–72, and "Resoluciones del Consejo Administrativo" for 1971–72, as well as unpublished statistics and internal memoranda and reports. Legally, Ex-Yarur represented a temporary state intervention in the management of S. A. Yarur, which began in April 1971 and came to an end in January 1974, and these documents may still be in its archive.

Instituto Textile de Chile. Unpublished statistics for 1962–72.

Manufacturas Textiles Forno. La Paz. Company reports and a typescript company history written in 1958.

Notario Abraham Del Río. Land purchases for 1935.

Notario Javier Echeverría Vial. Contract agreements for 1936.

Notario Jorge Gaete Rojas. Partnership agreements for 1936–37.

Oruro. Camara de Comercio. Registro Mercantil. Vols. I-II.

Said, S.A. La Paz. Company reports and a typescript company history written in 1973.

Said and Yarur Papers. Correspondence in S.A. Yarur archive.

Sindicato Industrial Yarur Hermanos. Minute book for 1939–41.

Sindicato Industrial S.A. Yarur, Manufacturas Chilenas de Algodón. Minutes of union meetings for 1961–71.

Sindicato Profesional de Empleados Particulares del Banco de Crédito e Inversiones. Correspondence; internal reports.

Sindicato Profesional de Empleados Particulares de S. A. Yarur, Manufacturas Chilenas de Algodón. Minutes for 1970–71.

Sindicato Unico de los Trabajadores de Ex-Yarur. Minutes for 1971–72.

Superintendencia de Compañías de Seguros, Sociedades Anónimas y Bolsas de Comercio. Departamento de Sociedades Anónimas. Corporation files contain prospectuses and statutes, company reports and state regulatory reports, correspondence and shareholder lists. Corporations whose files I researched include Algodones Hirmas, Distribuidora Talca, Empresas Juan Yarur, Manufacturas Sumar, Saavedra Benard, Tejidos Caupolican, Textil Viña, Textil Progreso and Yarur.

Tejidos Caupolican. Unpublished statistics and internal memoranda and reports.

Universidad Mayor de San Andrés de La Paz. La Paz. Repository for historical government documents. The most valuable for this book were the Ministerio de Hacienda reports and correspondence regarding commerce and industry for 1929–35.

Yarur Hermanos Papers. These include correspondence, contracts, inventories, and account books. In S.A. Yarur archive.

Yarur S. A., Manufacturas Chilenas de Algodón. Includes correspondence, company reports, internal memoranda, unpublished statistics, personnel records, company police reports, and the minutes of the meetings of the Board of Directors.

Printed Government and Organization Sources

Allende, Salvador. *Mensaje del Presidente . . . ante el Congreso Nacional*. Santiago, 1971, 1972, 1973.

Amnesty International. *Report*. London, 1973–84.

Asociación Chileno-Arabe de Cooperación. *Censo de la población de orígen árabe del Gran Santiago*. Santiago, 1970.

Brigada Ibañista de Yarur. *Camaradas: ¡Adelante!* Santiago, 1952.

British Chamber of Commerce of Chile. *Bulletin.* Santiago, 1947–52.

Central Unica de Trabajadores (CUT). *Primer Encuentro Nacional de Trabajadores Textiles. Participación es Poder.*

Chile, *El Diario Oficial.* Santiago, 1934–74.

Chile, Cámara de Diputados. *Diario de Sesiones.* Santiago, 1934–73.

Chile, Camara de Senadores. *Diario de Sesiones.* Santiago. 1934–73.

Chile, Corporación de Fomento de la Producción (CORFO). *Cinco años de labor, 1939–1943.* Santiago, 1944.

———. *Estudio provisorio de una política textil nacional.* Santiago, 1969.

———. *Geografía económica de Chile.* 4 vols. Santiago, 1950–60.

———. *Informe de la misión chilena al área andina.* Santiago, 1968.

Chile, Dirección General de Estadística. *Censo Industrial.* Santiago, 1938, 1948, 1958.

Chile, Instituto Nacional de Estadísticas. *IV Censo Nacional de Manufacturas.* Santiago, 1968.

Chile, Oficina de Planificación Nacional. *Antecedentes sobre el desarrollo chileno, 1960–70.* Santiago, 1971.

———. *Informe económico anual.* Santiago, 1971, 1972.

———. *Resumen del plan de la economía nacional, 1971–76.* Santiago, 1971.

Chile, Secretaria General de Gobierno. *Libro blanco del cambio de gobierno en Chile.* Santiago, 1973.

Consultores en Ingenería y Administración (CADE). *Situación actual y proyecciones futuras de la industria textíl chilena.* 8 vols. Santiago, 1968–69.

Frente de Trabajadores Revolucionarias (FTR) de Ex-Yarur. *Alerta.* Santiago, 1971–73.

Great Britain. Department of Overseas Trade. *Economic Conditions in Chile.* London, 1932–35.

———. *Report on Economic and Commercial Conditions in Chile.* London, 1936–39.

Instituto Textil de Chile. *Memorias.* Santiago, 1962–72.

MAPU. *El libro de las 91: las empresas monopólicas y el área social de la economía chilena.* Santiago, 1972.

———. *El primer año del gobierno popular.* Santiago, 1972.

———. *El segundo año del gobierno popular.* Santiago, 1973.

MAPU de Ex-Yarur. *De Frente.* Santiago, 1972.

Movimiento de la Izquierda Revolucionaria (MIR). *Chile: The MIR and the Tasks of the Resistance.* Oakland, Calif., 1976.

Municipalidad de Santiago, Comisión Especial. *El transporte colectivo de pasajeros en la Ciudad de Santiago.* Santiago, 1935.

Partido Comunista de Chile. *Documentos del cincuentenario del . . .* Santiago, 1972.

Sociedad de Fomento Fabril. *Boletín Mensual.* Santiago, 1914–73.

———. *Industria.* Santiago, 1938–54.

———. *Memorias.* Santiago, 1914–72.

Unidad Popular. *Programa de la Unidad Popular.* Santiago, 1972.

Unión Socialista Popular. *El nuevo sindicato del área social.* Santiago, 1972.

United Nations, Economic Commission for Latin America. *Economies of Scale in the Cotton Spinning and Weaving Industry.* New York, 1966.

———. *La industria textíl en América Latina.* Vol. 1. *Chile.* Vol. 12. *Informe Regional.* New York, 1962, 1968.

———. *Labour Productivity of the Cotton Textile Industry in Five Latin American Countries.* New York, 1951.

———. *Problems and Prospects of the Textile Industry in Latin America.* New York, 1965.

United States, House of Representatives. Committee on Foreign Affairs, Subcomittee on Inter-American Affairs. *United States and Chile During the Allende Years, 1970–1973.* Washington, D.C., 1975.

United States, Senate, Select Committee to Study Governmental Operations with Respect to Intelligence Activities. Interim Report. *Alleged Assassination Plots Involving Foreign Leaders.* Washington, D.C., 1975.

United States, Senate. Select Committee to Study Governmental Operations with Respect to Intelligence Activities. Staff Report. *Covert Action in Chile, 1963–1973.* Washington, D.C., 1975.

Newspapers and Periodicals

Ahora. Santiago, 1971.

Aurora de Chile, La. Santiago, 1973.

Boletín Arabe. Santiago, 1936–46.

Boston Globe. Boston, 1981–85.

Chile-América. Rome, 1974–76.

Chile Hoy. Santiago, 1972–73.

Christian Science Monitor. Boston, 1969–85.

Clarín. Santiago, 1969–73.

Crítica, La. Santiago. 1939–41.

Cuadernos de la Realidad Nacional. Santiago, 1969–73.

De Frente. Santiago, 1972–73.

Diario, El. La Paz, 1929–34.

Diario Ilustrado, El. Santiago, 1938–70.

Ercilla. Santiago, 1935–85.

Frente Popular. Santiago, 1936–40.

Germinal. Oruro, 1920.

Impacto. Santiago, 1971.

Imparcial, El. Santiago, 1947.

Industrial, El. Oruro, 1914–24.

Industrial, El. Santiago, 1938–39.

Latin America Reports. London, 1970–85.

Los Angeles Times. Los Angeles, 1970–85.

Marxismo y Revolución. Santiago, 1973.

Mayoría. Santiago, 1972.

Mercurio, El. Santiago. 1932–85.

Mercurio, El. Valparaíso, 1934.

Mensaje. Santiago, 1969–75.

Miami Herald. Miami, 1970–85.

Mundo Arabe. Santiago, 1935–36.

Nación, La. Santiago, 1932–73.

NACLA's Empire and Latin America Report. New York, 1971–85.

Nation, The. New York, 1970–85.

Newsweek. New York, 1970–85.

New York Times, The. New York, 1970–85.

News Journal. Wilmington, Del., 1976.

Norte, El. La Paz, 1928–34.

Noticias. Arequipa, 1927–28.

Nueva Economía. Santiago, 1972–73.

Panorama Económico. Santiago, 1964–73.
Patria y Libertad. Santiago, 1972–73.
PEC. Santiago, 1964–73.
Política Latinoamericana Nueva (PLAN). Santiago, 1972–73.
Portada. Santiago. 1972–73.
Posición. Santiago, 1972–73.
Prensa, La. Oruro, 1914–29.
Prensa, La. Santiago, 1972–73.
Principios. Santiago, 1946–73.
Pueblo, El. Arequipa, 1906–27.
Punto Final. Santiago, 1957–73.
Puro Chile. Santiago, 1970–73.
¿Qué Pasa? Santiago, 1972–75.
Ramparts. Berkeley, Calif., 1970–74.
Rebelde, El. Santiago, 1970–73.
Reforma/Al-Islah, La. Santiago, 1933–44.
Revista Latinoamericana de Estudios Urbano Regionales. Santiago, 1970–73.
Revista de la Universidad Técnica del Estado. Santiago, 1970–73.
Sepa. Santiago, 1973.
Siglo, El. Santiago, 1941–73.
Tarea Urgente. Santiago, 1973.
Tercera de la Hora, La. Santiago, 1962–74.
Times of the Americas. Washington, D.C., 1970–85.
Tizona. Santiago, 1973.
Tribuna, La. Santiago, 1971–73.
Ultima Hora, La. Santiago, 1947–73.
Ultimas Noticias, Las. Santiago, 1934–36, 1962, and 1970–73.
28 de abril, El. Santiago, 1971–72.
Vistazo. Santiago, 1962.
Wall Street Journal. New York, 1970–85.
Washington Post. Washington, D.C., 1970–85.

SECONDARY SOURCES

Books, Articles, Pamphlets, and Unpublished Writings

Affonso, Almino, et al. *Movimiento campesino chileno*. 2 vols. Santiago, 1970.
Agor, Weston H. *The Chilean Senate*. Austin, Tex., 1971.
Ahumada , Jorge. *En vez de la miseria*. 8th ed. Santiago, 1972.
Alaluf, David, et al. *Reforma agraria chilena; seis ensayos de interpretación*. Santiago, 1970.
Alba, Victor. *Politics and the Labor Movement in Latin America*. Stanford, Calif., 1969.
Aldunate Phillips, Arturo. *Un pueblo en busca de su destino*. Santiago, 1947.
Alessandri Palma, Arturo. *Recuerdos de gobierno*. 3 vols. Santiago, 1952.
Alexander, Robert J. *Labor Relations in Argentina, Brazil and Chile*. New York, 1962.
———. *Organized Labor in Latin America*. New York, 1965.
———. *The Tragedy of Chile*. Westport, Conn., 1978.
Allende, Salvador. *La historia que estamos escribiendo*. Santiago, 1972.
———. *La realidad médico-social chilena*. Santiago, 1939.

————. *Su pensamiento político*. Santiago, 1972.

Almeyda, Clodomiro. *Sociologismo e ideologismo en la teoría revolucionaria*. Santiago, 1972.

Altamirano, Carlos, *Decisión revolucionaria*. Santiago, 1973.

Alvarado, Edesio. *El turco Tarud*. Santiago, 1970.

Alvarez Andrews, Oscar. *Historia del desarrollo industrial de Chile*. Santiago, 1936.

Ampuero Díaz, Raúl. *La izquierda en punto muerto*. Santiago, 1969.

Amunátegui Solar, Domingo. *La segunda presidencia de Arturo Alessandri*. Santiago, 1961.

Angell, Alan. *Politics and the Labour Movement in Chile*. London, 1972.

Arrias Escobedo, Osvaldo. *La prensa obrera en Chile*. Santiago, 1970.

Arriagada, Genaro. *De la vía chilena a la vía insurreccional*. Santiago, 1974.

————. *10 años: visión crítica*. Santiago, 1983.

————. *La oligarquía patronal chileno*. Santiago, 1970.

Ayres, Robert L. "Electoral Constraints and the Chilean Way to Socialism." *Studies in Comparative International Development*, 8 (Summer 1973), 128–61.

Bahoz Ramírez, Julio. "Oruro en su apogeo mercantilista." *Boletín de la Camara de Comercio*, Edición Extraordinaria, 15 (July–December 1970), 33–38.

Baltra Cortés, Alberto. *Gestión econónomica del gobierno de la Unidad Popular*. Santiago, 1973.

Baraona Urzúa, Pablo, et al. *Visión crítica de Chile*. 3d ed. Santiago, 1972.

Bardón, Alvaro, et al. *Itinerario de una crisis; política económica y transición al socialismo*. Santiago, 1972.

Barraclough, Solon, et al. *Chile: reforma agraria y gobierno popular*. Buenos Aires, 1973.

————, and José A. Fernández, coords. *Diagnóstico de la reforma agraria chilena*. Mexico City, 1974.

Barrera, Manuel. *Chile, 1970–1972. La conflictiva experiencia de los cambios estructurales*. Caracas, 1973.

————. "Perspectiva histórica de la huelga obrera en Chile." *Cuadernos de la Realidad Nacional*, 9 (September 1971), 119–55.

————. *El sindicato industrial como instrumento de lucha de la clase obrera chilena*. Santiago, 1971.

Barría, Jorge. *El movimiento obrero en Chile*. Santiago, 1971.

————. *Historia de la CUT*. Santiago, 1971.

————. *Los movimientos sociales de Chile desde 1910 hasta 1926*. Santiago, 1963.

————. *Trayectoria y estructura del movimiento sindical chileno, 1946–1962*. Santiago, 1963.

Basso, Lelia, et al. *Transición al socialismo y experiencia chilena*. Santiago, 1972.

Bauer, Arnold J. *Chilean Rural Society from the Spanish Conquest to 1930*. New York, 1975.

Birns, Laurence, ed. *The End of Chilean Democracy*. New York, 1974.

Bitar, Sergio. *Transición, socialismo y democracia. La experiencia chilena*. Mexico City, 1979.

———— ed. *Chile: liberalismo económico y dictadura politica*. Lima, 1980.

Blanco, Hugo, et al. *La tragedia chilena*. Buenos Aires, 1973.

Bonilla, Frank, and Myron Glazer. *Student Politics in Chile*. New York, 1970.

Boorstein, Edward. *Allende's Chile*. New York, 1977.

Borón, Atilio. "Movilización política y crisis política en Chile." *Aportes*, 20 (April 1971), 41–69.

————."Notas sobre las raíces histórico-estructurales de la movilización política en Chile." *Foro Internacional* (July–September 1975), 64–121.

Bowers, Claude G. *Chile Through Embassy Windows*. New York, 1958.

Bray, Donald. "The Political Emergence of Arab-Chileans." *Journal of Inter-American Studies*, 4:4 (October 1962), 557–62.

Brunner, Karl H. *Santiago de Chile: su estado actual y futura formación*. Santiago, 1932.

Bunster, Enrique. *Un ángel para Chile*. Santiago, 1959.
Burbach, Roger. "The Chilean Industrial Bourgeoisie and Foreign Capital, 1920–1970." Ph.D. diss., Indiana University, 1975.
Burnett, Ben G. *Political Groups in Chile*. Austin, Tex., 1975.
Butland, Gilbert J. *Chile*. London, 1953.
Cademártori, José. *La economía chilena*. 2d ed. Santiago, 1971.
Campero, Guillermo. "Gestión de la empresa y participación de los trabajadores." *Nueva Economía*, 2 (January–April 1972), 3–19.
Campero, Guillermo, and José A. Valenzuela. *El movimiento sindical en el regímen militar chileno, 1973–1981*. Santiago, 1984.
Casanueva, Fernando, and Manuel Fernández. *El Partido Socialista y la lucha de clases en Chile*. Santiago, 1973.
Castells, Manuel. *La lucha de clases en Chile*. Buenos Aires, 1974.
———. "Movimiento de pobladores y lucha de clases." *Revista Latinoamericana de Estudios Urbanos y Regionales*, 2 (November 1972), 55–82.
Castillo, Leonardo, Arturo Sáez, and Patricio Rogers. "Notas para un estudio del movimiento obrero en Chile." *Cuadernos de la Realidad Nacional*, 5 (June 1970), 3–30.
Castillo Velasco, Jaime. *Las fuentes de la Democracia Cristiana*. 3d ed. Santiago, 1972.
Castro, Fidel. *Fidel en Chile. Textos completos de su diálogo con el pueblo*. Santiago, 1972.
Cavarozzi, Marcelo. "The Government and the Industrial Bourgeoisie in Chile, 1938–1964." Ph.D. diss., University of California, Berkeley, 1976.
Charlin, Carlos. *Del avión rojo a la república socialista*. Santiago, 1970.
Chelén, Alejandro, and Julio César Jobet, eds. *Pensamiento teórico y político del Partido Socialista de Chile*. Santiago, 1972.
Chuaqui, Benedicto. *Memorias de un emigrante*. Santiago, 1942.
Compa, Lance. *Labor and the Legal Way: Collective Bargaining in the Chilean Textile Industry under the Unidad Popular*. Program in Law and Modernization Working Papers, no. 23. Yale Law School, May 1973.
Cortázar, René, and Guillermo Campero. "Concertation Versus Confrontation: Logics of Union Action in Chile." Paper presented at the Workshop on New Labor Movements in Latin America, Kellogg Institute, Notre Dame University, 28 February–1 March 1985.
Cortés, Lia, and Jordi Fuentes. *Diccionario político de Chile (1810–1966)*. Santiago, 1967.
Corvalán, Luis. *Caminos de victoria*. Santiago, 1971.
———. *El poder popular*. Santiago, 1969.
Cruz-Coke, Ricardo. *Geografía electoral de Chile*. Santiago, 1952.
Cruz Salas, Luis. *Historia social de Chile: 1931–1945. Los partidos populares, 1931–1941*. Santiago, 1969.
Cuentas, J. Alberto. *Provincia de Chucuito*. Puno, 1928.
Cusack, David F. "Politics of Chilean Private Enterprise Under Christian Democracy." Ph.D. diss., University of Denver, 1970.
———. *Revolution and Reaction: The Internal and International Dynamics of Conflict and Confrontation in Chile*. University of Denver Graduate School of International Studies Monographic Series in World Affairs, vol. 14. Denver, Colo., 1977.
Dahse, Fernando. *Mapa de la extrema riqueza. Los grupos económicos y el proceso de concentración de capitales*. Santiago, 1979.
Darnton, Robert. *The Literary Underground of the Old Regime*. Cambridge, Mass., 1982.
Davis, Nathaniel. *The Last Two Years of Salvador Allende*. Ithaca, N.Y., 1985.
Debray, Regis. *The Chilean Revolution: Conversations with Allende*. New York, 1971.

De Shazo, Peter. *Urban Workers and Labor Unions in Chile, 1902–1927.* Madison, Wis., 1984.

Diccionario biográfico de Chile. 9th ed. Santiago, 1953–55.

Documentos secretos de la I.T.T. Santiago, 1972.

Drake, Paul W. "Journeys Toward Failure?: Political Parties and Labor Movements Under Authoritarian Regimes in the Southern Cone and Brazil. In *Partidos políticos y democracia en el Cono Sur*, ed. M. Cavarozzi and M. Garretón (forthcoming).

————. *Socialism and Populism in Chile, 1932–1952.* Urban Ill., 1978.

Duque, Joaquín, and Ernesto Pastrana. "La movilización de los sectores populares en Chile, 1954–1972." *Revista Latinoamericana de Ciencias Sociales*, 4 (December 1972), 259–94.

Edwards Bello, Joaquín. *El roto.* 2d ed. Santiago, 1968.

Edwards Vives, Alberto, and Eduardo Frei Montalva. *Historia de los partidos políticos chilenos.* Santiago, 1949.

Ellsworth, P. T. *Chile, an Economy in Transition.* New York, 1945.

Ericson, Kenneth, Patrick Peppe, and Hobart A. Spalding, Jr. "Research on the Urban Working Class and Organized Labor in Argentina, Brazil and Chile: What Is Left to Be Done?" *Latin American Research Review*, 9 (Spring 1979), 115–42.

Escobar, Aristodemo. *Compendio de la legislación social y desarrollo del movimiento obrero en Chile.* Santiago, 1940.

Espinosa, Juan G., and Andrew Zimbalist. *Economic Democracy: Workers' Participation in Chilean Industry, 1970–1973.* New York, 1978.

Evans, Les, ed. *Disaster in Chile.* New York, 1974.

Fagen, Richard R. "The United States and Chile: Roots and Branches." *Foreign Affairs* (January 1975), 297–313.

Falabella, Gonzalo. *Labor in Chile Under the Junta, 1973–1979.* University of London, Institute of Latin American Studies, Working Papers, no. 4., n.d.

Faletto, Enzo, Eduardo Ruíz, and Hugo Zemelman. *Genesis histórica del proceso político chileno.* Santiago, 1971.

Feinberg, Richard. *The Triumph of Allende.* New York, 1972.

Feliú Cruz, Guillermo. "La evolución política, económica y social de Chile." *Anales de la Universidad de Chile*, 119 (1960), 45–85.

Ffrench-Davis, Ricardo. *Políticas económicas en Chile, 1952–1970.* Santiago, 1973.

Flores, Benjamín. *Monografía de la Provincia de Compa.* Arequipa, 1928.

Foxley, Alejandro. *Latin American Experiments in Neo Conservative Economics.* Berkeley, Calif., 1983.

————, ed. *Chile: búsqueda de un nuevo socialismo.* Santiago, 1971.

————. *Reconstrucción económica para la democracia.* Santiago, 1983.

Frank, André Gunder. *Capitalism and Underdevelopment in Latin America.* New York, 1966.

————. "La política económica en Chile: Del Frente Popular a la Unidad Popular." *Punto Final*, 153 (March 14, 1972), Supplement.

Frei M., Eduardo. *Pensamiento y acción.* Santiago, 1958.

Furci, Carmelo. *The Chilean Communist Party and the Road to Socialism.* London, 1984.

Garcés, Joan. *Allende y la experiencia chilena: las armas de la política.* Barcelona, 1976.

————. *Chile: el camino político hacia el socialismo.* Barcelona, 1972.

————. *Desarrollo político y desarrollo económico. Los casos de Chile y Colombia.* Santiago, 1972.

————. *El estado y los problemas tácticos en el gobierno de Allende.* 2d ed. Buenos Aires, 1974.

————. *1970: La pugna política por la presidencia en Chile.* Santiago, 1971.

————. *Revolución, congreso y constitución: El caso Tohá.* Santiago, 1972.

————, ed. *Chile's Road to Socialism.* London, 1973.

García F., Patricio. *Los gremios patronales.* Santiago, 1973.

————.*El tancazo de ese 29 de junio.* Santiago, 1973.

Garretón, Oscar Guillermo, and Jaime Cisternas. "Algunas características del proceso de toma de decisiones en la gran empresa: la dinámica de la concentración." Mimeographed. Servicio de Cooperación Técnica, Santiago, 1970.

Giusti, Jorge. "La formación de las poblaciones en Santiago." *Revista Latinoamericana de Ciencias Políticas,* 2 (1971), 370–85.

Gil, Federico. *The Political System of Chile.* Boston, 1966.

Gil, Federico, and Charles J. Parrish. *The Chilean Presidential Election of September 4, 1964.* Washington, D.C., 1965.

Gil, Federico, Ricardo Lagos, and Henry Landsberger, eds. *Chile at the Turning Point. Lessons of the Socialist Years, 1970–1973.* Philadelphia, 1979.

Girard, Alain, and Raúl Samuel. *Situación y perspectivas de Chile de Septiembre de 1957.* Santiago, 1958.

Godoy Urzúa, César. *Estructura social de Chile.* Santiago, 1971.

González Díaz, Galo. *La lucha por la formación del Partido Comunista de Chile.* Santiago, 1958.

Goodman, Louis W. "Blue Collar Work and Modernization." Ph. D. diss., Northwestern University, 1970.

Grayson, George. *El Partido Demócrata Cristiano Chileno.* Buenos Aires, 1968.

Gregory, Peter. *Industrial Wages in Chile.* New York, 1967.

Griffin, Keith. *Underdevelopment in Spanish America.* London, 1969.

Gross, Leonard. *The Last Best Hope: Eduardo Frei and Chilean Christian Democracy.* New York, 1967.

Guilisasti Tagle, Sergio. *Partidos políticos chilenos.* 2d ed. Santiago, 1964.

Guíñez Carrasco, Julio. *Interpretación de la evolución social y política de Chile desde 1932 a 1952.* Concepción, 1963.

Guzmán, Antonio. *Historia de Bolivia.* La Paz, 1973.

Hakim, Peter, and Giorgio Solimano. *Development, Reform and Malnutrition in Chile.* Cambridge, Mass., 1978.

Halperin, Ernst. *Nationalism and Communism in Chile.* Cambridge, Mass., 1965.

Hammergren, Linn A. *Development and the Politics of Administrative Reform.* Boulder, Colo., 1983.

Hauser, Thomas. *The Execution of Charles Hormon: An American Sacrifice.* New York, 1978.

Heller Rouassant, Claude. *Política de unidad en la izquierda chilena (1956–1970).* Mexico City, 1973.

Herring, Hubert. *Chile en la presidencia de don Pedro Aguirre Cerda.* Buenos Aires, 1971.

Hersh, Seymour M. *The Price of Power: Kissinger in the Nixon White House.* New York, 1983.

Hirmas, María Eugenia, and Helia Henriquez. "La sociología de la gerencia: una analisis subcultural." Memoria de Licenciatura. University of Chile, 1970.

Hirsch, Fred. *An Analysis of Our AFL-CIO Role in Latin America.* San José, Calif., 1974.

Hirschman, Albert O. *Journeys Toward Progress.* Garden City, N.Y., 1965.

Hormachea R., Armando. *El Frente Popular de 1938.* Santiago, 1968.

Hoxie, Robert. *Scientific Management and Labor.* New York, 1921.

Ibañez del Campo, Carlos. *Lo que haremos por Chile.* Santiago, 1952.

Instituto de Economía, University of Chile. *Desarrollo económico de Chile, 1940–1956.* Santiago, 1956.

————. *La economía de Chile en el período 1950–1963.* 2 vols. Santiago, 1963.
————. *La economía chilena en 1971.* Santiago, 1972.
————. *La economía chilena en 1972.* Santiago, 1973.
————. *La migración interna en Chile en el período 1940–1952.* Santiago, 1959.
Jarpa, Sergio. *Creo en Chile.* Santiago, 1973.
Jobet, Julio César. *Ensayo crítico del desarrollo económico-social de Chile.* Santiago, 1955.
————. *Historia del Partido Socialista.* 2 vols. Santiago, 1973.
————. *Recabarren y los orígenes del movimiento obrero y el socialismo chilenos.* 2d ed. Santiago, 1973.
Johnson, Dale L. "Industrialization, Social Mobility and Class Formation in Chile." *Studies in Comparative International Development*, 3 (1967–68), 127–51.
————., ed. *The Chilean Road to Socialism.* New York, 1973.
Johnson, John J. *Political Change in Latin America.* Stanford, Calif., 1970.
Joxe, Alain. *Las fuerzas armadas en el sistema político de Chile.* Santiago, 1970.
Kaufman, Robert R. *The Politics of Land Reform in Chile, 1950–1970.* Cambridge, Mass., 1972.
Kay, Cristóbal. "Comparative Development of the European Manorial System and the Latin American Hacienda System." Ph.D. diss., University of Sussex, 1971.
————. *El sistema señorial europeo y la hacienda latinoamericana.* Mexico City, 1980.
Kinsbrunner, Jay. *Chile: A Historical Interpretation.* New York, 1973.
Kirsh, Henry W. "The Industrialization of Chile, 1880–1970." Ph.D. diss., University of Florida, 1973.
Klein, Herbert. *Bolivia, Evolution of a Multi-Ethnic Society.* New York, 1982.
————. *Parties and Political Change in Bolivia.* Cambridge, Eng., 1969.
Labarca G., Eduardo. *Chile al rojo. Reportaje a una revolución que nace.* Santiago, 1971.
————. *Corvalán, 27 horas.* Santiago, 1972.
Labrousse, Alain. *L'Expérience Chilienne: Réformisme ou Révolution?* Paris, 1972.
Lafertte, Elías. *Vida de un comunista.* 2d ed. Santiago, 1971.
Lagos E., Ricardo. *La concentración del poder económico. Su teoría, su realidad chilena.* 5th ed. Santiago, 1965.
Lagos V., Tulio. *Bosquejo histórico del movimiento obrero en Chile.* Santiago, 1941.
Lamour, Catherine. *Le pari chilien.* Paris, 1972.
Landsberger, Henry, Manuel Barrera, and Abel Toro. "The Chilean Labor Leader: A Preliminary Report on His Background and Attitudes." *Industrial and Labor Relations Review*, 17 (April 1964), 399–420.
Landsberger, Henry, and Timothy McDaniel. "Hypermobilization in Chile, 1970–1973." *World Politics*, 28 (July 1976), 502–41.
Larraín, Jorge, and Fernando Castillo. "Poder obrero-campesino y transición al socialismo en Chile." *Cuadernos de la Realidad Nacional*, 10 (December 1971), 161–98.
Latin American Bureau. *Chile: The Pinochet Decade. The Rise and Fall of the Chicago Boys.* London, 1983.
Layton, Edwin. *The Diffusion of Scientific Management and Mass Production from the United States in the Twentieth Century.* Proceedings of the 14th International Congress of the History of Science. Tokyo, 1974.
Lechner, Norbert. *La democracia en Chile.* Buenos Aires, 1970.
Loveman, Brian. *Chile, the Legacy of Hispanic Capitalism.* New York, 1979.
————. *Struggle in the Countryside: Politics and Rural Labor in Chile, 1919–1973.* Bloomington, Ind., 1976.
MacEoin, Gary. *No Peaceful Way: The Chilean Struggle for Dignity.* New York, 1975.

Maira, Luis. *Chile: dos años de Unidad Popular.* Santiago, 1973.

Mamalakis, Markos. *The Growth and Structure of the Chilean Economy from Independence to Allende.* New Haven, Conn., 1976.

————. *Historical Statistics of Chile.* 4 vols. Westport, Conn., 1978–83.

Mamalakis, Markos, and Clark W. Reynolds. *Essays on the Chilean Economy.* Homewood, Ill., 1965.

Marín, Germán. *Una historia fantastica y calculada.* Mexico City, 1976.

Marín, Juan Carlos. "Las tomas (1970–1972)." *Marxismo y Revolución,* 1 (July–September 1973), 49–78.

Marini, Ruy Mauro, et al. *¿Por qué cayó Allende? Autopsia del gobierno popular chileno.* Buenos Aires, 1974.

Martner, Gonzalo, ed. *El pensamiento económico del gobierno de Allende.* Santiago, 1971.

Mattelart, Armand, Carmen Castillo, and Leonardo Castillo. *La ideología de la dominación en una sociedad dependiente.* Buenos Aires, 1970.

Matellart, Armand, and Manuel Antonio Garretón. *Integración nacional y marginalidad.* 2d ed. Santiago, 1969.

Mattelart, Armand, and Michèle Mattelart. *Juventud chilena: rebeldía y conformismo.* Santiago, 1970.

————. *La mujer chilena en una nueva sociedad.* Santiago, 1968.

Matus, Carlos. *Estrategia y plan.* Santiago, 1972.

Medhurst, Kenneth, ed. *Allende's Chile.* New York, 1972.

Menges, Constantine. "Public Policy and Organized Business in Chile." *Journal of International Affairs,* 20 (1966), 343–65.

Millas, Hernán, and Emilio Filippi. *Chile 1970–1973: crónica de una experiencia.* Santiago, 1974.

Molina, Sergio. *El proceso de cambio en Chile: la experiencia 1965–1970.* Santiago, 1972.

Montero Moreno, René. *Confesiones políticas.* 2d ed. Santiago, 1959.

————. *La verdad sobre Ibañez.* Buenos Aires, 1953.

Moran, Theodore H. *Multinational Corporations and the Politics of Dependence: Copper in Chile.* Princeton, N.J., 1974.

Morris, David. *We Must Make Haste Slowly.* New York, 1973.

Morris, George. *The C.I.A. and American Labor.* New York, 1967.

Morris, James O. *Elites, Intellectuals and Consensus.* Ithaca, N.Y., 1966.

Morris, James O., and Roberto Oyaneder *Afiliación y finanzas sindicales en Chile, 1932–1959.* Santiago, 1962.

Moss, Robert. *Chile's Marxist Experiment.* Newton Abbot, Eng., 1973.

Muñoz, Oscar. *Crecimiento industrial de Chile, 1914–1965.* 2d ed. Santiago, 1971.

Mutchler, David E. *The Church as a Factor in Latin America.* New York, 1971.

Nash, June, and Juan Corradi, eds. *Ideology and Social Change in Latin America.* 2 vols. New York, 1977.

Navin, Thomas R. *The Whitin Machine Works Since 1831.* Harvard Studies in Business History, vol. 15. Cambridge, Mass., 1950.

Nehgme Rodríguez, Elías. *La economía nacional y el problema de las subsistencias en Chile.* 2 vols. Santiago, 1943.

Novoa M., Eduardo. *La batalla por el cobre.* Santiago, 1972.

North, Liisa. *Civil-Military Relations in Argentina, Chile and Peru.* Berkeley, Calif., 1966.

North American Congress on Latin America (NACLA). *New Chile.* New York, 1972.

Nun, José. "The Middle-Class Military Coup." in *The Politics of Conformity in Latin America,* ed. by Claudio Veliz. London, 1967.

Núñez, Carlos. *Chile: ¿la última opción electoral?* Santiago, 1970.

Nunn, Frederick M. *Chilean Politics, 1920–1931.* Albuquerque, N.M., 1070.

———. "New Thoughts on Military Intervention in Latin American Politics: The Chilean Case, 1973." *Journal of Latin American Studies,* 7 (November 1975), 271–304.

———. *The Military in Chilean History: Essays on Civil-Military Relations, 1810–1973.* Albuquerque, N.M., 1976.

O'Brien, Philip, ed. *Allende's Chile.* New York, 1976.

O'Donnell, Guillermo. *Modernization and Bureaucratic-Authoritarianism.* Berkeley, Calif., 1973.

Olavarría Bravo, Arturo. *Chile bajo la Democracia Cristiana.* 5 vols. Santiago, 1965–69.

———. *Chile entre dos Alessandri.* 4 vols. Santiago, 1962–65.

Orrego, Carlos. *La organización gremial y el poder político.* Santiago, 1932.

Orrego, Claudio. *El paro nacional: vía chilena contra el totalitarismo.* Santiago, 1972.

Orrego, Francisco, ed. *Chile: The Balanced View.* Santiago, 1975.

Ossandón, Jorge. *Economía de guerra: ¿vía chilena hacia el hambre?* Santiago, 1973.

Otero, Lisandro. *Razón y fuerza de Chile: tres años de Unidad Popular.* Havana, 1979.

Pardo Gómez, Adela, ed. *Guía de Oro de Arequipa.* Arequipa, 1944.

Peppe, Patrick. "Notes on a Visit to the Yarur Mill." Santiago, August 1968.

———. "Working Class Politics in Chile." Ph.D. diss., Columbia University, 1971.

Peralta, Ariel. *El mito de Chile.* Santiago, 1971.

Petras, James. *Politics and Social Forces in Chilean Development.* Berkeley, Calif., 1969.

Petras, James, and Betty Petras. "Ballots into Bullets: Epitaph for a Peaceful Revolution." *Ramparts* (November 1973), 21–28, 59–62.

Petras, James, and Morris Morley. *The United States and Chile: Imperialism and the Overthrow of the Allende Government.* New York, 1975.

Petras, James, and Maurice Zeitlin. *El radicalismo político de la clase trabajadora chilena.* Buenos Aires, 1969.

———, eds. *Latin America: Reform or Revolution?* New York, 1968.

Pierson,Richard. "Chile: Can the Junta Rule?" *Ramparts* (June 1974), 25–28.

Pike, Frederick B. *Chile and the United States, 1880–1962.* South Bend, Ind., 1963.

Pinochet Ugarte, Augusto. *Un año de construcción.* Santiago, 1974.

Pinto Santa Cruz, Aníbal, *Chile, un caso del desarrollo frustrado.* 2d ed. Santiago, 1962.

———. *Hacia nuestra independencia económica.* Santiago, 1953.

———, ed. *Antecedentes sobre el desarrollo de la economía chilena, 1925–1952.* Santiago, 1954.

Pinto Santa Cruz, Aníbal, et al. *Chile hoy.* Mexico City, 1970.

Pizarro, Crisostomo. "Sindicatos en la evolución de la sociedad chilena." *Ensayos,* 1 (1978), 89–122.

Plath, Oreste. *Aportes folkloricos sobre el tejido a telar en Chile.* Santiago, 1970.

Poblete Troncoso, Moisés, and Benjamin Burnett. *The Rise of the Latin American Labor Movement.* New Haven, Conn., 1960.

Prats, Carlos. *Memorias; testimonio de un soldado.* Santiago, 1985.

Portes, Alejandro. "Leftist Radicalism in Chile." *Comparative Politics,* 2 (January 1970), 251–74.

Prothro, James, and Patricio Chaparro. "Public Opinion and the Movement of the Chilean Government to the Left, 1952–1972." *Journal of Politics,* 36 (February 1974), 2–43.

Raczynski, Dagmar, et al. *Los actores de la realidad chilena.* Santiago, 1974.

Ramírez Necochea, Hernán. *Historia del movimiento obrero en Chile: siglo XIX.* Santiago, 1956.

———. *Orígen y formación del Partido Comunista de Chile.* Santiago, 1965.

Ramos, Sergio. *Chile: ¿una economía de transición?* Santiago, 1972.

Raptis, Michael. *Revolution and Counter-Revolution in Chile. A Dossier on Workers' Participation in the Revolutionary Process.* London, 1974.

Reully Guzmán, Victor. "Condiciones económicos-sociales de los obreros textiles, 1938–49." Memoria de Licenciatura, University of Chile, 1950.

Reyes, Enrique. *El desarrollo de la conciencia proletaria en Chile: el ciclo salitrero.* Santiago, 1970.

Rodríguez Grez, Pablo. *Entre la democracia y la tiranía.* Santiago, 1972.

Rojas Sandford, Robinson. *The Murder of Allende and the End of the Chilean Way to Socialism.* New York, 1976.

Romero, Emilio. *Monografía del Departamento de Puno.* Lima, 1928.

Romualdi, Serafino. *Presidents and Peons.* New York, 1967.

Rosenstein-Rodan, Paul N. "Why Allende Failed." *Challenge*, 17 (May–June 1974), 7–13.

Roxborough, Ian, Philip O'Brien and Jackie Roddick. *Chile: The State and Revolution.* New York, 1977.

Sader, E., et al. *Cordón Cerrillos-Maipú: balance y perspectivas de un embrión de poder popular.* Santiago, 1973.

Sanfuentes, Andrés. "La influencia de los árabes en el desarrollo económico de Chile." Memoria de Licenciatura, University of Chile, 1964.

Sanders, Thomas G. "Chile's Economic Crisis and its Implications for Political Change." *American University Field Staff Reports*, 30:4 (1983).

———. "The Process of Partisanship in Chile." *American University Field Staff Reports* 20:1 (October 1973).

———. "Urban Pressure, Natural Resource Constraints, and Income Redistribution in Chile." *American University Field Staff Reports* 20:2 (December 1973).

Sarah, Roberto. *Los turcos.* 2d ed. Santiago, 1961.

Segall, Marcelo. *Desarrollo del capitalismo en Chile.* Santiago, 1953.

Serra, José. "Economic Policy and Structural Change in Chile, 1970–1973." Ph.D. diss., Cornell University, 1976.

Sideri, Sandro, ed. *Chile, 1970–1973: Economic Development and Its International Setting.* The Hague, 1978.

Sierra, Enrique. *Tres ensayos de estabilización en Chile.* Santiago, 1970.

Sigmund, Paul E. "Allende in Retrospect." *Problems of Communism* (May-June 1974): 45–62.

———. "The 'Invisible Blockade' and the Overthrow of Allende." *Foreign Affairs* (January 1974), 322–40.

———. *The Overthrow of Allende and the Politics of Chile, 1964-1976.* Pittsburgh, Pa., 1977.

———. "Seeing Allende Through the Myths." *Worldview* (April 1974), 16–21.

Silva Solar, Julio, and Jacques Chonchol. *Desarrollo de la nueva sociedad en América Latina*, 2d ed. Santiago, 1969.

Silvert, Kalman. *Chile.* New York, 1965.

Simón, Raúl, et al. *El concepto de industria nacional y la protección del estado.* Santiago, 1939.

Smirnow, Gabriel. *The Revolution Disarmed: Chile, 1970–73.* New York, 1979.

Smith, Brian. *The Church and Politics in Chile.* Princeton, N.J., 1982.

Snow, Peter. *Chilean Radicalism: The History and Doctrine of the Radical Party.* Iowa City, Iowa, 1971.

Soares, Glaucio, and Robert Hamblin. "Socio-economic Variables and Voting for the Radical Left: Chile, 1952." *American Political Science Review*, 61 (December 1967), 1053–65.

Sofer, Eugene. "Recent Trends in Latin American Labor Historiography." *Latin American Research Review.* 15 (Spring 1980), 167–82.

Solaún, Mauricio, and Fernando Cepeda. "Alternative Strategies in Allende's Chile: On the Politics of Brinksmanship." Land Tenure Center Special Report. University of Wisconsin, Madison, Wis., 1973.

Solaún, Mauricio, and Michael A. Quinn. *Sinners and Heretics: The Politics of Military Intervention in Latin America*. Urbana, Ill., 1973.

Stallings, Barbara. *Class Conflict and Economic Development in Chile, 1958–1973*. Stanford, Calif., 1978.

Stallings, Barbara, and Richard Feinberg. "Economic Policy and State Power: A Case Study of Chile Under Allende." *Kapitalistate*, 3 (Spring 1975), 85–97.

Stallings, Barbara, and Andrew Zimbalist. "Political Economy of the Unidad Popular." *Latin American Perspectives*, 2 (Spring 1975), 69–88.

Steenland, Kyle. *Agrarian Reform Under Allende: Peasant Revolt in the South*. Albuquerque, N.M., 1977.

Stevenson, John Reese. *The Chilean Popular Front*. Philadelphia, 1942.

Sweezy, Paul, and Harry Magdoff, eds. *Revolution and Counter-Revolution in Chile*. New York, 1974.

Tagle, María A. "La calidad y el valor proteico de la dieta del proletariado chileno." *Revista Medica de Chile*, 98 (August 1970), 549–64.

Tapia Valdés, Jorge. *El terrorismo de estado: la doctrina de la seguridad nacional en el Cono Sur*. Mexico City, 1980.

Taylor, Frederick W. *The Principles of Scientific Management*. New York, 1911.

Thorpe, Rosemary, and Geoffrey Bertram. *Peru, 1890–1977: Growth and Policy in an Open Economy*. New York, 1978.

Tomic, Radomiro. *Intervención de . . . en reunión del Partido Demócrata Cristiana el 7 de noviembre de 1973*. Mexico City, 1974.

Touraine, Alain. *Vie et Mort du Chili Populaire*. Paris, 1973.

Uribe, Armando. *The Black Book of American Intervention in Chile*. Boston, 1975.

Urzúa Valenzuela, Gérman. *El Partido Radical: su evolución política*. Santiago, 1961.

————. *Los partidos políticos chilenos*. Santiago, 1968.

Valenzuela, Arturo. *The Breakdown of Democratic Regimes: Chile*. Baltimore, 1978. (Also published as Volume 4 of Juan Linz and Alfred Stepan, eds. *Breakdown of Democratic Regimes*. 4 vols. Baltimore, Md., 1978.)

————. *Political Brokers in Chile: Local Government in a Centralized Polity*. Durham, N.C., 1977.

Valenzuela, Arturo and J. Samuel Valenzuela, "Visions of Chile." *Latin American Research Review*, 10 (Fall 1975), 155–76.

————, eds. *Chile: Politics and Society*. New Brunswick, N.J., 1976.

Valenzuela, J. Samuel "Labor Movement Formation and Politics: The Chilean and French Cases in Comparative Perspective, 1850–1950." Ph.D. diss., Columbia University, 1979.

Vanek, Jaroslav. *The Participatory Economy*. Ithaca, N.Y., 1971.

Véliz, Claudio, ed. *Obstacles to Change in Latin America*. London, 1965.

————. ed. *The Politics of Conformity in Latin America*. London, 1967.

Vitale, Luis. ¿*Y después del 4, qué?* Santiago, 1970.

————. *Historia del movimiento obrero*. Santiago, 1962.

Vuskovic, Pedro. *Acusación al imperialismo*. Mexico City, 1975.

Vylder, Stefan de. *Allende's Chile: The Political Economy of the Rise and Fall of the Unidad Popular*. New York, 1976.

Wilson, James W. "Freedom and Control: Workers' Participation in Management in Chile, 1967–1975." 3 vols. Ph.D. diss., Cornell University, 1979.

Winn, Peter. "Consciousness and the Chilean Working Class: Creation, Diffusion, Transmission, Transformation." Paper presented at the Shelby Collum Davis Center of Historical Studies, Princeton University, December 1974.

———. "Economic Consequences of the Chilean Counter-Revolution." *Latin American Perspectives*, 1 (Summer 1974), 92–105.

———. "Loosing the Chains: Labor and the Chilean Revolutionary Process, 1970–1973." *Latin American Perspectives*, 3 (Winter 1976), 70–84.

———. "Oral History and the Factory Study: New Approaches to Labor History." *Latin American Research Review*, 14 (Summer 1979), 130–40.

———. "The Urban Working Class and Social Protest in Latin America." *International Labor and Working Class History*, 14/15 (Spring 1979), 61–64.

———. "Workers into Managers: Worker Participation in the Chilean Textile Industry." In *Popular Participation in Social Change*, ed. Jorge Dandler, Nicholas Hopkins, and June Nash. The Hague, 1976, pp. 577–601.

Winn, Peter, and Cristóbal Kay. "Agrarian Reform and Rural Revolution in Allende's Chile." *Journal of Latin American Studies*, 6 (May 1974), 140–53.

Wolpin, Miles. "La influencia internacional de la revolución cubana: Chile, 1958–1970." *Foro Internacional* (April-June 1972), 453–96.

Wright, Thomas C. *Landowners and Reform in Chile: The Sociedad Nacional de Agricultura, 1919–40.* Urbana, Ill., 1982.

Yepes del Castillo, Ernesto. *Peru, 1820–1920. Un siglo de desarrollo capitalista.*

Zammit, J. Ann, ed. *The Chilean Road to Socialism.* Austin, Tex., 1973.

Zañartu, Mario, and J. J. Kennedy, eds. *The Overall Development of Chile.* South Bend, Ind., 1969.

Zapata, Francisco. "The Chilean Labor Movement and Problems of the Transition to Socialism." *Latin American Perspectives*, 3 (Winter 1976), 85–97.

Zeitlin, Maurice, and Richard E. Ratcliff. "Landlords and Capitalists. Studies of the Dominant Class and the Historical Development of Chile." Princeton, N.J., forthcoming.

INDEX

317